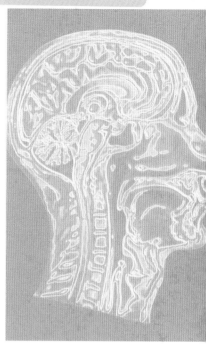

KU-222-083

This updated edition first published in Great
Britain in 2014 by Dorling Kindersley Limited
80 Strand, London WC2R 0RL
A Penguin Random House Company

Hardback edition first published
in Great Britain in 2002

2 4 6 8 10 9 7 5 3 1
001 – 196331 – 7/14

The CIP Catalogue record for this book
is available from the British Library

ISBN 978-1-4093-5070-5

Printed and bound in China

Discover more at
www.dk.com

Produced under license for SCMG
Enterprises Ltd. Science Museum® SCMG

Every purchase supports the museum.
www.sciencemuseum.org.uk

Introduction

Three million years of creativity and curiosity have produced tens of thousands of inventions and discoveries. Those that successfully met basic human needs – from the need to survive to the need to know – have played a big part in shaping our world.

Our world is very different from the world of our ancestors. Tens of thousands of inventions and discoveries have transformed the way we do things and the way we think. An invention is something new, created by arranging things in some novel way. A discovery is a thing or principle that already existed, needing only to be found. But it is often difficult to tell where invention ends and discovery begins. Whatever they are, few inventions or discoveries are made overnight. There is usually a period of preparation before they emerge. Even then, they take time to act. An invention may take years to displace existing methods. A discovery may take generations to change habits of thought.

WHEN DID IT HAPPEN?

This is not a book of "firsts". I have listed most inventions and discoveries under the date when they were first made public. But some dates relate to the beginning of something that only later became well known, or to a later stage of something that took time to influence people. It can also be difficult to say exactly who invented or discovered something. Often, when the time is right, many people come up with the same idea. And making an idea work can be more important than simply thinking of it. At the top of each invention or discovery, I have named the people who I think contributed most to it.

It is often difficult to tell where invention ends and discovery begins, and neither happens overnight.

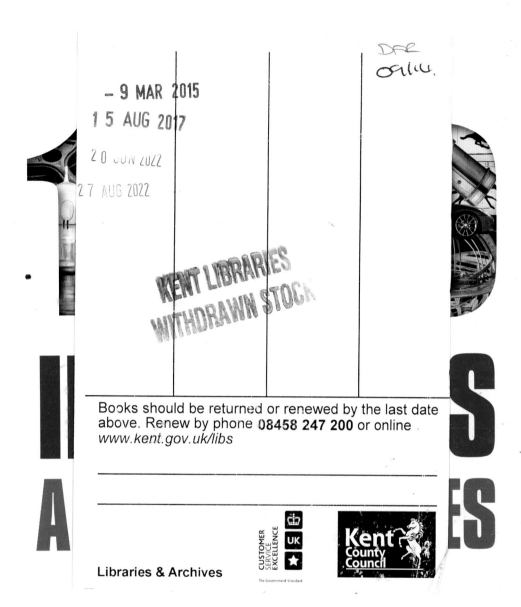

Written by
Roger Bridgman

In association with the

SCi
nce
mus
eum

DK

Contents

LONDON, NEW YORK, MUNICH,
MELBOURNE, and DELHI

NEW EDITION
Senior Editor Carron Brown
Designer Mary Sandberg
Managing Editor Linda Esposito
Managing Art Editor Michael Duffy
Category Publisher Andrew Macintyre
Production Controller Gemma Sharpe
Production Editor Ben Marcus
Picture Library Martin Copeland
Jacket Editor Maud Whatley
Jacket Designer Laura Brim
Jacket Design Development Manager
Sophia MTT
Publishing Director Jonathan Metcalf
Associate Publishing Director Liz Wheeler
Art Director Phil Ormerod

DK INDIA
Jacket Managing Editor Saloni Singh
Jacket Designer Suhita Dharamjit
Senior DTP Designer Harish Aggarwal

HARDBACK EDITION
Senior Editor Marie Greenwood
Senior Art Editor Clare Shedden
Designed and Edited by Bookwork
Editor Louise Pritchard
Art Editor Jill Plank
Assistant Editor Annabel Blackledge
Designer Kate Mullins·
Picture Research Marie Osborn
Picture Library Sally Hamilton,
Rose Horridge, Sarah Mills
Production Kate Oliver
DTP Designer Siu Yin Chan

We may soon know enough to control the machinery of life itself, making the future less certain.

Below, where possible, I have mentioned others who helped or attempted something similar. Some stories are too interesting to squeeze into a small space. I have given these either a separate box or two whole pages. These longer stories show how complicated inventing or discovering can be, and how it can change people's lives. Other aspects of these lives appear at the foot of most pages in a timeline, which records events in the wider world.

FASTER AND FASTER

Over the centuries, inventions and discoveries followed two main trends. Ancient ideas became modern science as measurement and mathematics improved on observation and argument, and the way things were made changed radically as scientific techniques displaced traditional crafts. These trends continue at an ever greater rate today. You may notice that while the first section of the book covers nearly three million years, the last covers only fifty. Despite this rapid change, many inventions and discoveries have had a lasting effect. Some, such as windmills or the theory of continental drift, vanished for a while but were born again. Others, such as pottery, have never been replaced. Inventions and discoveries like these were used or remembered because they met basic human needs. Until recently, these needs have not changed. But we may soon know enough to control the machinery of life itself, changing our basic needs and making the future less certain. I hope that this book will help you to understand how we got where we are now, and maybe even help you to guess where we are going next.

Roger Bridgman

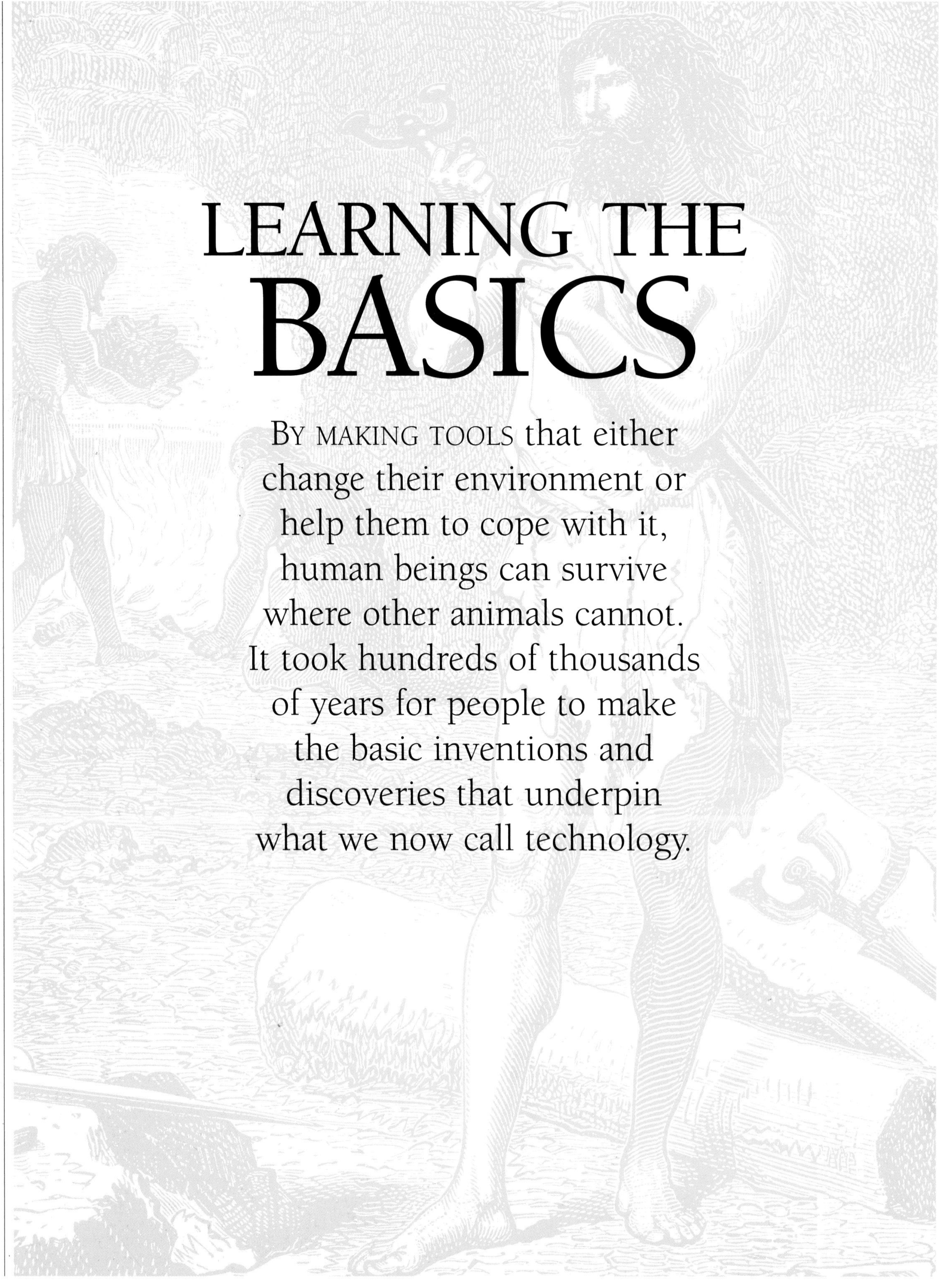

LEARNING THE
BASICS

By MAKING TOOLS that either
change their environment or
help them to cope with it,
human beings can survive
where other animals cannot.
It took hundreds of thousands
of years for people to make
the basic inventions and
discoveries that underpin
what we now call technology.

Stone tools

c 3,000,000 BC

The main difference between ourselves and most other animals is that we use tools. The oldest known tools, found in Africa, were made more than two million years ago. They are simply lumps of stone that have been shattered with another stone to make a sharp edge for chopping meat or wood. The people who made them would also have made tools from wood, but none have survived.

HAND AXE
The best stone for tools was flint. This flint hand axe, from about 1000–5000 BC, was found in Saint Acheul, near Amiens, France.

If flakes are chipped off, flint naturally forms sharp edges

Hand axe

c 1,800,000 BC

Over a period of more than one million years, the first crude stone tools evolved into beautifully shaped blades. Their makers flaked away the surfaces of a large flint pebble until its sides were sharp, for cutting or scraping, and one end was pointed, for piercing. The remaining blunt end fitted snugly into the hand, which is why the blades are called hand axes.

Use of fire

c 1,400,000 BC

People discovered the value of fire long before they found out how to make it. Fires can be started naturally by friction, lightning, or sunlight striking through a drop of water. The first people to use fire simply kept these natural flames going. They used fire for warmth and to cook food. Better still, fire could be used to clear away bushes and trees so that the grass grew thicker, attracting animals for people to catch and eat.

Cord attached to the ends of the crosspiece is also fixed to, and wrapped around, the shaft

Mining

c 40,000 BC

Early people made full use of everything around them, including rocks, which they used to make tools and to extract minerals. After a time, the good rocks on the surface were all used up, and people had to start digging to find what they wanted. The first mines were just shallow pits, but miners were eventually forced underground. One of the minerals they wanted was red ochre, which was used as a pigment for ritual purposes and for cave paintings. The oldest known underground mine was used for collecting red ochre. It is at Bomvu Ridge in Swaziland, Africa.

Wooden crosspiece was pumped downwards to turn the shaft via the cord

Stone weight was used to apply more pressure to the bit

Drill shaft, the end of which was fitted with a cast-iron bit

DRILL *The bow drill (right) is Egyptian. The drill (left) is a recent pump drill from New Guinea, which was used to drill holes in wood.*

Drill was kept upright by a piece of wood or stone held on top of it

Drill

c 35,000 BC

The earliest drills were probably pointed stones that people spun between the palms of their hands. Later, sticks were spun like this to make fire (✳ *see* **page 11**). People also discovered that they could spin the drill faster by wrapping a cord around it, tying the ends of the cord to a wooden bow, and pushing this back and forth. This bow drill was used in some parts of the world until recent times.

c 1,600,000 BC
Earth enters its most recent ice age. Ice will eventually cover northern Europe and North America. Most of it will have gone by 10,000 BC, leaving behind a changed landscape.

c 50,000 BC
A huge meteorite, the size of a building, falls on Earth in what is now Arizona, USA. The 400,000 tonne rock forms a crater 1.2 km (0.75 miles) wide and 150 m (490 ft) deep.

Fishing line is made from natural plant creeper

FISH HOOK *This modern fish hook from Hawaii was made in much the same way as the first fish hooks.*

Barb prevents the fish from escaping, once caught

Hook made from ivory

in bone or wood. This allowed people to create more precise tools, such as needles, and to engrave decoration on larger objects.

Fish hook

c 35,000 BC

The earliest method of catching a fish was with a piece of stone, pointed at both ends, baited, and tied to a line. This gorge, as it is called, simply jammed in the fish's throat. The first proper fish hooks were developed by the earliest "modern" humans, the Cro-Magnons. They caught their fish using a barbed bone hook, one of the many small, specialized tools they made using the versatile burin that they had perfected.

Handles for tools

c 35,000 BC

Attaching a wooden handle to a blade may not sound like a breakthrough, but it was. People could not hit things very hard with a tool held in their hands because it hurt. Nor could they swing the tool very quickly because their arms were too short. A handle, or haft, helped them to overcome both these limitations, protecting their arms from

HOUSE *After 20,000 years of development, houses began to be made of brick. This is a model of a house from the 6th century BC.*

Engraving tool

c 35,000 BC

As long as 40,000 years ago, people were making delicate objects and works of art using stone engraving tools called burins. Made by forming a sharp edge on a flake of flint, a burin could be used to scratch lines and cut grooves

impact and increasing the length of their swing. Hand axes (✳ *see* **page 7**) could be used to clear away bushes, but axes with hafts could be used to chop down trees.

Spear thrower

c 35,000 BC

By creeping along quietly, early hunters could often get close enough to an animal to throw a spear at it and kill it. But sometimes the animal would run away. What the hunters needed was a way of throwing spears from further off. The spear thrower was a piece of wood or antler with a notch at one end to hold the spear. It enabled hunters to hurl their weapons further and increased their chances of killing their prey.

Bow and arrow

c 30,000 BC

Bows and arrows were depicted in cave paintings from 30,000 BC onwards, but no actual examples survive today. By 18,000 BC, arrows were equipped with flint points, making them deadly to animals. Later, the bow came into use as a major military weapon and became deadly to people, too.

Cave painting

c 30,000 BC

Dramatic paintings made by people living more than 30,000 years ago lay forgotten until 1879, when a little girl, Maria de Sautuola, visited the

Bricks are moulded from mud and baked in the sun

Roof structure built from branches and reeds

c 35,000 BC
The first people to enter America travel on foot over a land bridge between Siberia and Alaska, which is exposed by the low sea level. The bridge will later disappear as ice melts worldwide.

c 27,000 BC
In what will become Germany, an unknown sculptor carves the Venus of Willendorf, one of the earliest known sculptures of a human. It has exaggerated female proportions and is painted red.

8

caves at Altamira in Spain with her father. She noticed the huge paintings of animals high above her head. Since then, even earlier paintings have been discovered at Chauvet in France. The artists of these early paintings had to invent paint, brushes, scaffolding, and even artificial lighting before they could begin painting.

Paintbrush

c 30,000 BC

The artists who created the cave paintings at Altamira in Spain, Lascaux in France, and in other places, probably put colour on to the walls in several different ways, including spitting it out. Some of the effects they produced must have needed a paintbrush. At its simplest, this could have been a twig chewed at one end to separate the fibres, but the world's first interior decorators may also have used bunches of feathers or bristles.

Rope

c 30,000 BC

It is difficult to say exactly when people first started to make rope because few early examples have survived, except in bogs, where the acid water has stopped it from rotting. But some early drawings and sculptures show it in use. It has also sometimes been preserved as an impression in clay, as in the caves of Lascaux, where archaeologists found evidence of a rope braided from three plant fibres. One early use of rope was for making nets and snares for catching food.

House

c 28,000 BC

People started to build houses about 30,000 years ago, but most people lived in shelters or caves. They also built simple huts, in which they probably lived for some time before moving on to find food. At Dolní Vestonice in the Czech Republic, archaeologists have found the remains of houses built from stone, wood, and mammoth bones, dating from about 25,000 BC.

Boomerang

c 19,000 BC

Used by hunters in Africa, India, and Australia, the boomerang was originally just a heavy stick thrown at an animal to injure it and make it easier to catch. Over the centuries, the stick was reshaped so that it would fly further and faster, and even return to its thrower. The first known boomerang was found in a cave in southern Poland, and it is probably about 21,000 years old. The Australian boomerang was in use by 8000 BC.

Pottery

c 13,000 BC

Having harnessed the power of fire, people were able to make pottery. The first potters only needed to find some soft clay, shape it, and then heat it in a fire. Because an ordinary fire did not heat the clay very evenly, the resulting pots were fragile and not completely waterproof, but they still proved extremely useful.

Pottery from about 15,000 years ago has been found in Japan.

Doorway supported by a large branch

Roof and walls plastered with mud

c 23,000 BC
Ice tightens its grip on Earth as the ice age reaches its peak. As more water is locked up in glaciers, the sea level continues to fall. By this time, it is 90 m (300 ft) below its level today.

c 18,000 BC
People in Australia cover rocks with thousands of elaborate engraved designs. They also create images in colour. For red, they use a rock called red ochre, or sometimes human blood.

Cutting holes in the skull
c 10,000 BC

People once thought that disease was caused by demons getting inside a person's head or gods stealing their soul. Their answer was to cut a hole in the head to let the demons out or the soul back in. Trephining probably took place as early as 10,000 BC, and a skull from about 5000 BC, found at Ensisheim in France, shows clear evidence of the operation. Other skulls show that people survived it: bone has grown around the hole, proving the patient lived.

Whistle
c 10,000 BC

The whistle could be the earliest musical instrument. Archaeologists have found examples more than 12,000 years old. People in China were using whistles with more than one note at least 9000 years ago. We don't know exactly how the whistle was invented, but it is likely that the first step was when someone blew across the end of a natural tube, such as bamboo or bone.

Agriculture
c 9000 BC

See **pages 12–13** for the story of how hunters became farmers.

Oven
c 9000 BC

The earliest method of cooking was to put food over an open fire and turn it occasionally. But this wasted fuel and someone had to do the turning. It was more efficient to put the fire inside a stone or clay chamber – an oven. Once the oven was hot, the cook could rake out the fire, put the food in, and seal it up until the food was ready. The first known ovens were found in the city of Jericho in ancient Palestine, where people have been living for more than 10,000 years.

Skull shows four circular holes, or trephinings

Bone shows signs of healing, indicating that this individual survived the process of trephining

CUTTING HOLES IN THE SKULL *This skull was trephined in 2200–2000 BC.*

FLINT MINING *This prehistoric pick is made from a deer's antler.*

Flint mining
c 8000 BC

For hundreds of thousands of years, people made tools from the stones that they found around them. As the need for tools grew, tool makers began to dig for suitable stones like flints. Fortunately, flints are found in soft chalk, which miners could cut away with picks made from antlers. Early flint miners in Britain and France sank complex mining shafts and galleries that went as deep as 13 m (40 ft).

c 11,000 BC People now occupy most of America, except the northern parts still covered by glaciers. Using stone-tipped spears, they hunt mastodons and mammoths (both similar to elephants) and even camels.

c 8300 BC A period of change known as the Middle Stone Age begins. World temperatures rise sharply and the great ice sheet covering Europe starts to shrink, opening up huge areas of land for people to occupy.

Sheep

c 8000 bc

About 10,000 years ago, sheep lived wild in western Asia and around the Mediterranean. They are now found in more countries than any other domestic animal. The first farmers may have favoured sheep because they tended to follow a leader, which made them easy to herd. They were also small and hardy, and produced valuable wool as well as meat and milk.

Wheat and barley

c 7500 bc

Wheat and barley are basically just types of grass. Modern varieties are the result of a continuous process of selection, which started when the first farmers chose to cultivate the plants with the most plentiful and largest seeds. The first crops were probably cultivated somewhere

in the Middle East, perhaps near Jericho, which had a large population to feed. Traces of wheat and barley seeds have been found buried under the modern town.

Chisel

c 7000 bc

About 9000 years ago, people began to grind stones to form a sharp edge, instead of flaking them. This meant they could use tough stones to make longer-lasting tools. One such tool was the chisel, a blade sharpened at the end, not the side. It gave better control for carving objects from wood or other soft materials.

Making fire

c 7000 bc

People have used fire for more than a million years, but only discovered how to make it about 9000 years ago. Two main methods were used. One was to hit a rock called pyrites with a flint, which produced sparks that could be used to start a fire. The other method was to spin a stick called a fire drill against a piece of wood until sparks flew. Archaeologists have found the equipment used for both methods throughout Europe.

Flax

c 7000 bc

By about 9000 years ago, people were growing plants to make their fibres into rope

SHEEP *Images of farmers with sheep and cows made 4500 years ago in the city of Ur, Mesopotamia.*

and cloth. The first plant to be cultivated for this reason was flax, a tall plant with blue flowers. Fibres extracted from its stems were spun into a thread called linen, which we still use today because it is much stronger than cotton. Archaeologists have found early flax plants and linen fishing nets and fabrics in Switzerland. The ancient Egyptians also used linen to wrap mummies.

c 8300 bc
The sabre-toothed tiger, a large ferocious cat with fangs, finally becomes extinct. Well equipped to hunt and kill large animals such as the mastodon, it cannot survive as this and many other prey die out.

c 8000 bc
After occupying many parts of the world for more than a million years, lions begin to disappear. By this time they have become extinct in North America. In another 8000 years there will be none left in Europe.

GOING FOR GROWTH

No going back as hunters become farmers

Flint blade (c 4000 – 2300 BC) in a modern handle

Ears of einkorn wheat

EARLY HARVEST
The first farmers grew einkorn, a type of wheat, and other crops. They harvested the wheat with a sickle, made by attaching a flint blade to a wooden handle. The sickle made it easy to cut down the tall, strong stems.

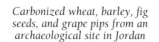

Carbonized wheat, barley, fig seeds, and grape pips from an archaeological site in Jordan

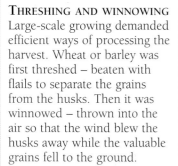

THRESHING AND WINNOWING
Large-scale growing demanded efficient ways of processing the harvest. Wheat or barley was first threshed – beaten with flails to separate the grains from the husks. Then it was winnowed – thrown into the air so that the wind blew the husks away while the valuable grains fell to the ground.

Some time after 10,000 BC, people made the first real attempt to control the world they lived in, through agriculture. Over thousands of years, they began to depend less on what they could hunt or gather from the wild, and more on animals they had tamed and crops they had sown. The abundant food that agriculture provided allowed small villages to grow into great cities.

It is not clear why people changed their lifestyle like this. We can only guess at what inspired them to try herding sheep or planting wheat. Whatever the reasons, there was no going back. Farming produced more food per person than hunting and gathering, so people were able to raise more children. And, as more children were born, more food was needed. Agriculture gave people their first experience of the power of technology to change lives.

The first people to become farmers lived in a huge, sunny, well watered area in the Middle East called the Fertile Crescent (now Iran, Iraq, Israel, Jordan, Syria, and Turkey), where the conditions were ideal for crops and livestock. But the story of the dawn of agriculture was repeated over and over again throughout the world. People invented agriculture independently in places as far

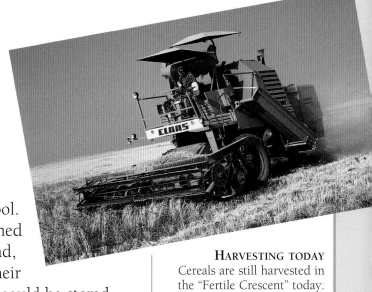

apart as China and South America. They may have started because people noticed that the grains they gathered sometimes sprouted, or that sheep liked to stick together and were easy to control.

By about 6000 BC, people had discovered that the best cereals to grow were wheat and barley, and that pigs, cows, and sheep returned the effort involved in rearing them by providing meat, milk, leather, and wool. Later, they used oxen for pulling ploughs. People learned to work with the seasons, planting at the right time and, in dry areas, making use of annual floods to irrigate their fields. They also invented granaries where the harvest could be stored.

This style of farming lasted for another 8000 years. Then, with the rise of science, changes began. New methods meant that fewer people were needed in farming. In the last century or so, these changes have accelerated. New power machinery, artificial fertilizers, and pesticides have now totally transformed a way of life that started in the Stone Age.

HARVESTING TODAY
Cereals are still harvested in the "Fertile Crescent" today. The principles of harvesting grain have not changed over the centuries, but in many areas the farmers now use machines like this combine harvester in Syria. This huge machine cuts, threshes, and winnows the crop.

As well as changing people's lives, agriculture gradually changed the landscape as farmers began to plough fields and channel water to their crops.

Mortise and tenon joint

c 7000 BC

Having learned how to make good tools, people could start to do precise woodwork. But first they had to solve the problem of how they could join together two pieces of wood. One method was with the mortise and tenon joint, in which one piece of wood has a tongue shape at the end, which fits into a matching hole in the other piece of wood. This joining method was also used for stone structures like Stonehenge, and is still the most widely used wood joint.

Sickle

c 7000 BC

Soon after people began to grow crops, they developed special tools for harvesting them. The first was a short, straight blade known as a sickle. Dating from about 7000 BC onwards, flint sickles were one of the inventions that made agriculture possible (✳ see pages 12–13). A later development was a curved blade, which could cut several stems at once. The curved sickle is still in use today in some places, but with a steel blade instead of a stone one.

COPPER *This copper is pure enough to be used almost as it is.*

TRADERS AND THEIR TRADES

SEVERAL EARLY settlements, such as Çatal Hüyük in Turkey (6500–5400 BC), and San Lorenzo in South America (1150–900 BC), owed their growth to trade. Çatal Hüyük's population grew to about 5000 at its height because it had access to the valuable material obsidian. Trading was also important for island dwellers, who could rarely find everything they needed locally but were able to produce specialized crops such as spices.

Cinnamon

OBSIDIAN
A natural glass formed by volcanoes, obsidian could be used to make much sharper cutting tools than flint or other stones. People living in what is now Turkey had plenty of this material but lacked precious metals, so they traded one for the other. Obsidian from this area has been found in ancient Palestine, 900 km (550 miles) away.

SPICES
Trading in spices such as cinnamon, cloves, ginger, and pepper goes back to 2000 BC or earlier. The spices originated in the East, and traders who knew where to get them made large profits by bringing them westwards. The traders kept their sources – places like the Spice Islands (now part of the Moluccas group of islands in Indonesia) – strictly secret.

Ginger

Peppercorns

Copper

c 6500 BC

The person who discovered copper, the first widely used metal, must have been thrilled. It is one of the few metals found in metallic form. People in Turkey were using it for small, precious objects by 6500 BC. By 3000 BC, with the development of ways to extract the metal from its ore, copper was in use all over the Middle East and the Mediterranean.

Lead

c 6500 BC

Lead is one of the most ancient metals. As with copper, people started to use it in about 6500 BC in Turkey. Unlike copper, lead is rarely found as a pure metal, and has to be extracted from its ore by roasting it in a hot fire to release the metal. The earliest known objects made of lead are beads, suggesting that at first people considered lead a precious material and used it only for display.

Painted pottery

c 6500 BC

Although early methods of firing were not very effective, even the earliest potters tried to make their wares look beautiful. Pots found in the ancient city of Çatal Hüyük, Anatolia (now Çumra in Turkey), dating from about 6500 BC, had been

BOAT *This boat from Lake Titicaca in the Andes mountains is made of reeds. The Egyptians were making boats from reeds by about 4000 BC.*

Ropes and sail made from reeds

washed over with a thin layer of cream clay called slip, and decorated with the natural pigment red ochre.

c 6800 BC
Methods of farming improve in villages in the Middle East. Farmers grow a wider range of crops and use land more efficiently. They domesticate what will become one of the most important farm animals – the pig.

c 6000 BC
Britain becomes cut off from Europe as the land link between what are now England and France is finally broken. Melting of the great glaciers has caused the sea to rise by hundreds of metres.

Trading

c 6500 bc

Few communities are able to produce everything they need. Trading allows people to exchange things they have too much of for things they lack, and probably make a profit at the same time. Trading became common when the first cities were established, and the profits from trading helped many cities to grow. As transport improved, trading spread more widely, exposing previously isolated groups of people to each other's knowledge and customs. (✳ *See also* **Traders and their trades**.)

Drum *This Sumerian vase from the end of the 4th century bc shows a musician playing a drum made from animal skin stretched across a wooden frame.*

Axe

c 6000 bc

From about 6000 bc, stone axe heads with a straight edge and heavy base began to appear, the earliest of which have been found in Sweden. Another basic tool, the adze, developed at about the same time. It was like an axe, but with the blade turned around to strike across, not along, the direction of swing. It was used to shape heavy timbers.

Drum

c 6000 bc

The remains of drums have been found dating from 6000 bc onwards. Drums have always had religious, political, or military significance, and the urge to influence a crowd with noise and rhythm has led people to develop the drum into many forms. The first drums were skins stretched over anything hollow, but now there are hundreds of varieties, such as African talking drums, classical kettle drums, and tambourines.

Boat

c 6000 bc

The first "boat" was probably just a dead tree on which someone hitched a ride downstream. But once tool makers had perfected stone axes, people used them to shape and hollow tree-trunks to make real boats – dugout canoes. Boat builders also covered wooden frames with animal skins to make lighter boats like the coracle, which is still used today. Later, people in ancient Egypt made boats by lashing reeds together.

High, domed shape keeps the sailor well out of the water

Bundles of reeds held by twine

c 6000 bc The city of Çatal Hüyük, in what is now Turkey, becomes one of the largest settlements of the Near East, after about 500 years of occupation. Its mud-brick buildings will survive for another 500 years.

c 6000 bc Chinese painters extend their range of pigments by heating mixtures of organic and inorganic materials to create new colours. They make these into paint with gum, egg white, gelatine, or beeswax.

Basket weaving
c 5500 BC

Basket weaving and cloth making were both common by 5000 BC. Baskets probably came first because weaving a basket was easier than weaving cloth. No loom was needed, and weavers could use whole plant stems instead of having to spin plant fibres into thread. Baskets were made using split bamboo in China, flax and straw in the Middle East, and willow in Europe. People in these areas also used the same materials to weave matting.

GRINDSTONE *This stone quern was used to make flour by grinding grain between the two stones.*

Grindstone
c 5000 BC

Cereal grains are difficult to digest unless they are cracked open. At first, people did this by pounding them with rocks. Then they used two stones, one on the ground and one in the hands. The flour produced was more nutritious than whole grains and could be made into bread. This type of grindstone is sometimes called a saddle quern because the lower stone gets ground into a saddle shape with use.

Leather
c 5000 BC

Early hunters knew that animal skins would be useful if they could stop them from decomposing. By about 5000 BC, they had worked out various ways of turning skin into leather. They started by drying the skin, then applied a range of substances, including urine. By about 800 BC, people in the ancient state of Assyria in northern Mesopotamia (Iraq) had developed a better process. They soaked the skin in a solution containing the chemical alum and vegetable extracts that were rich in the chemical tannin.

Irrigation
c 5000 BC

Irrigation is a means of getting water to plants so that they can grow, even when the land is dry. From about 5000 BC, the ancient Egyptians practised irrigation on a grand scale. Every year, the River Nile flooded, and the Egyptians used sluices and ponds to trap the water and its valuable nutrients, and send it to where it was needed.

Loom
c 5000 BC

To weave cloth, a thread called the weft is passed under and over alternate threads called the warp. The earliest weavers may have used a needle, but by 5000 BC, most looms allowed the weaver to avoid going under-and-over by lifting half the warp threads for the weft to pass straight through, then lifting the other half for the weft to pass back.

Plough
c 5000 BC

Seeds grow best in soil that has been broken up and turned over. Early farmers used sticks to prepare the soil. The plough, developed later, did the job better, although early ploughs did not turn the soil over. The first ploughs were pulled or pushed by people, but by 4000 BC oxen were doing the pulling and the farmer had only to steer.

Seal
c 4500 BC

The seal was the first security device used to protect goods and sign documents. In 4500 BC, people in Mesopotamia sealed packages by tying them with string, putting clay around the knot, and squashing the clay with a stone carrying their mark. A thousand years later, when people started writing on clay tablets, they signed their documents in a similar way.

PLOUGH *This model plough was found in an Egyptian tomb of 2000 BC.*

Ploughshare digs into the soil

Farmer steers the plough

c 5500 BC Chinese people begin to grow rice in the Huang He (Yellow River) valley in eastern China. Within five centuries, this small beginning will develop into a fully agricultural way of life.

c 5000 BC The fertile land to the north of the Persian Gulf is settled by the Ubaidians, the first of many occupants of the area that will become Sumer. They develop a rich culture that includes pottery and sculpture.

Scales
c 4000 BC

The simplest device for weighing things is the beam balance, a length of wood or metal hung from its centre with a pan hung from each end. The object to be weighed, in one pan, is balanced against weights in the other. It was developed in about 4000 BC in Mesopotamia. By 1500 BC, the ancient Egyptians had improved the accuracy of these early scales by passing the cords for the pans over the ends of the beam instead of through holes in it.

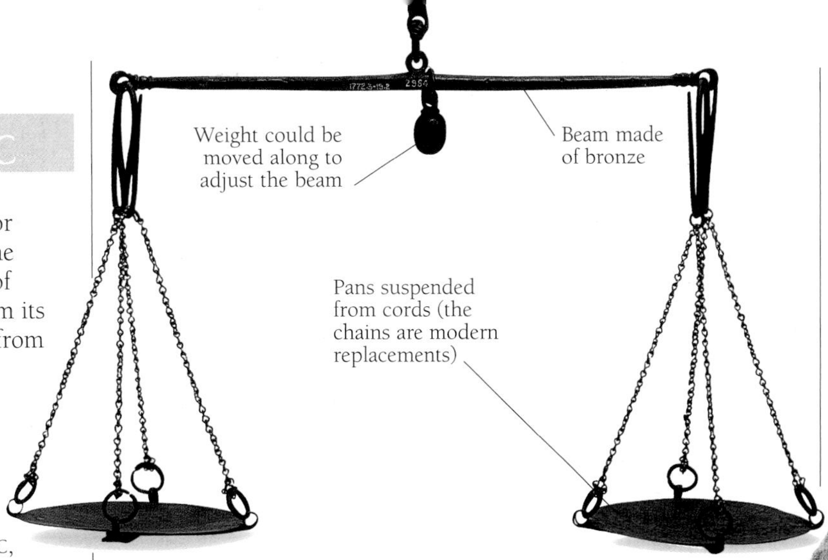

Weight could be moved along to adjust the beam

Beam made of bronze

Pans suspended from cords (the chains are modern replacements)

SCALES *These ancient Roman scales use the same principle as Mesopotamian scales. They are simple and very accurate. Similar ones remained in use until modern times.*

BRICK *Made in Mesopotamia in about 2500 BC, this mud brick was partly fired.*

Edges formed by the wooden mould

Silver
c 4000 BC

Silver is often found naturally with copper and lead, but it is more difficult to extract so it came into use rather later Archaeologists have found silver ornaments buried in tombs dating from 4000 BC. By 2500 BC, silver mines were in full production in the area now called Turkey. From the beginning, silver was valued for its rarity and beauty.

It was used as money, and this remained its main use until recent times, when it became the essential ingredient of photographic film.

Brick
c 3500 BC

People made the first bricks from mud. They mixed the mud with straw to reinforce it, then shaped the bricks in wooden moulds and dried them in the sun. Builders were using bricks of this kind 7000 years ago, but they were not very good because heavy rain could turn them back into mud. More practical bricks began to be made in the Middle East in about 3500 BC. They were made of clay and fired by heating them in a kiln, which made them as hard and as waterproof as pottery.

Oxen provide the power

c 4500 BC Farmers from south-west Asia migrate up the valley of the River Danube in Germany, mixing with people still only hunting for food. They settle here, build large wooden houses, and trade for tools.

c 3900 BC The Yangshao culture emerges in eastern China. Its people keep animals, practise simple farming, and later discover the secret of silkworms. Their other speciality is pottery painted in red, white, and black.

17

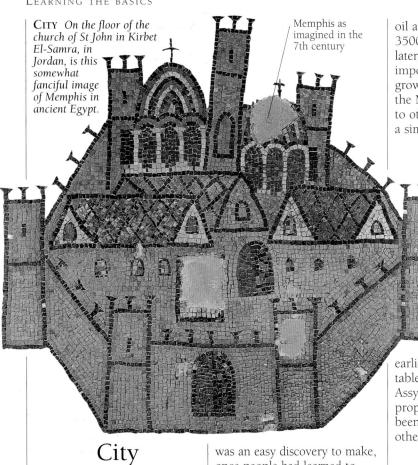

CITY *On the floor of the church of St John in Kirbet El-Samra, in Jordan, is this somewhat fanciful image of Memphis in ancient Egypt.*

Memphis as imagined in the 7th century

City

c 3500 BC

Because farming (✳ *see* **pages 12–13**) meant that fewer members of each community were needed to produce food, other members were free to develop cities. They were places where people gathered for security and to exchange goods and ideas, and were the foundations of civilization. The earliest large settlement was Jericho in the Middle East, which dates from about 7000 BC, but the first real cities, with streets and public buildings, were Thebes and Memphis in Egypt, both of which existed by 3500 BC.

Metal casting

c 3500 BC

Casting is a way of making objects by letting molten metal solidify in a mould. It was an easy discovery to make, once people had learned to melt metals, because any metal they spilled would have been shaped by what it fell on. The first known castings are axe heads made of copper from the Balkan region of south-east Europe. They were made between 4000 BC and 3000 BC. Later, copper was replaced by bronze (✳ *see* **page 20**), which is easier to cast and is much harder.

Olive

c 3500 BC

People on the island of Crete in the Mediterranean Sea were growing olive trees and harvesting olives for their oil and as a food by about 3500 BC. More than 5000 years later, olives are still Crete's most important crop, and olive growing has spread throughout the Mediterranean region and to other parts of the world with a similar climate.

Opium

c 3500 BC

Opium is a substance made from the unripe seed heads of poppies. It has been in use for more than 5000 years to relieve pain and help people sleep. Some of the earliest known writings – clay tablets of about 3000 BC from Assyria – refer to its medical properties. Since then, it has been used to make several other drugs, notably morphine, discovered by German chemist F. W. A. Sertürner in 1806, which is still one of the most potent painkillers available.

Pack-ass

c 3500 BC

Wheels are not always the best way to move things from place to place. In certain conditions, goods may travel more safely strapped to an animal. The first beast of burden was the donkey, domesticated from the African wild ass. In Sudan, in north-west Africa, people were using pack-asses, as they are often called, as early as 4000 BC, long before wheeled vehicles were invented. They probably chose the donkey because it is easy to tame, stands up well to harsh treatment, and can carry a load of up to 60 kg (132 lb).

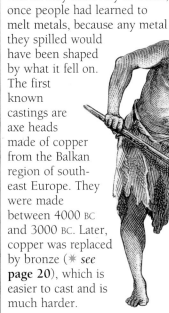

Bronze blade taken from the mould

Stone mould of a sword blade

Bronze melted in a furnace

METAL CASTING *Metalworkers discovered that bronze was easy to melt and cast into objects.*

---

c 3500 BC People in Europe begin to bury their dead in long barrows. These earth mounds are typically 70 m (230 ft) long and point east-west. An entire high-status family would be buried in a chamber at the east end.

c 3500 BC Sculptors in the Mesopotamian city of Uruk make outstanding items, such as a goddess's head in white limestone inlaid with other materials. They also carve vases from alabaster, a translucent stone.

Potter's wheel

c 3500 BC

People made the first pots with their bare hands. Later, they built up pots from a "worm" of clay. Neither method produced perfectly round pots. By about 3500 BC, potters were moulding clay on a turntable, possibly made from a round stone, which helped them to shape their pots more uniformly. Before long, they were using a heavy stone on an axle, which they spun with their feet. This left their hands free to work the clay on a smaller turntable above, and the potter's wheel was born.

Kiln-fired pottery

c 3500 BC

Clay heated in a fire does not get hot enough to change into really strong pottery. By about 3500 BC, potters had developed kilns, often fuelled with charcoal, in which hot gases rushed up through a stack of pots. Clay placed in such a kiln produced better pottery. Because kilns were expensive to run, potters who used them needed plenty of customers and usually operated in cities.

Road

c 3500 BC

Early roads were not surfaced like modern roads, but they could be just as long. The Persian Royal Road, built in about 3500 BC, stretched for 2857 km (1785 miles) between the Persian Gulf and the Aegean Sea. By 1050 BC, the Chinese were travelling on the Silk Road, which remained the world's longest road for 2000 years. Great roads were also built by the Incas in South America and by the ancient Egyptians, who needed to transport building materials for their pyramids.

Sail

c 3500 BC

Early boat users, noticing that the wind sometimes helped their progress, stretched skins or matting between poles to make the most of it. Sails made of cloth came later. They first appear in ancient Egyptian art from about 3300 BC.

Whatever they were made of, early sails worked only when the wind was behind them. Sails that could catch wind from the side, making sailors less dependent on the weather, were not invented for another 1500 years.

Wheel

c 3500 BC

Wheels were first used to move things around in Mesopotamia. It seems unlikely that the idea came from logs used as rollers, because the earliest wheels don't look anything like logs. People made them from planks, even in countries with trees that were large enough to slice into wheels. The wheel is more likely to have started life as an aid to potters in their quest to make perfectly rounded pots.

Wheeled vehicle

c 3500 BC

The first record of anything with wheels is a pictograph (picture-writing) found in Sumeria, an ancient civilization in southern Mesopotamia. It dates from about 3500 BC. The same pictograph shows that earlier vehicles had runners like a sledge. Within 500 years, wheeled vehicles were almost everywhere. They have been found in tombs and bogs and appear in wall-paintings and carvings. In China, vehicles have been found dating from 2600 BC onwards.

KILN-FIRED POTTERY *This beaker was made between 2500 and 1800 BC.*

---

c 3500 BC The first pottery on the continent of America is made in Ecuador and Colombia. The idea spreads northwards as new crops, such as beans, demand better storage. Pottery making will reach Mexico by 2300 BC.

c 3500 BC Corn, or maize, a basic Central American crop, begins to be grown on a large scale, displacing a more established cereal, millet. Beans and hot chilli peppers are already being grown in many places.

KINDS OF CALENDAR

A CALENDAR is like a clock that tells you what time of year it is, instead of what time of day. All calendars have to allow for the fact that a year does not contain a whole number of days or lunar months. Early calendars tended to run fast or slow, because their year was shorter or longer than the actual time it takes for Earth to go around the Sun.

This is an Aztec calendar stone. The Aztecs ruled most of Mexico in the 15th century. The calendar was based partly on a ritual cycle of 260 days.

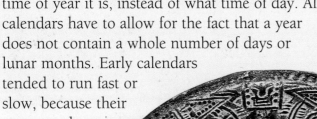

LUNISOLAR CALENDARS

These calendars were based on the lunar month, during which the Moon goes from new to full and back. This has no connection with the solar year, the time Earth takes to go exactly once around the Sun. So people using lunisolar calendars had to throw in an extra month every now and then to keep their months in step with the years.

Sun god surrounded by the 20 days of a month

THE EGYPTIAN CALENDAR

The Egyptians ignored the Moon and used 12 months of exactly 30 days each, plus 5 days at the end of the year, which didn't belong to any month. It was a simple method, but because this calendar gave a year of exactly 365 days, a quarter of a day shorter than the true solar year, it gained 25 days in every 100 years.

Writing numbers in tens
c 3400 BC

People were counting their possessions long before they began writing words. One way they did this was by cutting notches in a stick. Early counting methods like this gradually evolved into writing numbers. At first, people wrote 24 marks to represent the number 24. By about 3400 BC, the Egyptians had a more efficient system, with different symbols for 1, 10, 100, and so on. Using this system, they could write 24 using just six marks: two 10s and four 1s.

Bronze
c 3300 BC

People began to use metal instead of stone for the production of their tools in about 3500 BC. This happened when they discovered that copper could be extracted from certain rocks. Bronze, a harder metal, which was made by mixing copper with tin, was discovered several hundred years later. Easily shaped by casting (melting and pouring into a mould), and tougher than any stone, the discovery of bronze had a huge impact on human development.

Writing
c 3100 BC

See **pages 22–23** for the story of how Middle Eastern traders created the first permanent records.

Candle
c 3000 BC

Cave painters were using burning torches and crude oil lamps 30,000 years ago. Candles were better than these because their fuel did not spill, making them easy to carry around, and their wick gave a controlled flame. Candlesticks

CANDLE
Candles were originally formed from wax made by bees.

Ripples in wax show that the candle was hand-dipped

Tapered shape produced by dipping the wick repeatedly in molten wax

c 3200 BC
In England, work starts on a monument that will be known as Stonehenge. At this stage it does not have much stone, but is simply a "henge" – a sacred place surrounded by a bank and a ditch.

c 3200 BC
New people begin to arrive in the area to the north of the Persian Gulf. They speak a different language from the people already there, but together they form the Sumerian civilization.

dating from 3000 BC have been found in both Crete and Egypt. The candles they once held were made by dipping thin cords into molten wax.

Lubricants

c 3000 BC

The first wheeled vehicles needed lubrication because a wooden wheel rubbing on a wooden axle created a lot of heat. Any sort of oil or fat eased the problem for a while, but quickly burned away. The Egyptians, in about 1500 BC, were perhaps the first people to mix fat with lime and other substances, making lubricants that lasted.

Boat built from planks

c 3000 BC

The first boats built from planks are thought to have come from ancient Egypt. At Abydos, south of Cairo, archaeologists found 14 large boats, which had been made, almost 5000 years ago, by "sewing" planks together with ropes. The buried fleet was probably intended for use in the afterlife by a pharaoh. The boats' construction shows that the Egyptians still had a lot to learn – the boats had no frame and kept out water with reeds between the planks.

Calendar

c 3000 BC

The first calendars appeared in Babylonia, an ancient state in southern Mesopotamia. They were not very accurate because they were based on the Moon as well as the Sun, and

kept getting out of line with the seasons. The Egyptians, who had to know when to expect the annual flooding of the Nile, were the first to make a calendar based only on the Sun. (✳ *See also* **Kinds of calendar.**)

Cosmetics

c 3000 BC

People often feel the need to make themselves look more attractive or more frightening, and cosmetics have been used for these purposes since the earliest times. The oldest known cosmetics were found in ancient Egyptian tombs dating from about 3000 BC. They include perfume, skin cream (used by men as well as women), eye shadow, and mascara. Different minerals were ground up to make various colours, such as iron oxide for red and malachite for green. About 1000 years later, Britons daubed themselves with a blue dye called woad to frighten their enemies.

Cotton fibres grow from a seed

Strong fibres consist of 94 per cent cellulose

Ripe cotton pod is called a boll

Fibres begin to grow after the flower has fallen off

Fibres must be removed from the seed before being woven into fabric

Plants grow to about 1.6m (5.25 ft) high

Seeds can be cooked and pressed for their oil

COTTON *The textile fibre comes from various species of the plant* Gossypium.

Cotton

c 3000 BC

Cotton fabric starts out as a mass of silky fibres attached to the seeds of a plant belonging to the mallow family. It was probably discovered about 5000 years ago by people in the valley of the River Indus, in what is now called Pakistan. They found that the cotton seed fibres could be woven into much finer fabrics than could flax fibres (✳ *see page 11*). News of the discovery soon spread west into Mesopotamia, where the Assyrians welcomed cotton fabric as a substitute for rough wool. It then spread eastwards into China.

---

c 3000 BC On a group of islands in the Aegean Sea, the Cycladic culture emerges. Although based on seafaring and metalworking, the culture will be remembered for its simplified marble sculptures of females.

c 3000 BC The first known vet begins practising in the state of Mesopotamia (now mainly Iraq). His name is Urlugaledinna. He treats all kinds of animals, and in many cases he uses herbal medicines to cure them.

PUTTING IT IN WRITING

Middle Eastern traders create the first permanent records

CLAY SIGNATURE
Clay was used to carry information long before real writing began. People in Mesopotamia sealed packages with clay, then used a stone seal to impress their personal mark on it.

WRITING WITH A REED
The first "pencil and paper" was a stiff piece of reed and a soft piece of clay. The end of the reed was cut and used to make marks in the clay.

CUNEIFORM WRITING
Writing in Sumeria speeded up as curved lines gradually developed into wedges or triangles with short, straight sides. Later, signs were written from left to right, without any spaces between words.

EARLY GREEK WRITING
About 3000 years ago, people on the island of Crete used three different kinds of writing. In the 1950s, British architect Michael Ventris discovered how to read the kind seen here, called Linear B. The other two remain a mystery.

Writing, like so many inventions, came about by accident, and this one happened on the back of an envelope. About 6000 years ago in Mesopotamia, a group of people known as the Sumerians invented a new way of keeping track of trade. They made clay tokens shaped like animals, jars, and other goods, and recorded deals by wrapping the tokens up in clay envelopes. Once they'd sealed an envelope, they could no longer see what was inside it. So, using a pointed stick, they marked the soft clay with signs that showed its contents.

It didn't take them long to realize that, once they'd done this, they didn't need the tokens any more: just the marked envelope would do. So by about 3100 BC, the envelopes had turned into simple squares of clay recording trade deals in symbols. Writing had begun.

At first, the Sumerians used marks that were simplified pictures. To speed things up, they started jabbing the clay with the end of a reed instead of drawing with a stick. The pictures stopped looking like real things and became true writing. Archaeologists call it cuneiform. It was used for 3000 years.

There are some problems with writing in this way. Every time a new word is invented, someone has to invent a new mark. Some

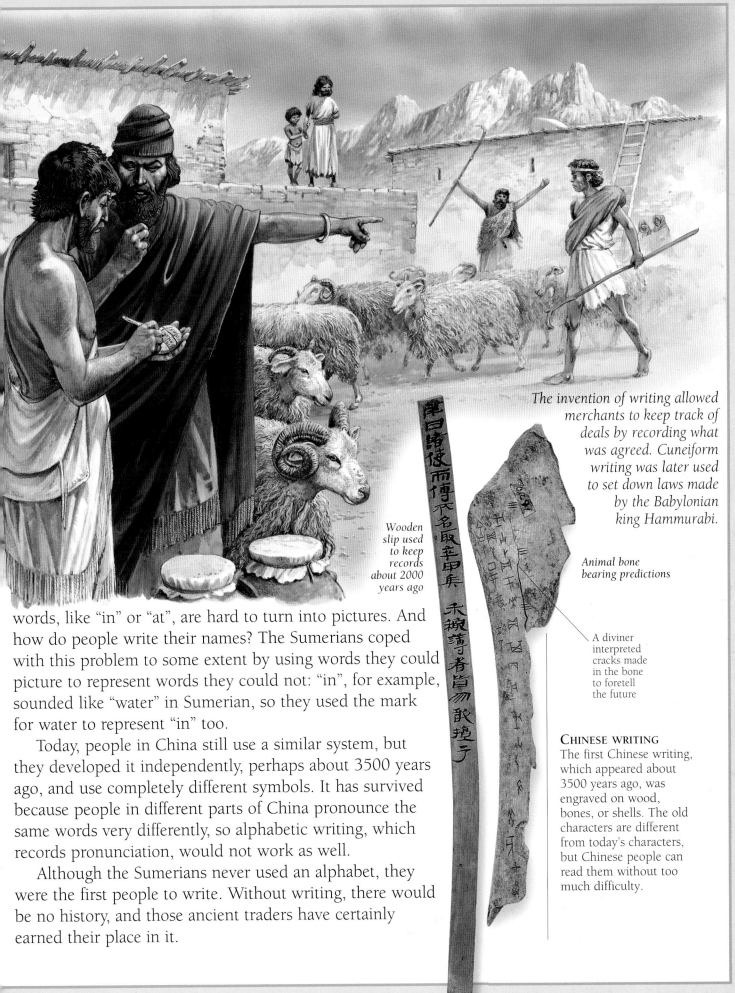

The invention of writing allowed merchants to keep track of deals by recording what was agreed. Cuneiform writing was later used to set down laws made by the Babylonian king Hammurabi.

Wooden slip used to keep records about 2000 years ago

Animal bone bearing predictions

A diviner interpreted cracks made in the bone to foretell the future

words, like "in" or "at", are hard to turn into pictures. And how do people write their names? The Sumerians coped with this problem to some extent by using words they could picture to represent words they could not: "in", for example, sounded like "water" in Sumerian, so they used the mark for water to represent "in" too.

Today, people in China still use a similar system, but they developed it independently, perhaps about 3500 years ago, and use completely different symbols. It has survived because people in different parts of China pronounce the same words very differently, so alphabetic writing, which records pronunciation, would not work as well.

Although the Sumerians never used an alphabet, they were the first people to write. Without writing, there would be no history, and those ancient traders have certainly earned their place in it.

CHINESE WRITING
The first Chinese writing, which appeared about 3500 years ago, was engraved on wood, bones, or shells. The old characters are different from today's characters, but Chinese people can read them without too much difficulty.

23

Ramp
c 3000 BC

By about 3000 BC, people were using the basic elements of machines: wheels, levers, and inclined planes, or ramps. The inclined plane makes it easier to lift a heavy object by allowing it to be pushed or pulled gradually up a slope, instead of heaving it straight up. The 2-tonne stone blocks of Egypt's Great Pyramid of Giza were lifted into place in about 2500 BC by workers pulling them up ramps.

Lathe
c 3000 BC

The lathe, perhaps 5000 years old, allows its user to form a piece of material into a circular shape by spinning it against a cutting edge. The mechanism of the earliest lathes was like that of early drills (✳ *see* **page 7**). A cord was wrapped around the piece to be shaped and pulled back and forth by a bow to make it rotate. Marble vases turned on a lathe, dating from before 2000 BC, have been found on some islands in the Aegean Sea.

Harp
c 3000 BC

The harp is one of the oldest musical instruments. It first appeared in Sumeria and Egypt about 5000 years ago. Early harps resembled bows used to fire arrows, but had several strings stretched across instead of one. These were plucked to sound notes. Although the harp has developed over the centuries into something almost as complicated as a piano, it is still played in its simplest form in parts of Africa and Afghanistan.

Lever
c 3000 BC

A simple lever is a rod or bar that turns around a pivot called a fulcrum. It changes the force exerted on one end into a greater force, but with smaller movement, at the other end. People were using levers by 3000 BC, and probably long before that. They may have discovered that a rock that was impossible to lift directly could be levered up with a tree branch resting on a smaller stone, which acted as the fulcrum. It wasn't until about 250 BC that Archimedes came up with a full explanation of how levers worked.

Lyre
c 3000 BC

The lyre is a musical instrument that is closely related to the harp. The strings are stretched between two arms attached to a box or bowl. People were playing lyres in Sumeria by 2800 BC. The instrument remained a favourite with the ancient Greeks, who linked it to the god Apollo, a handsome and gifted musician. Unlike the harp, the lyre did not make it into the modern orchestra.

Decorated base strengthens the sound

HARP *A harpist of c 2500 BC is shown here in a picture from Ur in Mesopotamia.*

Papyrus
c 3000 BC

The ancient Egyptians used papyrus much as we use paper. They made it by squashing and drying a mat of reed fibres until they stuck together, then polishing them with a stone to form a smooth sheet. Papyrus was too stiff to fold, so the Egyptians joined the sheets together to make long scrolls. It was on these scrolls that they wrote and drew much of what we now know about ancient Egypt from about 2600 BC onwards.

Painting with wax
c 3000 BC

The ancient Egyptians liked art. By about 3000 BC, they had developed a new technique of painting on walls, using a mixture of pigments and melted beeswax. When the painting was complete, they heated it to make it melt into the surface of the wall. This method is called encaustic painting. The result was rich and colourful, and many of the paintings can still be seen today. The technique was revived by US artist Jasper Johns in the 1960s.

Stone buildings
c 3000 BC

In 2600 BC, the Egyptian pharaoh Djoser and his architect Imhotep created the step pyramid at Sakkara – the first pyramid to be made entirely of stone. It was designed to be Djoser's tomb and rose in six steps to a height of 60 m (200 ft). At that time, nearly all buildings were made of bricks or wood. Small stone buildings did exist, but Djoser's gigantic pile of square-cut stone blocks must have seemed truly

---

c 3000 BC The Egyptians establish the first widely used unit of length, the cubit. It is the distance between the elbow and the end of the middle finger, usually about 450 mm (18 in), but sometimes longer.

c 3000 BC Merchants in the state of Babylonia begin to use bottomry, a form of insurance. They take out a loan to equip a ship. The interest rate is steep, but if the ship sinks they don't have to pay the money back.

amazing. The pyramids of Egypt are still some of the world's most impressive stone buildings. The tallest one is the Great Pyramid of Khufu at Giza. It is made from about two million huge blocks of limestone and stands 147 m (482 ft) high.

Venus

c 3000 BC

Although it is never visible in the middle of the night, the planet Venus is often the brightest object in the evening or morning sky. So it is not surprising that it was one of the first heavenly bodies to be studied. It features in the ancient astronomical records of China, Egypt, Greece, and South America, and the Babylonians made records of its movements as early as 3000 BC.

Dam

c 2900 BC

Dams are among the largest constructions that ancient people built. Probably the earliest was a 15 m (49 ft)

PAPYRUS *Artists working on papyrus could include fine detail. In this ancient Egyptian illustration, the heart of a dead person is being weighed to see if he is worthy of eternal life.*

mound raised beside the River Nile in Egypt in about 2900 BC. It was built to protect the city of Memphis from flooding. The remains of another dam almost as old can still be seen today at Wadi Gerrawi in Egypt. Instead of providing protection from floods, this one was built in 2500 BC to catch the seasonal flood in a dry river bed feeding the Nile. It is 90 m (295 ft) thick.

Clay tablet book

c 2800 BC

The first books were not made of paper. Instead, their writers, working in Mesopotamia in about 2800 BC, used rectangles of soft clay called tablets. One tablet could contain quite a lot of information, but not enough to be called a book. To write something longer, people did exactly what we do today. They used several tablets and numbered them to keep them in the right order.

c 2800 BC

People in northern Europe start to switch from mass burials in "houses for the dead" to graves that hold only one person. Not just anyone gets a grave to themselves. They are confined to high-ranking men.

c 2800 BC

Tree-lined walks and ponds with water birds appear in ancient Egypt as the first garden designers get started. Working for wealthy clients, they use a system of rectangular walled enclosures, and include small pavilions.

ACUPUNCTURE *This set of eight acupuncture needles and their protective case are from 19th-century China.*

Needles made of steel

Protective case made of mahogany

Lost-wax casting
c 2800 BC

Lost-wax casting is a way of making hollow objects. A lump of clay is covered with wax, which is then modelled and covered with plaster. When the mould is heated, the wax runs out, leaving a gap between the clay and plaster. Molten metal is poured into the gap and left to cool. This process is thought to have been invented by the Sumerians. The ancient Egyptians, who probably learned the technique from them, were using it by 2200 BC, and it is still used today.

Tea
c 2700 BC

Shen Nong

Tradition says that the Chinese emperor Shen Nong was boiling water beneath a camellia tree in about 2700 BC when a leaf fell in, creating the first cup of tea. The new drink, however, was not mentioned in a book until about AD 800, and it took another 800 years for tea to reach Europe. By 1657, the first "cuppa" had been sold in London, and tea became wildly fashionable.

Acupuncture
c 2700 BC

Sticking needles into certain places in the body can relieve pain and may restore health. Acupuncture was developed in China before 2500 BC, and has changed little, except that stone needles have now been replaced by stainless steel. Acupuncture is based on the idea that the life force, or *chi*, of the body flows in certain channels, which can become blocked. Twirling a needle in the right place is thought to make the *chi* start flowing smoothly again.

Chair
c 2600 BC

People were probably sitting on chairs well before 2600 BC, but the first chairs we actually know about were found in the tombs of ancient Egyptian kings. Placed there for their owner's comfort in the afterlife, these chairs had soft, padded seats and legs carved in the shapes of animals. The Egyptians also used folding stools of a design that can still be bought today.

Leavened bread
c 2600 BC

The first bread was rather hard to chew because it wasn't made lighter, or leavened, with yeast or other agents. The ancient Egyptians were the first people to produce leavened bread. They kept a stock of "sour

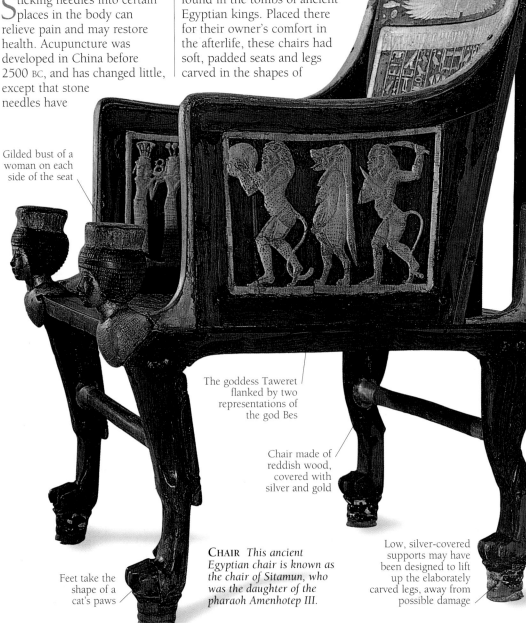

Gilded bust of a woman on each side of the seat

The goddess Taweret flanked by two representations of the god Bes

Chair made of reddish wood, covered with silver and gold

Feet take the shape of a cat's paws

CHAIR *This ancient Egyptian chair is known as the chair of Sitamun, who was the daughter of the pharaoh Amenhotep III.*

Low, silver-covered supports may have been designed to lift up the elaborately carved legs, away from possible damage

c 2800 BC
Cannabis, or hemp, begins to be grown in China. It is valued for its oily seeds and as a source of fibres for cloth and ropes, rather than as a drug. Centuries pass before it is grown in the Western world.

c 2700 BC
Egyptian farmers dance to make the rains come, and are recorded in paintings placed in tombs. Their dances are intended to bring the community not only rain, but also health and plenty of children.

dough", in which fermenting organisms were at work, and mixed in some of this whenever they made fresh dough. As the organisms from the sour dough multiplied, they produced bubbles of carbon dioxide gas, making the finished bread much lighter.

Silk

c 2600 BC

Silk is still considered to be the most desirable of fabrics. It was first made in China about 46 centuries ago, and its origin was a closely guarded secret. The silkworm and the luxurious, fibrous covering of its cocoon are said to have been discovered by a 14-year-old girl called Xilingshi, who was the wife of the emperor Huang Di. Nearly 3000 years passed before the secret was revealed, spreading to India, Japan, and eventually Europe.

Arch

c 2500 BC

Without arches, the only way to hold up doorways and roofs is with straight beams. An arch can span a greater distance than a straight beam, allowing wall openings to be larger. The first arches, built in India and Mesopotamia in about 2500 BC, were produced simply by building the top of the walls out towards each other until they met. By 100 BC, Roman builders were using semi-circular arches in almost all their buildings.

Carpet

c 2500 BC

The ancient Egyptians were weaving carpets of a sort by about 2500 BC, but nomadic tribes in eastern countries, such as Turkestan, soon became the greatest carpet makers. One carpet found preserved by the cold in Siberia had been buried with a nomad chieftain 2500 years previously, showing that carpets were highly prized. Carpets have often been associated with magic and romance. In 48 BC, the Egyptian queen Cleopatra introduced herself to the Roman emperor Julius Caesar by jumping out of a rolled-up carpet.

Glass

c 2500 BC

Glass had humble beginnings. It was probably discovered by accident. Made by heating sand with limestone and wood ash, it first appeared in the form of small ornamental beads in about 2500 BC. The basic formula may have been discovered in Mesopotamia, but it was the ancient Egyptians who began to develop it into the material we know today. By 1450 BC, they were making glass bottles in moulds, and over the next 1000 years their techniques spread to Europe and the East.

Ink

c 2500 BC

The first ink came in the form of a solid block made from soot mixed with glue, and had to be wetted before it could be used for writing. The ancient Egyptians wrote on papyrus with ink and a pen made from a reed, using a flowing style of writing called hieratic. In China, scribes wrote their characters with a brush. You can still buy blocks of Chinese ink exactly like those made 4500 years ago.

Mirror

c 2500 BC

Although chimpanzees enjoy looking at themselves in mirrors, humans are the only animals that do it every day. This began four or five thousand years ago, with discs of polished copper or bronze. A hand mirror was an essential fashion accessory in ancient Egypt, and the Romans gazed at themselves in mirrors made of silver. The first glass mirrors were made by Venetian craftsmen in about AD 1300.

Mirror was shaped in a mould

Hercules' lion skin

Silver handle was made separately

MIRROR *The reflecting surface of this ancient Roman mirror is polished silver. The handle is in the form of the club and lion skin of the ancient Greek mythical hero Hercules.*

c 2700 BC
A Chinese book of herbal medicine describes one of the first laxatives – rhubarb. It is taken as the powdered root of the plant. Rhubarb will not be cultivated for this purpose in the West until the 18th century AD.

c 2500 BC
A colossal pyramid is built in Egypt by the pharaoh Khufu. Future generations will know the Great Pyramid of Giza, near Cairo, as one of the most amazing structures in the history of architecture.

Potato

c 2500 BC

Farmers in Peru, South America, were cultivating potatoes in the high Andes mountains more than 4000 years before Spanish invaders discovered the strange new vegetable and took it back to Europe. Potatoes ceased to be important in Peru, but became a major crop elsewhere. By the middle of the 19th century, Ireland was so dependent on the potato that a series of crop failures led to famine.

Skis

c 2500 BC

As people in the northern hemisphere spread north towards the Arctic, they had to

SKIS *There is plenty of snow in Scandinavia, so it was an obvious place for skis to develop. Both the Vikings and Lapps used them.*

learn to cope with deep snow. Skis started out as something more like snow shoes: short, wide, wooden frames covered in leather. In time, they became the longer, more rigid devices we know today. The oldest known skis, found in the bogs of Finland and Sweden, date from about 2500 BC, and a Norwegian rock carving from about the same date clearly shows people using skis.

Welding

c 2500 BC

Welding is the process of joining metal parts together using heat or pressure. It is used today for making

large things like cars and ships, but it was first used with jewellery. Queen Pu-abi of Sumeria was buried about 4500 years ago with all her finery. This included some exquisite necklaces, the pieces of which, unlike earlier jewellery, were welded together. They are still in one piece today.

Parchment

c 2400 BC

Parchment is a smooth, white leather on which people write. It is supposed to have been invented in 200 BC, when King Ptolemy of Egypt banned exports of papyrus, forcing the ruler of a rival kingdom, Eumenes of Pergamum, to find a substitute. Although the word "parchment" is derived from "Pergamum", parchment books are known to have existed well

before this alleged incident, and ancient Egyptians had been writing on something very similar since 2400 BC.

Horse

c 2300 BC

Horses, more wild and wilful than sheep or pigs, took time to tame. The first people to get them under control lived in eastern Europe, around the area that is now called Ukraine. We don't know exactly when horses were domesticated, but by 2000 BC they were being used in Babylonia. Three hundred years later, they were also being used in Syria and ancient Palestine. They arrived in Egypt when a tribe of nomads, the Hyksos, used horse-drawn chariots to capture the city of Memphis and eventually most of Egypt.

---

c 2500 BC People in northern Peru build downwards and live in stone-lined pits. They know nothing of pottery, but weave baskets for containers. They also grow gourds (hollow fruits) and store things in these.

c 2500 BC Flower arranging thrives in Egypt. Bowls of flowers decorate banqueting tables, and bouquets are offered at funerals. Special vases are used to hold up the heavy heads of the most widely used flower, the lotus.

Barrel vault
c 2000 BC

Once builders had discovered how to make arches, they were soon using them to hold up the most crucial and awkward part of any building – the roof. By building a row of arches one behind the other, they created a strong, tunnel-shaped structure. Because of its shape, this is called a barrel vault. It was in use soon after the arch was invented, and remained a favourite feature with builders until modern times.

Bathroom
c 2000 BC

A bathroom was considered essential by some builders as long as 4000 years ago. Even relatively humble houses excavated at Mohenjo-Daro in the Indus valley (in what is now Pakistan), and dating from about 2000 BC, had bathrooms with drains. Some even had toilets, of a sort, with seats to sit on. Further west, in about 1700 BC, the wealthier Minoans of ancient Crete had more lavish bathrooms to which they could creep off for a quiet soak.

Bell chime
c 2000 BC

Clocks that strike use an idea that started in China before 2000 BC. Bells or blocks of stone tuned to musical notes were hung from a frame. They were hit with hammers to add music to religious ceremonies or simply to play tunes. The idea spread to Japan, India, and the West, where monks were playing rows of bells by about AD 850. Five hundred years later, the idea was adapted for public time-keeping, with the monks replaced by clockwork.

Chariot
c 2000 BC

Four-wheeled battle wagons were in use in Mesopotamia by 3000 BC. They developed from lumbering oxcarts, and although clumsy, they gave the Mesopotamian armies an advantage over their enemies. With the introduction of horses, and a switch to two wheels instead of four, the chariot, with its high-speed mobility, was born in about 2000 BC. (✻ *See also* **Wheels of war.**)

WHEELS OF WAR

As WITH many inventions, military commanders were pioneers in the development of wheeled transport. Large vehicles were probably first used for royal funerals, but soldiers soon saw that wheels could deliver men and materials to the battle front more quickly than feet or pack-animals. It was only later that chariots were used for fighting. Eventually, as soldiers became more skilful at riding horses, chariots went out of use.

Chariots were used for sport as well as war. Here, Assyrian king Ashurnasirpal II hunts lions.

Wheel with separate rim, spokes, and hub

Pole for attaching horses

Fast, manoeuvrable Roman chariots were highly developed fighting and racing vehicles.

CHARIOTS AS TRANSPORT
The first chariots had heavy bodies made of wood and leather, and four solid wooden wheels. The front axle pivoted for mobility, and was attached to a long pole, to which two oxen were attached by a wooden yoke. The charioteer rode in a raised section at the front that pivoted with the axle.

THE FIGHTING CHARIOT
The introduction of horses and a lighter construction, including spoked wheels (✻ *see* **page 31**), made the chariot into a formidable fighting platform for one or two soldiers. It had only two wheels, allowing it to take sharp turns, but could be pulled by as many as four horses. These lightweight chariots helped win many battles.

c **2400** BC On the island of Malta, a complex "cult of the dead" develops. It starts with shared tombs cut into the rock near Xagra and Zurrieq, and ends with an amazing underground burial chamber near Rahal Gdid.

c **2300** BC The Sumerian empire, weakened by internal strife, is taken over by an invader, Sargon I. He founds a new city, Agade. It becomes the wealthiest in the world, and the Sumerians become the Akkadians.

Iron

c 2000 BC

When iron was first discovered in south-east Asia, about 4000 years ago, it was considered more valuable than gold. As ways of extracting it and working it improved, people were able to make better use of its strength and flexibility. By about 1200 BC, the Iron Age had begun, pushing humanity faster than ever towards the modern world. Because iron is hard to melt, early users had to invent new techniques, such as shaping it by hammering rather than casting.

Paved road

c 2000 BC

The first road known to have been surfaced and drained so that it was usable in all weathers was built by the Minoans on the Mediterranean island of Crete in about 2000 BC. It was paved with stone and made higher in the centre so that water would drain to the edges, which had gutters in some places. One feature of this road seems odd today: the pedestrian walkway was in the middle, not at the sides.

Dice

c 2000 BC

It is thought that the ancient Egyptians were the first people to play with dice like the ones we use now. Before dice were given their spots in about 2000 BC, they existed in many other forms. People originally threw dice to try to predict the future, using objects such as bones or teeth. Perhaps it was inevitable that prediction soon led to gambling. Today, people still place bets on the throw of a dice.

Lock

c 2000 BC

Most locks today are based on an idea from about 2000 BC. The ancient Egyptians invented a wooden lock in which a bolt was held by pins that dropped into holes in it. Only a key shaped to push all the pins out of the way would free the bolt. Modern Yale locks and keys work in much the same way (✳ see page 144).

Blades operated by a spring action

IRON *Suitably treated iron is springy and takes a sharp edge – ideal for making shears like these from ancient Rome.*

Saw

c 2000 BC

Unlike an axe or knife, a saw can cut cleanly through any thickness of

Mast and sail on the model were missing upon discovery, but were replaced by replicas based on other ships of the same time

Square sail

Sailor at the bow with a plumbline to test the depth of the water

Men pull the rope to adjust the position of the sail

SHIP *Ancient Egyptian ships, like this model found in a tomb of c 2000 BC, needed paddles to help the sails propel the craft through the water. It was a common custom to place models of boats in the tombs of kings and nobles, for their transport in the afterlife.*

c 2000 BC People of the Celtic race build "beehive" houses in Scotland and Ireland. The houses, constructed from rough stone blocks, are circular in shape and rise to a point in the centre like a straw beehive.

c 2000 BC The world's first written language, Sumerian, ceases to be spoken because the Sumerians, now the Akkadians, switch to the language of their conquerors. Sumerian will live on in written form for 2000 years.

wood. Its angled teeth cut in easy stages and create a gap wide enough for the blade to pass right through. The invention of the saw was made possible by the discovery of copper and, by 1500 BC, the ancient Egyptians were sawing planks. Modern saws cut on the push stroke, but to stop them from buckling, early saws worked the other way around.

Sexagesimal number system

c 2000 BC

Our 60-minute hour and 60-second minute come from a system devised about 4000 years ago by the Babylonians. It was the first to use a basic feature of the decimal system we use today: the value of each digit depended on where it was placed. The Babylonians based their system on 60 instead of

10, so a 1 in the first position meant 1, but in the second position it meant 1 × 60, or 60, and in the third position it meant 1 × 60 × 60, or 3600.

Male and female plants

c 2000 BC

The Babylonians were expert farmers and gardeners. They found out early on that some kinds of plant can, like people, be either male or female. The female plant produces fruit, but only when fertilized by pollen from a male plant. Illustrations on Babylonian seals show fertilization being done artificially, and by 1800 BC, people were buying and selling male date-palm flowers for this purpose.

Support for steering oar

Passengers seated at the stern

The Egyptians used planks of cedar wood for the best real ships

Large oar used for steering

Ship

c 2000 BC

It is hard to say when a boat becomes a ship, but a ship needs to be large enough to cross open water safely. The

ancient Egyptians built the first ships well suited to the sea about 4000 years ago. They had already discovered how to arrange their sails to cope with winds coming from the side. To deal with winds coming from in front of them, they kept paddles on board, too.

Tongs

c 2000 BC

Tongs were probably first made for handling hot metal. They could have appeared at any time after people started melting metals, from about 3000 BC onwards. The earliest evidence is an ancient Egyptian wall-painting from about 1450 BC. It shows a metalworker blowing through a tube to make a fire hot while he holds an object over it with an unmistakable pair of tongs.

Sling

c 2000 BC

A sling is a weapon made from a piece of leather with two cords attached. Its user puts a stone on to the leather,

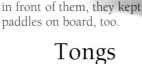

SLING *The young Israelite David challenges the Philistine giant Goliath with his trusty sling.*

whirls the sling around with the cords, then releases one cord to launch the stone. It was with a sling that David famously killed Goliath in the Old Testament of the Bible. The Old Testament was written in about 1000 BC, so the sling must date back to before then. It was used by the ancient Egyptian army in about 750 BC, and can still be seen today.

Spoked wheel

c 2000 BC

The first wheels were solid and heavy, but it didn't take vehicle builders long to work out that the important parts were the rim and the hub. They made the rest of the wheel lighter by cutting holes in it, forming crude spokes. Stronger spokes, usually four, made from separate pieces of wood, were being used in Mesopotamia by 2000 BC, but it was another 1000 years before this type of wheel reached northern Europe.

---

c 2000 BC The Aleutian Islands, off the coast of Alaska in North America, are colonized by people from the mainland. They build villages on the seashore near fresh water, travel in skin boats, and hunt seals and bears.

c 2000 BC An event similar to throwing the hammer starts at the Tailteann Games in Ireland, but with a chariot wheel, not a hammer. Celtic hero Chulainn grabs the wheel by the axle and hurls it as far as he can.

Corset

c 1900 BC

People have never been satisfied with the shape of their bodies. Four thousand years ago, Minoan women living on the island of Crete in the Mediterranean Sea were wearing corsets to pinch in their waists. And it may not just have been the women who wanted to accentuate their curves: wall-paintings from about 1500 BC, excavated at the palace of King Minos, also show Minoan men looking suspiciously wasp-waisted.

Running water

c 1700 BC

The ancient bathrooms of Mohenjo-Daro in the Indus valley had everything but running water. This wasn't good enough for wealthy Minoans on Crete. They wanted their water on tap, and excavations show that they got it. Pipes and drains ran throughout the great palace of King Minos at Knossos, making bath time more of a pleasure than a chore.

Child's swing

c 1600 BC

Nobody really knows when the swing was invented or, more probably, developed from a dangling creeper. But a purpose-built swing was found in excavations of Minoan Crete dating back to 1600 BC. The swing is just one of the ancient amusements, like jacks (fivestones) or blind man's buff, that have kept children happy for countless generations.

Brass

c 1500 BC

Brass is an alloy, or mixture, of copper and zinc. Its strength, bright colour, and resistance to corrosion make it a good material for many objects. Its early history is difficult to trace because it was often confused with bronze. As late as the 18th century, many people used brass that was made by a method dating back to its discovery. In this process, copper and zinc ore were heated together, producing brass. Because the zinc ore that they used was called calamine, the product was known as calamine brass.

Flag

c 1500 BC

We don't treat flags with such great respect today, but when they were invented in China they had life-or-death significance and played a vital part in battles. If a leader's flag was captured by the enemy, it was all over. Strangely enough, the first important flag we know about, which belonged to the first ruler of the Zhou dynasty in about 1100 BC, was white – a colour that people in the West now associate with surrender and defeat.

Gloves

c 1500 BC

Although the weather does sometimes get cold in Egypt, the fine linen gloves found in the tomb of the boy king Tutankhamun were probably more ceremonial than practical. They show, however, that even in this generally hot country, some people were wearing gloves by 1350 BC. People in colder places must have worn them too, but we do not have any evidence of this before about AD 700.

Secret writing

c 1500 BC

As soon as people began to write, they started to worry that the wrong people would read what they had written. Secret writing, or encryption, has a long history. The first known example is in ancient Egyptian hieroglyphs of about 1500 BC. It may have been

---

c 1900 BC
Interior decorators are hard at work for wealthy people in Egypt. They paint patterns on plaster, hang textured matting screens, add red, white, and black striped dados, and install painted wooden ceilings.

c 1900 BC
The cities of Sodom and Gomorrah near the Dead Sea in Israel are destroyed in an earthquake. Later, the book of Genesis in the Bible will say that God destroyed them because their people were so sinful.

Trumpet
c 1500 BC

A trumpet is any kind of tube that you sound by squeezing air into it through your lips. The Australian didgeridoo is technically a trumpet, as is the shofar, made from a ram's horn, which is still used in Jewish rituals. The earliest existing silver trumpet dates from about 1500 BC and comes from ancient Egypt. It was probably used for ritual purposes. The Romans developed trumpets for use in battle, but it was another 1000 years before the trumpet really began to develop into the musical instrument that is played today.

Armour
c 1100 BC

Body armour was worn in battle until the 17th century, when firearms made it useless. It developed bit by bit – helmets, belts, reinforced shirts – over thousands of years. In about 1100 BC, Chinese soldiers were wearing armour made from layers of rhinoceros hide. By 800 BC, Greek warriors were wearing substantial bronze helmets, metal shin guards, and bronze items called cuirasses, which totally covered their chest.

TRUMPET *The Australian didgeridoo, made from a eucalyptus branch, produces a deep droning sound. It is usually about 1.5 m (5 ft) long.*

Clepsydra
c 1500 BC

The Egyptians usually told the time from the Sun, but were also using a clock called a clepsydra by about 1500 BC. The basic model was just a pot of water with a hole near the bottom and marks down the side. As the water ran out, its level showed the time. The flow slowed as the pot emptied, so the marks had to be closer together near the bottom, making them hard to read. An improved model, invented in about 270 BC, worked the other way around: water ran into the pot, moving a pointer to show the time.

Marks show the approximate time

Ankh symbol was the Egyptian sign of life

CLEPSYDRA *This is a cast of a clepsydra found at the ancient Egyptian temple at Karnak. The clepsydra dates from 1415–1380 BC.*

intended to amuse rather than conceal. But some writers of books in the Old Testament in the Bible did try to hide the meaning of their text by reversing the entire alphabet.

Shoes
c 1500 BC

The earliest shoes were sandals, but by about 1500 BC, in Mesopotamia, people were wearing shoes that completely enclosed their feet. They were similar to what we would now call moccasins – single pieces of soft leather drawn up around the ankles with a rawhide thong. At about the same time, the Minoans of Crete were stepping into calf-length boots for winter wear.

c 1600 BC A scribe in Egypt prepares a new edition of a 1500-year-old medical manual. The papyrus scroll gives instructions for examining patients with a range of conditions, and details the treatment for each case.

c 1400 BC Greek people begin to write their language, using a script quite unlike the alphabet they will develop later. In 3350 years' time, a cryptographer will decipher it, and it will be called Linear B.

ICE SKATES This skate is made from a leg bone of a horse. Dating from about AD 1200, it was inexpensive and did not rust.

Oars

c 1100 BC

Oars of a sort are as old as boats, but were probably perfected by the Phoenicians, seafarers who came from an area that is now mainly Lebanon. By 1100 BC, they were the greatest traders in the eastern Mediterranean, and by 700 BC they had developed the bireme, a ship with an extra deck to allow for twice as many oars. Later, the Greeks developed this into the formidable trireme, a fighting ship with oars on three levels.

Camel

c 1000 BC

The ancient Egyptians knew about camels as early as 3000 BC, but they do not seem to have used them to carry anything. The idea of loading this unfriendly but almost desert-proof beast with up to half a tonne of goods came from Mesopotamia about 2000 years later. The people here also bred the camel into a lighter, faster animal for riding.

Ice skates

c 1000 BC

You would expect ice skates to come from somewhere with plenty of ice, and it does seem likely that skating began in Scandinavia

about 3000 years ago. Metals were a luxury there, so the first ice skates were made from bones of animals such as reindeer and horses. Developed as a practical necessity, skating eventually became a sport, with the canals of the Netherlands providing ideal ice rinks from medieval times.

Knitting

c 1000 BC

A disadvantage of woven fabrics is that people need a loom to make them. Although early looms were portable, clothes that could be made using nothing but a pair of needles had obvious appeal to nomadic people. So it is likely that knitting originated among the nomads of the deserts of north Africa in about 1000 BC. It seems to have reached Europe by way of Egypt, where archaeologists have found knitted items dating from about 450 BC.

Magnet

c 1000 BC

Some time before 800 BC, the Greeks discovered a curious black rock in the plains of northern Greece. Thales of Miletus may later have written about the rock's strange attraction to iron, but the Greeks do not seem to have discovered its ability to

point north. Chinese explorers discovered this some 300 years later (✳ *see* **page 37**). The place where it was first found, Magnesia, gave its name to the mineral (magnetite) and to anything with the same property (a magnet).

OARS This is a model of a Phoenician bireme of c 700 BC.

Square-rigged sail adds speed

Hull probably made in one piece from a tree-trunk

Upper deck fits above the heads of the inner oarsmen

Bow shaped to form a ram

c 1100 BC The circle of stones now known as Stonehenge is still in use. It gets a facelift in the shape of a much longer entrance avenue, stretching 2.8 km (1.7 miles) east and then south-east to the River Avon.

c 1000 BC A new Hindu calendar is adopted in India. Its year is 12 Moon months. An actual year is longer than this, so one extra month is added in every 30. The calendar will still be in use 3000 years later.

Iron-tipped ploughshare

c 900 BC

The part of a plough that lifts and turns the soil, the ploughshare, wore away quickly when it was made of wood or bronze. Iron is harder than bronze, but was an expensive material in ancient times. The answer was to continue to use a wooden ploughshare but use iron to protect the tip. Ploughs of this type were probably being used in ancient Palestine by 900 BC.

Alphabet

c 900 BC

An alphabet contains symbols for individual speech sounds. Early writers did not use an alphabet: their symbols stood for whole words or, later, syllables. An alphabet with symbols for consonants appeared in Syria or ancient Palestine in about 1600 BC. By about 900 BC, the Greeks had adapted this to their own language by adding vowels. This was the first alphabet that recorded speech accurately, and it became the ancestor of several others, including the alphabet used for English.

Socks

c 800 BC

Once they started wearing shoes, people must have felt the need for socks. We don't know when they first started wearing them, but the earliest mention of socks was in a poem by the Greek poet Hesiod, who was working in about 700 BC. These early socks were probably made of felt rather than knitted, so they wouldn't have been very comfortable.

Oil lamp

c 700 BC

People have been making artificial light by burning oil sucked up by plant fibres for at least 30,000 years. But true oil lamps, with a reservoir that could be refilled and a fibrous wick that gave a controlled flame without burning away itself, came much later. Simple lamps, with a spike or channel to hold a wick, existed in ancient China and Egypt, but the first really practical lamps – they even had handles – appeared in ancient Greece in about 700 BC. They usually ran on olive or nut oil. None of these early lamps gave out enough light for detailed work after dark. (✳ *See also* **New lamps for old**.)

NEW LAMPS FOR OLD

TO MAKE a successful lamp, three things have to be just right: the fuel, the fuel reservoir, and the wick. Oil burns with less smoke than fat. The reservoir should be easy to fill and convenient to carry. The wick is needed to spread the oil into a thin film so that it will vaporize and burn. A good wick will feed the flame without burning away rapidly itself.

This ornate bronze oil lamp was used by rich people in the late AD 900s in the Afghan empire of central Asia.

THE FIRST LAMPS

The first cave painters may have worked by the light of burning branches. It is possible that while they were cooking they noticed that a branch burned for longer if it was soaked in fat. From there, it would have been a short step to the first lamp – a container of moss or twigs dipped in fat or oil. Moss or twigs spread the oil but they tended to burn away.

LATER OIL LAMPS

Improving on the fat-soaked bunch of twigs, called a lampas, the ancient Greeks developed oil lamps shaped like a teapot with a fibrous wick in the spout. No great improvements were made until 1784 when Swiss inventor Aimé Argand produced a lamp with a cylindrical wick and a glass chimney.

Stays hold up the heavy mast

Shields protect the oarsmen

Steering oars

c 1000 BC

A big, white, shaggy breed of dog known as the great Pyrenees or Pyrenean mountain dog reaches Europe from Asia. It is used to guard sheep from wolves and bears, which are common in the region.

800 BC

The population of China reaches 14 million as the country continues to grow. Over the next 800 years, it will increase more than fourfold to 60 million, and after a further 2000 years it will be about one billion.

Shadow clock
c 700 BC

People knew at least 3500 years ago that the shadow cast by a vertical pole could be used to indicate the time. By 700 BC, at the latest, the ancient Egyptians had perfected the shadow clock. It had a straight scale of hours, probably with a raised part at one end to cast a shadow on the scale, and it had to be turned to point the opposite way after half a day. Astronomers, including Berosus from Babylonia, made curved sundials several hundred years later.

Archimedean screw
c 600 BC

The Archimedean screw is a kind of pump that is still used today for irrigating the land (✳ see page 16). A cylinder with a large screw inside has its bottom end dipping into water. As the screw is turned, it pushes water up the cylinder in the same way that a wood screw is pulled into wood. Archimedes did not invent the screw himself, but he wrote about it, probably after seeing one being used in Egypt in about 260 BC. The date of the screw's actual invention is uncertain.

Rotary quern
c 600 BC

After 3000 years in which generations of women laboriously ground corn by hand between two stones, an improvement, known as the rotary quern, was developed. It had a heavy, circular top stone that fitted snugly into a hole in a stone base. Grain was fed through a hole in the centre of the top stone, which was turned round and round with a wooden handle. The two stones crushed the grain between them,

Farmer uses a handle to turn the screw

Water flows out of the cylinder

Irrigation channel

Cobalt blue
c 650 BC

The deep blue colour known as cobalt blue, still widely used on pottery, seems to have been discovered by the Assyrians in about 650 BC. The use of minerals containing cobalt to give a blue colour is part of one of their glass recipes. They knew nothing, of course, about the chemical element cobalt, which was not discovered until 1742. Although cobalt blue is used to decorate Chinese porcelain today, Chinese potters did not begin to use it until AD 800 at the earliest.

Screw lifts water up through the cylinder

Wooden cylinder (cut away) prevents water from escaping

c 700 BC People in Assyria (now mainly northern Iraq) hunt with hawks and falcons. All kinds of hunting are popular with royalty. The Assyrian king Ashurbanipal has himself portrayed in stone with the words, "I killed the lion."

c 650 BC The famously pessimistic biblical prophet Jeremiah is born in Anathoth, a village near Jerusalem. He will condemn his people for worshipping false gods and proclaim his vision of a terrible invasion from the north.

grinding it into flour. The flour came out of the narrow gap around the edge of the top stone. This useful device was probably invented before 500 BC, but nobody really knows where.

Metal coins

c 600 BC

Before about 600 BC, people often exchanged pieces of precious metal in return for goods. It was easy to cheat by handing over impure metal or too small a quantity, so traders wasted time checking the quality and weight of all the different pieces. The Lydians, from what is now western Turkey, stopped this. They standardized the quality and weight of the pieces, and stamped them with the king's mark as proof of their value. They had invented coins.

Shop

c 600 BC

According to the Greek historian Herodotus, who lived in about 450 BC, the people who invented coins also invented shops. The Lydians certainly had a talent for making money. Their capital city, Sardis, was known for its magnificence, and one of their kings gave his name to the expression "rich as Croesus", which means very rich indeed.

Attraction of objects to amber

c 600 BC

Thales of Miletus

The history of electricity starts with a yellow fossil resin called amber. In about 600 BC, the Greek philosopher

MAGNETIC COMPASS *This Chinese sundial includes a built-in compass.*

Magnetic compass

c 500 BC

When and where the compass was invented depends on what is meant by compass. The north-seeking properties of the magnetic rock called lodestone (or magnetite) were used hundreds of years before a magnetized needle was pivoted in a case. The earliest records are from China in

---

ARCHIMEDEAN SCREW *The cylinder is cut away in this model of an Archimedean screw to show how the screw lifts water as it turns.*

Fixing post holds the screw in place

Thales observed that amber rubbed on cloth attracted small, light objects. What he saw was the result of static electricity, but it was more than 2000 years before an English doctor, William Gilbert, investigated this thoroughly (✳ *see* **page 85**). He coined the term "electric", for the attracting effect, from the Greek word "elektron" meaning "amber".

Musical ratios

c 520 BC

Pythagoras

See **pages 38–39** for the story of how Pythagoras and his followers discovered the harmony of the universe.

WRITING BRUSH *Used in 19th-century Japan, this writing brush is made of hair set in a bamboo shaft.*

Pythagoras' theorem

c 520 BC

Pythagoras

Pythagoras' theorem states that in a right-angled triangle, the square of the longest side is equal to the sum of the squares of the other two sides. Pythagoras may not have thought of it himself: it could have been any member of the group he founded in Italy in about 530 BC (✳ *see* **pages 38–39**). But no matter who invented it, the theorem often crops up in the mathematics of the modern world, and we couldn't do without it.

about 500 BC, where pieces of lodestone were used to guide mineral prospectors. The first real compass did not appear until AD 1100 or later.

Writing brush

c 500 BC

Before the invention of the writing brush, in about 500 BC, people in China wrote on bamboo with a stiff stylus. The writing brush, with its pencil-sized bamboo shaft and pointed tip, could be used on silk. A brush is well suited to the complexities of Chinese script. It came into its own two or three hundred years later, when it was used for *li-shu*, the first writing to make full use of the elegant brush strokes we now associate with Chinese calligraphy (✳ *see* **page 50**).

---

c 600 BC Seafarers from Phoenicia (now Lebanon) regularly make the 6000 km (3750 mile) journey to Britain to collect tin from Cornwall. To do so, they have to work out ways of navigating the open ocean.

c 500 BC The last Irish elk, a type of deer similar to a moose, dies out. With it go the largest antlers ever known. The Irish elk's antlers measured up to 4 m (13 ft) across, and had sharp points all around the edge.

THE MUSIC OF NUMBERS

Pythagoras and his followers discover the harmony of the universe

Two and a half thousand years ago, a small town in southern Italy was home to an extraordinary group of thinkers. As well as discovering facts about music and mathematics that we still use today, they created a philosophy that has had a deep influence on the way we see the world – in particular our belief that physics and mathematics can explain most things.

The Greek philosopher Pythagoras was about 50 years old when he crossed the Ionian Sea to settle in Crotona (now Crotone) and gather his students around him. Bound together by vows of loyalty and secrecy, the Pythagoreans held beliefs that amounted to a mathematical religion. Because they also believed that human souls could live on in animals, they were strict vegetarians.

Pythagoras is best known for the theorem that bears his name (✳ *see* page 37) but this was just one of many relationships that his group found between numbers. The Pythagoreans were fascinated by the fact that 1 + 2 + 3 + 4 = 10, and that these numbers can be arranged into a triangle, which they called the *tetraktys*. Their belief that the whole universe was based on a mystic order, or *kosmos*, was greatly strengthened when they discovered that there was a link between the *tetraktys* and music.

Starting with a musical string that had a length of one unit, they found that dividing it into two, three, or four parts produced new notes that all harmonized perfectly with each other.

ANCIENT JOURNEY
Pythagoras was born on the island of Samos in the Aegean Sea. In about 530 BC he sailed westwards to Crotona, in the south of what is now Italy.

SOLID SCIENCE
Pythagoras got the idea of musical ratios by listening to blacksmiths hammering on anvils, and then applied it to strings. This woodcut of about 1490 shows two ways of demonstrating that his theory still applies to three-dimensional objects.

SECRETIVE SCIENTIST
This bust portrays Pythagoras as a great man of science, but in reality he forbade his followers to publish any of their discoveries.

This discovery not only laid the foundations of the science of music, but also led the Pythagoreans to a new view of the universe.

The Pythagoreans were among the first thinkers to contemplate an Earth that was not at the centre of everything. They said that the planets revolved around a "central fire". And, because the universe was ruled by numbers, the distances between the planets were in the same proportions as those that produced harmonious sounds, creating an unearthly "music of the spheres".

THE DEBATER
This detail from a frieze at the University of Athens probably shows an accurate view of how the Pythagoreans formed their theories, basing them on belief and fierce argument rather than on cold contemplation of abstract symbols.

The tetraktys was a triangle of ten dots. The Pythagoreans must have known of other triangular numbers, because two of them, 3 and 6, form part of the tetraktys.

THE MATHEMATICIAN
We don't know what Pythagoras looked like, but many artists through the ages have used their imagination to portray him as a man fascinated by his mystic symbols and books.

We have moved on since Pythagoras' time, but not by that much. Physicists and cosmologists (who get their name from the Greek word *kosmos*) are still looking for much the same thing as Pythagoras and his followers: a reassuring mathematical order in the universe – the elusive "theory of everything".

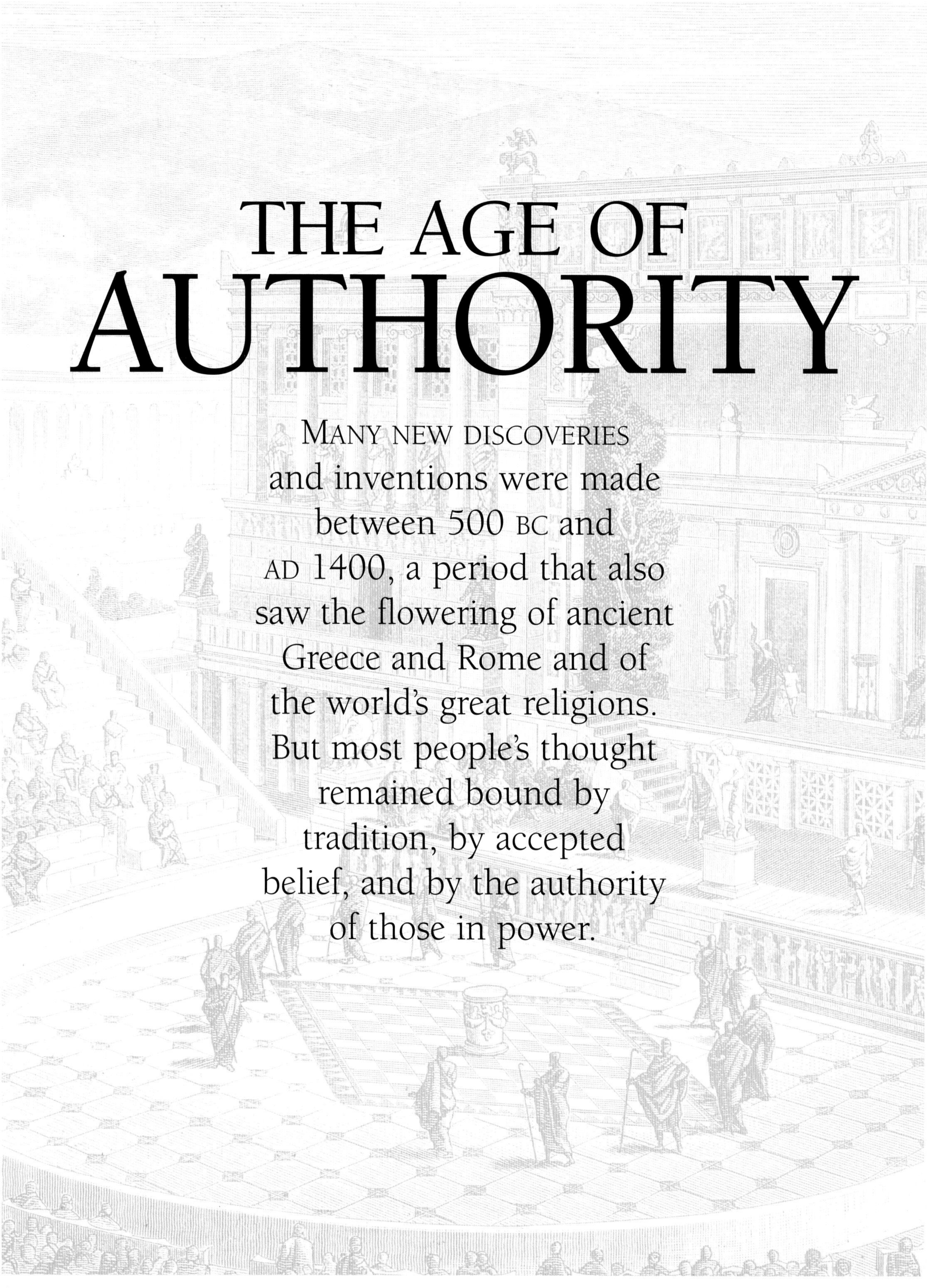

THE AGE OF
AUTHORITY

MANY NEW DISCOVERIES
and inventions were made
between 500 BC and
AD 1400, a period that also
saw the flowering of ancient
Greece and Rome and of
the world's great religions.
But most people's thought
remained bound by
tradition, by accepted
belief, and by the authority
of those in power.

IRON IN BUILDING *This is the Temple of Concord, one of about 20 temples in Agrigento dating from the 5th and 6th centuries BC.*

Sturdy column with a flat top, or capital, known as the Doric style

Ancient Greek buildings may have been inspired by earlier buildings whose roofs were supported by tree-trunks

Iron in building

c 470 BC

The Victorians are usually thought of as being the first people to use iron as a structural material. But 2300 years before Queen Victoria, ancient Greek builders in Agrigentum (now Agrigento, Sicily) installed a huge iron beam 5 m (16 ft) long in one of the city's many temples. The ancient Greeks were also using other, smaller beams and all sorts of iron fittings to hold their blocks of stone together.

Theatre scenery

458 BC

Aeschylus

The word "scenery" comes from the dressing room, or "skene", once used by actors in ancient Greece. It was in a building at the back of the stage and, by the time of the playwright Aeschylus, it was also being used to support

coloured panels, which formed a background for the actors. For the first performance of his trilogy of plays the *Oresteia*, Aeschylus created an even better background. He had the plain panels painted with colourful pictures to create what we now call scenery.

CENTRAL HEATING *The Greeks may have circulated hot air around these pillars in the ruined city of Phaselis to heat the room above.*

Cause of solar eclipses

c 450 BC

Anaxagoras

Even the sophisticated people of Athens regarded eclipses of the Sun with fear, until the Greek philosopher Anaxagoras explained them. Anaxagoras came to Athens from what is now Turkey. He said that a solar eclipse was just the Moon getting in the way of the Sun. This was true, but he also thought that the Sun was a white-hot rock less than half the size of Greece.

Central heating

c 450 BC

Most people think the Romans were the first builders of central heating systems, but the Greeks may have built them first. The Romans called their under-floor hot air system a hypocaust, and

"hypocaust" is actually a Greek word meaning "burning below". The ruined Greek city of Phaselis, now in Turkey, has buildings with hollow floors, just like a Roman hypocaust. This suggests that the Greeks were using central heating as early as 450 BC.

Earth, air, fire, and water

c 450 BC

Empedocles

Ancient Greek philosophers spent centuries wondering what the universe was made of. By about 350 BC, most of them had accepted a theory put forward by the statesman and poet Empedocles about 100 years earlier. He said that everything was made of earth, air, fire, and water mixed in various proportions. His theory may seem funny to us, but it was the first one that suggested the existence of chemical elements, and it eventually led to modern chemistry.

490 BC The first ever marathon is run in Greece when a soldier staggers 42 km (26 miles) from Marathon to Athens to bring news of a victory over the Persians. A race of this distance will become a sporting event 2386 years later.

450 BC Responding to popular demand, the Romans move towards more open government by writing down and publishing their laws. Before this, the laws were known only to a select few, so justice was rarely seen to be done.

Signs of the zodiac

c 450 BC

It was probably the Babylonians who devised the signs of the zodiac. These represent the 12 groupings of stars through which the Sun seems to travel during the year. A cuneiform tablet dated 419 BC carries a horoscope using the signs. It was the ancient Greeks, however, who named the band of sky that contains the Ram, the Bull, and the other constellations. They called it *"zodiakos kyklos"*, or "circle of animals".

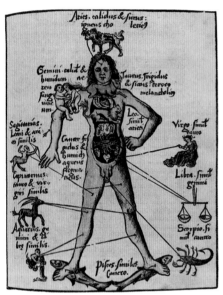

SIGNS OF THE ZODIAC
This 16th-century woodcut gives one of many theories that developed linking the zodiac with the body.

Flying actor

c 450 BC

Sophocles

When an ancient Greek playwright got into an impossible tangle with a plot, the usual way out was to have a god descend from heaven and sort out the mess. The god was played by an actor hoisted into the air with a crane. The same device, called a mechane, was also useful for comic effects: a character in one play by Aristophanes flies up to heaven on a dung beetle.

Grid-plan city

c 450 BC

Hippodamus of Miletus

Many ancient cities have some sort of regular grid plan, but Hippodamus of Miletus was the first real town planner. He was a colourful and influential character who believed that buildings should be grouped according to their function. He put his thoughts into practice when he became involved in the rebuilding of the Greek port of Piraeus and the construction of a new Greek settlement in southern Italy.

Knitted socks

c 450 BC

After enduring scratchy felt socks for centuries, feet finally got some loving care in the shape of knitted socks.

Knitting is ideal for making snugly shaped garments like gloves and socks, and allows them to be made in one piece instead of being stitched together from separate pieces of cloth. Some wealthy ancient Egyptians were buried in their knitted socks in about 450 BC, and 800 years later, people in Saudi Arabia wore knitted socks with their sandals.

Mule

c 450 BC

Horses are not well suited to hot, dry climates. Donkeys are better suited, but are often too small and slow. We don't know who came up with the idea of crossing a horse with a donkey to get the best of both, or whether it occurred naturally, but it probably happened in or around Turkey. The result was the tough, strong mule, an animal that was first recorded by the ancient Greek historian Herodotus in about 450 BC.

Throwing arm has a cup at the end to hold the missile

Skein of twisted sinews provides pulling power

---

c 450 BC Chinese military expert Sunzi writes the first book on spying. It shows how to organize intelligence and counter-intelligence systems with secret agents, including double agents who spy for both sides.

443 BC Censorship begins in Rome with the appointment of the first censor. At first, his job is just to count people, but it soon gets extended to looking after public morality and suppressing unwanted publications.

University

c 450 BC

If we take a university to be any centre of learning, then the world's first university was probably Nalanda in the north of India's Bihar state. This Buddhist monastic institution may well have been in existence while Gautama the Buddha, founder of the Buddhist religion, was still alive. It survived until after 1100, when invaders from Turkey destroyed it.

Coded correspondence

c 410 BC

The first secret messages were exchanged by the Spartan army chiefs of ancient Greece, using a tapered rod called a scytale. They wound a strip of leather around the rod, then wrote on the leather. When unwrapped, the strip displayed a meaningless jumble, but when wrapped around an identical scytale, it revealed what had been written. It was thanks to a scytale message that Lysander of Sparta avoided defeat by the Persians in 404 BC.

Catapult

c 400 BC

Long before gunpowder was invented, huge wooden catapults were used to hurl missiles, such as iron-tipped darts or boulders. The first examples may have been used in 399 BC in the war between Rome and the ancient empire of Carthage in north Africa. A pair of arms were swung back to hold the missile, twisting and tightening cords made of animal sinews. When the tension in the cords was released, the arms sprang forwards, launching the missile up to 500 m (1640 ft) away, but not very accurately.

Crossbow

c 400 BC

A soldier could shoot an arrow further with a crossbow than with an ordinary bow. The first crossbow was the gastrophetes – a stiff bow of ancient Greece. The "gastro" part of its name means "stomach", because the soldier had to rest one end of the bow in the pit of his stomach. He rested the other end on the ground and bent the bow into the firing position, ready to be released by a trigger. It was a deadly weapon, as long as there was time to load it.

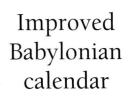

CROSSBOW *By the 15th century, the crossbow had developed into a long-range weapon that was aimed like a rifle.*

CATAPULT
The catapult was still used as a weapon in the Middle Ages. It was useful if there was time to get it into place and the target was easy to hit.

Rope to winch down the arm

Heavy base to keep the catapult on the ground

Improved Babylonian calendar

c 380 BC

The early Babylonian calendar started a new month with every new moon (✳ **see page 21**). To keep it in step with the seasons, extra months had to be added now and then. Confusingly, different cities added months at different times. Some might even add two months in the same year. In 541 BC, everyone was ordered to add months at the same times, but it was not until about 380 BC that astronomers worked out a cycle of extra months that really kept the calendar on track. Then, for a while, the Babylonian calendar became the best in the world.

---

c 430 BC A giant statue of the Greek god Zeus is completed by Phidias. Nearly 12 m (40 ft) high, it shows Zeus on a throne encrusted with gold and precious stones. It becomes one of the Seven Wonders of the World.

390 BC The Gauls, a Celtic race living in what is now northern Italy and France, sweep down the valley of the River Po and overwhelm Rome. The city is ransacked, but after a pay-off of gold the invaders depart.

Pen nib

c 380 BC

Scribes in ancient Egypt wrote on papyrus (✳ *see* **page 24**) with a pen made from a reed. This had a soft point, rather like a modern felt-tip. The first pens with a hard tip, split at the end to channel the ink, came from ancient Greece. They were still made from reeds, but scribes could produce finer writing with them. With the introduction of parchment (✳ *see* **page 28**), which was smoother than papyrus, most writers eventually switched to using the more flexible quill pens, which were made from long feathers.

Reed cut and split at the end to hold the ink

PEN NIB
Early Greek documents were written with pens made from stiff reeds. Scribes often kept their pens in a wooden case. This one has a space for ink at one end.

CELESTIAL SPHERES *In this 16th-century view of the universe, Atlas holds up Earth surrounded by the planets on their spheres.*

Automaton

c 370 BC

Archytas of Tarentum

An automaton is a machine that imitates the actions of a living creature. The earliest was a pigeon built in about 370 BC by the ancient Greek scientist Archytas of Tarentum. It "flew" around on an arm driven by steam or air. Influenced by Pythagoras, much of Archytas' work involved music. But he was also interested in the mathematics of mechanical devices, which may explain why he designed the pigeon.

Celestial spheres

c 360 BC

Eudoxus of Cnidus

Planets and other celestial bodies seem to move irregularly against a smoothly revolving background of stars. The ancient Greek astronomer Eudoxus offered the first explanation for this. He said that everything astronomers saw was carried around Earth on 27 spheres. The outermost sphere held the stars, while the Sun, the Moon, and the planets had several spheres each. Their combined steady motions created the observed irregular motion. Despite numerous flaws, Eudoxus' theory was, with some refinements, the best on offer for 2000 years.

c 350 BC Greek philosopher Aristotle puts forward six arguments for a spherical Earth. His reasoning is generally accepted, putting an end to centuries of speculation about the shape of the world.

330 BC As the final act of his conquest of the Persian empire, the Macedonian king Alexander the Great burns down the palace in the city of Persepolis. From now on, Greek culture will begin to influence the Middle East.

Atomic theory

c 350 BC

Democritus

The ancient Greek philosopher Democritus held views that have influenced the whole of modern science. He was probably the first person to put forward the idea that the world is made of atoms, the smallest things that can exist. He said that there were countless numbers of them, all made of the same stuff, but with different shapes. They could be arranged in different ways to produce everything in the world. This theory is close to the truth, and not bad for someone who lived about 2400 years ago.

Cookery book

c 350 BC

Archestratus

Throughout history, people have tried to find better ways of preparing food. As long ago as 350 BC, the ancient Greek writer Archestratus produced a book about the joy of food called *Pleasant Living*. About 200 years later, an enthusiast called Athenaeus produced a book containing, among other things, several recipes for cheesecake.

Coal

c 350 BC

Archaeologists believe that coal may have been burned in Wales as long as 4000 years ago. But the first written record of coal is a mention by the ancient Greek philosopher Aristotle in a book he wrote on geology in about 350 BC. His interest in coal came from his theories about Earth. Later people, from the Romans onwards, were more interested in coal as a source of heat or for use in smelting metals. In about 1200, a monk called Reinier of Liège wrote about metalworkers using a black earth similar to charcoal.

Iced dessert

c 350 BC

The ancient Romans enjoyed their food, especially anything cold and sweet. Sugar was a rarity and refrigeration unknown, but from the 4th century onwards, they used natural ice and honey. This was a problem in summer, so the emperor Nero had snow brought from the mountains and served with sweetened fruit juice. Meanwhile, people in China were eating ice cream, invented there in about 2000 BC. This reached Europe in about 1300, when the Italian traveller Marco Polo returned with recipes from the Far East.

Mercury

c 350 BC

Mercury is the only metal that is liquid at room temperature. It may have been known to the ancient Egyptians, but was definitely being mined and refined by about 350 BC. From the start, probably because of its seemingly magical properties, it was an important ingredient in alchemy, in which people tried to make gold out of cheaper metals. It also featured in early medical treatments although people knew it was poisonous.

Formal logic

c 350 BC

Aristotle

Everyone needs to know how to argue logically. The ancient Greek philosopher Aristotle was the first to set out clear rules for argument. He pointed out, for example, that an argument like "Fish can swim; I can swim, so I am a fish" is false. (A true statement would be "Fish can swim; I am a fish, so I can swim.") He also pointed out that all of science depends on a set of principles that can be accepted as true without proof. His rules were so good that, for centuries, people believed he had said all there was to say on the subject. Many of his ideas on logic are still essential to science.

Euclidean geometry

c 300 BC

Euclid of Alexandria

Euclid was possibly the greatest maths teacher ever. His way of explaining geometry in about 300 BC was still being used in the 20th century. He collected together earlier texts and rearranged them with his own work so that they made more sense. The result, called *The Elements*, takes readers on a journey from basic ideas to surprising outcomes. Its clarity is still hard to beat. In fact, there are a lot of Euclid's ideas in maths books used today.

Lead pipe

c 300 BC

Plumbers get their name from "plumbum", which was the Roman word for lead. Roman engineers brought water from the surrounding hills into their cities, then sent it to where it was needed through pipes. They sometimes made these from wood, but more often used lead because it lasted longer and was soft and easy to roll up into tubes. Lead pipes were still in use in the 20th century, but most have now been replaced because unfortunately, as the Roman engineer Vitruvius pointed out, lead is poisonous.

LEAD PIPE *In ancient Rome, city dwellers often had their name put on their own lead water pipes.*

320 BC Cities continue to grow, and with them the problem of waste disposal. In Athens, a law is passed preventing people from throwing their rubbish into the streets. The first waste collection systems are also organized.

c 304 BC In Rome, Gnaeus Flavius erects a permanent calendar showing the days on which legal business can be conducted. Before this, the days were just read out each month, making justice uncertain.

MOSAIC *A tessera mosaic made between 250 and 50 BC shows how well this seemingly rigid technique could show detail and movement.*

Mosaic
c 300 BC

Mosaics are pictures made up using small pieces of coloured stone or glass cemented to walls or floors. The first mosaics were probably made using natural pebbles. By 300 BC, the "tessera" technique had been invented, in which tiny tiles cut from stone or glass were used to give fine detail and rich colour. This beautiful, hard-wearing form of interior decoration went down well with the Romans. Many of their mosaics still exist today.

Scientific botany
c 300 BC

Theophrastus

After thousands of years spent using and cultivating plants, people began to wonder where the plants came from and how they worked. The scientific study of plants is called botany, and the ancient Greek philosopher Theophrastus was the first real botanist. Between about 320 and 280 BC, he wrote more than 200 books on the subject. Only two, which deal with the origin and growth of plants, have survived. Modern botanists no longer use his work, but without him they might never have got started.

Saddle
c 300 BC

The first horse riders rode bareback, clinging on without the help of saddle or stirrups. They sat on some kind of blanket or cloth, and this eventually evolved into the padded leather saddle used today. Chinese riders were using saddles by about 50 BC, but it is thought that saddles were invented at least 250 years earlier than this by a group of nomads called the Scythians, who lived in what is now mostly Ukraine.

Lighthouse
c 280 BC

Sostratus of Cnidus

Ancient mariners often relied on fires to guide them into harbour. These showed smoke by day and a light to aim for at night, and were simply placed on hilltops. The first purpose-built lighthouse was created in Egypt, on the island of Pharos, off Alexandria. When its Greek engineer Sostratus of Cnidus finished it in about 280 BC, it was probably about 125 m (410 ft) high – almost as high as the pyramids (✳ *see* **page 24**). It had stairs inside and fuel for its fire was hoisted up by pulley.

Compressed air
c 270 BC

Ctesibius of Alexandria

Ctesibius of Alexandria discovered that air can be compressed and will then exert a force. He may have done this by plunging a pot into water with its mouth downwards and noticing that this required a bit of force. Seeing that the inside of the pot stayed dry, he would have realized that the air inside

Padded saddle made riding more comfortable

SADDLE *This model of a horse, complete with a saddle and bridle, was made in China during the Tang Dynasty (AD 618–907).*

c 300 BC Geographer Pytheas becomes the first Greek to describe northern Europe after sailing to Land's End in Cornwall and exploring much of Britain on foot. On the way, he enjoys the local honey-based drink, mead.

293 BC Hygeia, the goddess of health, reaches Rome. With her husband Asclepius, the god of medicine, she will watch over the well-being of Roman citizens. She is depicted giving her snake a drink from a saucer.

was pushing the water out. We do know that Ctesibius used his discovery in several air-powered inventions.

Bridge for boarding ships

c 260 BC

Gaius Duilius

Military leaders have always been called upon to solve practical problems. Second World War soldiers erected "instant" steel bridges to help them get across rivers, and the Roman commander Gaius Duilius had organized bridges more than 2000 years before. In 260 BC, he found himself fighting a battle at sea with soldiers trained to fight on land. So he brought some "land" on to his ships in the form of wooden bridges that hooked on to the enemy ships. His soldiers could then rush across and fight as usual. They won the battle.

Archimedes' principle

c 250 BC

Archimedes

See **pages 48–49** for the story of how Archimedes solved a weighty problem and discovered how things float.

Size of Earth

c 250 BC

Eratosthenes of Cyrene

The astronomer Eratosthenes of Cyrene (now Shahhat in Libya) was the first person to work out the size of Earth. He found that on Midsummer's day, at noon, the Sun shone straight down a well at Aswan, in Egypt, so the Sun there was directly overhead. But at

exactly the same time, the shadow of a vertical stick about 800 km (500 miles) north at Alexandria showed that the Sun was not overhead, but angled at about seven degrees from the vertical. Eratosthenes realized that the difference was caused by the curvature of Earth. Using the idea that there were 360 degrees in a circle, and knowing the distance between Aswan and Alexandria, he was able to calculate Earth's circumference as the distance between Aswan and Alexandria × 360 ÷ 7. Eratosthenes' calculation came up with the answer of about 41,143 km (25,700 miles). The true value is about 40,000 km (25,000 miles), so he wasn't too far off.

Compound pulley

c 250 BC

Archimedes

A simple pulley is a rope passed around a wheel, and it is useful for lifting things vertically. One end of the rope is attached to the load and the other end of the rope is pulled to lift the load. Greek inventor Archimedes developed the compound pulley from the simple pulley by wrapping the rope around several wheels instead of one, which enabled people to lift heavier loads. It meant pulling the rope further, but this was better than not being able to pull it at all. Compound pulleys, using chains rather than ropes, are still used for heavy lifting jobs.

Heart valves

c 250 BC

Erasistratus of Ceos

An ancient Greek doctor called Erasistratus of Ceos was one of the first people to

Diaphragm separates the thorax from the abdomen

Model shows the internal organs of a female

think about how the human body works. Although we have different theories today, his ideas did make sense. He gave the first correct account of how valves inside the heart prevent blood from flowing backwards. His name for one of the valves, the tricuspid, is still used today.

Human anatomy based on dissection

c 250 BC

Herophilus of Chalcedon

Anatomy is the study of the structure of living bodies. Early anatomists were often forbidden to cut open dead bodies, so some of their descriptions and diagrams of the internal organs of humans were based on guesswork. The ancient Greek doctor Herophilus was one of the first scientists to base his anatomy on real observations, and he accurately described the brain, nerves, blood vessels, eyes, and other parts of the body.

HUMAN ANATOMY BASED ON DISSECTION *This 15th-century model for teaching anatomy probably shows more detail than was known to Heophilus.*

---

c **287** BC The ordinary people of Rome, the plebeians, gain a great victory in their campaign for recognition, as plebeian Quintus Hortensius becomes "dictator". He decrees that plebeian laws must apply to rich people too.

282 BC After 12 years' work, Greek sculptor Chares of Lyndus completes a 32 m (105 ft)-high bronze statue of the Sun god Helios, on the island of Rhodes. An earthquake destroys it within 60 years and it is sold for scrap.

DOING SCIENCE IN THE BATH

Archimedes solves a weighty problem and discovers how things float

Why do some things float and others sink? This is an important question for ship designers, but the ancient Greek scientist Archimedes may have found the answer while he was checking the quality of a king's jewellery.

Archimedes was born in Syracuse, Sicily, in about 290 BC. He was related to the king, Hieron II, so had plenty of time to think and write about mathematics and mechanics. Hieron often called upon Archimedes to help him with problems. He had a gold wreath that he thought contained some silver, and he asked Archimedes to find out exactly how much. Archimedes knew he could check the wreath if he could measure its density (its mass in relation to its volume) because silver is less dense than gold. The obvious way to find the density of something is to measure its weight (which is proportional to its mass) and volume, but Archimedes didn't know how to measure the volume of the wreath.

One day he noticed the water rising as he got into his bath. He realized that he could fill a bath to the top, lower Hieron's wreath into it to make the water overflow, then take the wreath out and see how much water was needed to fill the bath again. That would be the volume of the wreath.

Archimedes may also have noticed that he felt lighter in his bath. Left to itself, bath water doesn't rise or fall, so every part of it must get an upward push that balances its own weight. The same force must push on anything placed in the water. When anything is immersed in a fluid (a liquid or a gas), even partly, it feels an upward push

Golden leaves used to adorn a religious statue

GOLD FOR GODS AND KINGS
Ancient craft workers fashioned gold into decorations that were not only beautiful but also indicated the importance of the wearer. That is why Hieron wanted to make sure that his wreath was made of pure gold.

EUREKA!
It is said that Archimedes was so excited by his discovery that he leaped out of his bath and ran naked through the streets shouting "Eureka!" ("I've found it!"). This probably never happened, but people still shout "Eureka!" at moments of discovery.

TESTING THE PRINCIPLE
Two identical containers filled to the brim with water will balance exactly. When an apple is carefully lowered into one of them, so that the container stays full, the balance is unchanged. Archimedes' principle says that the floating apple will push its own weight of water out of the container, making the total weight the same as before.

Identical containers on an accurate set of scales

equal to the weight of fluid it displaces. We now call this Archimedes' principle. Using this, Archimedes could have immersed the wreath in water and noted how much weight it lost, then have worked out how much silver the wreath contained, without measuring its volume at all.

Archimedes probably didn't do this. Nevertheless, he had solved Hieron's problem. He may also have discovered why things float or sink. Objects placed in water move downwards until their weight is balanced by the weight of the water they displace, then stay at that level. If their average density is higher than that of water, they cannot float. They sink.

Hieron also had more serious problems. Later, when Archimedes was an old man, the Romans besieged Syracuse. Once again, he was called upon. He used his scientific knowledge to design ships, catapults, and even, it is said, giant mirrors to burn Roman ships with the Sun's rays. In 211 BC, the city was eventually captured. The Roman soldiers rampaged through it, burning and killing. Sadly, one of their victims was Archimedes, the genius who did science in his bath.

Greek trireme of about 450 BC

GREEK WARSHIP
The magnificent trireme, a Greek ship with three layers of oars, showed how much importance the Greeks attached to winning battles at sea. It was extremely fast, and could sink an enemy ship with its built-in battering ram. Fighting techniques moved on, and the trireme evolved into a ship that could carry large numbers of heavily armed soldiers.

Archimedes was a genius who needed only the simplest of equipment to make profound discoveries.

Pipe organ
c250 BC

Ctesibius of Alexandria

The Greek inventor Ctesibius was the first person to put together all three parts of an organ: pipes, a keyboard, and a supply of air. To get a steady sound from the pipes, Ctesibius realized that he needed to supply air to them at a steady pressure. So he attached them to a large container, open at the bottom and standing in a tank of water. As he pumped air into the container, the weight of water pressing on the air kept the pressure fairly constant, even though the amount of air in the container varied. His organ, called a hydrolos because of the water (from *hydro*, the Greek word for "water"), was loud enough to play outdoors.

Simple pattern carved in the bronze clasp

SAFETY PIN *This Hungarian brooch dates from about 50 BC. It fastens using the same principle as a safety pin.*

Safety pin
c250 BC

The modern safety pin was invented in 1849 by US mechanic Walter Hunt, but this useful fastener has a much longer history. A clothing clasp called a fibula is thought to have been invented by a group of people called the Phrygians in about 1100 BC. It was worn by the ancient Greeks and Romans, often in elaborately decorated form. By 250 BC, the pin had become recognizable as the object that Hunt re-invented more than 2000 years later.

SAFETY PIN *This type of early pin of about 750 BC was found in Italy. It is a brooch that was probably worn by someone of high rank.*

Spring mechanism

Surface area and volume of a sphere
c250 BC

Archimedes

The formulas for calculating the surface area and volume of a sphere are used throughout science. The first person to work them out was the Greek mathematician Archimedes. He proved that a sphere has four times the surface area of a circle the same size. He also proved that a sphere has two-thirds the volume of the cylinder that just contains it. These are easy problems to solve using modern mathematical tools, but Archimedes had to use imaginary

Front of brooch made from glass discs

spheres, which he sliced, weighed, and measured in his imagination to get the answers. His methods, lost for centuries, anticipated 17th-century calculus (✳ *see* **page 96**).

Standardized Chinese writing
c220 BC

Shi Huangdi

In Chinese writing, each character stands for a word, not a sound. It works like numbers in Western languages. People in different Western countries all understand the symbol "2", but pronounce it "two", "deux", and so on, depending on their language. This principle is useful in China, because speakers of its many local dialects can all read the same writing, but only if the same characters are used everywhere. The standardization of Chinese writing was just one of the many reforms that the forceful emperor Shi Huangdi introduced in about 220 BC, as part of his plan to turn the separate states of China into one nation.

Three finger holes allowed only a few different notes to be played

Tram
c220 BC

Shi Huangdi

Today, electric trams run in many of the world's cities. Chinese emperor Shi Huangdi did not have electricity in 220 BC, but he saw the need for orderly, smoothly flowing traffic. He decreed that all carts should have their wheels the same distance apart, and had matching grooves put in the streets. This may have been the world's first tram system.

---

222 BC After four centuries of occupation by Celtic tribes, the city of Mediolanum in the north of Italy is overrun by Romans from the south and becomes part of their empire. It will eventually be known as Milan.

218 BC Using elephants to carry heavy equipment, Carthaginian general Hannibal leads 40,000 soldiers over the snowbound Alps into Italy in an attempt to conquer Rome. He wins some battles but fails in the end.

STANDARDIZED CHINESE WRITING *Each Chinese character consists of a number of lines. Early Chinese characters were simplified pictures, but they gradually evolved into the shapes of today. These characters mean "football".*

Strokes must be written in the correct order

Characters written with a brush made from animal hair

Each character is contained within an imaginary square

There are five basic strokes

Natural gas
211 BC

People in the Middle East worshipped "eternal flames" escaping from the ground 5000 years ago. But the first people to use natural gases seeping out of rocks were the Chinese. In 211 BC, they sunk their first gas well using a drill mounted on bamboo poles. By AD 200, they were making salt by using gas to boil brine.

Punctuation
c 200 BC

Aristophanes of Byzantium

The rules of punctuation can make writing more difficult, but punctuation does make life easier for readers. The idea came to us through Greek and Latin. Early Greek writers used hardly any punctuation, and didn't even put spaces between words. Aristophanes of Byzantium, who was Librarian of the library of Alexandria in about 200 BC, was the first to put this right. By adding punctuation to Greek text, he began the trend that led to modern punctuation, including one mark that has a Greek name – the apostrophe.

Chain mail
c 200 BC

The ancient Greek warrior's bronze chest protector, or cuirass, was heavy and restricted its wearer's

Chain store
c 200 BC

A chain store is a shop that is part of a group run by the same company and selling the same goods. They became a prominent feature of towns and cities everywhere in the 20th century. But the Hudson's Bay Company was operating a chain of stores in the USA before 1750, and the earliest-known chain stores were selling their wares in China as long ago as 200 BC.

Flute
c 200 BC

The flute that musicians play today is held sideways rather than lengthways. This "transverse" flute may have developed independently in both China and Europe. Pipes played sideways were known in China as early as the 9th century BC, but the instrument now known in China as the *di*, or *dizi*, was not perfected until about 200 BC. It has six finger holes,

FLUTE *Almost any tube can form a flute. This bone was made into a musical instrument by a 10th-century Viking.*

plus an extra hole, with a thin piece of bamboo or reed over it. When a musician blows into the pipe, the bamboo vibrates to create the plaintive sound typical of Chinese flute music. At about the time that this pipe began to be heard, musicians in what is now Tuscany, in Italy, also seem to have taken up the transverse flute. In Germany, it was used in military bands from about AD 1100.

movement. From perhaps 200 BC onwards, Greek soldiers increasingly wore chain mail in battle, and soldiers in Sumeria may already have been using it a few years earlier. Made of thousands of iron rings looped together over a leather or cloth backing, chain mail offered protection against swords and spears. It was more flexible than a cuirass so it was relatively comfortable, although a shirt could weigh 10 kg (22 lb). Chain mail eventually became standard equipment for Roman legionnaires.

215 BC Rome passes laws ruling that women must not wear more than half an ounce of gold jewellery or have tunics of more than one colour. The laws also limit the number of guests at banquets and prevent men from wearing silk.

213 BC Wise men repeatedly tell Chinese emperor Shi Huangdi that he is a fool to look for alchemists or magicians who can give him eternal life. The emperor gets his own back by having all their books burned.

Sari

c 200 BC

Indian women were wearing the elegant sari as long ago as 200 BC. This single piece of fine cloth, worn wrapped around the body and sometimes over the head, appears in Indian sculptures dating from about 150 BC. Women depicted in the sculptures from this period are typically shown wearing a sari, a headscarf, and lots of jewellery. Today, saris are made from synthetic fabrics as well as traditional silk or cotton.

Steel

c 200 BC

Once people had discovered iron, they accidentally made steel, which is iron containing a little carbon. It is much stronger than pure iron. The carbon could have come from the charcoal the people burned with iron ore to extract the iron. Steel making started in several places at about the same time. China and India had real steel industries from about 200 BC. They heated iron with charcoal to get carbon into it, then reheated and hammered the metal until the carbon was mixed throughout.

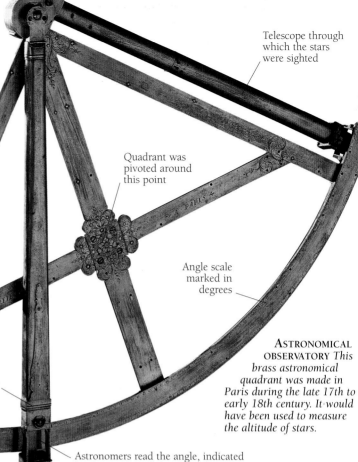

ASTRONOMICAL OBSERVATORY *This brass astronomical quadrant was made in Paris during the late 17th to early 18th century. It would have been used to measure the altitude of stars.*

Telescope through which the stars were sighted

Quadrant was pivoted around this point

Angle scale marked in degrees

Enclosed plumb line hung vertically

Astronomers read the angle, indicated by the position of the plumb line on the scale, and then calculated the star's altitude

Piston

c 150 BC

Pistons working in cylinders drive many machines today, using compressed air or fuel. Pistons are difficult to make accurately enough to stop leaks, so early inventors tried to avoid them. For example, the pumps that blew air into metalworking furnaces from about 1000 BC were usually just bellows. But as early as 150 BC, or even earlier, some metalworkers were using better air pumps using the piston-and-cylinder principle.

PISTON *Early water pumps often used pistons because the water acted as a lubricant, and leaks didn't matter very much.*

Astronomical observatory

c 150 BC

Hipparchus

Basic astronomical observatories existed in Babylonia in 2500 BC, but they did not have any instruments. A great observatory built at Alexandria in Egypt in about 300 BC did not have many instruments either. The first observatory with fairly accurate instruments for measuring star positions was probably on the Greek island of Rhodes, where the astronomer Hipparchus worked between about 134 and 129 BC. Much later, in the 9th or 10th centuries, splendid new observatories were established at Damascus and Baghdad.

c 200 BC
Rome suffers from success as the city's population grows out of control. Poorer people are packed into wooden buildings three floors high, which often collapse or catch fire. Within 20 years, plague sweeps the city.

c 150 BC
Wealthy Romans become convinced that dancing is a shameful and dangerous activity. To protect their children from what they see as its anti-Roman influence, they order that all dancing schools should close.

Horseshoes
c 150 BC

People were riding horses by 2000 BC, but it was 150 BC before they began to think of ways to protect horses' feet so they could ride them on rocky ground and roads. Shoes for horses and mules were developed by the people in eastern Europe who had first tamed the horse. Most early shoes were made of leather. Metal shoes, nailed to the hoof, were being used in western Europe by about AD 450.

Precession of the equinoxes
c 150 BC

Hipparchus

The equinoxes are the times of the year when day and night are the same length. Their dates shift slightly each year – an effect called precession. This was discovered by the Greek astronomer Hipparchus, who noticed that his star positions had all moved by the same amount from those measured by earlier Greek and Babylonian astronomers. With a little scientific detective work, he found out that the change was caused by a very slow shifting of Earth's axis of rotation.

Trigonometry
c 150 BC

Hipparchus

Trigonometry is a method of calculating angles from distances and distances from angles. It can solve such problems as how high or how far away a building is, without actually taking these measurements. Trigonometry was started by astronomers, because they could not measure distances in space directly. The first step was to find out how the distance between two lines drawn from the centre to the edge of a circle varied with the angle between them. The astronomer Hipparchus founded modern trigonometry with a table giving this information in such detail that it filled 12 books.

Stirrups
c 150 BC

Stirrups, those useful footrests for riders, were almost certainly invented by people from the same area – modern Ukraine – as those who tamed the horse in the first place (✳ see page 28). This simple invention made a huge difference to the way horses were used in war. It is very hard to stay on a galloping horse without stirrups, let alone fight for your life at the same time.

Star magnitudes
c 130 BC

Hipparchus

Some stars look brighter than others, so astronomers classify them on a magnitude scale, which records their brightness as seen from Earth. The astronomer Hipparchus began this system when compiling a star catalogue. Working on the island of Rhodes, he listed 850 stars so accurately that his observations were useful until as late as the 17th century.

Groin vault
c 100 BC

The barrel vault, a tunnel-like structure made from a series of arches, could be used to create buildings of any length. But unfortunately, its walls could contain only small openings. Large ones made the arches collapse. The Romans, masters of the arch, found a solution: they made each opening into the start of another barrel vault. In this way they could make buildings of any size from a grid of vaults crossing each other to form self-supporting "groin vaults".

Iron ploughshare
c 100 BC

We don't know if the Romans used iron ploughshares in the light soils of southern Europe, but the implements were ideal for cutting through the heavier soils found in the north. While some people in the north continued with wooden ploughs, others, including the invading Romans and local people such as the Celts, switched to iron. Efficient agriculture may have been one of the things that helped the Celts build a strong culture – and make themselves a nuisance, if not a threat, to the Romans.

Loops that held leather straps have rusted away

Triangular shape used less iron than the modern rounded shape

Decorative points may also have been used as spurs

STIRRUPS *These stirrups were used by Vikings between AD 850 and 1050.*

c 150 BC Philosopher Crates of Mallus takes time off from his usual work on Greek grammar to make one of the first ever geographical globes. It shows that by this time the Greeks are convinced the world is round.

124 BC Two scholars, Gonsun Hong and Dong Zhongshu, found China's first university. Its job will be to teach civil servants how to run the Chinese empire, including skills like interpreting portents and omens.

53

Wheel is screwed down to lower the board

Holes for the juice to run through

Grapes or olives placed between the boards

SCREW PRESS *This small wooden press was used to crush grapes for wine or olives for oil.*

Screw press
c 100 BC

The screw press used a large wooden screw to squeeze things between two boards. It was probably invented by the Greeks in about 100 BC for pressing olives or grapes. The Greeks and the Romans also used it to press their clothes. Its real importance, however, comes from what it was used for 1500 years later: pressing type on to paper to print books (✳ *see* **pages 76–77**).

Water-wheel
c 100 BC

Grinding corn in a hand-powered mill, or quern, (✳ *see* **page 36**) was tiring work, and was often left to women. Ancient Greek women must have welcomed the first water-powered quern in about 100 BC. The top stone was connected to horizontal paddles turned by a fast-flowing stream. Within 70 years, the Romans were building large vertical water-wheels like those seen today.

Tin can
c 100 BC

Cans made from tin-coated steel were first used to preserve food in 1810. But about 2000 years earlier, the Romans already knew that tin was ideal for lining metal food containers because it was resistant to corrosion and easy to apply. They made their tin cans from copper and used them for cooking, not storage. Tin-lined copper pans can still be bought today.

Shorthand
63 BC

Marcus Tiro

Politicians like their words to be remembered, and the great Roman statesman Cicero was no exception. In 63 BC, he

WATER-WHEEL *These water-wheels of the late 16th century were used to power a mill grinding corn into flour.*

Woodworking plane
c 100 BC

The traditional way to get a flat surface on wood is with a plane. A plane is a block of wood or metal, with a blade set into it sticking out slightly. The blade takes a thin shaving off the surface of the wood as the plane is pushed across it. The origin of the plane is a mystery, but the Romans were the first to use it. The earliest planes, which were very like the modern tool, were found at Pompeii, an ancient city in southern Italy, which the Romans colonized in 80 BC and which was buried by the eruption of Mount Vesuvius in AD 79.

100 BC China's Silk Road extends westwards to reach the Roman Empire as Chinese emperor Wudi conquers or makes alliances with large areas of central Asia. Ideas and luxury goods will travel the 6000 km (3700 mile) route.

67 BC After decades in which its citizens have seen their coinage fall in value, Rome solves the problem by introducing a gold coin, the aureus. Seventy years later, Emperor Nero will steal the gold to prop up his empire.

asked his friend Marcus Tiro to invent a shorthand system so that the important speeches he made in the senate could be recorded for ever. Tiro did a good job. His system was still in use centuries after the Roman Empire had collapsed.

News bulletin
59 BC

There has always been a demand for news. Without printing, the only way to get it to people was to write it out and pin it up where everyone could see it. *Acta Diurna* (Daily Acts) was started by Julius Caesar in 59 BC as an official propaganda sheet. It quickly expanded, and was soon offering the latest news on births, marriages, horoscopes, and public executions.

Paper
c 50 BC

It is easy to forget what marvellous stuff paper is. Light, strong, and cheap, it quickly displaced other writing materials as it spread from China to the West. The story is that a Chinese courtier invented it in AD 105 as a substitute for silk, but archaeologists have found paper dating from 49 BC in the Shanxi district of China. Paper has been a key component of many later inventions, from printing to teabags. (✳ *See also* **The paper makers.**)

Julian calendar
45 BC

Julius Caesar

By 45 BC, the Roman Empire's calendar was in a mess. Extra days were added in a confusing way and dates were counted backwards from

certain special days. When officials began mismanaging it to suit themselves, reform became urgent. Julius Caesar introduced a year of 365 days with a leap year every fourth year. While he was at it, he rearranged the months, naming July after himself and August after Augustus, who was later to be his successor. The result was very close to the calendar we use now.

THE PAPER MAKERS

Traditional paper makers dip a frame with a mesh bottom into a vat containing water and plant fibres. As the water drains away, the fibres cling together on top of the mesh. Further drying and pressing form the paper into a sheet. Modern paper is made from wood fibres using huge machines, but the first paper was handmade with fibres from Chinese hemp and ramie plants.

Some copies of this 1455 Bible, the first book to be printed, were on vellum, others on paper.

PAPER AND PRINTING
The invention of letterpress printing in about 1450 made it easier for people to produce multiple copies of a book. But if books had continued to be printed on vellum (a kind of leather), they would have remained expensive. Paper arrived just in time to turn a good invention into a great one.

HOW PAPER REACHED THE WEST
It took 12 centuries for paper making to complete its journey from China to Europe. Spreading first to Korea, it reached Japan in about AD 650. Paper mills in Syria were exporting to Europe by the 8th century, but Europeans did not start making their own paper until about 400 years later.

Glass blowing
c 10 BC

Centuries after the ancient Egyptians had discovered how to shape glass by blowing it into moulds (✳ *see* **page 27**), people still did not realize that it could be shaped using air alone. It was in Syria, probably in about 10 BC, that someone

first put a blob of molten glass on to the end of a tube, blew hard, and watched the glass swell into a bubble without any mould to shape it. For some time, glassworkers continued to shape glass in moulds, but the glass-blowing process eventually became as important as moulding. The resulting smooth, rounded vessels were shipped all over the Roman Empire.

44 BC On 15 March a group of senators including Gaius Cassius and Marcus Brutus kill Julius Caesar as he enters the senate house in Rome. His assassins believe that he wants to make himself king, destroying Rome as a republic.

c 19 BC Roman engineers in the south of France complete a huge aqueduct with three layers of arches. It channels water over the River Gard to the city of Nimes. The Pont du Gard will survive for more than 2000 years.

Dome

c AD 50

A dome is just an arch that arches in all directions. Sumerian builders were putting up domes of a sort more than 4000 years ago, but the first great dome builders were the Romans. They made extensive use of concrete. One of their earliest domes, which roofed a palace for the emperor Nero in AD 68, was 15 m (50 ft) in diameter. The dome of the Pantheon in Rome, which was completed 60 years later and still stands today, is nearly three times as wide.

Screw

c AD 50

A screw thread can exert a large force when turned with a small force, making screws ideal for holding things together. The thread is quite difficult to make, especially the female thread on the inside of a nut, which is used in conjunction with the male thread on a screw. By about AD 50, a tool for cutting these, called a tap, was in use. At about the same time, the Greek scientist and inventor Hero of Alexandria was writing about machines with parts that had to be held together with well made screws.

Street lamp

c AD 50

People in large cities today depend on good street lighting. By about AD 50, some public places in Rome had lighting after dark. It cannot have been very bright. The street lamps were just giant, metal versions of the teapot-shaped pottery oil lamps invented in Greece about 750 years earlier (✳ *see* **page 35**).

Topiary

c AD 50

Topiary, the art of clipping shrubs into geometric shapes, was a fashionable pastime in Rome in about AD 50. It is most likely to have begun as a bit of pruning that got out of hand, although a friend of the emperor Augustus claimed to have invented it. As well as being interesting in its own right, Roman topiary also suggests that the Romans had developed a form of shears suitable for use in the garden.

Wheelbarrow

c AD 50

The wheelbarrow should have been an obvious invention once the wheel had arrived (✳ *see* **page 19**), but it appears that no one thought of it for another 3500 years.

Chinese labourers were trundling barrows around from about AD 50 onwards, but people still didn't catch on in the West. The earliest evidence we have of European builders and miners using this versatile one-wheeled vehicle are depictions of some in medieval illustrations.

Vending machine

c AD 60

Hero of Alexandria

The first known vending machine was designed by the Greek inventor Hero of Alexandria in about AD 60. The idea was that when someone dropped in a coin the machine would release a shot of holy water. Hero described his machine in a book. We don't know whether he ever built one – or if it would have been reliable!

AD 60 The British Queen Boudicca, wife of a local ruler put in place by the Romans, leads a rebellion against them. After early successes, Boudicca is defeated near Towcester by the Roman army under Suetonius Paullinus.

AD 64 After ten years under the tyrannical Roman emperor Nero, a fire sweeps through Rome. Although Nero probably started the fire himself, he blames it on the Christians, and uses it as an excuse to persecute them.

Steam aeolipyle

C AD 60

Hero of Alexandria

Often said to be the first steam engine, the aeolipyle was built by Hero of Alexandria and was really just a toy. It was a metal ball set on a hollow spindle. Steam rushed into the ball through the spindle and out again through two nozzles at the sides. These acted like little rockets, and made the ball spin around. Probably named after Aeolus, the Greek god of the winds, the aeolipyle didn't do anything useful, but it did demonstrate the power of steam. It would be another 17 centuries before this power was unleashed.

DOME *The dome of the Pantheon in Rome was the world's largest until modern times.*

Formula for the area of a triangle

C AD 60

Hero of Alexandria

There is a well known formula for working out the area of a triangle – half the base times the height – but if the height isn't known, it has to be calculated before the formula can be applied. Nearly 2000 years ago, Hero of Alexandria discovered a different formula that doesn't involve knowing the height of the triangle, just the length of its three sides. His formula is: area = $\sqrt{[s(s-a)(s-b)(s-c)]}$ – where a, b, and c are the sides and s is half the perimeter. Despite its simplicity, the formula is not widely used.

Scissors

C AD 100

Scissors are ideal for cutting floppy things such as cloth, paper, or hair. The scissor principle was known in 3000 BC, but scissors like those used today, with two separate blades pivoted at the centre, were invented by the Romans in about AD 100. Until steel became cheaper in the 16th century, scissors remained a specialized tool used only by professionals like tailors and barbers.

Steam escaped through vents, forcing the ball to rotate

Water was heated in the boiler

Truss bridge

C AD 100

When someone stands on a plank laid across a gap, only the top and bottom of it do much to hold them up. The wood in the middle adds weight but not strength. A truss, which is a framework with most of its strength at the top and bottom, is more efficient at bearing weight. The Romans had grasped this concept by AD 100 and were using truss bridges to get their armies across rivers. By AD 300, they were also using trusses to support roofs up to 23 m (75 ft) wide.

Earthquake detector

C AD 130

Chang Heng

It is obvious when a major earthquake is happening, but smaller warning shocks can go unnoticed without the help of a detector, or seismoscope. In about AD 130, Chinese scientist Chang Heng invented what may have been the first of these. It was certainly one of the strangest. It had eight bronze dragons arranged in a circle, and eight bronze frogs, one below each dragon, with their mouths pointing upwards. Each of the dragons held a ball in its mouth. Because of the way the dragons were arranged, at least one of them would feel the slightest tremor. When this happened, its ball would drop, clanging into the mouth of the frog below and raising the alarm.

STEAM AEOLIPYLE *This is a modern reconstruction of Hero of Alexandria's toy.*

AD79 After an earlier earthquake, the southern Italian city of Pompeii is destroyed by the eruption of nearby Mount Vesuvius. Its inhabitants, including wealthy Roman holidaymakers, are buried alive in ash and lava.

AD115 Chinese scholar, poet, and single mother Ban Zhao dies at the age of 70. Her career, following marriage at 14 and the early death of her husband, included completing a history of the Han dynasty and writing many poems.

Epicyclic universe

c AD 140

Ptolemy

Ptolemy was an astronomer and mathematician who lived in ancient Egypt. Five centuries before him, the Greek astronomer Eudoxus had explained the movements of the stars and planets with his theory of celestial spheres (✳ *see* **page 44**), but this did not account for the way some planets appeared to stand still or move backwards at times. Other astronomers tried explanations based on planets moving in circular orbits around Earth, but the errors remained. Ptolemy solved the problem by suggesting that each heavenly body moved in small circles, or epicycles, at the same time as it orbited Earth. His new system was generally accepted as the truth by astronomers for the next 1500 years.

Crank

c AD 150

A crank converts a to-and-fro movement into a rotary movement. For example, bicycle pedals convert the up-and-down motion of the legs into the rotary motion of the wheels. The date for when the crank was invented depends on how it is defined. The first rotary querns (✳ *see* **page 36**) could qualify as early cranks, and they go back to 600 BC, but it is not until AD 150 that there is evidence of the first "bent rod" crank being used. One is depicted in a Chinese tomb-model of a winnowing machine.

Bucket was found at Pompeii, Italy

SOAP
The image on this Roman bucket shows the goddess Venus using soap to wash her hair.

Soap

c AD 150

People seem to have made soap from about 1000 BC onwards, by boiling fat with wood ash. Soap was originally used for medicinal purposes, and was not really the sort of soap that makes a good lather. It was probably the Romans, in about AD 150, who first started using soap to wash things, and Roman women were using a kind of soap as a shampoo one hundred years earlier.

Sympathetic nervous system

c AD 170

Galen

Many parts of the body are not under conscious control, but are operated by the sympathetic nervous system. This system automatically readies us for action by, among other things, speeding up the heart and shutting down the digestion. The influential Greek physician Galen studied the human body extensively, including its nerves. Some of the nerves he identified in about AD 170 are now known to form part of the sympathetic nervous system.

Cataract operation

c AD 200

Cataract is a condition of the eye in which the lens becomes cloudy, leading to blindness. Surgeons today can usually restore sight by removing the damaged lens. Amazingly, the same operation was being done about 2000 years ago. An Indian medical encyclopedia, the *Susruta-samhita*, which is thought to have been compiled by an Indian surgeon called Susruta, gives detailed instructions for the procedure. The only method he suggested for anaesthetizing patients seems to have been to give them alcohol.

Algebra

c AD 250

Diophantus of Alexandria

No single person invented algebra. The art of doing arithmetic without actual numbers developed slowly, starting in Babylonia and ancient Egypt, with calculations expressed entirely in words. When Diophantus wrote his book *Arithmetica* in about AD 250, he introduced symbols to replace some of the words. He also worked out the rules for powers, and explained how negative quantities behave when multiplied. His book also contained some difficult mathematical problems, which became known as Diophantine equations and are still of interest today.

AD 136 The Roman emperor Hadrian completes a great wall to keep out barbarians from the north of Britain. It stretches 118 km (73 miles) from Bowness on the Solway Firth to Segedunum (now Wallsend) on the River Tyne.

AD 184 The Yellow Turbans, a religious peasant movement in north-east China, start a rebellion that will cause the collapse of the Han dynasty. They aim to replace the Han "Green Heaven" with a "Yellow Heaven" of perfect peace.

Book with pages

C AD 350

The first books had no pages – they were written on a continuous scroll. Roman emperor Julius Caesar is sometimes credited with having been the first to fold a scroll into pages instead of rolling it, making it easier for a messenger to carry. Both the ancient Greeks and the Romans had ring-bound notebooks with wooden pages, but it wasn't until about AD 350 that the book with pages, or codex, became the standard way of storing words. The early Christians found the more compact codex useful for hiding their forbidden texts under their clothes. (✴ *See also* **Birth of the book**.)

BIRTH OF THE BOOK

FROM ABOUT 50 BC, books, particularly religious texts, started getting longer and the codex gradually became more attractive. Papyrus, the usual writing material at that time (✴ *see* **page 24**), tended to crack when folded into pages, so most of the new codexes were made from parchment (✴ *see* **page 28**), a material that was known in 2400 BC but had been little used.

WHY PAGES WON
As well as being a handy shape, a codex allows people to turn to any section instantly or flip the pages to scan the contents. Because the pages of books can have writing on both sides, it is also possible to pack in twice as many words as on a scroll of the same size.

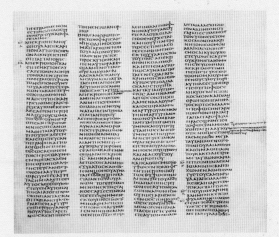

A page from a Greek Bible of the 4th century

THE OLDEST CODEXES
The oldest surviving book with pages is a Greek Bible written between AD 300 and 400. It is known as the Codex Sinaiticus because it was found near Mount Sinai, Egypt. Another Bible, the Codex Alexandrinus, was written a century later. Both are kept in the British Museum.

Jointed fishing rod

C AD 350

Fishing rods have probably been around nearly as long as fish hooks (✴ *see* **page 8**). It was only when wealthy Romans began to take up fishing as a pastime in the 4th century AD that rods more than about 1 m (3 ft 3 in) long came into use. They were made of wood, and because they were long they had to be made in several sections. So they were quite like a modern, jointed fishing rod to look at.

JOINTED FISHING ROD
This floor mosaic was found in the Roman town of Leptis Magna, now in Libya, Africa. It clearly shows people fishing with rods.

AD 250 The Roman Catholic Church creates a new class of priests known as exorcists. Their job is to persuade demons to leave people or places thought to be under their power, especially as a preliminary to baptism.

AD 330 In Constantinople (now Istanbul), the world's largest racetrack is finally completed after 127 years. With room for 60,000 spectators, this "hippodrome" will host chariot races, political rallies, and public executions.

Public hospital
C AD 397

St Fabiola

Temples may have been used as refuges for the sick as long ago as 4000 BC, but it is thought that the first public hospital opened in Rome in about AD 397. It was founded by a woman who did so much good that she was made a saint. Fabiola was a highly educated Roman aristocrat who became a Christian. She created several hospitals and also gave help to monasteries. The monks in turn started more hospitals.

Plough with wheels
C AD 500

A basic plough doesn't have wheels. The person doing the ploughing holds it upright as an animal pulls it along. This is fine on light soils, but in the heavy soils of northern Europe, something sturdier was needed. In about AD 500, heavy wheels were added to the basic plough, making it easier to handle and stable enough to be pulled by several animals.

Horse collar
C AD 500

The first animals used for hauling things were oxen, which pushed on a wooden bar, or yoke. This didn't suit horses. The yoke pressed on their throats so they couldn't pull very hard. A padded collar that fitted around the neck was better. Its origins are not clear, but it may have been invented in China in about AD 500. Horse collars were being used in the West by the 12th century.

ASTROLABE *This invention let people find their latitude or local time by studying the stars' position.*

Quill pen
C AD 500

Quill pens came into use in about AD 500 and were in use until the 19th century. They were usually made from one of the larger wing feathers of a goose. The feather was prepared by cutting the tip to a sharp point then making a slit to channel the ink. The hollow quill held enough ink for a line or two of writing.

BC and AD dates
AD 525

Dionysius Exiguus

The year numbers used today were laid down by the Christian Church: BC means "before Christ" and AD stands for *anno Domini*, meaning "in the year of the Lord". In AD 525, a monk named Dionysius Exiguus had the idea of using the birth of Christ as a starting point (AD 1), and calculated that this was 754 years after the founding of Rome. This is now thought to be several years too late but the error has never been corrected.

Astrolabe
C AD 550

The astrolabe was an astronomical calculator and star finder used by travellers and astronomers. Its star map could be turned to match the sky at any time, and adjustable sights allowed stars to be located accurately. The earliest surviving examples were made in the Middle East in the 6th century AD. By the mid 15th century, wealthier travellers might have taken an astrolabe with them.

Block printed book
C AD 600

Books were being printed in China long before movable type was perfected ( *see **pages 66–67**). The printers wrote their books by hand on thin paper, then stuck each page face down on a block

BLOCK PRINTED BOOK *Patterns and symbols are carved into this wooden printing block.*

of wood. The writing, visible through the paper, showed them where to carve the wood to leave text standing proud. They inked the block and

AD 400 The first inhabitants of Hawaii reach the island from the Marquesas Islands more than 3200 km (2000 miles) away. They bring with them no written language, but a rich oral culture of myth and practical knowledge.

AD 476 The Western Roman empire comes to an end. German chieftain Odoacer deposes its last emperor, Romulus Augustulus, 66 years after the city of Rome was overrun by the Germanic people known as the Visigoths.

Scenes painted on silk

FOLDING FAN This 18th-century folding fan would have been the height of fashion. It features the first free ascent of a hydrogen-filled balloon, which took place over Paris in 1783.

Sticks of carved ivory

pressed paper on it to create copies of the original writing. Things were printed in this way from about AD 600 onwards.

Tapestry
C AD 600

True tapestries are woven on a loom using different coloured threads. The first tapestries were made in China about 1500 years ago. Some, made of fine silk, looked almost like painted pictures. Others, designed as wall-hangings, were coarser but larger. Tapestry was invented independently in Europe possibly in the 8th century. The famous French Bayeux tapestry, which tells the story of the invasion of Britain by William

the Conqueror in 1066, is not a tapestry at all – it's a piece of embroidery, which is fabric decorated with needlework.

Windmill
C AD 600

The first windmill, invented in 7th-century Persia, consisted of a simple wheel with cloth sails and was used to drive a millstone to grind grain. The wheel was mounted on a vertical shaft directly above a millstone mounted on the same shaft. These windmills were giant, upside-down versions of the early water-wheels invented

seven centuries before (✳ *see* **page 54**). They developed into today's wind turbines used to generate electricity.

Folding fan
C AD 650

Folding fans, as opposed to rigid ones, were invented in Japan in the 7th century. This clever accessory became especially popular in medieval China and Japan, where there was more to fans than simply keeping cool – they were important social items. In 18th-century Europe, where all things Chinese were fashionable, folding fans were also carried by wealthy women.

Zero to represent nothing
C AD 650

Brahmagupta

Zero is a difficult idea. How can you count something that isn't there? It was a long time before mathematicians could accept a number that stood for nothing. One of the first scholars to accept the concept was the great Hindu astronomer Brahmagupta, who worked in the 7th century. The English word "zero" comes, in a roundabout way, from the Hindu word "*sunya*", meaning "empty". Hindu mathematicians wrote zero as a circle, the same symbol that is used today.

AD 529 As part of a drive to rid his empire of non-Christian thinking, Byzantine emperor Justinian closes the 900-year-old Academy in Athens, a centre of thought and learning founded by the great Greek philosopher Plato.

AD 604 In London, now under the rule of King Ethelbert, the first of five cathedrals dedicated to St Paul is built on the site of an old Roman temple. During the next 1100 years, three will be destroyed by fire and one by Viking raiders.

Flame-thrower

c AD 670

Callinicus of Heliopolis

Setting fire to an enemy's property usually means having to get close to it, but a weapon that shoots a jet of flame can do damage at a distance. The first people to try this were the Byzantines from Constantinople (present-day Istanbul in Turkey) in the 7th century AD. Their "Greek fire" – a sticky, flaming liquid squirted from pumps – was much feared by their enemies. Possibly invented by a Syrian architect called Callinicus, Greek fire helped the Byzantines to defeat a Saracen (Arab) fleet in AD 673.

Paddlewheel

c AD 780

Ships with paddlewheels have a long history. They may have existed towards the end of the 5th century AD, but the first clear description of one is given by the writer Li Kao in about AD 780. It was a Chinese warship with twin paddlewheels turned by sailors walking on treadmills. It was said to be as fast as a sailing ship. In 1130, Chinese peasant Yang Yao led a revolt backed up by paddle warships. In 1838, British engineer Isambard Brunel launched the first transatlantic steamship service with the paddle-powered *Great Western*.

PADDLEWHEEL *This is a model of the giant wheels that drove Brunel's ship the* Great Eastern, *launched in 1858.*

The original paddlewheels were 17 m (56 ft) in diameter

STAINED-GLASS WINDOW *This window was created in about 1330.*

Kimono

c AD 700

The Japanese kimono – a long, wide-sleeved robe – dates from about AD 700. It has no buttons or other fastenings, and is simply wrapped around the body in a particular way and tied with a sash, which is called an *obi*. The kimono developed from a similar garment worn by courtiers in China as early as 200 BC. By the 17th century, 1000 years of further development had turned it into the beautiful garment we know today.

Porcelain

c AD 800

Porcelain is no ordinary pottery. It is pure white, translucent, and very strong. Its secret ingredient is a mineral called petuntse, which is a kind of granite. When mixed with china clay and fired at a high temperature, it turns to glass. Porcelain was discovered in China in about AD 800, and was perfected by about AD 1300. From then on, China exported vast quantities to the West, where potters struggled to imitate it.

Stained-glass window

c AD 800

In the 7th century, glass windows were rare, although they did exist in churches. By the end of the century, church builders were using coloured glass in windows, but they did not create pictures for another 200 years. Two more centuries went by before the glorious stained glass of Europe's 12th-century Gothic cathedrals was in place. Painted glass appeared in the 14th century.

Systematic use of zero

c AD 820

Muhammad al-Khwarizmi

It is accepted today that a zero at the end of a number makes it ten times bigger: e.g. 20 is ten times bigger than 2. But early number systems were rather vague about using zero in this way. They used it to show that the tens column, for example, had nothing in it, but rarely used it in the units column. The first mathematician to use zero in

AD 691 Caliph Abd al-Malik finishes the Dome of the Rock, a shrine in Jerusalem. It stands where it is said Muhammad, founder of Islam, ascended into heaven, and Abraham, ancestor of the Jews, prepared to sacrifice his son.

AD 750 At Tegernsee, on the River Isar in Germany, a Benedictine monastery is founded. It becomes known as München, meaning "home of the monks". It will grow to become Germany's third largest city, Munich.

62

today's systematic way was Muhammad al-Khwarizmi, in about AD 820. His ideas reached the West through the efforts of the French scholar Gerbert of Aurillac, who became Pope in AD 999.

Diagnosing smallpox

C AD 900

Smallpox and the less dangerous disease measles have similar early symptoms. Persian physician ar-Razi, known in the West as Rhazes,

told doctors how to tell the difference in about AD 900. He said that "inquietude, nausea, and anxiety are more frequent in the Measles than in the Small-Pox; while the pain in the back is more peculiar to the Small-Pox than to the Measles."

Cyrillic alphabet

C AD 900

Russian and some related languages are written with the Cyrillic alphabet. It was named after St Cyril, one of the

people who preached Christianity in eastern Europe in the 9th and 10th centuries. Like the rather different alphabet used for English, it is derived from the Greek alphabet that St Cyril knew, but has several extra letters, which were needed to represent the speech sounds of the region.

Gunpowder

C AD 900

Gunpowder was the first known substance that would burn when packed into a tube. In about AD 900,

Chinese alchemists were surprised to discover that when three well known ingredients were mixed in the right proportions, they could produce an intense flame or explosion. They put their discovery to work in fireworks for fun and rockets for war. From the 14th century onwards, the Europeans used gunpowder in cannons and firearms and this changed the whole nature of warfare. Gunpowder remained the only known explosive until the 17th century. (✳ *See also* **Explosive events**.)

EXPLOSIVE EVENTS

THE HISTORY OF GUNPOWDER is not clear. The secret was certainly known first in China, but nobody is sure whether people in the West learned it from the East or discovered it for themselves. English scientist Roger Bacon recorded the formula for making gunpowder in the 13th century, but it is possible that he discovered it by studying the works of Arabs, who had themselves learned it from the Chinese.

Medieval engraving of workers packing gunpowder into a tube

CANNONS AND ROCKETS
Gunpowder packed into a tube burns so intensely that it can throw objects out of the tube, forming a crude cannon, or propel the tube itself through the air as a rocket. Chinese scientists used both of these effects for military purposes, and may also have used gunpowder to make bombs.

FIREWORKS
Gunpowder was probably first used in fireworks. Even an inaccurate rocket made a good display, experimental cannons could throw decorative balls of fire, and the explosive properties could provide fun in firecrackers.

12th-century Chinese emperor Wu-Wang entertains guests with gunpowder.

AD837 Planet Earth has a near miss on 9 April as Halley's comet makes its closest ever approach. The wandering ball of dust and ice strays to within 494,000 km (310,000 miles) of the planet. It will return in about 76 years.

AD874 Ingólfr Arnarson reaches Iceland from Norway and becomes its first inhabitant. He starts a farm, which he calls Reykjavík, meaning "smoky", because of the steam from nearby hot springs. It will become Iceland's capital.

Movable type

1045

Bi Sheng

Printing with movable type – separate letter blocks that can be assembled to form text – revolutionized Western communication in the 15th century (✳ see **pages 76–77**), but as early as 1045, Chinese alchemist Bi Sheng was moulding types from clay and glue, then assembling them by sticking them down with resin. The types could even be reused by heating the resin to release them. Unfortunately, Chinese uses thousands of characters and doesn't really suit movable type. Bi Sheng had got the right idea, but in the wrong place.

Paper money

c AD 900

PAPER MONEY *13th-century Mongol emperor Kublai Khan watches as officials pay his bills with paper money.*

As China grew wealthier, increasing amounts of cash were needed to keep trade going. Paper money was used occasionally before AD 900, but it only really became common when merchants in the great trading city of Chengdu began to use it in the 10th century. Within 300 years, under the rule of the Mongol emperor Kublai Khan, China had practically replaced metal coins with paper money.

Mental hospital

AD 918

Attitudes towards mental illness have varied from place to place and time to time. In many countries, people have often put unusual behaviour down to possession by demons, or treated disturbed people like animals. But the people of 10th-century Baghdad (now the capital of Iraq) thought differently. Despite being constantly under attack from their enemies, they managed to set up the first known mental hospital in AD 918. Their policy was to treat disturbed people with respect.

Andromeda galaxy

AD 965

as-Sufi

A galaxy is a system of stars. Our Sun is just one star among hundreds of millions in the Milky Way galaxy. The Andromeda galaxy is 2.3 million light-years away. Islamic astronomer as-Sufi recorded it in AD 965. Although it is quite easy to see, it was not recorded again until 1612, after observation with a telescope.

Theory of vision

c 1000

Alhazen

See **pages 66–67** for the story of how an Arab scientist faked madness to found modern optics.

Fireworks

c 1000

Fireworks were developed by the Chinese about 1000 years ago, following the invention of gunpowder (✳ see **page 63**). Chinese fireworks came in just one colour – yellow – but in about 1800, the French chemist Claude Berthollet discovered potassium chlorate, which made multicoloured fireworks possible. Firework makers eventually discovered that strontium compounds produce crimson, while barium compounds produce green.

Musical notation

c 1050

Guido of Arezzo

Some music doesn't need to be written down because people can just remember it. But the complicated choral music of 9th-century Europe needed to be written down to

FIREWORKS *A Chinese family honours its kitchen god with a shower of sparks.*

AD 968 On 22 December, Byzantine historian Leo the Deacon observes a total eclipse of the Sun. Writing a description of what he sees, he is the first to record the glow, or corona, that surrounds the Sun at totality.

AD 986 Bjarni Herjulfsson from Greenland is the first European to sight the mainland of North America when his ship is blown off course in a storm. He sails along what is now the Atlantic coast of Canada before returning home.

indicate where voices should rise and fall. The squiggles people used at the time didn't look much like music until about 1050, when Guido of Arezzo, a Benedictine monk and music teacher, placed the marks on a grid of five lines, or stave. It was, however, another 500 years before people were writing music as we do today.

Mechanical clock

1088

Su Sung, Henry De Vick

The first mechanical clock, built in 1088, did not use clockwork. Its Chinese inventor, Su Sung, designed a water-wheel that paused to empty a bucket after it filled, marking intervals of time. The first clockwork clock was put in the Palais de Justice, Paris, by Henry De Vick in about 1360. It had only one hand, and with errors of up to two hours a day was probably less accurate than Su Sung's clock.

Three-field system

c1100

The same crop grown year after year in the same field will eventually exhaust the soil. Early farmers just moved on and used new land, but this was impossible in medieval Europe because farmers had to stay in one place. From about 1100, European farmers began using a three-field system. They planted one-third of their land in the autumn, another third in spring, and left the rest unplanted for a year to recover, rotating the use of the patches of land each year. In this way, the farmers got two harvests a year, and by planting a spring crop of peas or beans, which

increase nitrogen in the soil, they increased the fertility of the land as well.

Gothic arch

c1140

The pointed Gothic arches in cathedrals made these medieval buildings lighter and more spacious than earlier ones. Roman arches were semicircular, so tall arches had to be wide, which created design problems. They also needed heavy walls to stop them from spreading. Gothic arches could be made taller without making them wider, and their sideways push was smaller so walls could be thinner and windows larger.

MECHANICAL CLOCK *This is a model of Su Sung's mechanical clock tower.*

Fireplace

c1150

The first fireplaces were put in the middle of the floor, and smoke went out through a hole in the roof. A few

fireplaces with tall chimneys appeared in the 12th century. They carried smoke away and created a draught to make the fire burn well. With a raised iron grate, which let air reach the fire from below as well as from above, they made a dent in the winter chill.

Metal sphere represents Earth

Sphere turns once every 24 hours

Decorative dragons

Gears inside casing transmit motion to the sphere

AD**996** On 1 November, Holy Roman Emperor Otto III seals a document granting some land in Bavaria. It is the first time the name "Ostarrîchi", meaning "eastern realm", is used. The land will eventually became Austria.

1066 On Wednesday, 27 September, William, Duke of Normandy, invades England with about 6000 soldiers. He travels east towards Hastings, where on 14 October he will defeat Harold II's army and change English history.

65

VISION OF THE FUTURE

Arab scientist Alhazen fakes madness to found modern optics

Photography, telephones, and television are just a few of the inventions that depend on optics – the science of light. For hundreds of years, the subject was in confusion. Then, about 1000 years ago, a "mad" Arab scientist called Alhazen helped everyone to see things more clearly.

The story is that Alhazen went to Cairo, Egypt's fastest-growing city, to advise the notoriously cruel ruler al-Hakim on how to control the flow of the all-important River Nile. But Alhazen's ideas didn't work, and the Nile flowed on as usual. He thought that the only way to escape the wrath of the terrifying leader – who had once had all the dogs in Cairo killed just to stop them barking – was to pretend to be mad. Fortunately, his idea worked, and al-Hakim left him to get on with his studies in mathematics and physics.

Alhazen stopped thinking about water and started thinking about light. What happened when he saw something? Did feathery feelers come out of his eyes to explore the surface of objects, as Pythagoras had thought? Or was ancient Greek philosopher Epicurus right to think that light, from a source like the Sun, bounced off objects and entered the eye?

To a scientist like Alhazen, Pythagoras' ideas seemed ridiculous. If they were true, why couldn't people see in the dark? So he sided with Epicurus, but took his ideas a lot further. Using his mathematical skills, Alhazen worked out much of what is known today about the way light is reflected by flat and curved mirrors, and bent by glass or the atmosphere. He even explained why two eyes work better than one.

CITY OF CAIRO
Cairo, the capital of Egypt, is on the River Nile, 160 km (100 miles) south of the Mediterranean coast. In the 10th century, it became a walled city, one of the greatest of the medieval world. Its name comes from the Arabic words *al-Qahhirah*, which mean "victorious".

Greek philosopher and mathematician Pythagoras.

SENSE OF SIGHT
Pythagoras, who lived from about 580 to 500 BC, was one of the first people to think about how the eye worked. About two hundred years later, Epicurus realized that sight was caused by light entering the eye.

Epicurus (c 341 – c 270 BC) was, like Pythagoras, born on the Greek island of Samos.

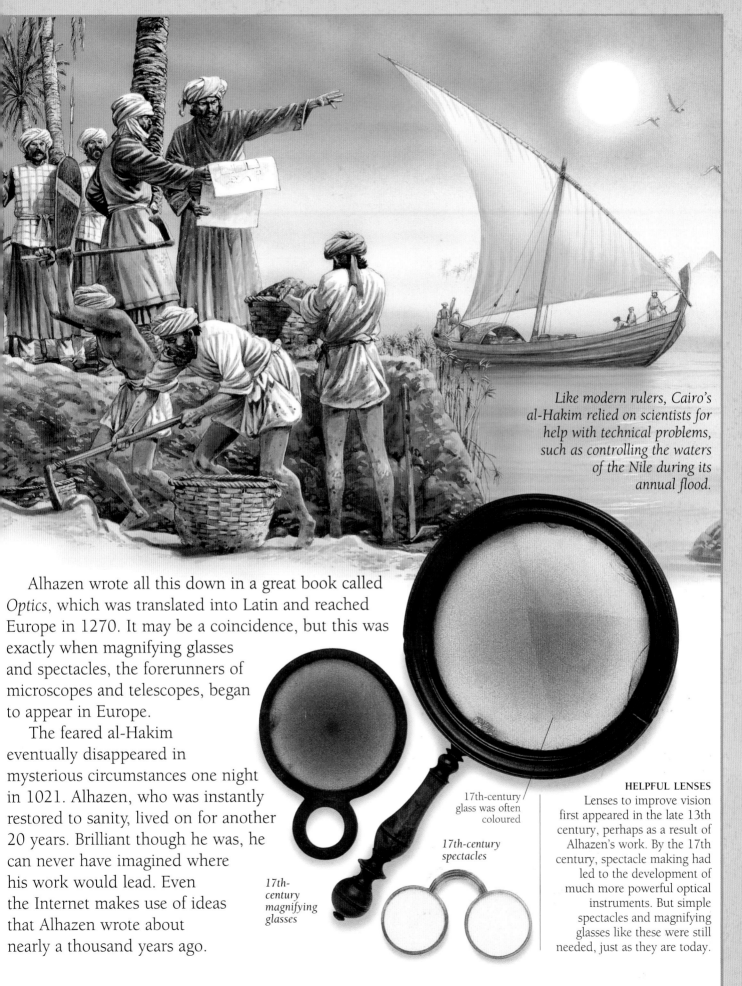

Like modern rulers, Cairo's al-Hakim relied on scientists for help with technical problems, such as controlling the waters of the Nile during its annual flood.

Alhazen wrote all this down in a great book called *Optics*, which was translated into Latin and reached Europe in 1270. It may be a coincidence, but this was exactly when magnifying glasses and spectacles, the forerunners of microscopes and telescopes, began to appear in Europe.

The feared al-Hakim eventually disappeared in mysterious circumstances one night in 1021. Alhazen, who was instantly restored to sanity, lived on for another 20 years. Brilliant though he was, he can never have imagined where his work would lead. Even the Internet makes use of ideas that Alhazen wrote about nearly a thousand years ago.

17th-century magnifying glasses

17th-century glass was often coloured

17th-century spectacles

HELPFUL LENSES
Lenses to improve vision first appeared in the late 13th century, perhaps as a result of Alhazen's work. By the 17th century, spectacle making had led to the development of much more powerful optical instruments. But simple spectacles and magnifying glasses like these were still needed, just as they are today.

RUDDER *This model of an English ship of about 1430 has a fully developed rudder. Copied from a small image, it does not show the tiller that would have been used to control it.*

Crow's-nest, from where the ship's lookout would have kept watch

Stay to hold up the mast

Rudder was placed amidships at the stern of the ship, and extended the depth of the hull

Rudder

c 1200

It is thought that some early Chinese boats were steered with simple rudders, but until about AD 1200, most boats around the world were steered by sailors trailing oars over the side. The modern rudder arrived in stages. First, a large steering oar was fixed near to the back, or stern, of the boat. In about 1200, it was moved right to the stern to become a simple rudder. By about 1300, a long steering lever, called the tiller, had been added to complete the rudder.

Modern numerals

1202

Leonardo Pisano

The modern number system arrived in the West after a long, slow trip from India. The system, which was started in the 6th or 7th centuries in India, was taken up by Arab mathematicians in the 9th century and reached the West during the 10th century. It made little impact until Leonardo Pisano wrote *Liber Abaci* (Book of the Abacus) in 1202. The book explained everything about Arabic numerals, from how to write them to the mysteries of hundreds, tens, and units. The new system made calculations much easier.

Propaganda dropped from the air

1232

Military commanders have often tried to win battles with words instead of weapons. One way is to drop leaflets from the air. This tactic was tried as early as 1232, when the Mongols (nomads of central Asia) besieged the Chinese city of K'ai-feng. They used kites to drop leaflets on the people inside. It is not known whether any of the citizens read the leaflets, but by 1234 the Mongols had taken over the city.

1215 Supported by the Archbishop of Canterbury, England's barons demand a declaration of rights from King John. The Magna Carta (great charter) is drafted at Runnymede, near Windsor, and sealed by John on 15 June.

1225 On the Île de la Cité in the centre of Paris, the great cathedral of Notre Dame (Our Lady) is completed after 65 years' work. It sets a new standard for cathedrals and will become one of the world's most visited buildings.

Buttonhole

c1250

You might think that buttons and buttonholes were invented together, but buttons actually came first. The ancient Greeks and Romans used buttons to fasten their clothes at the shoulder, but these went through loops, not holes. Buttonholes were invented in Europe in the 13th century. They made buttons so popular that laws were passed to limit the number that people could have, to prevent rich people having too many.

Magnetic poles

1269

Petrus Peregrinus de Maricourt

French engineer Petrus Peregrinus de Maricourt did the first known scientific experiment on a magnet. He put a sliver of iron in various places on a round lump of magnetic rock called lodestone, and marked the stone to show how the iron positioned itself each time. His lines converged at opposite sides of the stone. The marked stone looked like a globe with lines of longitude radiating from the north and south poles. He called these points the magnetic poles, a term that is still used today.

Spectacles

c1280

Spectacles, in the form of a pair of lenses clipped on to the nose, appeared in the 13th century, but nobody is sure where they came from. The English scientist Roger Bacon described a magnifying glass for reading small print in 1268, but this is not quite the same thing. In Italy, where spectacle making was established by 1301, two men from Florence, Alessandro di Spina and Salvino degli Armati, have been credited with the invention. But, like so much else at this time, spectacles may have been invented in China as early as the 10th century.

SPECTACLES
Medieval spectacles were pivoted to grip the nose.

Mathematics of the rainbow

c1280

Qutb ash-Shirazi, Kamal Farisi

Working out what's going on when we see a rainbow requires advanced trigonometry (✳ *see* **page 53**), and by about 1280, Muslim astronomers had created the maths they needed. At an observatory financed by a grandson of the 13th-century Mongol ruler Genghis Khan, two students, Qutb ash-Shirazi and Kamal Farisi, applied the new maths to the optical theories of Alhazen (✳ *see* **pages 66–67**) to explain the way rain bends sunlight into a multicoloured circle.

Rocket

c1300

Although the Chinese may have made simple rockets as fireworks soon after the invention of gunpowder, serious military use came only later. "Arrows of flying fire" were used when the Mongols besieged the Chinese city of Kai-feng in 1232, but these were probably just fireworks tied to arrows. Chinese soldiers are not thought to have begun using rockets as weapons until 1300 at the earliest, but by 1330, rockets were equipped with explosive warheads and were no longer toys.

Shoe sizes

c1305

The earliest system of standard shoe sizes may possibly date back to 1305, when King Edward I of England decided that the inch should be fixed at the length of three barleycorns. This made the official barleycorn one-third of an inch long. It has been said that children's shoes then began to be based on this barleycorn measure. As a large child's foot at that time was about 13 barleycorns (11 cm/ 4.33 in) long, a shoe to fit it was called size 13.

NAVIGATION CHART *This 1375 chart centres on the Mediterranean Sea. The many straight lines aided navigation.*

Navigation chart

1311

Petrus Vesconte

Map makers began to produce charts towards the end of the 13th century. The earliest dated chart was made in 1311 by Petrus Vesconte of Genoa, Italy. Like most early charts, it shows only the Mediterranean Sea. It was drawn using information collected by sailors, and was not based on measurements.

Printer's type case

c1313

Wang Chen

Unaware of Bi Sheng's failure with movable type in 1045 (✳ *see* **page 64**), Chinese magistrate Wang Chen tried something similar in about 1313. He needed 60,000 wooden Chinese characters to print a book. To store these, he invented the first printer's type case, which had a compartment for each character. Because he needed so many cases, Wang Chen stacked them in layers on a spindle so that he could swivel one out as needed.

1275 Venetian explorer Marco Polo crosses Asia's Gobi desert into China, where he travels to the court of Kublai Khan, ruler of China and lands beyond. Polo will later recount this meeting, and more, in *The Travels of Marco Polo*.

1306 A small town protected by a dam on the River Amstel in the Netherlands finally gets official recognition after being granted privileges in 1275. Its name, Amsterdam, from "Amstel dam", will become familiar to millions.

Practical manual of anatomy

1316

Mondino de' Luzzi

Doctors today know about people's insides only because other doctors have cut dead people open to study them. An Italian doctor, Mondino de' Luzzi, did a lot of this, and often gave public lectures while he dissected corpses. Although he tended to see what his predecessor Galen (✴ *see* **page 58**) told him he should, his 1316 book *Anathomia Mundini* was the first European anatomy book since ancient times that was based on observation of human bodies. It was the first systematic guide to human dissection, and remained the standard manual until 1543, when Andreas Vesalius' manual was published (✴ *see* **page 80**).

CANNON *This French print shows highly developed cannons being used during the siege of Paris by the German Empire, 1870–1871.*

Cannon

c1320

The Chinese made cannons (large guns that stand on the ground) soon after they invented gunpowder (✴ *see* **page 63**), but because they were made only of bamboo they were really just oversized fireworks. Only cannon barrels made of bronze or iron were strong enough to withstand a powerful explosion. They were not made until about 1320, when techniques for casting and boring them were perfected. The new weapons were rushed into action all over Europe. By the 15th century, the cannon had grown into a monster that could fire balls weighing more than 25 kg (55 lb).

Alchemy textbook

c1320

Geber

The first popular books on alchemy – the study of base metals and theories for turning them into gold – were published in 1320 under a false name. By 1300, several books written by 8th-century Arab alchemist Jabir ibn Hayyan had been translated into Latin. The books had made Jabir famous, so an unknown alchemist pretended to be Jabir when he wrote *De Investigatione Perfectionis* (The Study of Perfection) to make people read it. He wrote several other books under the name Geber (his version of Jabir), but he could really have used his own name. His books were so good that alchemists everywhere used them anyway.

Striking clock

1335

Early clocks just rang a bell to mark the beginning of each hour. The first clock to sound out the actual time was built in Milan, Italy, and started striking in 1335. It was a major achievement for medieval technology – a machine that could count. The Milan clock was quickly followed by others throughout Europe, including one in Salisbury cathedral, England, which was installed in 1386 and is still working today.

Chromatic keyboard

c1350

The first keyboard instrument was the organ, but it couldn't play all the

1321 Italian poet Dante Alighieri dies on 14 September at the age of 56. His *Divine Comedy*, written in Italian, not Latin, describes a journey through hell, purgatory, and paradise. It is one of the greatest poems in all literature.

1333 A catastrophic flood sweeps through the Italian city of Florence as the River Arno overflows its banks. All of the city's bridges are destroyed. Despite this, Florence grows and prospers, becoming one of Italy's finest cities.

different sharps and flats, or semitones. It was therefore a great step forward when, in about 1350, organs in Europe began to be equipped with chromatic keyboards. These did have semitones, allowing them to play in any key. But the keyboards were designed for chubby fingers, and it was the end of the 15th century before organ keys slimmed down to their present size.

Firearms
c1350

Cannons were fairly easy to design, but working out how smaller, portable weapons could be charged with powder, aimed, and fired proved more difficult. The earliest attempts, used in Europe from about 1350, had no triggers and were held under the arm, making it impossible to aim them accurately. The first firearm that looked anything like a modern weapon was the harquebus. This didn't reach the battlefield until about 1470, and it was useless against fast, accurate bows and arrows.

Clavichord
c1360

The clavichord is a distant ancestor of the piano. The first reference to what was probably a clavichord is in a French account book of about 1360, although the instrument did not get its modern name until later. The clavichord's mechanism is very simple: when a key is pushed down at one end, the other end goes up, making a metal blade strike a string. The sound is very quiet because the blade stops the string from vibrating freely – a definite advantage for musicians who like to practise playing at night.

Canal lock
c1373

Canal locks are pieces of medieval technology that can still be seen in action. They move boats up and down between stretches of canal with different water levels, trapping boats in a basin that fills to raise them or empties to lower them. The first is said to have been built at Vreeswijk in the Netherlands, in 1373, but there were certainly locks at Viterbo, Italy, by 1481.

Woodcut
c1400

A woodcut is a picture carved on a piece of fine-grained wood, which is then used for printing. Whole books were being printed from wood blocks in China by AD 600, but the woodcut has a different history. It began to be used in about 1400, especially for the production of playing cards. But it really came into its own after 1450, when printing from movable types had been perfected. Readers wanted to see the same sort of pictures they had always had in handwritten books, and the woodcut was there to provide them.

Players used a bat resembling a modern tennis racket

Tennis
c1400

Tennis today is a very different game from the French pastime jeu de paume (palm game) that started it all.

As the name suggests, the French game was played with hands, not rackets. By about 1400, wooden bats had replaced hands, and a game resembling tennis emerged. In the 16th century, it was played indoors with rackets. Then, about 300 years later, a British army officer, Walter Wingfield, adapted the game to outdoors, creating "lawn" tennis as it is now known.

TENNIS The game of jeu de paume was popular in 18th-century France.

Carpenter's brace
c1400

A type of drill invented in about 1400, the brace is also the ancestor of the car-engine crankshaft. It is a rod with a U-shape in the middle, a hand-rest at the top, and a drill bit at the bottom. The carpenter steadies it with the hand-rest, grasps the U, and moves it around with the same action as a piston in a car.

1347 Germ warfare hits Europe as soldiers from the East catapult corpses infected with Black Death into a trading post in southern Ukraine. The virulent disease spreads rapidly, killing a third of Europe's population in four years.

1362 For the first time since 1066, English court proceedings are conducted in English instead of Latin or Norman Frenech. The Statute of Pleadings, which makes this possible, says that proceedings must still be recorded in Latin.

NEW WORLDS, NEW IDEAS

HUMAN UNDERSTANDING of the world grew enormously between 1400 and 1750. Our planet ceased to be seen as the centre of the universe, and seemed to grow as explorers reached new lands. New discoveries, and new means to communicate them, led to an age of reason and the beginnings of modern science.

METAL MOVABLE TYPE *These casts are from Korean bronze type used in about 1406.*

Metal movable type
1403
Htai Tjong

People in Korea started working on movable metal types in the 14th century, and in 1403, King Htai Tjong of Korea had the first true font of metal type made. One hundred thousand bronze characters were cast, and that was just the start. The king had two more complete fonts ready long before movable type was perfected in Germany (✳ *see* **pages 75 and 76–77**).

Water-powered iron works
1408
Walter Skirlaw

Medieval iron workers heated iron ore with charcoal in a furnace to produce a spongy lump of iron called a bloom. The hotter the fire was, the better the furnace worked, so air was pumped in with bellows to feed the flames. As demand for iron grew and furnaces got larger, something more than muscle power was needed to work the bellows. In England, which would become the largest iron producer in the world, the problem was tackled by Walter Skirlaw, the Bishop of Durham. He set up a water-powered bloomery in 1408.

Code breaking
1412
al-Kalka-shandi

Early attempts at secret writing were not effective, but by the late 14th century Arab code writers and breakers, called cryptographers, were getting serious. They invented systems for changing each letter into a different one, and used the fact that some letters occur more often than others to decipher supposedly secret messages. These tricks of the trade were published in 1412 by Egyptian scholar al-Kalka-shandi, forming the first reliable set of instructions for code makers and breakers.

Perspective
c1412
Filippo Brunelleschi, Leon Alberti

The Italian architect Filippo Brunelleschi discovered perspective – the art of drawing objects in a way that gives an impression of their size and relative position – between 1410 and 1415. The discovery revolutionized the way artists drew pictures. Until he invented the "vanishing point", to which all parallel lines converge, pictures were built up from flat shapes. Twenty years later, his friend Leon Alberti wrote a book giving detailed instructions on how to create the correct perspective. This enabled painters to produce pictures with a realism that was surpassed only by 19th-century photography.

Tower windmill
c1420

One problem with windmills is that the wind doesn't always blow from the same direction. Early windmills contained their entire mechanism in a huge wooden box mounted on a pivot, so it was difficult to swing the sails into the wind. The tower mill, invented in about 1420, had all its heavy machinery in a fixed tower.

Only the sails, which were mounted on a movable cap, had to be moved to track the wind – a much easier task.

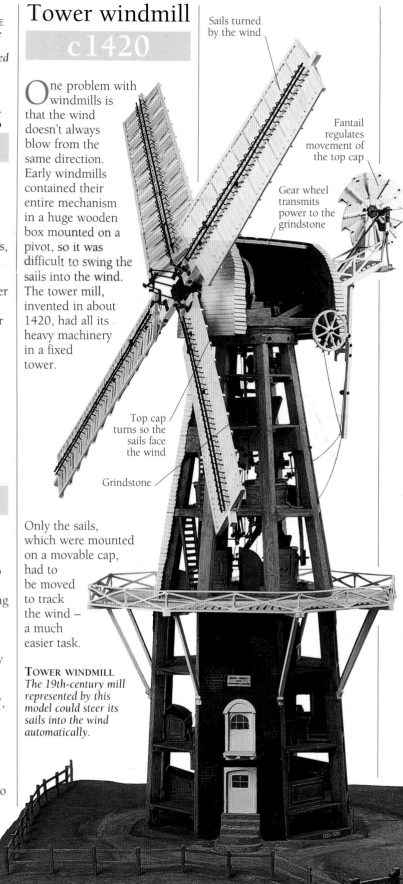

Sails turned by the wind

Fantail regulates movement of the top cap

Gear wheel transmits power to the grindstone

Top cap turns so the sails face the wind

Grindstone

TOWER WINDMILL *The 19th-century mill represented by this model could steer its sails into the wind automatically.*

1405 Chinese admiral Zheng He ends China's isolation with the first of a series of missions to countries around the South China Sea, which he knows as the Western Oceans. Sixty-two ships reach Indochina, Java, and Sri Lanka.

1418 Italian architect Filippo Brunelleschi is asked to design the dome of Florence's cathedral. His highly original solution, octagonal in form, with its white structural ribs exposed on the outside, will dominate the city's skyline.

Flywheel
c1430

A car engine (✽ see **page 150**) wouldn't work without its flywheel, a heavy wheel that stores energy during the brief bursts of burning inside the cylinders, then releases it to keep the engine running smoothly. Although early devices like the potter's wheel incorporated a kind of flywheel action, separate flywheels first appeared in the early 15th century. They evened out the jerky rhythm of machines powered by feet moving up and down on a treadle.

Oil painting
1430

Robert Campin, Jan van Eyck

Although the Romans knew about oil paint, it was the French and Flemish painters Robert Campin and Jan van Eyck who perfected its use in art. Both were attracted by the realism that oil paint allowed. Earlier paints, such as tempera, which was made with eggs, couldn't produce the same smoothly graded tones. Using the new paint and the new laws of perspective (✽ see **page 73**), van Eyck painted pictures with a realism never seen before.

Peep show
1437

Leon Alberti

Having studied perspective, Leon Alberti realized that he could apply the same laws to a three-dimensional model to make it more realistic. The peep show was a box with a hole in one end. Inside was a three-dimensional scene modelled in perspective. When the model was viewed through the hole, it leapt to life with startling realism. Alberti made his first peep shows in 1437. He even painted the scenery on glass to allow for lighting effects.

Harpsichord
c1450

The harpsichord was king of the keyboards from about 1500 until well after the piano was invented in 1709

HARPSICHORD *This harpsichord was made in Belgium in about 1600. It has two keyboards, known as manuals.*

Beautifully decorated case indicates the status of the harpsichord's owner

(✽ see **page 100**). Unlike the piano, its strings are plucked, not struck with hammers, as the keys are pressed. Because of this, it is not possible to vary the loudness of a note by striking the key with more or less force. Some harpsichords have several sets of strings so that pieces of music can be played at different volumes. The instrument was first described in about 1450. It spread rapidly throughout Europe and is still played today.

Anemometer
c1450

Leon Alberti

Weather watchers measure the speed of the wind with an anemometer (from the Greek word "*anemos*", meaning "wind"). The type with cups attached to a vertical shaft dates from about 1850, but the first anemometer was devised 400 years earlier. Italian artist and mathematician Leon Alberti's instrument was much simpler – just a rectangular metal plate, hinged at the top. When the wind blew, the plate tilted, giving a rough indication of the speed. Alberti described it in about 1450 in his book *The Pleasures of Mathematics*. This type of anemometer was re-invented in a more accurate form by the 17th-century British scientist Robert Hooke.

Trombone
c1450

Originally called the sackbut, the trombone was invented in France in about 1450. It is basically a tube that produces sound from vibration of the lips. The simplest instruments of this type can play only a few notes because their length is fixed. A trombone can play a full range of notes because its length can be changed with tubes that slide in and out. The modern trombone has not changed much since the original instrument was designed more than 550 years ago.

1431 French military leader Joan of Arc is burned at the stake by the English in Rouen on Wednesday 30 May. Guided by inner voices, she had incited the French to expel the English. She was convicted of denying true religion.

1435 Italian sculptor Donatello completes a nearly life-size bronze statue of the biblical hero David, the first nude figure made since ancient times. People are astonished by the expressive realism of this free-standing work of art.

Early printing was hard work. Type was set and inked by hand, and it took two or three people to produce each page.

he persuaded businessman Johann Fust to make him two large loans. By 1455, Gutenberg's first book was ready. He showed it off at the trade fair in nearby Frankfurt, where visitors commented on the book's clarity.

It was then that Fust suggested it was time he got his money back. But Gutenberg couldn't or wouldn't pay. Once again he found himself facing a judge in court. This time, he didn't win. Fust got control of everything. Pausing only to steal Gutenberg's best assistant, he set himself up as the world's first successful printer.

Fust didn't keep his lead for long. Within 25 years, there were printers all over Europe. By 1500 they had printed 30,000 books, spreading new ideas far and wide and helping to launch the age we call the Renaissance.

And Johann Gutenberg? He kept on printing, but didn't make much money. The Archbishop of Mainz gave him food and clothing, but by 1468, Gutenberg was dead. The future he had helped to create was on its way without him.

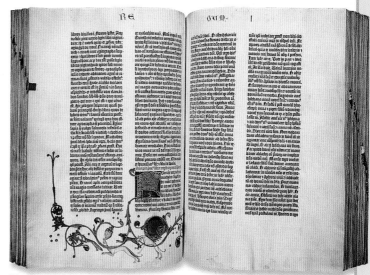

FIRST BOOKS
The first books, like this Gutenberg Bible, were designed to imitate handwritten work. The printed letters were often embellished by hand with elaborate coloured decoration.

Cryptographic frequency table
1465

Leon Alberti

A frequency table shows how often each letter of the alphabet is used. With this table, anyone can crack a simple substitution cipher. For example, in English, "e" is the most often-used letter. If "k" is the most common letter in a ciphered document, it must represent "e". The first frequency table was published in 1465 by the Italian architect Leon Alberti. Because it made simple ciphers useless, Alberti also invented a cipher wheel that encrypted messages more securely.

AMERICA
Columbus sailed westwards on 3 August, 1492, in this ship, the Santa Maria.

The *Santa Maria* was a caravel from northern Spain

Carillon
c1480

Visitors to the Netherlands and Belgium can still enjoy the haunting sound of the carillon, a set of bells that plays tunes. Developed from earlier devices that produced simple clock chimes, it appeared in about 1480. The secret of the carillon lies in the careful shaping of the bells. If this is not done correctly, they generate discordant tones that ruin the music.

Square sails carried on the main mast and foremast

Stove
1490

An open fire wastes energy, so people put their fires in stone or brick boxes called stoves. These trapped the heat of the fire before it went up the chimney. The first stove was built in Alsace, France, in 1490. Later stoves had iron fins placed to regulate the flow of the smoke and extract heat from it. In Russia, the stove was often part of the building, with flues heating all the rooms.

Short, stocky body

America
1492

Christopher Columbus

In the 15th century, a young Italian sailor made a miscalculation that led him to America. Christopher Columbus thought Earth was smaller than it really is. Because it was round, he said, a quicker way of getting to China and India in the east would be to sail westwards. Most people thought he was crazy, but in 1492 Queen Isabella of Spain paid for him to try out his idea. He never reached India, but landed instead in the West Indies. Columbus made four voyages to this "New World" and reached mainland America, at what is now Venezuela, on his third voyage, in 1498. Although he was proved wrong about his route to Asia, he did take European ideas across the Atlantic, changing the New World forever.
(✳ *See also* **Europe's New World**.)

Automatic keyboard instrument
c1500

Before about 1500, musicians were needed to make instruments play music. Then instruments that played themselves began to appear. One had a cylinder the width of the keyboard with pins sticking out of it, one for each note to be played. Someone turned a handle to make the cylinder revolve, and the pins worked the keys to make them play harpsichord or organ music. King Henry VIII of England had an automatic keyboard instrument, and street entertainers are still using them in the 21st century.

1455 The Wars of the Roses, a series of civil wars fought over who should rule England, begins with a battle at St Albans. On this occasion, York, whose emblem is a white rose, defeats Lancaster, with their emblem of a red rose.

1475 In Bruges, Flanders, William Caxton publishes the first book to be printed in English. Having learned about printing in Germany, he uses it to produce *Recuyell of the Historyes of Troye*, which he has translated from French.

EUROPE'S NEW WORLD

AMERICA WAS NEW ONLY to Columbus and other non-Americans. Both the north and south of the continent were inhabited by people who had lived there for thousands of years and built advanced cultures of their own. Once the New World was discovered, other people flooded in, creating new colonies. Some of these became the United States of America, which within a few centuries would dominate the world's science, technology, and industry.

Columbus greets the inhabitants of the New World

THE MEDIEVAL WORLD
Before Columbus sailed west, the entire world known to Europeans consisted of Asia, Africa, and Europe. China dominated Asia, while power in Europe was shared by many countries, including England, France, and Spain.

COLUMBUS' BIG IDEA
Trade with the East was important in the 15th century, but getting there was difficult. Columbus thought he could reach the East by sailing west. Expert sailors told him he was wrong, but failed to stop him attempting it.

THE GROWTH OF AMERICA
Part of North America was temporarily colonized by England in 1587 and named Virginia. Later, the same name was used for one of the states in the USA, which by 1880 had overtaken Britain to become the world's industrial leader.

PINEAPPLE
A pineapple's fruit is formed by a number of separate flowers fusing together.

Pineapple
c1500

A native of South America, the pineapple was unknown to Europeans before Columbus' discovery of America in 1498. Europeans then began to transport the fruit and grow the plants elsewhere. By 1502, Portuguese explorers had found pineapples in the West Indies. They were soon growing them 7000 km (4400 miles) away on St Helena, an island in the South Atlantic, which was trading with Europe by 1590. By this time, the English adventurer Sir Walter Raleigh had discovered the pineapple on one of his voyages to North and South America.

Halftone woodblock print
1510

Lucas Cranach, Hans Burgkmair

Early printing could produce pictures only in stark black and white. Cross-hatching could be used to suggest in-between tones, but it was not very convincing. Two German artists, Lucas Cranach and Hans Burgkmair, were the first to solve this problem. They made several woodcuts for each picture, one for black, one for grey, one for a lighter grey, and so on. Printed on top of each other, they gave realistic results.

Watch
1500

Peter Henlein

The first watch was the size of a hamburger. Invented by German locksmith Peter Henlein, it used a spring instead of weights to drive clockwork inside. Henlein's "Nuremberg egg'" had a metal cover, which had to be lifted to see the time, and no minute hand. Despite these shortcomings, people could at last carry the time with them.

1478 King Ferdinand V and Queen Isabella of Spain, tell Pope Sixtus VI to set up the Spanish Inquisition. Its aim is to seek out and destroy enemies of the Roman Catholic Church. It will become notorious for its use of torture.

1510 In the Netherlands, painter Hieronymus Bosch completes his strange and disturbing triptych (picture in three sections) called The *Garden of Earthly Delights*. Its nightmare symbolism will influence painters 400 years later.

Laudanum

c1520

Paracelcus

From the early 16th century, doctors used laudanum as a painkiller, until other drugs became popular nearly 400 years later. Made by dissolving opium in alcohol, it was introduced by Paracelcus, a Swiss physician. In England, Thomas Sydenham pioneered its use about a century after Paracelcus. Laudanum was freely available in the 18th and 19th centuries, and patients often became addicted to it.

LAUDANUM *These laudanum bottles were essential items in the 19th-century medicine chest.*

Music type

c1525

Pierre Attaignant

Printing music from movable type was, to begin with, done in two steps: first the five-line stave, then the notes. By 1525, French printer Pierre Attaignant had invented a better system. Each note carried a bit of stave, so lines and notes were printed together. Within ten years, Attaignant was printing music by every leading composer.

Fluorspar

1529

Georgius Bauer

As well as being a beautiful crystal, fluorspar, or fluorite, is important in making steel and aluminium. It is a compound of calcium and fluorine, often found near hot springs. The German scholar and scientist Georgius Bauer, usually known as Agricola, described it first in 1529. He regarded it as a fossil, the term that scientists used then for anything found in the earth.

Scientific study of human anatomy

1543

Andreas Vesalius

For centuries, what doctors knew about the structure of the human body was largely based on the work of the Greek physician Galen (✳ *see page 58*). Then, Flemish physician Andreas Vesalius took a fresh look at human anatomy. From his own dissections, he discovered that Galen had based his work on animals, not humans. In 1543, Vesalius produced a book describing human anatomy in detail. It showed what could be done by daring to dissect.

Solar system

1543

Nicolaus Copernicus

In the 16th century, most people believed that the planet Earth stood still at the centre of a moving universe.

SOLAR SYSTEM
Users turned the handle of this 18th-century orrery to show the annual rotation of Earth around the Sun and the Moon's rotation around Earth.

When Nicolaus Copernicus published a book in 1543 saying that Earth orbits the Sun and revolves daily on its own axis, few believed him. By the late 17th century, however, most scientists in Britain, France, Denmark, and the Netherlands agreed with Copernicus, and in 1758 the Roman Catholic Church finally allowed its members to read what he had written.

Botanical garden

1543

Botanical gardens are not just places to stroll. They are also living libraries of scientific knowledge, often gathered over centuries. The first public botanical garden was opened at Pisa, Italy, in 1543. Two years later, another was opened by the University of Padua in Italy. Modern botanical gardens, such as Kew Gardens in England, maintain seed banks to help to save plants from extinction.

Complex numbers

1545

Gerolamo Cardano

Complex numbers are used in advanced mathematics. Without them, problems that involve the square root of a negative number cannot be solved. This is because the squares of negative numbers are always positive, so there is

1535 French explorer Jacques Cartier, trying to find a route to China through North America, sails up a river he names the St Lawrence to a hill he calls Mont Réal and a village that will become Quebec. It is the beginning of Canada.

1535 The Inca empire of Peru is destroyed by Spanish conqueror Francisco Pizarro. Having executed chieftain Atahualpa two years earlier, he sacks Cuzco, capital of the Inca Empire, and founds the modern city of Lima.

"real" number that can be a square root of a negative number. In 1545, Italian mathematician Gerolamo Cardano swept this difficulty aside by inventing a new number to represent the square root of -1. Combined with ordinary numbers, it gave what are now called complex numbers, allowing Cardano to solve a wide range of mathematical problems.

Stage lighting
1545

Sebastiano Serlio

In the early 16th century, the stage of most theatres in Europe was lit by daylight, but Italian architects were hoping to create a type of theatrical lighting to control stage effects.

In 1545, Sebastiano Serlio suggested placing a globe of coloured water in front of a torch or candle to tint and concentrate the light.

Railways in mines
c1550

Trains pulled by locomotives did not appear until the 19th century, but rail transport was used much earlier. Wheels roll more easily on rails than on a road, which allows heavier loads to be pulled. Railways first appeared in mines, where tonnes of rock had to be moved through narrow tunnels. The earliest was built in France in about 1550. Similar railways existed in England by 1605.

Occupational disease
1556

Georgius Bauer

People are not designed to work in mines and factories, where dust and chemicals can attack them at close quarters and make them ill. One of the first people to recognize this was Georgius Bauer, better known as Agricola. In his great book *De Re Metallica* (About Metallurgy) he described the appalling conditions that existed in 16th-century mines, and the occupational diseases, such as "difficulty in breathing and destruction of the lungs" that miners suffered.

Camera obscura
1558

Giambattista della Porta

The term "camera obscura" means "a dark room", and the modern camera started as a darkened room with a tiny hole in it. On the wall opposite the hole, a faithful, though upside-down, image of the outside world appeared. It was fuzzy and dim until 1558, when Italian physicist Giambattista della Porta suggested changing the hole to a lens. The lens let in more light and focused it to a sharp image, which an artist could trace accurately.

BOTANICAL GARDEN *The Jardin des Plantes, Paris, was opened to the public in 1650.*

1536 When the Roman Catholic Church will not allow him to divorce his wife, King Henry VIII of England says that he will no longer obey the Pope. He closes down nunneries, monasteries, and similar places, and confiscates their property.

1555 French astrologer and doctor Nostradamus publishes his book *Centuries*. Its verses, written in language that can be interpreted in different ways, are said to predict the future. One says the end of the world will be in 3797.

Condom
1564

Gabriel Fallopius

In 1564, an Italian doctor, Gabriel Fallopius, described a condom in writing for the first time. Early condoms were made from animal gut, like sausage skins, because there was no rubber in the 16th century. People didn't see any need to limit the size of their families in those days, so condoms were almost always used as protection against disease rather than as contraceptives.

Pencil
1565

Conrad Gesner

Conrad Gesner, a German-Swiss naturalist, was the first person to identify graphite as a distinct mineral. And he was also the first to think of using this soft, slippery form of carbon for writing. In 1565 he had the idea of placing it in a wooden holder to form a writing instrument. An abundant source of graphite was discovered in England at about this time, but pencils as we know them, with their "lead" glued into place, were not made until 1812.

Mercator map projection
1568

Gerhard Mercator

Map makers have to show the curved Earth on flat paper, called a projection, so they cannot avoid distorting it in some way. The Flemish geographer Gerhard Mercator was the first person to tackle this systematically. He knew that for easy navigation, sailors needed a map that showed constant compass directions as straight lines. His way of representing the world does this perfectly. Although it makes countries near the poles look much too big, it is still used for many maps today.

Supernova
1572

Tycho Brahe

A central point of the teachings of Aristotle was that the stars never changed. So the Danish astronomer Tycho Brahe got a big shock on 11 November, 1572, when he noticed that the constellation of Cassiopeia had acquired a bright new star. We know now that it was a supernova – a star destroying itself in a massive explosion. Tycho confirmed that the star was beyond the Moon, therefore in the realm of the "fixed" stars. When he published this observation in 1573, his reputation was made. His star had exploded those ancient beliefs.

GREGORIAN CALENDAR This 18th-century perpetual calendar gives the date of Easter each year either in the Julian or Gregorian calendar.

Instructions for finding the date of Easter are given on the back

Bottle cork
c1580

For centuries, wine came in jars or barrels, which did not usually have corks. When bottles appeared, their stoppers were often made of cork. It is not clear when this material became widely used, but in about 1600 Shakespeare wrote his play *As you Like it*. One character says to another, "Take the cork out of thy mouth, that I may drink thy tidings," showing that Shakespeare's audience must have been familiar with the invention.

Gregorian calendar
1582

Pope Gregory XIII

Although Julius Caesar improved the calendar enormously in 45 BC (✳ *see* **page 55**), by 1582 it had fallen behind the seasons again. The reason was that an Earth year is 365.242 days, not 365.25 as Caesar had assumed. Pope Gregory XIII sorted things out once and for all. First he chopped out ten days to reset the calendar. Then, by decreeing that one leap year should disappear in three out of every four centuries, he corrected the error, creating the calendar we use today.

Constant swing of a pendulum
c1583

Galileo Galilei

The time a pendulum takes to swing from side to side is the same whatever the size of the swing, provided it is not too large. The great Italian scientist Galileo was the first to notice this in about 1583, supposedly while watching a lamp swinging in Pisa cathedral during a boring service. The problem of accurate time-keeping was solved in principle, but a practical pendulum clock was not available until Christiaan Huygens of the Netherlands built one in 1657 (✳ *see* **page 92**).

1564 On 26 April, a baby who will become the world's most famous writer is christened in Stratford-upon-Avon, England. His father, merchant John Shakespeare, and mother, Mary Arden, call their first son William.

1570 A new architecture based on clean, classical lines and simple layout is born in Italy as Andrea Palladio completes the Villa Rotunda in Vincenza. Thousands of "Palladian" buildings will appear in the centuries to come.

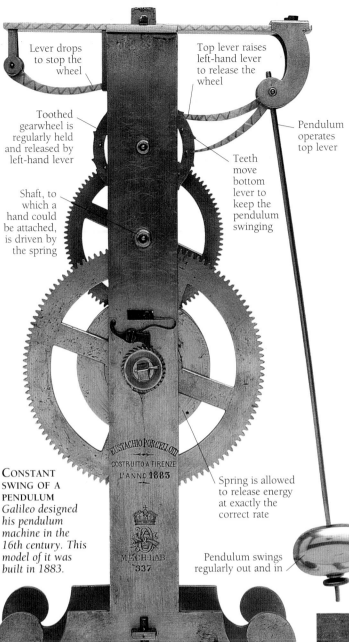

Lever drops to stop the wheel

Toothed gearwheel is regularly held and released by left-hand lever

Shaft, to which a hand could be attached, is driven by the spring

Top lever raises left-hand lever to release the wheel

Teeth move bottom lever to keep the pendulum swinging

Pendulum operates top lever

CONSTANT SWING OF A PENDULUM *Galileo designed his pendulum machine in the 16th century. This model of it was built in 1883.*

EUSTACHIO PORCELLOTTI
COSTRUITO A FIRENZE
L'ANNO 1883

MECH·LAB
337

Spring is allowed to release energy at exactly the correct rate

Pendulum swings regularly out and in

Decimals
1585
Simon Stevin

The idea of decimals was known but not much used until the Flemish mathematician Simon Stevin published a little pamphlet called *La Thiende* (The Tenth) in 1585. He proposed a complicated way of writing decimal fractions, which we no longer use. He also advocated the use of decimal coins, measures, and weights – a suggestion that has been taken up, with varying degrees of enthusiasm, almost everywhere.

Triangle of forces
1586
Simon Stevin

A problem in mechanics is how an object will move when pulled or pushed in two directions at once. We can solve it with something called a parallelogram of forces, in which the strength and direction of forces acting on an object are represented by the sides of a parallelogram. This technique was developed from the slightly simpler triangle of forces invented by Simon Stevin in 1586. It was a new departure at the time, as were many of Stevin's discoveries, some of which put him ahead of the more famous Galileo.

Book carousel
1588
Agostino Ramelli

These days, we can access a range of information without leaving our seats, using CD-ROMs and the Internet. This is not a new idea. In 1588, Italian engineer Agostino Ramelli realized that readers were natural couch potatoes, and designed a large wooden gadget like a fairground big wheel, with shelves that stayed horizontal as the wheel turned. Users could stay seated while they spun the wheel to consult any one of ten volumes. Ramelli recommended it particularly for "those who are suffering from indisposition".

Infinity of the universe
1584
Giordano Bruno

Astronomical references in the Bible reflect the current beliefs of the time, that Earth is the centre of the universe. The Italian philosopher and poet Giordano Bruno had other ideas, and was burned at the stake in 1600 for views that now seem normal. It was bad enough that he believed that Earth orbited the Sun. It was unforgivable of him to say that the universe contained an infinity of worlds like our own. What really sealed his fate was his statement that the Bible should guide morality, not astronomy.

INFINITY OF THE UNIVERSE *The universe is much bigger than early astronomers, such as Hipparchus, once thought.*

1577 El Greco, a painter with a unique, almost mystical style, arrives in Toledo, Spain. The Cretan-born artist expresses his spirituality by crowding his pictures with elongated figures stretching towards heaven.

1588 In May, Philip II of Spain sends a heavily armed fleet of 130 ships – the Spanish Armada – to invade England. It anchors off Calais, but the ships are forced to flee towards Scotland, where rocks and storms destroy 63 of them.

KNITTING MACHINE *This 19th-century machine is a development of Lee's design.*

Knitting machine

1589

William Lee

When English clergyman William Lee realized that his girlfriend liked hand knitting more than him, he set out to change this. He designed a knitting machine in 1589, which remained in use until the 19th century. Some of its principles are still used today. Lee asked Queen Elizabeth I to protect his ideas. First she said the machine was no good, then she said it was too good and would ruin hand knitters. Lee died in poverty.

Flush lavatory

1591

John Harington

Toilet humour goes back to the inventor of the flush lavatory, or water closet, John Harington. He was a famous wit at the court of the English queen Elizabeth I, and he published his design under the title *The Metamorphosis of Ajax*, a pun on the word "jakes" – Elizabethan slang for a lavatory. Harington installed the first water closet in England at Richmond Palace, but his invention was not much used

before the late 18th century, when the U-bend and cistern were invented.

Modern algebraic notation

1591

François Viète

The first person to write algebra more or less as we do today was the French mathematician François Viète. His book *Introduction to the Analytical Arts* was the first to use letters consistently to represent numbers. Viète also sometimes used words instead of signs, such as "quadratus", which indicated a squared quantity.

Water-filled globe focuses flame on to lens below

Reservoir of oil

Oil lamp used to light specimen

Thermoscope

1592

Galileo Galilei

Galileo is famous for revolutionizing physics with his experiments, and for insisting that Earth orbited the Sun. He also made several useful inventions, including the thermoscope. Noticing that air expanded when it got warm, he dipped the neck of a bottle into liquid. As the air in the bottle warmed or cooled, the liquid was pushed out or sucked in, indicating the temperature.

Wind-driven sawmill

1592

Cornelis Cornelisz

Windmills for grinding grain and windmills for pumping water – that was

Lens to focus light on specimen

Objective lens

about it until a Dutch painter with the memorable name of Cornelis Cornelisz thought of applying wind power to another industrial task: sawing wood. Like other mills, the one he built in 1592 needed to be turned to face the wind. It was so big that he had to float it on a raft to make this possible.

Southern star constellations

1595

Pieter Keyser

From any one point on Earth, only half the stars are visible. Earth gets in the way of the rest. So until explorers ventured south of the equator,

Microscope was turned up and down a screw-thread to focus the image

COMPOUND MICROSCOPE *During the 1660s, Englishman Robert Hooke made compound microscopes, such as this one, containing two or sometimes three lenses.*

1591 The Rialto Bridge, one of the best-loved bridges in Venice, Italy, is completed, replacing an earlier bridge. Antonio da Ponte, who won a competition with his design, gives it a single stone arch and a double row of shops.

1597 One of the greatest singer-songwriters of the Elizabethan age, John Dowland, publishes his *First Book of Songs or Ayres*. It will be the best-selling song book of its time. Many of the lyrics express unbearable sadness.

European astronomers knew nothing about large areas of the heavens. In 1595, Pieter Keyser, a Dutch navigator, named 12 new constellations,

Eyepiece lens inside base of eye cup

Pasteboard barrel covered with fine leather

which he had discovered while he was sailing to the East Indies. By 1603, these had found their way into the latest celestial globes and atlases.

Compound microscope

c1600

Hans Janssen

It's possible to magnify things with a single lens, but in theory it's better with two. The first microscope with two lenses, called a compound microscope, was built in about 1600, possibly by Dutch spectacle maker Hans Janssen. Hampered by poor lenses, early compound microscopes didn't give such clear images as the single-lens instruments created later by Dutch naturalist Antoni van Leeuwenhoek.

Magnetism of Earth

1600

William Gilbert

Magnetism was a mystery until the English physician William Gilbert started his experiments. He published the results in 1600. His book on the magnet took the first steps towards modern electromagnetic theory and also contained many observations about the magnetism of Earth. Gilbert concluded that compass needles point north because Earth itself is a giant magnet whose north and south poles roughly coincide with its geographic poles. In an age without Newton's theory of gravity (* see pages 98–99), Gilbert was not the only scientist who concluded that the whole universe was held together by magnetic attraction. (* See also **Magnetic planet**.)

MAGNETIC PLANET

WILLIAM GILBERT BELIEVED that Earth contained a huge bar magnet, but in reality its core is too hot to allow this. The modern theory is that electric currents circulating in its liquid iron core create the magnetic field. However this field arises, navigators have been using it for centuries, whenever they use a magnetic compass to guide them. We now know that its influence extends far beyond Earth.

William Gilbert (1544–1603)

THE MAGNETIC COMPASS

The principle of the compass may first have been used by the Chinese for land exploration and in their *feng shui* philosophy for checking the orientation of buildings. The difference between magnetic and geographic north was understood by 1050, and compasses with iron needles floating on water were in use at sea by the 12th century.

THE NORTHERN LIGHTS

Early sailors would have been familiar with the northern lights – eerie, dancing curtains of light that sometimes appear in the night sky of the far north. But they would not have connected them with the behaviour of their compasses. In fact, both reveal the existence of Earth's magnetic field.

Lights, or auroras, like this can be seen near both north and south poles.

1598 In England, the Poor Laws are passed to deal with people who are old, sick, or have no money. The laws provide money for them, but say that if people can work they must go into a workhouse – often little better than going to prison.

1599 The Globe Theatre opens near the River Thames in south London with a performance by the Chamberlain's Men. The company's leading playwright is William Shakespeare, who has shares in the theatre.

NAMING OF STARS *Before Bayer published* Uranometria, *there was no systematic way of naming the stars. The book's ornate title page is typical of the period.*

Naming of stars

1603

Johann Bayer

Thousands of stars can be seen without a telescope, so astronomers need a system for naming them all. The standard way is to label the stars in each constellation with Greek letters: our nearest star (actually three stars close together) is called alpha Centauri because it is the brightest star in the Centaurus constellation and alpha is the first letter of the Greek alphabet. This system was invented by German lawyer Johann Bayer for a guide to the stars, *Uranometria*, which was published in 1603. It was the first really accurate star atlas. Where there were more visible stars than letters in the Greek alphabet, Bayer continued with Latin characters. His system has since been extended to cover about 1300 stars.

Convex objective lens gathers light and bends it to form an upside-down image

Valves in the veins

1603

Hieronymus Fabricius ab Aquapendente

Once blood has done its job of transporting important substances around the body, it goes back through the veins to the heart to be pumped around again. But gravity and friction are against it. Without one-way valves in veins, it might go the wrong way. In 1603, the Italian surgeon Hieronymus Fabricius ab Aquapendente published details of the valves that he had discovered in human veins. He didn't quite understand why they were there, but his observation helped William Harvey to prove that blood circulates (✳ *see* **page 89**).

Theory of shadows

1604

Johannes Kepler

The recording of light and shade, so easily done by the camera today, demanded

Thermostat

c 1600

Cornelis Drebbel

A thermostat keeps something at a constant temperature by turning the heat up and down. In about 1600, Dutch inventor Cornelis Drebbel made a mechanical thermostat by coupling the damper of a furnace, which regulates the flow of air, with a thermometer. This was significant because it was one of the first examples of a feedback control system.

TELESCOPE *This is a replica of one of Galileo's telescopes, which he made in 1610.*

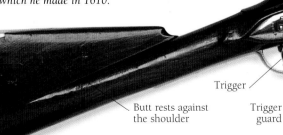

Cock holds flint, which strikes frizzen, making sparks to ignite powder

Trigger

Frizzen

Trigger guard

Butt rests against the shoulder

1600 Shakespeare writes what will become one of his greatest plays, *Hamlet*. With ten years of experience behind him, he produces a tragedy that presents, like no other play, the highs and lows of human existence.

1605 Roman Catholic soldier Guy Fawkes is arrested on 5 November in London. He and other conspirators had placed barrels of gunpowder in the House of Lords to blow it up during the state opening of parliament.

careful thought from 16th-century artists. The key is that light travels in straight lines, illuminating some areas but being blocked from others. Much of the theory of shadows was worked out by the Renaissance genius Leonardo da Vinci, but it was a German astronomer, Johannes Kepler, who produced a complete scientific theory in 1604.

Telescope
1608
Hans Lippershey

In 1608, Dutch spectacle maker Hans Lippershey discovered that if you look through the right pair of lenses, distant objects appear bigger. He had invented the telescope. Following his discovery he may also have invented a microscope, which, like the telescope, involves looking through two lenses. He offered his telescope, or "looker", as he called it, to the government, but they said they would prefer binoculars. However, within a year, the Italian scientist Galileo had recognized the importance of the telescope and was using his own to make startling discoveries about our galaxy.

Newspaper
1609
Johann Carolus

Newspapers started as private newsletters circulated between company offices. They gradually turned into publications of political news. Either of two German papers that started in 1609 could have been the world's first: the *Relation* (published by Johann Carolus) or the *Avisa Relation oder Zeitung*. By 1650, all the major cities in Europe had newspapers, usually only a single sheet without headlines or pictures.

Moon craters
1609
Galileo Galilei

Everyone believed the Greek philosopher Aristotle's theory that the Moon was a perfect sphere – until 1610, when Galileo pointed a telescope at it. He saw that the Moon was far from perfect, being pock-marked with clearly visible craters. It was just one of many observations that began to shake the certainties of the ancient world.

Moons of Jupiter
1610
Galileo Galilei, Simon Marius

Galileo became expert at making telescopes, and eventually built one that made objects look 20 times bigger. In January 1610, he trained it on Jupiter and saw the planet's four largest moons. He published this observation, and much else revealed by the telescope, in a book called *The Starry Messenger*. The moons were given their names – Io, Europa, Ganymede, and Callisto – by the German astronomer Simon Marius.

Orion nebula
1610
Nicolas de Peiresc

Stargazing became a popular occupation once the telescope was invented. In 1610, a French scholar, Nicolas de Peiresc, aimed his telescope at the constellation of Orion and was the first to notice what looked like a cloud. We now know this to be a mass of glowing gas containing new stars, which we call a nebula. It is strange that nobody recorded the Orion nebula before, because it is visible without a telescope.

Maths for fun
1612
Claude-Gaspar de Méziriac

One of the first and most successful puzzle setters was the French mathematician Claude-Gaspar de Méziriac, with his 1612 book *Pleasing and Delightful Number Problems*. As well as the usual brain-teasers involving weighing things with strange sets of weights and getting awkward combinations of objects across rivers, it included a number of intriguing card tricks. Its last reprint was in 1959.

Flintlock musket
c 1612

The first portable firearms were made in the 14th century, but it was not until the 17th century that the first really effective ones appeared. They used a trigger mechanism to set off the powder, allowing a soldier to hold the weapon with both hands and aim it accurately. The best of them was the flintlock musket. The first true flintlock may have been made by a French gun maker called Marin de Bourgeoys for Louis XIII of France, in about 1612. Its trigger released a spring-loaded flint, which struck a steel plate, creating sparks to light the gunpowder and fire a bullet. By 1630, the flintlock musket was being used throughout Europe.

Sliding tube for focusing

Eyepiece contains a concave lens, which bends the light into parallel lines to clarify the image

Wooden stock

Spiral grooving, or rifling, cut inside the musket barrel spins the musket ball so that it flies in a straight line

FLINTLOCK MUSKET *The flintlock musket was loaded from the muzzle end. This made it slow in action, but it remained the standard long-range firearm until cartridges pre-loaded with powder and a bullet made it obsolete.*

1605 Spanish writer Miguel de Cervantes publishes his comic masterpiece, *The History of Don Quixote de la Mancha*. Its central character, Don Quixote, and his faithful servant Sancho Panza, overcome many imaginary enemies.

1607 On Thursday 14 May, a band of colonists found Jamestown, on an island in the River James, Virginia. It is the first permanent English settlement in America. The colonists have been led there by a guide, Christopher Newport.

Index to a book
1614
Antonio Zara

A book without an index is like a website without a search engine. This applies especially to large, factual books, so it's not surprising that the first index was compiled by an encyclopedia maker. When Antonio Zara, Bishop of Petina, now in Croatia, compiled his *Anatomy of the Arts and Sciences* in 1614, he took pity on his readers and included a list of words and where to find them.

Laws of planetary motion
1619
Johannes Kepler

In the early 17th century, people accepted Copernicus' theory that the planets orbited the Sun at a constant speed and in perfect circles. Then the astronomer Johannes Kepler showed that they didn't. Using the excellent data gathered by his former employer Tycho Brahe, he calculated that the planets' paths were ovals, or ellipses, not circles, and that their speed was not constant. The universe was turning out to be more complicated than people thought.

Structure of a candle flame
1620
Francis Bacon

The English statesman and philosopher Francis Bacon believed that people could learn more about Nature by observing things and thinking about them than by reading books and making hasty judgements. In 1620, he published details of a revealing observation he had made: a candle flame has a distinct structure, with a dark centre and a bright edge. This simple fact eventually helped scientists to understand combustion. Bacon's way of thinking about observations has become a key method of science.

Submarine
1620
Cornelis Drebbel

English mathematician William Bourne described a submarine in 1578, but Dutch engraver Cornelis Drebbel was the first person to build one. His "diving boat" of 1620 was made of wood and covered in greased leather to stop leaks. Powered by 12 oarsmen, it made trips up and down the River Thames at a depth of about 4.5 m (15 ft). Passengers breathed through tubes held up on the surface of the water by floats. The passengers once included the man who paid for the invention, King James I.

Law of refraction
1621
Willebrord Snell

Light normally travels in straight lines, but when it enters something like glass, its direction can change, in an effect called refraction. In 1621 Dutch astronomer Willebrord Snell discovered the law that governs this change in direction. Once people knew the law, scientists eventually began to use it to design more effective lenses. Later, French mathematician Pierre de Fermat showed that Snell's law amounted to saying that light always takes the quickest route.

Systematic study of metabolism
1614
Santorio Santorio

Italian physician Santorio Santorio spent much of his life on a giant pair of scales. He was trying to find out whether the solids and liquids leaving his body weighed the same as the food and drink he consumed. He found that they didn't: there was something missing. We now know the missing ingredient is carbon dioxide, but Santorio called it "insensible perspiration". His 30-year experiment was the first in which detailed measurements of the body's metabolism were made.

Logarithms
1614
John Napier, Joost Bürgi

Logarithms simplify calculations by converting multiplication and division into addition and subtraction. Scottish mathematician John Napier started working on the idea in about 1594 and published it in 1614. Further details followed in a second book that came out two years after his death. Swiss mathematician Joost Bürgi published the same idea independently in 1620.

Convection heating

1624

Louis Savot

The Romans used warm air for heating, but it travelled under the floor, not inside the room. The alternative method of heating was an open fire, which sent most of its warm air up the chimney. French architect Louis Savot thought he could combine both ideas to heat rooms. In 1624, he designed a fireplace that drew in air under the floor, heated it, then wafted it into the room. He published the idea in 1685.

Circulation of the blood

1628

William Harvey

In 1628, English physician William Harvey made one of the most important discoveries in the history of medicine. Through observation and experiment, he proved that our blood circulates. Before this, doctors believed that blood was made in the liver and then turned into flesh. Harvey's idea seems obvious today, but that's only because we live in the era of scientific medicine that he helped to create.

SMELTING IRON WITH COKE
Flames light the sky as coal is heated to make coke for smelting iron in 18th-century Britain.

Smelting iron with coke

1621

Dud Dudley

Iron is made by heating its ore with carbon, and until the 17th century, the carbon came from wood charcoal. By 1620, trees were getting scarce, so English iron maker Dud Dudley began to experiment with coal. Coal contains a lot of sulphur, which would ruin the iron, so Dudley devised a way of removing the sulphur and other unwanted elements by roasting the coal. The solid that remained, which we call coke,

was almost pure carbon. Dudley got a patent for his process in 1621, but coke was not widely used in smelting iron until 1709, when English iron master Abraham Darby started using it on a large scale.

Dictionary

1623

Henry Cockeram

The first dictionary actually called a dictionary was published by an Englishman, Henry Cockeram, in 1623. His *English Dictionarie* contained only "hard" words. He didn't see the point of listing words that everybody knew. John Kersey, however, in his *New English Dictionary* of 1702, did give definitions of everyday words, creating one of the first modern dictionaries.

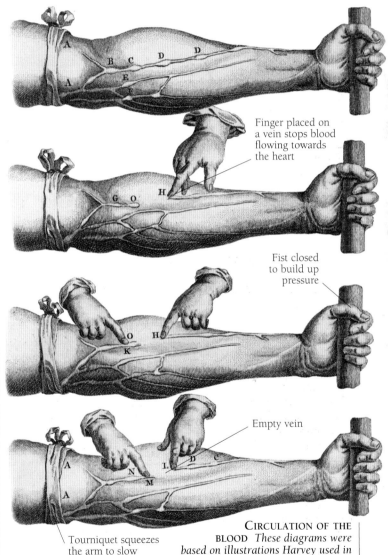

Finger placed on a vein stops blood flowing towards the heart

Fist closed to build up pressure

Empty vein

Tourniquet squeezes the arm to slow blood flow

CIRCULATION OF THE BLOOD *These diagrams were based on illustrations Harvey used in 1628 to explain blood circulation.*

1620 One hundred Puritans escape persecution by leaving England for America. The Pilgrim Fathers, as they will be known, set sail from Plymouth on 16 September, heading for Virginia, but get lost and settle at Cape Cod.

1624 Dutch painter Frans Hals, a master of the quick, bold brushstroke, paints his best-known picture, *The Laughing Cavalier*. Unusually, its subject – an extravagantly dressed soldier – is smiling, as if for a photograph.

Vernier scale
1631

Pierre Vernier

Readings from a graduated scale can be inaccurate because the position of a pointer has to be estimated by eye. In 1631, French civil servant Pierre Vernier invented an improved scale, which is still used today. Instead of a simple pointer, it has a second smaller scale with slightly narrower divisions than the main scale. By noting which of these lines up exactly with the main scale, its user can obtain an exact readout.

Slide rule
1633

William Oughtred

An English vicar, William Oughtred, turned maths into mechanics in 1633 by making two scales showing the logarithms of numbers (✳ see page 88). Users could multiply and divide by sliding the scales to a certain position and reading off the answer.

Robert Bissaker improved the sliding action in 1654, and the slide rule became a basic tool for scientists and engineers until the invention of calculators made it obsolete.

X–Y coordinates
1637

René Descartes

Graphs turn pairs of numbers represented by x and y into meaningful shapes. This idea was invented by the French philosopher René Descartes, who is perhaps more famous for saying "I think, therefore I am." It allowed people to solve geometric problems with algebra and algebraic problems with geometry.

Descartes also started the convention of using letters from the end of the alphabet to represent unknown quantities, and letters from the beginning of the alphabet to represent known ones.

Umbrella
1637

The first written evidence of umbrellas dates from 1637. King Louis XIII of France was reported as having sunshades and "umbrellas of oiled cloth". These would probably have looked like traditional Chinese and Japanese parasols, with a folding wooden frame. The steel-ribbed device we use now was invented by Samuel Fox of England in 1874.

Parabolic path of a projectile
1638

Galileo Galilei

Until the 17th century, people believed that things kept moving only if something kept pushing them. Galileo

Ivory globe represents Earth

Support placed where Venus' and Earth's orbits cross

Brass ball represents the Sun

Ring rotates slowly to represent change in Venus' orbit

Bar supporting Venus rotates quickly

TRANSIT OF VENUS *This model, made in about 1760, shows how Venus can seem to move across the Sun.*

Engraved line shows the path of Venus

1632 Overweight but agile, Sumo wrestler Akashi Shiganosuke forces his opponent out of the ring to become the world's first Yokozuna, or grand champion of Sumo, after the revival of public matches 32 years earlier.

1642 The great Dutch artist Rembrandt van Rijn paints a huge group portrait called *The Night Watch*. The painting shows an army company marching out from its headquarters in the shadowy gloom of early morning.

showed that this was untrue: a moving object carries on moving forever unless something stops it. Objects in the real world slow down and stop because of friction. Galileo did further experiments that proved that a falling object speeds up as it falls. He went on to study projectiles – objects that are thrown into the air. He deduced that a projectile moves forwards at a constant speed but accelerates downwards. It therefore follows a curved path called a parabola.

Transit of Venus
1639

Jeremiah Horrocks

A "transit" of Mercury or Venus occurs when one of them appears to travel across the face of the Sun. Transits of Venus happen only in June or December, and always in pairs eight years apart. They are very rare, the pairs occurring at intervals of well over a century. English clergyman Jeremiah Horrocks was an amateur astronomer. Using standard astronomical tables, he calculated that there would be a transit of Venus in December 1639. He also noted that it happened on schedule – the first ever recorded.

Mezzotint engraving
1642

Ludwig von Siegen

There was no good way of printing all the tones of a picture until Dutch artist Ludwig von Siegen invented the mezzotint, a variation on the ordinary engraving process used with metal printing plates

MEZZOTINT ENGRAVING
Mezzotints were used to publish pictures of many celebrities, including chemist Humphry Davy.

(✳ *see* **page 75**). Instead of drawing directly on the metal plate, the artist first roughens its entire surface. Printed, this would give solid black, because the roughened surface traps the ink. By smoothing different areas of the plate to varying degrees however, the artist can produce lighter tones where required – completely smooth areas do not print at all. Mezzotint reproductions of paintings were popular until the invention of photography.

Barometer
1643

Evangelista Torricelli

Italian physicist Evangelista Torricelli helped Galileo in the last months of the great scientist's life. Galileo suggested the experiment that made Torricelli famous. Torricelli filled a tube with mercury, then

BAROMETER *This is a replica of the barometer invented by Torricelli.*

upended it in a dish. The mercury started to drop out, then stopped. Torricelli realized that the mercury was prevented from falling further by the pressure of the atmosphere. As the air pressure rose and fell, so did the mercury in the tube. Torricelli had invented the barometer, although it was French physicist Edmé Mariotte who named it in 1676.

Torricelli's column of mercury could reach a height of about 760 mm (30 in)

Revolving stage
1645

Giacomo Torelli

Behind every stage show is machinery that the audience never sees, including the revolve. With this huge turntable, a scene can be changed in seconds. The first revolve was probably built by an Italian architect, Giacomo Torelli. He built a theatre containing one in Venice, Italy, in about 1645. He then worked at a theatre in Paris, France. His work there was so good that when he returned to Italy, his successor in Paris destroyed the machinery in a fit of jealousy.

Recognition of gases as distinct from air
1648

Jan Baptista van Helmont

Jan Baptista van Helmont was an alchemist. He believed in the "philosopher's stone", which was supposed to turn ordinary metals into gold. He also made a real discovery: that the gases given off by two different processes – burning charcoal and fermenting grape juice – were actually one and the same. He recognized, too, that it was a distinct gas, not just another form of air. We now call this gas carbon dioxide. Helmont's works, published in 1648, show that he also came across another gas, nitric oxide.

1643 Louis XIV, who will later be known as the Sun King, becomes king of France. He regards himself as having absolute power over his subjects. As well as spending hugely on war, he will also be an extravagant patron of the arts.

1647 In India, the Taj Mahal is completed. Built by the emperor Shah Jahan in memory of his favourite wife, Mumtaz Mahal, it is made of white marble, inlaid with semi-precious stones. It will attract visitors for centuries to come.

Strength of a vacuum

1654

Otto von Guericke

Torricelli's barometer (✳ *see* **page 91**) showed that the atmosphere exerts a force. Engineer Otto von Guericke of Magdeburg in Germany showed just how large that force could be. In 1654, he gave an amazing demonstration to Emperor Ferdinand III. He took two metal bowls, put them together to form a sphere, and pumped the air out with a pump he had developed. With no air inside the bowls, the air pressure on the outside held them together so strongly that teams of horses could not pull these "Magdeburg hemispheres" apart. (✳ *See also* **Working in a vacuum**.)

Pendulum clock

1657

Christiaan Huygens

Galileo realized as early as 1583 that a pendulum would make an excellent timekeeper, but he never managed to turn it into a practical clock. The Dutch mathematician Christiaan Huygens solved the problem in 1657 when he designed a mechanism that allowed the swing of a pendulum to control the rotation of weight-driven gearwheels. He also devised a pendulum that would swing at exactly the same rate whatever the size of its swing. The pendulum improved the accuracy of timekeeping so much that it was at last worth giving clocks a minute hand.

many new facts. Unfortunately, his father thought this was all a waste of time, and stopped his allowance. Swammerdam died an unhappy man.

Rotation of Mars

1659

Christiaan Huygens

Squinting through what would today be considered very poor telescopes, 17th-century astronomers made many discoveries. In 1659, Christiaan Huygens managed to sketch surface features on Mars. He noticed that the features moved between his observations, and he realized that the planet was rotating. Seven years later, the

Italian-born French astronomer Gian Cassini measured the length of a day on Mars – the time the planet takes to make one rotation. He found it was just 40 minutes longer than a day on Earth.

Capillaries

1661

Marcello Malpighi

The microscope helped to solve many mysteries. One of them was the missing link in William Harvey's theory of the way blood

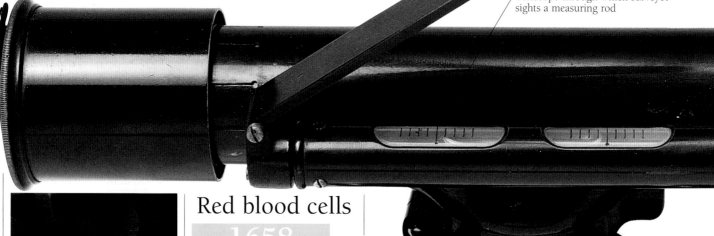

SPIRIT LEVEL *This early 20th-century instrument uses the principle of the spirit level to measure small changes of height of plots of land.*

Telescope through which surveyor sights a measuring rod

Red blood cells

1658

Jan Swammerdam

Blood is red because it is full of red cells. Nobody knew this until the Dutch naturalist Jan Swammerdam looked at blood under a microscope in 1658. One of the best microscopists of his day, he used the instrument to discover

RED BLOOD CELLS *A scanning electron microscope reveals the dish shape of red blood cells.*

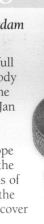

1652 Dutch commander Jan Van Riebeeck lands at Table Bay in the Cape of Good Hope to set up a supply station for Dutch ships on their way to the Dutch East Indies. The country of South Africa will develop from this settlement.

1655 The island of Jamaica becomes an English colony. An expedition led by Admiral William Penn and General Robert Venables overwhelms the Spanish settlers who have been there since the time of Christopher Columbus.

irculates (✴ *see* **page 89**). How
did blood get from arteries to
veins? Marcello Malpighi,
working in Bologna, Italy, in
1661, found the answer. The
blood travelled through tiny
vessels, which were visible only
under a microscope: capillaries.

Spirit level
1661

Anything affected by gravity
can be used to check
whether something is level.
The best thing is a bubble in a
liquid, which always rises to
the highest point. In a slightly
barrel-shaped tube, this is in
the centre when the tube is
level. If the tube is mounted in
a suitable holder, the user only
has to place it on an object and
centre the bubble to ensure the
object is level. This gadget, the
spirit level, first appeared in
1661, and builders still use
spirit levels today.

contract if the pressure is
raised and vice versa. In
France, this principle is called
Mariotte's law, because Edmé
Mariotte not only discovered it
for himself but also noted that
the law is not true if the
temperature changes.

Life table
1662

John Graunt

People who study
population are known as
demographers. They use
statistics, such as how many
people live in an area and how
many births and deaths per
thousand. English shopkeeper
John Graunt founded the
subject by studying death
records. In 1662, he published
tables showing the probability
that someone of a given age
would live to some greater age.
"Life tables" like these are now
the basis of life insurance.

Boyle's law
1662

Robert Boyle,
Edmé Mariotte

Robert Boyle worked with
the English physicist Robert
Hooke, who helped him to
build an effective air pump.
Boyle used the new pump to
make all sorts of discoveries
about air, but the one
everybody remembers is Boyle's
law. This says that the volume
of a given mass of gas varies
inversely with its pressure,
which means that the gas will

Reflecting telescope
1663

James Gregory

Early telescopes used lenses
to refract light from a
distant object before it reached
the observer. The lenses
produced colour fringes, which
made the images indistinct.
Mirrors didn't do this, so a
telescope that used mirrors
promised clearer vision. Italian
astronomer Niccolò Zucchi
suggested this in 1616, but the

WORKING IN A VACUUM

The ancient physics of Aristotle said that a
vacuum was impossible. In the 17th century,
improved technology
could challenge this
directly. Once Guericke
had demonstrated an
effective air pump, other
people, such as Irish
chemist Robert Boyle, built
them too. With the ability
to move air around at will,
they began to find out
more about combustion,
sound, weather, and
much else.

Otto von Guericke was a
great showman as well as a
good scientist.

*Replica
Boyle-Hooke
vacuum pump
of 1659*

Glass chamber
fitted on top
of this cylinder

Handle
moved
to force
piston in
or out

Rack turned
by gearwheel
to move piston

MAKING A VACUUM
Simple pumps use pistons to
suck out air. One-way valves
stop it from rushing back in.
Because a piston sucks out only
a fraction of the remaining air
on each stroke, the vacuum is
never perfect, even if the valves
and seals don't leak. This did
not worry early experimenters.

THE SCIENCE OF AIR
With air under control,
scientists like Guericke, Boyle,
and Edmé Mariotte could
find out some facts about it.
For example, without air,
candles don't burn and
there is no sound; and
reducing the pressure of
moist air makes clouds
form. Mariotte and
Boyle also discovered
the law that links air
pressure and volume
(✴ *see* **this page**).

first practical design came from
Scottish mathematician and
astronomer James Gregory in
1663. In 1668, Isaac Newton
produced his own design,

which drew the reflecting
telescope to the attention of
scientists, but the Gregorian
reflector is still useful. One was
launched into space in 1980.

1660
Britain's premier
scientific association,
the Royal Society, is founded in
London after 15 years of informal
meetings between prominent
English scientists. Two years
later, it will receive a royal
charter from King Charles II.

1661
King Louis XIV of
France sets up the
Royal Academy of Dancing to
improve ballet training. Under its
first director, Pierre Beauchamps,
professional standards improve.
Centuries later, it will become the
Paris Opéra Ballet.

Polar caps of Mars
c 1666

Gian Cassini

Mars has polar ice caps like Earth. At least they look like them but they are probably thinner and made mainly of frozen carbon dioxide. In about 1666, Gian Cassini, who made some of the earliest telescopic observations of Mars, was the first person to report the caps. In spite of his pioneering work, Cassini was rather old-fashioned in his approach. He later rejected Isaac Newton's theory of gravity (✳ *see* **page 98**).

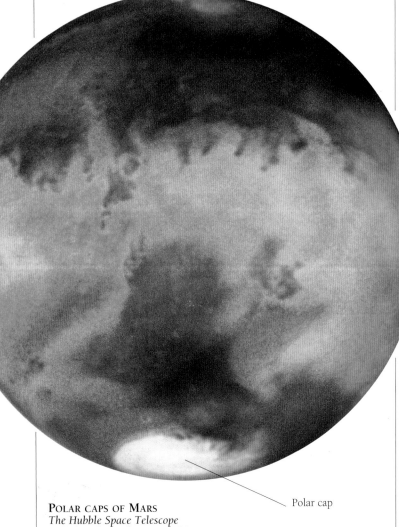

POLAR CAPS OF MARS
The Hubble Space Telescope took this photo of Mars in 1997.

Polar cap

Phosphorus
1669

Hennig Brand, Robert Boyle

Phosphorus makes matches burn. It is also an essential part of the chemistry of our bodies. German alchemist Hennig Brand discovered it in 1669 when, for some reason, he made an extract of his own urine. To his amazement, the extract glowed in the dark: it was phosphorus. Hennig kept his discovery secret, but in 1680, Robert Boyle also discovered the new element for himself.

Shop scales
1669

Gilles de Roberval

Old-fashioned scales with separate weights use a mechanism devised by French mathematician Gilles de Roberval in 1669. The pans are supported from below with a system of arms that makes them move vertically. Objects do not have to go exactly in the centre of the pans, making the scales ideal for shops and other places where speed and simplicity matter.

Champagne
c 1670

Dom Pérignon

Winning racing drivers can never resist shaking the bottle of champagne they get, and squirting its overflowing contents everywhere. The trick works because champagne contains carbon dioxide, which is formed by a special method of fermentation called *méthode champenoise*. It was invented, it is said, by a Benedictine monk called Dom Pérignon, in about 1670. But he was probably only one of many winemakers in the Champagne region of France who contributed to the development of this unique drink.

Diffraction of light
1672

Robert Hooke

Light travels in straight lines. This is almost true. At the edges of objects it actually bends very slightly, so shadows are a little smaller than the simple straight-line idea would suggest. This effect is called diffraction, and was discovered in 1672 by the English physicist Robert Hooke. Hooke's discovery supported the theory that light travelled in waves (✳ *see* **page 97**) because light waves would bend around objects in exactly this way.

Protozoa
1674

Antoni van Leeuwenhoek

Dutch naturalist Antoni van Leeuwenhoek was not a trained scientist, but he was lucky enough to have a job that left him plenty of spare time. He spent it making ever better lenses with which he could see ever smaller things. In 1674, he became the first person to see protozoa – tiny, single-celled creatures that swim around in ponds and water butts. His descriptions of the hidden world around us made a big impact on science.

Speed of light
1676

Ole Rømer

Light travels so fast that it's difficult to measure its speed. It helps if you work with light that has to travel a long way. Danish astronomer Ole Rømer found this out by accident in 1676, when he noticed that the time between eclipses of Jupiter's moons (when they are hidden behind the planet) varied throughout the year. Rømer realized that this must be because the distance from Earth to Jupiter varied throughout the year, and so did the distance that light from the moons had to travel. Rømer calculated that the speed of light was 225,000 km (137,000 miles) per second. This was 25 per cent too slow, but a good start.

1666 On 2 September, a small blaze in a bakery in London gets out of control, starting the Great Fire of London. Four days later, more than 13,000 houses and many public buildings, including St Paul's Cathedral, lie in ashes.

1675 After the Great Fire, mathematician and architect Christopher Wren designs a bold new replacement for St Paul's Cathedral. Some of the boldness is removed by his client, the Church, whose tastes are rather old-fashioned.

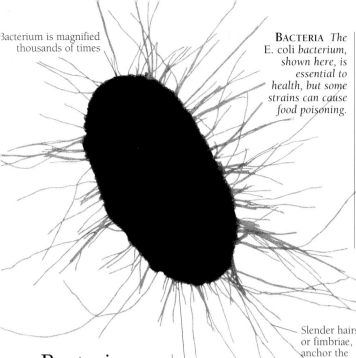

Bacterium is magnified thousands of times

Slender hairs, or fimbriae, anchor the bacterium to a surface

Rigid cell wall with slimy outer covering

BACTERIA *The E. coli bacterium, shown here, is essential to health, but some strains can cause food poisoning.*

Bacteria
1676

Antoni van Leeuwenhoek

Bacteria are even smaller than protozoa. So it wasn't until 1676, when Antoni van Leeuwenhoek had made a lens that magnified 280 times, that he saw some of the larger types of bacteria, collected from his own mouth. To see them, he used some secret techniques, which probably included lighting his tiny subjects from the side so that they stood out sharply like dust in a sunbeam.

Lemonade
1676

Lemon juice must have been used in drinks for a very long time, but the first commercial lemonade appeared in Paris in 1676. Thirsty Parisians could buy it from roaming sellers belonging to the *Compagnie de Limonadiers*, which had an exclusive licence to distribute the drink. Lemonade sellers dispensed the refreshing mixture of water, lemon juice, and honey from tanks strapped to their backs.

Binary system
1679

Gottfried Leibniz, Shao Yung

The binary system records numbers by using just two symbols, such as 0 and 1. The system is essential to modern computers, but it may go back more than 3000 years. The Chinese book *I Ching*, written in the 12th century BC, showed how to make predictions from binary patterns. The 11th-century Chinese philosopher Shao Yung was influenced by the book, and it is possible that German mathematician Gottfried Leibniz was made aware of the binary system through his writings. Leibniz loved the beauty of the binary system. To him its two digits stood for nothingness and God. He thought it could form a universal language, something that never occurred to the writer of *I Ching*.

LEMONADE *By the 19th century, lemonade was big business. This Italian lemonade seller is no longer roaming the streets, but has a permanent stall.*

1678 Puritan preacher John Bunyan writes the first part of *The Pilgrim's Progress*, the story of the journey of a soul seeking salvation. His rich, biblical prose conveys the ideas of vice and virtue through the book's human characters.

1679 The onion-shaped domes and twisted, brightly coloured turrets of St Basil's Cathedral, Moscow, are finally completed after 124 years of work. The building is a high point of Russian Orthodox church architecture.

Gilt balance-wheel cover

Plate supporting wheels

REPEATING WATCH
The exquisite mechanism of this Quare repeating watch was normally hidden from its user.

Pressure cooker
1679

Denis Papin

Food cooks more quickly in water that is hotter than its normal boiling point. In 1679, French-English physicist Denis Papin made water hotter than hot with his "digester", a closed vessel with a safety valve. When water was heated inside it, the pressure rose. The increased pressure stopped the water from boiling until it was hotter than normal.

Repeating watch
1680

Daniel Quare

Owners of early watches had to take them out of their pocket and open a protective

cover before they could read the time – assuming there was enough light. In 1680, English clockmaker Daniel Quare made life easier when he invented his "repeater". Its owner had only to reach into a pocket and touch a button or move a lever to hear the approximate time ring out on a tiny bell inside the watch. This was especially useful at night.

Tunnelling with explosives
1681

Pierre Riquet

The mountains of Europe are riddled with tunnels, many of which were blasted through the solid rock with the help of explosives. According to one

authority, the first major tunnel made this way was for the Canal du Midi, which crosses France, linking the Atlantic Ocean and the Mediterranean Sea. Between 1666 and 1681, French engineer Pierre Riquet cleared a 160 m (515 ft) path for the canal through a sandstone hill by setting off gunpowder in hundreds of holes, which he had drilled into the rock.

HALLEY'S COMET *All comets are giant dirty snowballs made of ice and dust.*

Halley's Comet
1682

Edmond Halley

It used to be thought that comets appeared only once. Then English astronomer Edmond Halley showed that they could orbit the Sun, coming back repeatedly. He studied the path of a comet that appeared in 1682, and was able to show that this, and two earlier comets, were in fact the same comet. In 1705, he predicted that it would return again in 1758. It did, and was named in his honour.

Calculus
1684

Gottfried Leibniz, Isaac Newton

Calculus is the mathematics of change: physical change, such as movement, or mathematical change, such as increasing area. It was invented independently by Gottfried Leibniz in Germany and Isaac Newton in England. Newton created a special method to solve problems in mechanics. Leibniz produced something more like modern calculus.

Newton had the basics by 1666, but in 1684 Leibniz became the first to publish his work, making Newton his lifelong enemy.

Laws of motion
1687

Isaac Newton

English scientist Isaac Newton formulated three laws of motion, which he published in 1687. The laws are still used to get people to the Moon. The first law states that the velocity of an object (its speed and direction) will change only if a force acts on it. This was discovered by Galileo, but the other two laws are all Newton. The second says how

1682 The Palace of Versailles is ready at last on a site just south-west of Paris, after 21 years of building that at times involved 30,000 workers. King Louis XIV moves his court into the extravagantly furnished new buildings.

1688 England's first female novelist, Aphra Behn, publishes *Oroonoko*, the story of an African prince who is made a slave. Some people do not believe a woman could have written anything so good, and accuse her of copying.

uch an object's velocity will e changed by a given force, hile the third says that ushing on an object makes push back equally hard in he opposite direction.

Gravity
1687
Isaac Newton

See **pages 98–99** for the story of how Newton discovered the glue that holds the universe together.

Wave theory of light
1690
Christiaan Huygens

Light has puzzled scientists since the earliest times. Although the law of refraction was known by 1621, nobody

could explain why light obeyed it. Christiaan Huygens provided the first good theory: light was a stream of waves, with each wave made up of smaller wavelets. When light hit glass at an angle, the wavelets that reached it first were slowed down, making the light bend. Huygen's theory conflicted with Newton's ideas, so was not accepted until the 19th century.

Clarinet
c1700
Johann Denner

The clarinet is a woodwind instrument with a wide range of notes and a smooth, distinctive tone. It was developed from an earlier musical instrument, the chalumeau, by the German musician and instrument maker Johann Denner, in about 1700. To extend the range of the chalumeau, Denner added

three extra keys to bridge the awkward gap between the instrument's lower and upper registers. The lower register of a clarinet is still sometimes called the chalumeau.

Phlogiston theory of combustion
c1700
Georg Stahl

When something burns, flames come out, so people naturally thought that combustible substances lost something when they burned. In about 1700, German chemist Georg Stahl called this "phlogiston". A problem with this theory is that things get heavier when they burn, so phlogiston would have to weigh less than nothing. By 1783, French chemist Antoine

Lavoisier had substituted gain of oxygen for loss of phlogiston, which is the true explanation of burning.

Seed drill
c1701
Jethro Tull

Seed drills sow seed in neat rows instead of scattering it. The Babylonians had them, but in about 1701, English farmer Jethro Tull invented the first automatic seed drill. It was part of a system of farming that he developed after seeing grapevines flourishing in rows with the soil between them loose and weed-free. Not all his ideas were accepted, but the benefits of precise drilling were. The successors to Tull's drill are at work in fields today.

SEED DRILL *Jethro Tull shows off his seed drill in this mural from the Science Museum in London.*

Seed drill sowed three rows at a time

1694 The Bank of England is founded on Friday, 27 July. Although private, it lends all its money – £1.2 million – to the government, and is in turn granted the right to issue banknotes and do all the country's company banking.

1697 "Sleeping Beauty", "Cinderella", and other fairy tales reach a wide public for the first time, as French writer Charles Perrault publishes *Tales of Mother Goose*. He collected them from people who knew them by heart.

THE MOON IS FALLING

*Isaac Newton discovers the glue that
holds the universe together*

TRINITY COLLEGE
Trinity College, Cambridge, was founded by King Henry VIII in 1546. Isaac Newton went there to study in 1661.

When Isaac Newton was only three years old, his father died and his mother married again. She went to live in the next village, leaving him with his grandmother. Isaac was not happy. He often sat in the orchard behind his home, Woolsthorpe Manor in Lincolnshire, England, smouldering with hatred for his new stepfather. In 1653, when Isaac was ten, his mother came back. She expected him to make himself useful, but he only wanted to read. In the end, she packed him off to school.

Isaac didn't learn much at school except Latin, but Latin was the language of science. He certainly needed it when he got to Cambridge

Newton knew his orchard well. It was an ideal spot for the intense thought that led him to the idea of universal gravitation.

University. There was so much to read.
The official teaching was old-fashioned,
but Newton taught himself the new science
of Galileo, Descartes, and others. "Plato is
my friend, Aristotle is my friend," he wrote
in his notebook, "but my best friend is truth."

UNIVERSAL LAW
The mass of the Moon is unimaginably greater than that of an apple. Yet both obey the same law of gravity.

No sooner had he got his degree, in 1665,
than the Plague came, which forced everyone to leave Cambridge.
Newton returned to Woolsthorpe. The orchard was still there, and
Newton still went to sit there, his mind now full of scientific questions.
One of them was "What keeps the planets in their orbits?" As Newton
pondered this among the old trees, with heavenly bodies like the Moon
uppermost in his thoughts, an apple fell. It took a genius like Newton to
see the connection. The Moon kept circling Earth because, like the apple,
it was falling. Gravity made the Moon curve towards Earth instead of
continuing in a straight line. And what worked for the Moon could
work for the planets circling the Sun.

REFLECTING TELESCOPE
Newton believed that lenses would never make a good telescope, so he designed one that used a mirror instead. It is still a popular design.

Newton was able to show that the force of gravity got weaker
in proportion to the square of distance. In other words,
a planet twice as far from the Sun as
another will experience only one
quarter of the force; if it is three
times as far away, the force will
be one ninth, and so on.
Other people had suggested
this, but Newton went further.
Using powerful new maths he'd
invented, together with his laws of
motion, he proved that gravity
could account for the orbits of all
the planets. It was the glue that held the
universe together.

Replica of Newton's reflecting telescope

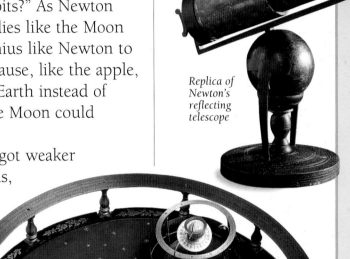

In 1687, Newton published his book
Mathematical Principles of Natural Philosophy, usually
known as the *Principia*, a shortened form of its Latin
title. In it he explained his three basic laws, which govern
the way objects move, and his theory of gravity and the universe. But
his personal universe was not so well ordered. Just before publication,
another scientist, Robert Hooke, accused him of copying his ideas.
Newton never forgave him. Just as he hated the man who stole his
mother, he now despised the rival who was trying to steal his glory.

SOLAR SYSTEM
This clockwork model of the solar system was built in about 1712. Newton thought of the solar system as a giant machine. He was never sure that God would not have to intervene to keep it running.

Two separate plant groups
1703

John Ray

Plants come in two kinds: the ones that look like grasses or palms, and the rest. Scientists call them monocotyledons and dicotyledons – monocots and dicots for short. The baby seedlings in the first group have only one leaf, while the others have two. These important plant groups were first recognized by English naturalist John Ray, in 1703, after a lifetime of study.

Composition of white light
1704

Isaac Newton

For thousands of years, white has symbolized purity. Imagine the upset when Isaac Newton announced to his students at Cambridge University, where he was professor of mathematics, that white light was anything but pure. He said that it was a mixture of every colour in the rainbow. He proved it in experiments in which he separated and recombined white light with prisms. Newton's announcement came in 1670, but nobody took much notice until 1704, when he published the findings in his book *Opticks*.

Piano
1709

Bartolomeo Cristofori

Today, most keyboard instruments play louder when the keys are struck harder. The best keyboard of 300 years ago, the harpsichord, did not do this because it plucked its strings with a mechanism that was unaffected by the force applied. Italian harpsichord builder Bartolomeo Cristofori invented touch-sensitivity in 1709 with his *gravicembalo col piano e forte* (harpsichord with soft and loud), which eventually became the piano. Cristofori's keyboard instrument hit its strings with hammers, giving more control over the sound.

STEAM ENGINE *The piston of a Newcomen engine was connected to the rods of a water pump by a rocking beam.*

Steam engine
c1710

Thomas Newcomen, John Calley

English engineer Thomas Newcomen designed his steam engine in about 1710 and built the first one in 1712. It was based on an earlier pump invented by Thomas Savery, which used the vacuum created by condensing steam to suck water out of mines. Working at first with another inventor, John Calley, Newcomen made the vacuum move a piston, which then drove a separate pump to remove the water. Although incredibly inefficient, the Newcomen engine remained the best available for 50 years.

Laws of chance
1713

Jakob Bernoulli, Abraham de Moivre

Guessing and gambling might not suggest the precision of mathematics, but top mathematicians like Pierre de Fermat and Blaise Pascal were studying the laws of chance as early as the 17th century. The first important book on the subject came from Swiss mathematician Jakob Bernoulli, and was published in 1713. Then, in 1718, came another by French mathematician Abraham de Moivre, which revealed most of today's basic probability theory.

MERCURY THERMOMETER *This early English thermometer has its tube fixed to a scale marked on a separate piece of wood.*

1703 Peter the Great, the tsar of Russia, founds the city of St Petersburg, which he calls his "window on Europe". Thousands of Russian serfs die in the building of the city which, in 1712, will become Russia's capital for two centuries.

1707 England and Scotland become the Kingdom of Great Britain with the passing of the Act of Union. Scotland agrees to be governed by parliament in England, but keeps it own legal system and Presbyterian Church.

THE CLAY MOULDING PROCESS

During the same period when William Ged was working on his plaster-moulding method for casting stereotypes, a French printer, Gabriel Valleyre invented, in 1730, a method of casting molten copper into a mould made from a type of clay. The letters, however, were not always clearly defined and some lines appeared broken.

This development was later revived and improved upon by the Government Printing Office in Washington, U.S.A. The modified method employed the movable bed of an iron moulding press on which was laid the former. An iron plate was screwed to the underside of the top of the press and a layer of clay spread over. The surface of the type was treated with benzine.

After the top of the press had been closed on to the former and secured by a lever, the bed of the press was raised and the impression obtained. The mould was dried in a warm oven. When casting, the plate holding the mould was clamped to a companion plate and into the opening was poured stereotype metal, thus forming the plate.

Aberration of light

1728

James Bradley

There was no evidence that Earth is speeding through space until English astronomer James Bradley discovered the aberration of light in 1728. Imagine a car standing in the rain. Streaks of rain run vertically down the windows. When the car moves, the streaks slope backwards. This is what Bradley saw, only the car was Earth, the rain was light from a star, and the slope was an extra tilt of his telescope.

Achromatic lens

1729

Chester Hall

Isaac Newton said that lenses would always produce images with colour fringes. In 1729, English judge Chester Hall proved him wrong. By gluing a convex lens made of ordinary glass to a concave lens made of heavy flint glass (✳ *see* **page 94**), he cancelled out the fringes to create a colour-free, or achromatic, lens. English optician John Dollond later did the same. The lenses led to the first really good microscopes.

Cobalt

1730

Georg Brandt

In the early 18th century, chemistry was shaking off the last of alchemy. Georg Brandt, a metallurgist from Sweden, used the more scientific approach. He was rewarded in 1730 with the discovery of cobalt. He later exposed alchemists claiming to make gold as frauds. Cobalt is now essential to advanced magnets and radiotherapy.

Mercury thermometer

1714

Daniel Fahrenheit

German physicist Daniel Fahrenheit invented two things at once: a more useful thermometer and a temperature scale which was later named after him. Early thermometers either relied on the expansion of air or allowed alcohol to expand from a small bulb into a fine tube. Fahrenheit's thermometer, which he produced in 1714, used the second of these methods, but with mercury instead of alcohol. This allowed him to measure higher temperatures.

Diving bell

1717

Edmond Halley

A diving bell is a chamber in which people can stay under water without diving equipment. In 1687, William Phips, the future governor of the state of Massachusetts, USA, made one to recover sunken treasure in the West Indies, but his divers wouldn't use it. The first long periods spent under water were in a bell invented by English astronomer Edmond Halley. In 1717, he described how people had survived at a depth of 17 m (55 ft) for an hour and a half. He supplied air to the bell by sending it down in weighted barrels.

STEREOTYPE *This is a clay stereotype mould. The metal stereotype made from it is reversed.*

Stereotype

1727

William Ged

Once a book was printed, early printers broke up the type and reused it. If a reprint was needed they had to set up the pages again. Scottish goldsmith William Ged saved labour in 1727 by inventing the stereotype, a copy of a page of type made by pouring metal into a plaster mould. French printer Gabriel Valleyre had a similar idea, but used clay. With stereotypes, printers did not have to lock up tonnes of type.

1726 Anglo-Irish writer Jonathan Swift writes *Travels into Several Remote Nations of the World*, later known as *Gulliver's Travels*. His satire about countries called Lilliput, Brobdingnag, Houyhnhnms, and Laputa will become a classic.

1729 At Oxford University, England, John Wesley, with his brother Charles, founds the Methodist Church. Preaching personal salvation through faith, Wesley's new, less formal Church appeals strongly to working people.

Sextant
c1730

John Hadley, Thomas Godfrey

Sailors can navigate by measuring the height of the Sun. Simple ways of doing this are inaccurate, and looking straight at the Sun can damage the eyes. In about 1730, John Hadley in Britain and Thomas Godfrey in North America both found a better method: looking at a reflection of the Sun in a movable mirror. The instruments that they invented were called octants,

because the mirror swung over one-eighth of a circle. A later version, the sextant, gave even greater accuracy.

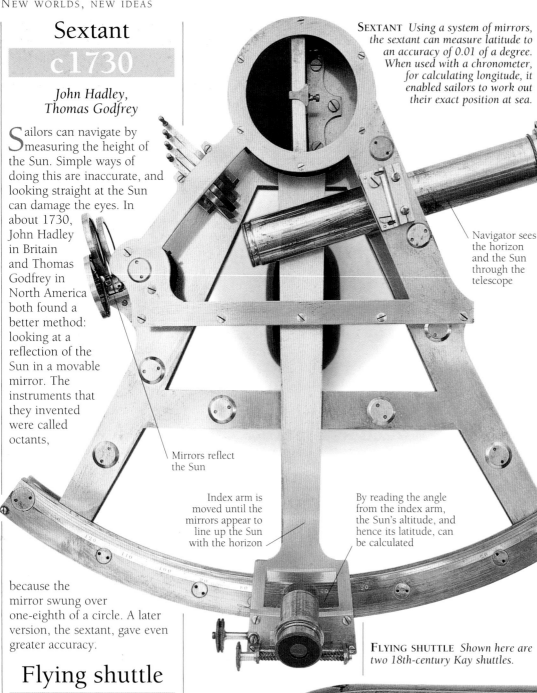

SEXTANT *Using a system of mirrors, the sextant can measure latitude to an accuracy of 0.01 of a degree. When used with a chronometer, for calculating longitude, it enabled sailors to work out their exact position at sea.*

Navigator sees the horizon and the Sun through the telescope

Mirrors reflect the Sun

Index arm is moved until the mirrors appear to line up the Sun with the horizon

By reading the angle from the index arm, the Sun's altitude, and hence its latitude, can be calculated

FLYING SHUTTLE *Shown here are two 18th-century Kay shuttles.*

Rollers underneath reduce friction

Flying shuttle
1733

John Kay

In weaving, thread on a reel in a holder called a shuttle is shot back and forth. John Kay, the son of an English woollen manufacturer, invented the flying shuttle in 1733. Before then, for wide cloth, a solitary weaver had to walk from one side of the loom to the other to pick up the shuttle and throw it back, so it was more economical to have two weavers. Kay added rollers to the shuttle so that it ran on a track. It was operated by one weaver, halving the labour needed for broad cloth. It was a key to the Industrial Revolution in Britain (✳ *see* **page 111**), but brought Kay neither fame nor fortune.

Measurement of blood pressure
1733

Stephen Hales

Stephen Hales was an English clergyman and also an expert scientist. He specialized in taking measurements of living things and was the first person to measure blood pressure. His technique, revealed in 1733, was brutally straightforward: he simply stuck a tube into a horse's artery and measured the height to which the blood rose.

Rubber
1736

Charles-Marie de la Condamine

Rubber got its name in 1770 when British chemist Joseph Priestley found it would rub out pencil. Rubber trees, with their sticky sap, had been discovered earlier by the French scientist Charles-Marie de la Condamine, while he was on an expedition in South America. Rubber wasn't really new to Europeans – even Christopher Columbus knew about it – but it was

1731
The first magazine to be called a magazine is published in Britain. At this time, magazine means "storehouse", and *The Gentleman's Magazine* is a sort of storehouse of articles collected every month from other publications.

1737
Government censorship of the stage begins in England after playwright Henry Fielding produces a wicked send-up of prime minister Robert Walpole. Until 1968, the lord chamberlain will have to check all new plays.

Bernoulli effect
1738
Daniel Bernoulli

Swiss scientist Daniel Bernoulli worked out that if a stream of fluid (a gas or liquid) speeds up, its pressure drops. This "Bernoulli effect" can be seen in a popular science exhibit – a ball suspended on a stream of air from a blower. The air coming out of the blower is moving faster than the air that went in, so its pressure is lower than the surrounding air. If the ball moves from the air stream, the higher pressure pushes it back.

Franklin stove
1740
Benjamin Franklin

Benjamin Franklin was a writer, scientist, and diplomat, who played a leading part in creating the USA. He still found time to create a simple invention that would warm thousands of homes in the republic: the Franklin stove. It was marketed as the "Pennsylvania Fireplace" and was the ancestor of the wood-burning stoves of today. Made of cast-iron, it had a hinged door to enclose the fire and an adjustable ventilator to control the rate of combustion.

High-quality steel
c1740
Benjamin Huntsman

Mass-produced steel is good enough for most things, but sometimes a more personal touch is needed. English clockmaker Benjamin Huntsman, finding that ordinary steel made poor watch springs, began to make his own steel in Sheffield in about 1740. He was the first to make steel hot enough to melt, allowing it to form a perfectly even alloy. Huntsman's work helped make Sheffield famous for fine steel.

Celsius scale of temperature
1742
Anders Celsius

Inventors of temperature scales hate doing the obvious. Daniel Fahrenheit set the freezing and boiling points of water at a seemingly strange 32 and 212 degrees. In 1742, Swedish astronomer Anders Celsius went decimal with a scale that ran from 0 to 100, but made freezing point 100 and boiling point 0. Eventually, his thermometer was turned upside-down to produce the Celsius scale used today.

Silver-plated tableware
1743
Thomas Boulsover

There has always been a demand for anything that looks like solid silver but costs less. In 1743, English cutlery maker Thomas Boulsover discovered that he could make copper look and behave like silver. Working in Sheffield, Boulsover heated copper between thin sheets of silver, then rolled the hot sandwich to produce Sheffield plate. It quickly pushed solid silver off all but the wealthiest tables.

Slip casting
c1745
Ralph Daniel

Some earthenware items are made by slip casting. A suspension of clay in water, called slip, is poured into a mould. When dry, the shape is removed and fired. English potter Ralph Daniel invented the process in about 1745. He started with iron moulds, but soon discovered that plaster moulds worked better because they sucked out water from the slip and speeded up drying.

Leyden jar
1745
Ewald von Kleist, Pieter van Musschenbroek

In the 18th century, electricity was often regarded as a fluid – something that has no definite shape, but takes on the shape of its container – so where better to store it than in a jar? This may have been the thinking behind German physicist Ewald von Kleist's invention of the Leyden jar in 1745. The jar was covered with metal and made

Metal-covered glass

LEYDEN JAR
This jar is charged by bringing a source of electricity into contact with the central rod.

of glass so that electricity could not leak out. The following year, physicist Pieter van Musschenbroek of the University of Leiden in the Netherlands invented the jar independently. He named it and told other people about it. A charged jar could give a mighty shock. One demonstration involved 1000 hand-holding monks. When the jar was connected to the first and last monk, all of them jumped.

With two pins, this shuttle weaves two-ply thread

Pointed end helps the shuttle to pass through the threads

1742 On 13 April, in Dublin, Ireland, German composer George Frideric Handel's choral and orchestral work *Messiah* is performed for the first time. An instant success, it will be a hugely popular work for centuries to come.

1745 Charles Edward Stuart, known as Bonnie Prince Charlie, lands on the isle of Eriskay, off western Scotland, on 25 July. He will lead an unsuccessful attempt to put him on the British throne in place of the German George II.

Condamine's samples, sent back to France in 1736, that put this unique natural product on the scientific map.

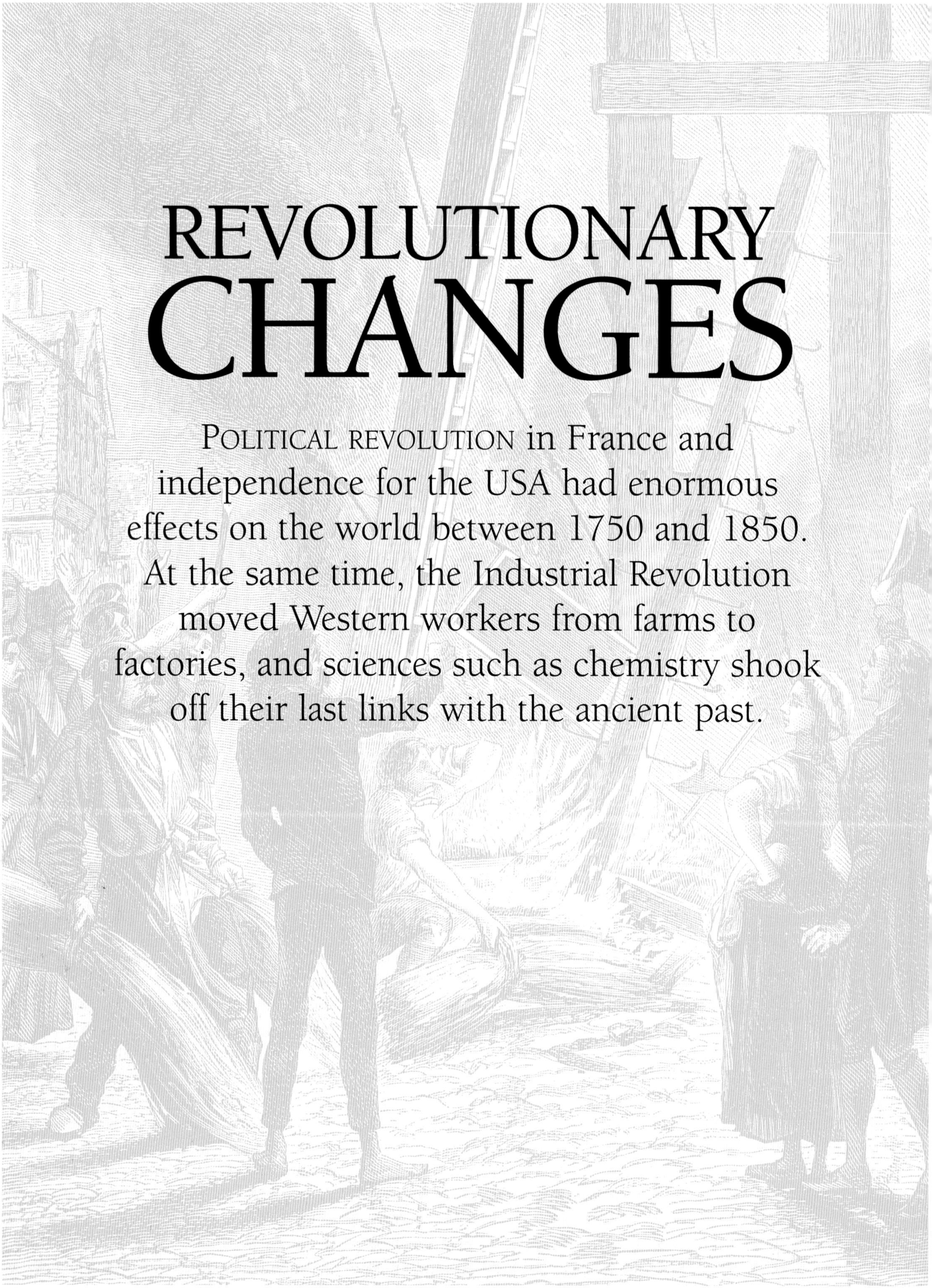

REVOLUTIONARY CHANGES

POLITICAL REVOLUTION in France and independence for the USA had enormous effects on the world between 1750 and 1850. At the same time, the Industrial Revolution moved Western workers from farms to factories, and sciences such as chemistry shook off their last links with the ancient past.

ELECTRICAL NATURE OF LIGHTNING *Thunderclouds threaten as Franklin flies his kite.*

Electrical nature of lightning

1752

Benjamin Franklin

US scientist Benjamin Franklin could have killed himself when he flew a kite in a thunderstorm. He did it to prove that lightning is caused by electricity. Electric charge from the thunderclouds passed down the string and Franklin collected it in a Leyden jar (✳ *see* **page 103**). Amazingly, he lived to show that the charge behaved just like electricity from other sources.

Scientific names for plants

1753

Carolus Linnaeus

Until Swedish botanist Carl von Linné published his *Species Plantarum* (Kinds of Plants) in 1753, botanists described plants using very long-winded names. Linné, known as Linnaeus, classified plants into closely related groups, or genuses, then gave each one the genus name plus its own species name. For example, *Taraxacum officinale* is the dandelion. Linnaeus' system is still in use today.

Carbon dioxide

1756

Joseph Black

Carbon dioxide was recognized by the alchemist Jan Baptist van Helmont in 1648, but the first person to investigate it systematically and relate it to other chemical substances was the British chemist Joseph Black. In 1756, he announced his discovery that carbonates release what he called "fixed air" (carbon dioxide) on heating. Black's work eventually helped chemists to gain a new understanding of air and also of combustion.

Prevention of scurvy

1757

James Lind

Scurvy is caused by lack of vitamin C. The gums swell, joints get stiff, and there may be bleeding beneath the skin. In 1757, British naval surgeon James Lind published a book recommending that sailors should receive rations of citrus fruits, which contain vitamin C. At that time more British sailors died from scurvy than in battle. The navy thought about Lind's idea for 40 years, then tried it. Scurvy disappeared like magic.

Indestructible lighthouse

1759

John Smeaton

Lashed by storms off the coast of England, the Eddystone rock has been feared by sailors for centuries. The weather had destroyed two lighthouses there before British engineer John Smeaton discovered how to defy Nature. He cemented together interlocking blocks of stone with concrete that would set under water. His lighthouse lasted more than 100 years. Even then it was the rock that crumbled, not the lighthouse.

Improved blast furnace

1760

John Smeaton

When Abraham Darby started using coke to smelt iron (✳ *see* **page 89**), he needed a better blast furnace. British engineer John Smeaton, one of the first to apply science to engineering, made the furnace larger and blew air through it with a fan powered by an efficient new water-wheel. Water rushed over the top of the new "overshot" wheel instead of underneath it.

PREVENTION OF SCURVY *James Lind tells sick sailors that limes are the answer to their problems.*

1752 In August, the bell that will be known as the Liberty Bell arrives in Philadelphia, USA, from England where it was made. It will be rung on 8 July, 1776 to celebrate the first public reading of the Declaration of Independence.

1759 French writer Voltaire, a critic of those who try to restrict others' freedom of thought, writes his novel *Candide*. Its central character, Candide, fights against the stupidity of the world but is forced in the end to give up.

Faller wire guided the thread

Pulleys rotated the spindles

Clove helped to twist the fibres together

Creels held the fibres to be spun

Driving wheel was turned to make the spindles rotate

Spinning jenny
1764

James Hargreaves

Until the middle of the 18th century, people spun thread with a spinning wheel, which could spin only one thread at a time. James Hargreaves' spinning jenny (said to be named after his daughter) could spin several threads at once. Traditional spinners were alarmed about the machine, because it could put them out of work, but it helped to start the Industrial Revolution in Britain and brought greater prosperity in the end.

SPINNING JENNY *This replica of Hargreaves' machine shows that it was basically the older spinning wheel rearranged to drive several spindles.*

FINDING LONGITUDE AT SEA *The fourth version of Harrison's chronometer looks quite like a modern watch, but bigger. It is shown here at about two-thirds its actual size.*

Latent heat
1761

Joseph Black

When water is heated, it goes on getting hotter until it boils, then stays at the same temperature. Heat that changes the state of something (from water to steam in this case) instead of its temperature is called latent heat. It was discovered by British chemist Joseph Black in 1761. Three years later he explained the effect to James Watt, who had noticed it independently while working on a steam engine.

Finding longitude at sea
1761

John Harrison

Early sailors navigated by the Sun and the stars. This was all right for determining their latitude (position north or south), but measuring longitude (position east or west) was difficult. One way was for them to compare the time at home, shown by a clock, with the time where they were at sea, shown by the Sun. But no clock existed that would work at sea and keep accurate enough time. The government offered £20,000 to anyone who solved the longitude problem. Between 1735 and 1761, British clockmaker John Harrison built four chronometers. The fourth model was tested on a trip to Jamaica and proved accurate to within five seconds. Although Harrison had solved the problem, the government was reluctant to give him his full reward, and he was an old man before it finally paid up.

1762
Ideas about education change with the publication of *Émile* by the French thinker Jean-Jacques Rousseau. His argument that true education can be built only on children's natural impulses will greatly influence later educators.

1765
British writer Samuel Johnson gains an honorary Doctor of Laws degree from Trinity College, Dublin, Ireland. Although he will never use the title Dr Johnson himself, it will be made famous by his biographer, James Boswell.

Dividing engine

1766

Jesse Ramsden

Accurate maps depend on accurate angles, and map makers measure angles with an instrument called a theodolite. Before British instrument maker Jesse Ramsden perfected his dividing engine in 1766, angles on theodolites and other instruments were marked out by craftsmen and could be somewhat hit-or-miss. The dividing engine produced scales for scientific instruments mechanically. It was faster and more accurate than craftsmen, and meant that maps, as well as astronomical and navigational measurements, were more reliable.

Hydrogen

1766

Henry Cavendish

British scientist Henry Cavendish was the first person to show that hydrogen was a distinct gas, not just a sort of air. He released hydrogen from sulphuric acid by dissolving metal in it, then measured its density. He found that it was lighter than any other gas. Later, he confirmed that hydrogen forms water when it burns. This led French chemist Lavoisier to call it hydrogen, from the Greek for "water maker".

Improved steam engine

1769

James Watt

The first steam engines were built to pump water out of coal mines. It was lucky there was plenty of coal, because the engines wasted a lot of fuel.

James Watt discovered how to reduce the waste, allowing steam engines to compete with water-wheels in powering the new factories. He also invented better ways of controlling steam engines and connecting them to other machines. (✳ *See also* **The story of steam**.)

Steam tractor

1769

Nicolas Cugnot

Early steam engines were huge, heavy, and underpowered, but by 1769 they were good enough for Nicolas Cugnot, a French army engineer, to build a three-wheeled steam tractor. The following year, he built a bigger one to pull heavy guns. Its single front wheel, which was used for steering, was driven by a two-cylinder high-pressure steam engine. Although the later machine successfully pulled a three-tonne cannon at walking speed, Cugnot never got the money he needed to solve its problems, such as how it could carry enough water to keep the engine going, and how to stop the high-pressure steam from leaking out.

Water frame

1769

Richard Arkwright

Before fibres can be woven into cloth they have to be spun into threads. To keep up with the demands of new weaving machinery, such as the flying shuttle (✳ *see* **page 102**), spinning had to speed up. In 1769, Richard Arkwright invented a high-speed spinning machine that made really strong thread. He called it a water frame because it was driven by water power.

THE STORY OF STEAM

THOMAS SAVERY'S STEAM ENGINE, which he patented in 1698, simply sucked up water with the vacuum created when steam condenses. Thomas Newcomen's engine, built in 1712, had a piston and could operate a mechanical pump, but wasted fuel because its cylinder had to be warmed up from cold after every stroke. James Watt added a separate cooling chamber, allowing the main cylinder to stay hot all the time.

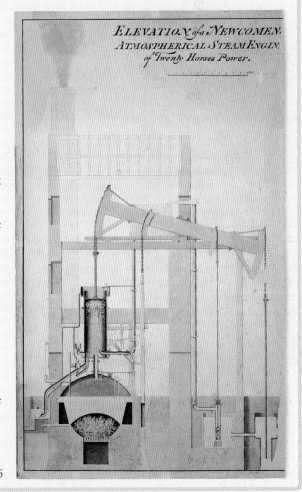

SAVERY'S ENGINE
Steam entered a chamber, forcing water out through a valve. The steam was then cooled, creating a vacuum that sucked water in through another valve, ready to be forced out during the next cycle.

NEWCOMEN'S ENGINE
Steam entered a cylinder, causing a piston to move upwards. The steam was then cooled, creating a vacuum that allowed the atmosphere to push the piston down. This operated a pump through a rocking beam.

WATT'S ENGINES
Having added a separate cooling chamber, Watt further improved Newcomen's engine by letting steam push the piston down as well as up, and adding gears that allowed the engine to drive rotating machinery.

Drawing of a Newcomen engine of about 1826

1768 English painter Joseph Wright questions the growing fascination with science. His dramatic picture *The Air Pump* shows people being "entertained" by an experiment in which a bird is deprived of air and dies.

1769 San Francisco Bay in the USA, one of the world's best natural harbours, is discovered by people arriving on foot. Led by Spanish explorer Gaspar de Portolá, they were sent to look for Monterey Bay but missed it and went too far north.

Factory
c1770

Richard Arkwright

Richard Arkwright realized that his water-powered spinning machine (✱ see **page 107**) meant that spinners would have to gather where there was a water-wheel. In about 1770, in partnership with two local stocking makers, Samuel Need and Jedediah Strutt, he opened a water-powered mill at Cromford in Derbyshire, England. This was the first real factory, and marked the start of the industrial age.

Oxygen
1772

Carl Scheele, Joseph Priestley

Oxygen has a complicated history. Swedish chemist Carl Scheele discovered it in 1772, but waited five years before publishing the fact. Meanwhile, British chemist Joseph Priestley discovered a gas in which things burned fast. Believing that burning things gave out "phlogiston" (✱ see **page 97**), he called it "dephlogisticated air". But the French chemist Antoine Lavoisier proved that the gas combined with burning substances rather than sucking phlogiston out. Lavoisier's new name for it, oxygen, means "acid maker", which it isn't.

Bode's law
1772

Johann Titius, Johann Bode

There's something odd about the planets from Mercury to Uranus. There seems to be a relation between their distances from the Sun. This was first noticed by German astronomer Johann Titius, and his formula was published by fellow astronomer Johann Bode in 1772. At that time, there were gaps where the formula predicted there should be planets. When later astronomers found that the asteroids and Uranus filled the gaps, it seemed to prove Bode's law. Then Neptune and Pluto were discovered, and these planets don't obey the law, so the relationship is probably just an amazing coincidence.

Carbonated drinks
1772

Joseph Priestley

The first fizzy drinks flowed out of the ground – natural carbonated water from health-

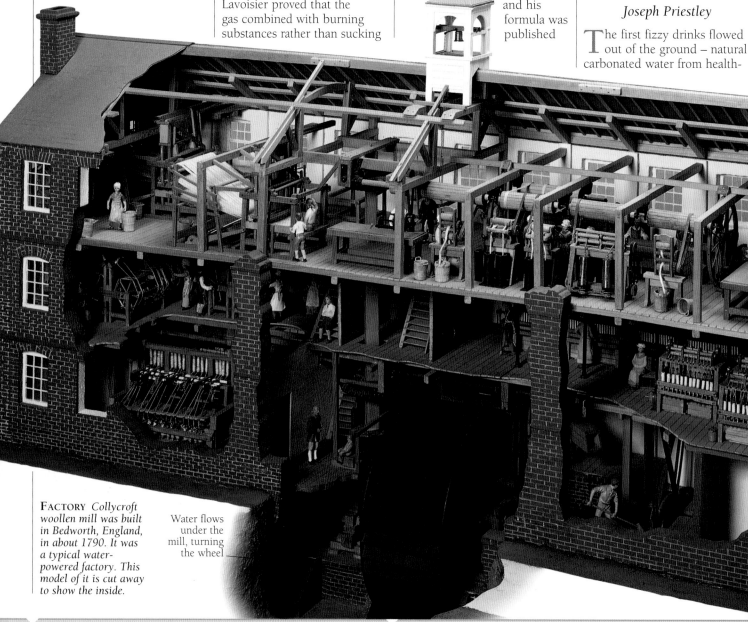

FACTORY *Collycroft woollen mill was built in Bedworth, England, in about 1790. It was a typical water-powered factory. This model of it is cut away to show the inside.*

Water flows under the mill, turning the wheel

1770 London's Bethlem Royal Hospital, an asylum for mentally ill people that is better known as Bedlam, shuts its doors to fee-paying spectators. The behaviour of its inmates is no longer regarded as a form of entertainment.

1772 John Fielding, chief magistrate of the Bow Street Police Court, London, starts issuing the *Quarterly Pursuit*, an information sheet detailing current stolen property and wanted persons. It will become the daily *Police Gazette*.

...iving springs. The first to imitate them was Joseph Priestley. In 1772, he started producing "soda water" in quantity. He had found out how to make it several years earlier, and in the process had made important discoveries about the gas carbon dioxide.

Precision boring machine
1775

John Wilkinson

Early steam engine builders were hampered by the difficulty of making the huge cylinders the engines required. British ironmaster

John Wilkinson improved matters greatly with the precision boring machine he built in 1775 at his father's factory in Wales. It could bore deep, wide holes in large pieces of iron to form much more accurate cylinders than before. James Watt used the machine when building his later engines (✳ *see* **page 107**).

Division of labour
1776

Adam Smith

To make a sandwich, bread has to be buttered and filled. If two people have to make a pile of sandwiches, is it quicker if both people butter and fill complete sandwiches, or if one butters and the other fills? The second way is quicker because doing just one job is simpler. This principle, called division of labour, was identified in 1776 by Scottish economist Adam Smith. He saw its extra productivity as the true source of prosperity.

Photosynthesis
1779

Jan Ingenhousz

In sunlight, green plants take in more carbon dioxide than they give out, and give out more oxygen than they take in. In darkness, the reverse is true. Dutch doctor Jan Ingenhousz published this discovery in 1779 under the delightful title *Experiments Upon Vegetables, Discovering Their Great Power of Purifying the Common Air in Sunshine, and of Injuring It in the Shade and at Night*. This was the first description of the basics of photosynthesis.

Iron bridge
1779

Abraham Darby, Thomas Pritchard

A metal bridge seemed revolutionary at a time when stone, bricks, and wood were the only materials used for large structures. Abraham Darby built the world's first iron bridge in 1779 to the design of Thomas Pritchard. Its 30.5 m (100 ft) arch spans the River Severn at Coalbrookdale, Shropshire, in England. Having survived disastrous floods in 1795, Darby's bridge is still being used today.

Mule spinning machine
1779

Samuel Crompton

Samuel Crompton's "mule" could draw, twist, and wind fibres into a fine thread. Unlike a hand spinner, though, it could work on a thousand reels at the same time. Like the animal of the same name, the mule was a hybrid, using ideas from Hargreaves' spinning jenny and Arkwright's water frame (✳ *see* **pages 106 and 107**). It soon replaced both of them.

Uranus
1781

William Herschel

The planet Uranus is just visible to the naked eye, but British astronomer William Herschel discovered it with a telescope. On 13 March, 1781, he spotted what he thought might be a comet, but the way it moved convinced him it was a planet. He wanted to name it after the king, while French

astronomers generously insisted it should be called Herschel. In the end it was decided to stick to naming planets after gods, and it became Uranus.

Paper balloon

HOT-AIR BALLOON *The first demonstration of a Montgolfier balloon took place in June 1783.*

Hot-air balloon
1783

Joseph Montgolfier, Étienne Montgolfier

The first hot-air balloons were made by two French paper makers, Joseph and Étienne Montgolfier. In September 1783 they sent three animals on a successful 3 km (2 mile) trip in a balloon. Then, in November, they organized the first human escape from Earth's surface. Two volunteers remained aloft for 25 minutes, climbing to 450 m (1500 ft) above Paris and travelling 8.5 km (5.3 miles). Strangely, the brothers never risked a flight themselves.

1776 On Thursday 4 July, the Declaration of Independence is approved in the USA. It notes why 13 British colonies "ought to be Free and Independent States". Independence Day will later be celebrated as a national holiday.

1777 Europeans learn of the existence of New Zealand when British explorer James Cook publishes *A Voyage Towards the South Pole and Round the World*. Cook spent a year charting its islands and getting to know its Maori people.

Hydrogen balloon
1783
Jacques Charles

While the Montgolfiers were experimenting with hot air over Paris (✳ *see* **page 109**), the French scientist Jacques Charles was working with the lightest of all gases, hydrogen, to get a balloon airborne. In 1783, he ascended in a hydrogen balloon to nearly 3 km (10,000 ft). Charles is also known for a law describing how gases expand when heated.

Parachute
1783
Louis Lenormand

Frenchman Louis Lenormand invented his parachute as a means of escape from a burning building. After testing it by jumping from trees, he made his first serious trial in December 1783. He leaped from the top of the Montpelier observatory in France with a 4.3 m (14 ft) 'chute and landed safely on the ground. The first person to jump from the air was another Frenchman, André Garnerin, who took the plunge in 1797 after his hot-air balloon burst over Paris.

Tungsten
1783
Juan D'Elhuyar, Fausto D'Elhuyar

Tungsten is the metal that glows white-hot inside a light bulb. It has the highest melting point of any metal that can be made into wire, is extremely dense – making it good for fishing-weights – and is an important ingredient of cutting-tools. It was first isolated by the Spanish D'Elhuyar brothers, Juan and Fausto, in 1783, although it was already known to the Swedish chemist Carl Scheele.

Bifocal spectacles
1784
Benjamin Franklin

Older people can find it hard to see things close up as well as far away. Reading glasses make nearby objects clearer, but make distant ones less clear. In his old age, US scientist Benjamin Franklin solved the problem with the bifocal lens. This has a section for distant vision mounted above one for near vision. When wearers of bifocal spectacles look down to read, they automatically see through the near vision part of the lens; when they look up, the distant vision section comes into play.

Pick-proof lock
1784
Joseph Bramah

Picking a lock means opening it without the key. Some locks are harder to pick than others, but one of the hardest was invented as long ago as 1784. British engineer Joseph Bramah offered £210 to anyone who could pick his lock, but it was 67 years before anyone claimed the reward. Even then it took US locksmith A. C. Hobbs 51 hours – hardly feasible for a burglar.

Heddle raised and lowered the warp threads

Gear wheels drove cams to move the different parts

Finished cloth wound on to a roller

POWER LOOM *By the mid-19th century, the power loom had been developed into a highly effective, reliable machine. British looms like this one by Harrison and Sons produced cloth for sale worldwide.*

1784 Jedidiah Morse, father of the inventor of Morse code, publishes the USA's first geography textbook, *Geography Made Easy*. It is a great success, and Morse writes several more books on US geography.

1786 On 1 May, an audience in Vienna, Austria, gives a warm reception to *The Marriage of Figaro*, a new opera by Wolfgang Amadeus Mozart. Its comic scenes disguise an attack on the foolishness and corruption of the nobility.

Puddling process for wrought iron

1784

Henry Cort

Iron with too much carbon in it is brittle. Before British ironmaster Henry Cort invented his "puddling" process in 1784, the only way to produce flexible, or wrought, iron was to hammer freshly smelted iron while it was still hot, squeezing out carbon. Cort melted iron with iron oxide to form a puddle, then stirred it while hot gases burned off the carbon. The purer metal gathered into a large ball that, with just a little hammering, became wrought iron.

Power loom

1785

Edmund Cartwright

The designer of the first power loom, Edmund Cartwright, was a British country parson. He was, in his own words, "totally ignorant of the subject, having never at that time seen a person weave". He realized, though, that cheap yarn from powered spinning machines could transform cloth making. His first loom, built in 1785, was very crude, but by 1787 he had improved it enough to start a weaving factory in Doncaster. The government later awarded him £10,000 in recognition of his pioneering work. (✳ *See also* **Weaving a new world**.)

WEAVING A NEW WORLD

BETWEEN ABOUT 1750 AND 1850, in a process known as the Industrial Revolution, Britain transformed itself from a largely agricultural nation into the world's leading industrial power. The industry that led the way was cloth making. Attracted by higher wages, workers moved from farms into the new factories. These were made possible by water power, steam power, new machines, and more adventurous ways of raising money.

This 1834 drawing of a Lancashire cotton mill cannot convey the deafening noise of the many power looms.

SPEEDING UP SPINNING
Until about 1770, spinning was a cottage industry. Merchants delivered raw wool and picked up finished yarn made at home. This changed when powered machines forced spinners to work in a factory, or starve.

LOOMING LARGER
Weaving, too, was done at home until looms in factories started to threaten cottage weavers. Although the change was slower than in spinning, by 1825 half the cloth in Britain was coming from power looms.

FROM COUNTRY TO CITY
Early factories were noisy and dangerous, but offered regular work at better wages than farm labouring. Even skilled craft workers, unable to compete with factory prices, were forced into the fast-growing industrial cities.

Stability of the solar system

1786

Pierre-Simon Laplace

Although gravity explains the way the planets move, Newton (✳ *see* **pages 98–99**) was not sure they would go on forever. He suggested that God intervened from time to time to keep them on track. A century later, people did not believe so readily in divine intervention. In 1786, French mathematician Pierre-Simon Laplace proved that Newton's theory, properly applied, does predict a stable solar system: in the long run, any wobbles cancel out.

Centrifugal governor

1787

James Watt

The governor was one of James Watt's more significant additions to the steam engine. It kept the engine's speed constant as conditions varied. Watt adapted it from a device used in windmills. Weights mounted on a spindle flew out sideways if the engine speeded up, closing the steam valve and slowing down the engine. Like Cornelis Drebbel's thermostat of 1600 (✳ *see* **page 86**), it was an early example of feedback control.

CENTRIFUGAL GOVERNOR *Watt based his governor on this windmill regulator.*

1787 Marylebone Cricket Club is founded at Lord's cricket ground in Marylebone, London. It will soon become Britain's premier club and the world's authority on the laws of the game. Its ground will move to St John's Wood in 1811.

1787 During the summer, the Constitution of the United States of America is written by 55 delegates meeting in Philadelphia. It defines the various parts of the USA's system of government and the basic rights of its citizens.

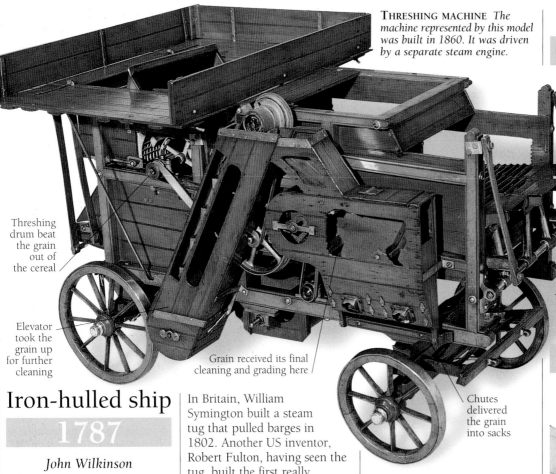

THRESHING MACHINE *The machine represented by this model was built in 1860. It was driven by a separate steam engine.*

Threshing drum beat the grain out of the cereal

Elevator took the grain up for further cleaning

Grain received its final cleaning and grading here

Chutes delivered the grain into sacks

Platinum
1789

P. F. Chabaneau

The valuable, silvery-grey metal platinum was known as long ago as 700 BC, although only as an impurity in gold. Pure platinum was first produced in 1789 by the French physicist P. F. Chabaneau. Instead of using it for some sensible laboratory apparatus, he had it made into a decorative cup, which he gave to the Pope.

Uranium
1789

Martin Klaproth

Uranium, essential to nuclear power, was discovered in 1789

Iron-hulled ship
1787

John Wilkinson

John Wilkinson had iron in his soul. When he was 20 years old he built an iron furnace. Later, as well as making a machine to bore holes in iron (✳ *see* **page 109**), he was involved in building the first iron bridge. He used his boring machine to make iron cannons, and in 1787 built an iron barge to carry them down the River Severn in Britain – the first ever iron ship. He was even buried in an iron coffin.

Steam ship
1787

*John Fitch,
William Symington,
Robert Fulton*

The first working steamboat, built in France, shook to pieces in 15 minutes. In 1787, US clockmaker John Fitch built a more robust craft that made several 30 km (20 mile) trips.

In Britain, William Symington built a steam tug that pulled barges in 1802. Another US inventor, Robert Fulton, having seen the tug, built the first really successful steam ship, the *Clermont*, in 1807. With its sister ship *Phoenix*, it plied the Hudson River for many years.

Threshing machine
1788

Andrew Meikle

Corn was traditionally beaten, or threshed, with sticks to separate the grain from its straw and outer covering, known as chaff. The wind was then used to blow away the smaller chaff. In 1788, Scottish millwright Andrew Meikle invented a machine to do the threshing. The wheat was trapped between a rotating drum and a close-fitting cover, to strip the chaff from the grain. There was no wind inside the machine, so the mixture had to be separated afterwards.

Modern chemistry
1789

*Antoine Lavoisier,
John Dalton*

Before French chemist Antoine Lavoisier cleaned it up, chemistry was full of old-fashioned names and notions. As well as overturning mistaken theories, he and his followers renamed the known elements and compounds, and established the basic naming system used today. After this, Lavoisier's 1789 *Elementary Treatise of Chemistry*, together with British schoolmaster John Dalton's 1808 *New System of Chemical Philosophy*, laid the foundations of modern chemistry. Lavoisier's brilliance did not save him from the French Revolution though: he was guillotined in 1794.

1787 Eleven ships sail from England, carrying the first white settlers to Australia. They arrive at Botany Bay, but later divert to a new site, Port Jackson. Of the 1030 people who land there on 26 January 1788, 736 are convicts.

1788 On New Year's Day, John Walter produces the first issue of the London newspaper called The *Times*. An update of the earlier *Daily Universal Register*, it includes gossip and scandal as well as trade and business news.

y the German chemist Martin Klaproth. He named it after the planet Uranus. Although he believed that he had isolated a new element from the mineral pitchblende, in reality he had only extracted uranium dioxide. The French chemist Eugène Péligot, realizing this in 1841, was the first to produce uranium as pure metal.

Printing ink roller
1790

William Nicholson

In the 18th century, printing ink was dabbed on to the type with leather pads. This was a slow process and required some skill to get the type inked evenly. In 1790, British engineer William Nicholson came up with an improvement that was literally revolutionary: a leather roller. When printing presses were mechanized in the 19th

century, the leather on the roller was replaced by a strange but effective mixture of glue and treacle.

Speech synthesizer
1791

Wolfgang von Kempelen

If your computer can talk, it's thanks to research that goes back to the 18th century. By the 1770s, the basics were understood well enough for Hungarian engineer Wolfgang von Kempelen to start building the first speech synthesizer. He published details of his machine in 1791 in his book *The Mechanism of Human Speech and a Description of a Speaking Machine.* His machine could produce sentences, but it needed a lot of skill to "play". The original machine, with nostrils and a mouth, bellows for lungs, and a reed for the voice, is now in the Deutsches Museum, Munich, Germany.

Titanium
1791

William Gregor, Martin Klaproth

Titanium dioxide is what makes white paint white. Pure titanium and its alloys are used inside jet engines because they stand up well to the enormous heat. This versatile element was first discovered, as an ore called menachanite, by British clergyman William Gregor on a Cornish beach in 1791. Three years later, German chemist Martin Klaproth confirmed Gregor's discovery and chose the name titanium for the new element.

Ambulance
1792

Dominique Larrey

The ambulance was a military invention. Before French surgeon Dominique Larrey's work, few armies had even a first-aid kit. In 1792,

Larrey organized the "flying ambulance" – a mobile team of paramedics supporting Napoleon's troops in battle. They carried medical supplies with them and could get some of the wounded back to hospital on a lightweight vehicle. Larrey became chief surgeon of the French army, and later devised ambulances to get the wounded into field hospitals.

Gas lighting
1792

William Murdock

In the 19th and 20th centuries, coal gas was used for lighting. Early experiments were carried out in Belgium and Scotland by chemist J. P. Minckelers and the Earl of Dundonald, but the gas industry owes more to Scottish engineer William Murdock. In 1792, he lit his cottage in Cornwall, England, by heating coal in a closed vessel and piping the gas to lights. Later, he developed a complete system for making and storing gas.

AMBULANCE *By 1915, during the First World War, the military ambulance really could fly. But only the favoured few went by air.*

1788 After years of odd behaviour, King George III of England becomes so deranged that parliament passes a bill to remove him from the throne and replace him with his son. He will recover the next year before the law comes into effect.

1789 The French Revolution begins in earnest on Tuesday 14 July, when the people of Paris storm the Bastille, a royal prison, and organize a people's militia. The hated King Louis XVI is forced to withdraw his troops.

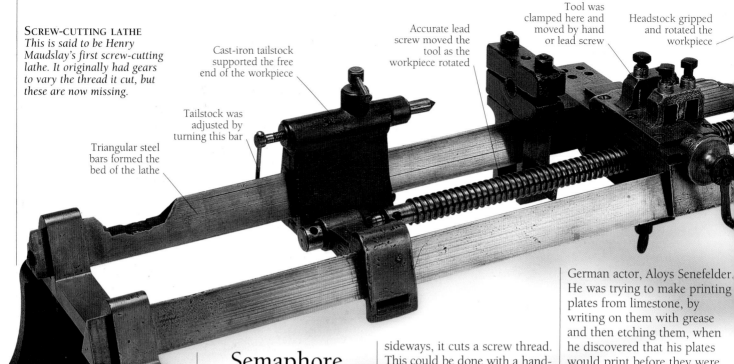

SCREW-CUTTING LATHE
This is said to be Henry Maudslay's first screw-cutting lathe. It originally had gears to vary the thread it cut, but these are now missing.

Triangular steel bars formed the bed of the lathe

Tailstock was adjusted by turning this bar

Cast-iron tailstock supported the free end of the workpiece

Accurate lead screw moved the tool as the workpiece rotated

Tool was clamped here and moved by hand or lead screw

Headstock gripped and rotated the workpiece

Cotton gin
1793

Eli Whitney

Cotton is the fibre attached to the seeds of the cotton plant. It cannot be used until the seeds have been removed. In 1793, US engineer Eli Whitney invented the first machine to remove the seeds – the cotton gin. A revolving cylinder covered with rows of hooks forced the cotton through a comb to rake out the seeds. It was so successful that it made the USA the world's leading cotton producer, overtaking other regions such as Egypt and India. Despite this, it brought Whitney little profit.

Semaphore telegraph
1794

Claude Chappe

Between 1792 and 1814, France was usually at war with Austria. Some of the fighting was near Lille in northern France. To speed up communication with Paris, engineer Claude Chappe built a chain of towers. Each one had movable arms to signal letters and numbers, which could be seen from the next tower using a telescope. In August 1794, this semaphore telegraph sent news of a victory over a distance of 205 km (128 miles) in less than an hour.

Screw-cutting lathe
1797

Henry Maudslay, David Wilkinson

A lathe spins metal against a tool to give it a circular shape. If the tool also moves sideways, it cuts a screw thread. This could be done with a hand-operated screw mechanism, but in 1797 Henry Maudslay in Britain and David Wilkinson in the USA invented lathes where the tool was driven by a screw geared to the lathe. They cut accurate threads with ease.

Chromium
1797

Nicolas Vauquelin

Chromium can prevent corrosion of other metals, either as plating or in stainless steel. French chemist Nicolas Vauquelin discovered the element in 1797 as an impurity in lead ore. He called it chromium, from the Greek word for colour, because its compounds are brightly coloured. This makes them especially useful in paints.

Lithography
1798

Aloys Senefelder

Most printing today relies on a process invented in 1798 by an unsuccessful German actor, Aloys Senefelder. He was trying to make printing plates from limestone, by writing on them with grease and then etching them, when he discovered that his plates would print before they were etched because the printing ink stuck to the grease but not to the wet stone. In today's lithography, the plates are metal and the image is formed photographically, but the principle remains the same.

Beryllium
1798

Nicolas Vauquelin

Perhaps the best known beryllium compound is the green gemstone called emerald. Electrical contacts made of copper also contain beryllium, which makes the copper springy without reducing its conductivity. Beryllium was first identified as beryllium oxide by French chemist Nicolas Vauquelin in 1798. This compound conducts heat well but does not conduct electricity, making it useful today in certain electronic components. Pure beryllium metal was prepared in 1828 by German chemist Friedrich Wöhler and, independently, by French chemist Antonine Bussy. It is often used in the space and nuclear industries.

1794 What will become one of the world's best loved poems, "The Tyger", which begins "Tyger, tyger, burning bright / In the forests of the night", is printed by British artist and poet William Blake in *Songs of Innocence and Experience*.

1795 France replaces its old weights and measures with the metric system. Its basic unit, the metre, is taken to be one 40-millionth of the circumference of Earth, but it will be several years before this is known really accurately.

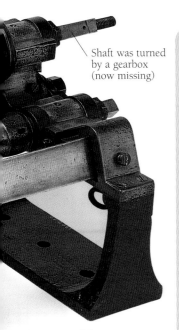

Shaft was turned
by a gearbox
(now missing)

Smallpox vaccine

1798

Edmund Jenner

Edward Jenner

Smallpox was a deadly viral infection common 200 years ago. British surgeon Edward Jenner noticed that people who caught cowpox, a similar but milder disease, never got smallpox. In 1796, he scratched a boy's skin, then applied fluid from a girl with cowpox. It was the first vaccine. The boy later survived deliberate smallpox infection, and in 1798 Jenner published the first book on vaccination. (✳ *See also* **Protection for life**.)

Laughing gas

1799

Humphry Davy

Joseph Priestley discovered nitrous oxide in 1772, but it was 1799 before Humphry (later Sir Humphry) Davy found that the gas could make people laugh. While suggesting that it might be useful in surgery, he also liked to throw parties at which he used nitrous oxide to give his guests a good laugh.

PROTECTION FOR LIFE

EDWARD JENNER HIT ON THE PRINCIPLE by which all vaccines work. The body creates different antibodies to destroy specific viruses or other invaders. But making the right antibody takes time, so a big infection can overwhelm the system. It works better with advance warning in the shape of harmless vaccine particles resembling the unwanted guest. Then, if the real thing comes along, the body is ready for it.

Edward Jenner

Simple tools used by Jenner for his early work

Cupping horn

SMALLPOX BEFORE JENNER
Before vaccination, the only known precaution against smallpox was a dangerous procedure called variolation. Infectious matter from a person with smallpox was applied to a scrape in the skin of someone who wanted to be protected from the disease. The procedure produced either immunity or smallpox.

VACCINATION FOR ALL
Jenner's work stirred up a lot of opposition, but his ideas began to take hold as deaths from smallpox dwindled. In 1881, the French biologist Louis Pasteur created a vaccine against anthrax, a fatal disease caught from animals. Today, we can be vaccinated against a wide range of once deadly infections.

Vaccine points

Vaccination lancets

Lancet and vaccinator

Stratigraphy

1799

William Smith

Stratigraphy, a key way to understand Earth, was developed by British surveyor William Smith. He noticed the same sequence of rock layers in different places. Tracing these over a wide area, he drew the first geological maps. He also saw that each rock had its own fossils, and that those in higher layers were more complex life forms. This lets geologists group rocks by age, according to the fossils they contain.

LAUGHING GAS *In this 1802 cartoon, James Gillray suggests a possible danger of playing with laughing gas. Davy is wielding the bellows.*

1796
A new medical system called homeopathy is introduced by a German doctor named Samuel Hahnemann. It treats an illness with tiny doses of drugs that produce effects similar to the symptoms of that illness.

1798
British poets William Wordsworth and Samuel Taylor Coleridge together produce the slim volume *Lyrical Ballads*. It opens with Coleridge's "Rime of the Ancient Mariner" and marks the start of poetry's Romantic Movement.

Battery
1800

Alessandro Volta

In 1780, Italian doctor Luigi Galvani noticed that a frog's leg in contact with two different metals would twitch, and found that the effect was electrical. His friend Alessandro Volta proved that it was the metals, not the animal tissue, that produced the electricity. In 1800 he made the first battery, a stack of silver and zinc discs separated by brine-soaked cardboard, and showed that electricity from his "pile" behaved like static electricity.

Electrolysis of water
1800

William Nicholson, Anthony Carlisle

British engineer William Nicholson and surgeon Anthony Carlisle began to use Volta's new battery. They found that bubbles formed when they put wires from the battery into salt water. Investigation revealed that the bubbles from one wire were hydrogen. Oxygen was liberated at the other wire, but it combined with the wire rather than forming bubbles. This was the start of electrochemistry, which would reveal much about the nature of chemical compounds.

Iron-framed printing press
1800

Charles Stanhope

In printing, the bigger the area of type, the greater the force needed to squeeze the paper into contact with it. Wooden presses couldn't stand the force needed to print a large sheet. Charles Stanhope, a scientifically minded aristocrat, improved things by making the first cast-iron press. Stronger than a wooden press, it could print large sheets in one pull.

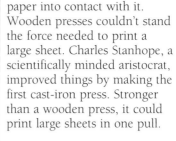

CHROMATIC HARP *This French pedal harp dates from about 1810.*

Strings stretched between the neck and the sound box

Pedals for retuning the strings

Asteroid
1801

Giuseppe Piazzi

Italian astronomer Giuseppe Piazzi discovered the first asteroid in 1801, but soon lost it again as it moved into the daytime sky. It fitted just where Bode's Law said there was a missing planet (❋ *see* **page 108**). German mathematician Carl Gauss invented a way of calculating its orbit from Piazzi's few observations. Using this information, German astronomer Franz von Zach later found the missing asteroid. Piazzi named it Ceres.

Chromatic harp
c1801

Sébastien Érard

Simple harps have one string per note, and can normally play in only one key. Adding too many extra strings would make the instrument unplayable, so attempts to solve the problem have all been based on rapid retuning. The first harp that could play in every key was designed by Sébastien Érard in France

between 1801 and 1810. Its double-action pedal mechanism can instantly retune any of its seven sets of strings.

Jacquard loom
1801

Jacques de Vaucanson, Joseph-Marie Jacquard

By raising and lowering the warp (lengthways) threads on a loom in the right sequence, elaborate patterns can be woven. In the 18th century, this was done manually by a "drawboy". Inventor Jacques de Vaucanson replaced the boy with a punched-card mechanism in 1745, but this was ignored until 1801, when Joseph-Marie Jacquard turned it into the Jacquard loom. As well as weaving under the control of punched cards, it acted as an inspiration to the earliest computer pioneers.

Ultraviolet light
1801

Johann Ritter

Radio waves, X rays, and many other kinds of radiation, including light, the only visible kind, are electromagnetic waves. They can be arranged in order of wavelength to form a spectrum. The part of the electromagnetic spectrum that we can see, the visible spectrum, has red at one end and violet at the other. In 1800, William Herschel discovered infrared radiation beyond the red end of the visible spectrum when he put a thermometer there and noted that it heated up. This made German physicist Johann Ritter have a look beyond the violet end. There he found that silver chloride, which darkens in light, darkened more quickly, again revealing the presence of radiation – ultraviolet light.

1800 In the USA, the Library of Congress is founded. Like the British Museum library, founded 41 years earlier, its aim is to collect at least one copy of everything published in the USA, as a way of establishing copyright.

1801 Following a decree of the revolutionary government of France, seven years earlier, what were once the royal art collections of France at last become fully accessible to the public. They are displayed at the Louvre palace in Paris.

High-pressure steam engine

1802

Richard Trevithick, Oliver Evans

James Watt would never try steam at high pressure because he was convinced it was too dangerous. British engineer Richard Trevithick had no such fears. He made his cylinders extra thick and the pressure ten times higher. In 1802, he patented the resulting smaller, more powerful engine, which made steam power far more versatile. At about the same time, Oliver Evans was pioneering high-pressure engines in the USA, where they were taken up with even greater enthusiasm.

Mass production

1802

Marc Brunel, Henry Maudslay

Mass production reduces a complex operation to simpler operations, each carried out by a separate machine. The first true mass production system made wooden blocks for the rigging of sailing ships. It was designed by French engineer Marc Brunel and built by British engineer Henry Maudslay. Each of its 45 machines carried out a single operation, such as drilling a hole. It increased output per person by more than ten times.

Names for clouds

1803

Luke Howard

Clouds tell us a lot about the weather, so it's not surprising that meteorologists recognize many types. Most of the names they use, such as cirrus and cumulus, were invented in 1803 by British chemist Luke Howard. His lifelong interest in the weather led him to lecture on meteorology and to publish the first book about it. In recognition of his work, he was elected to the Royal Society (a leading scientific society founded in 1660) in 1821.

Railway locomotive

1804

Richard Trevithick

In 1804, when Richard Trevithick added wheels to his high-pressure engine and used it on a tramway, he created the first steam locomotive. It pulled 70 people and 10 tonnes of iron 16 km (10 miles) at a speed of 8 km/h (5 mph). Its advanced features included blowing used steam up its own chimney to make the fire burn faster. Unfortunately, the locomotive destroyed the cast-iron tracks on which it ran, so Trevithick was forced to abandon it.

RAILWAY LOCOMOTIVE
This is a model of Trevithick's locomotive Catch-Me-Who-Can, *which he built in 1808.*

Rods powered by the piston drove the rear wheels

Strongly built boiler

Pump fed water into the boiler

1802 After the break-up of her marriage, Marie Tussaud, an expert in wax modelling, arrives in Britain from France, with several models and two children. She will tour Britain for 33 years, then start a waxwork museum in London.

1804 Tsurya Namboku IV, chief playwright of the Kawarazaki Theatre in Japan, scores his first big hit with *Tokubei of India: Tales of Strange Lands*. Written for top actor Onoe Matsusuke I, it is full of the macabre and the grotesque.

Arc light

c1807

Humphry Davy

By 1807, British chemist Humphry Davy had demonstrated a sensational effect to an audience at the Royal Institution of Great Britain. He brought together two carbon rods connected to a colossal 3000-volt battery, then drew them apart to produce a blinding white flame 10 cm (4 in) long. It was another 70 years before electric generators were good enough to turn this bold experiment into practical lighting for streets and warehouses.

ARC LIGHT *In Minneapolis, USA, the first electric arc lights were illuminated in February 1883.*

Sodium and potassium

1807

Humphry Davy

Volta's battery (✳ *see* **page 116**) brought a flurry of new discoveries. Two of them, sodium and potassium, were made by Humphry Davy at the Royal Institution. Because these elements are so reactive, they are never found uncombined. In separate experiments, Davy melted sodium hydroxide and potassium hydroxide, then connected a battery across the molten masses to extract the metals from their different compounds electrically.

Atomic weights

1808

John Dalton

In 1808, British schoolmaster John Dalton helped to create the formulas and equations of modern chemistry. In his *New System of Chemical Philosophy* he said that chemical elements consist of atoms, each element having atoms of a different weight. The ratios of these weights, and the proportions in which atoms combined, were whole numbers. Ignored for nearly 50 years, Dalton's work eventually had a great effect.

Lace-making machine

1809

John Heathcoat

Lace was originally made by clever hands manipulating lots of bobbins. Only rich people could afford to buy it. In 1809, British inventor John Heathcoat patented a machine that could imitate handmade lace. With his partner Charles Lacy, he set up a mill to turn out the new product. It was wrecked in 1816 by Luddites – organized groups of workers who tried to stop machines forcing workers into factories.

Canning

1810

Nicolas Appert, Peter Durand

Canned food started with an attempt to provide better food for French soldiers. The idea was developed by French confectioner Nicolas Appert, in

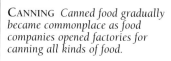

CANNING *Canned food gradually became commonplace as food companies opened factories for canning all kinds of food.*

1809. He put jars of food into boiling water, then sealed them while still hot. Although Appert didn't know it, this killed bacteria and prevented reinfection. In 1810, British inventor Peter Durand replaced the jars with tin-coated iron containers, creating the first canned food. By 1820, it was feeding the British navy.

Compound steam engine

1811

Arthur Woolf

In a high-pressure steam engine, the steam released after each stroke of the piston is still under pressure, and therefore contains wasted energy. By feeding it into a second cylinder, much of this

---

1807 Three years after all states of the USA north of Maryland abolish slavery, British anti-slavery reformers William Wilberforce and Thomas Clarkson finally succeed in making it illegal to import slaves into any British colony.

1812 In Germany, language and folklore researchers Jacob and Wilhelm Grimm publish the first of a two-volume set of folktales called *Kinder- und Hausmärchen*. The stories will appear 45 years later as *Grimms' Fairy Tales*.

Cylinder printing press

1811

Friedrich König, Andreas Bauer

Early 19th-century printing presses worked in much the same way as the one used by Gutenberg in 1455 (✳ *see* **page 76**). Then, with better engineering, faster machines became possible. The first was designed by German engineers Friedrich König and Andreas Bauer in 1811. The paper was wrapped around a cylinder that rotated as the type rolled under it. In 1814, a steam-driven König and Bauer at the offices of *The Times* newspaper in London hit a record-breaking total of 1100 sheets an hour.

Tube in which coloured fragments are viewed

can be recovered. British inventor Jonathan Hornblower patented the idea in 1781, but was prevented from developing it by James Watt, who claimed that it infringed his own steam engine patent. (✳ *see* **page 107**). However, British engineer Arthur Woolf rediscovered the principle in 1804 and produced the first successful compound engine in 1811, after Watt's patent had expired.

Sensory and motor nerve fibres

1811

Charles Bell

Scottish anatomist Charles Bell did fundamental research on the human nervous system. Working in London, he investigated the structure of the brain and spinal nerves. His biggest discovery was that there are two kinds of nerve fibres: sensory fibres that bring in messages to the spinal cord and brain, and motor fibres that send out instructions. Bell's findings were later confirmed by the French physiologist François Magendie.

KALEIDOSCOPE *Brewster's kaleidoscope was far more elaborate than today's toy.*

Object plates containing loose coloured fragments

Miner's safety lamp

1816

Humphry Davy, George Stephenson

See **pages 120–121** for the story of how Davy and Stephenson fought to save miners' lives.

Kaleidoscope

1816

David Brewster

In 1816, Scottish physicist David Brewster took time off work to invent the optical toy called a kaleidoscope. Multiple reflections between a pair of mirrors set at an angle to each other turn a collection of coloured fragments into a constantly changing symmetrical pattern. Its name is Greek, meaning "see beautiful shapes".

Lockable case

1813 Jane Austen sees her novel *Pride and Prejudice* in print at last, 17 years after she started writing it.

Austen declares the book's central character, Elizabeth Bennett, to be her favourite among the many heroines she has created.

1815 On 18 June, Napoleon suffers his final defeat, at the Battle of Waterloo in Belgium. As well as

making some tactical errors, he is heavily outnumbered by 133,000 men led by General von Blücher and the Duke of Wellington.

MAKING THE MAGIC LAMP

*Humphry Davy and George Stephenson
fight to save miners' lives*

Monday, 25 May, 1812, was a terrible day for the mining village of Felling, near Newcastle, England. A massive underground explosion killed 92 miners, some of them only ten years old. It was one of a series of disasters caused by the flame in miners' lamps making "firedamp", or methane gas, explode. In the previous ten years, 108 miners had died in the north-east alone. Now the number had risen to 200. Something had to be done.

A committee was formed to investigate the problem. It asked the advice of William Clanny, a local doctor, Humphry Davy, a chemist, and George Stephenson, a self-educated mine mechanic.

Both Clanny and Stephenson started work on a safer lamp. Clanny sealed his with water, but miners had to pump air in by hand, so it wasn't very useful. Stephenson tried letting the air in through small holes. Firedamp got in too, and burned, but the metal around the holes cooled the flame, preventing explosions. Stephenson's lamp was tested in October 1815, and it worked.

Back in London, Davy experimented with firedamp from a mine. Like Stephenson, he fed in air through small holes, but he realized that the holes had to be very small indeed. His lamp had copper gauze around the flame. It was tested in January 1816, and was a success. The mine owners held a celebration dinner and gave Davy some silverware worth 50 times a miner's yearly pay.

The miners were not impressed. They resented a southerner getting credit for something one of their own people had already invented. Many wouldn't use Davy's lamp, and stuck to their "geordie" – Stephenson's design. Davy said that

BEING A MINER
A section through Bradley mine in Staffordshire, in 1808, shows the rock strata and the jobs of miners. As well as coping with rock fall and floods, early miners worked in almost total darkness. Any light came from candles, which could cause devastating explosions.

THE COMPETITORS
Humphry Davy and George Stephenson were very different people. Davy, born in the south-west of England, was a well educated gentleman and a skilled scientist. Stephenson, who came from the north-east, was a tough, practical mine mechanic who had never been to school.

Humphry Davy was a chemist, but he turned his hand to scientific matters of many kinds.

George Stephenson pioneered the first public steam railway as well as inventing a safety lamp.

Stephenson had stolen the idea from him and that the geordie wouldn't work because it wasn't scientific.

In the end, most miners' lamps incorporated ideas from all three inventors. They had glass instead of gauze around the flame, so they gave more light than Davy's lamp, but the air was still fed in through gauze to prevent explosions. The problem was solved.

Or was it? Unfortunately, the new lamps encouraged mine owners to send miners into areas that were previously thought too dangerous. And because the lamps weren't totally safe, there were just as many deaths as before. Davy and Stephenson may have fought each other for nothing.

The industrial world of the 19th century was powered by coal. The safety lamp, which made it possible to work in dangerous areas, helped coal owners to get a lot more coal out of their mines.

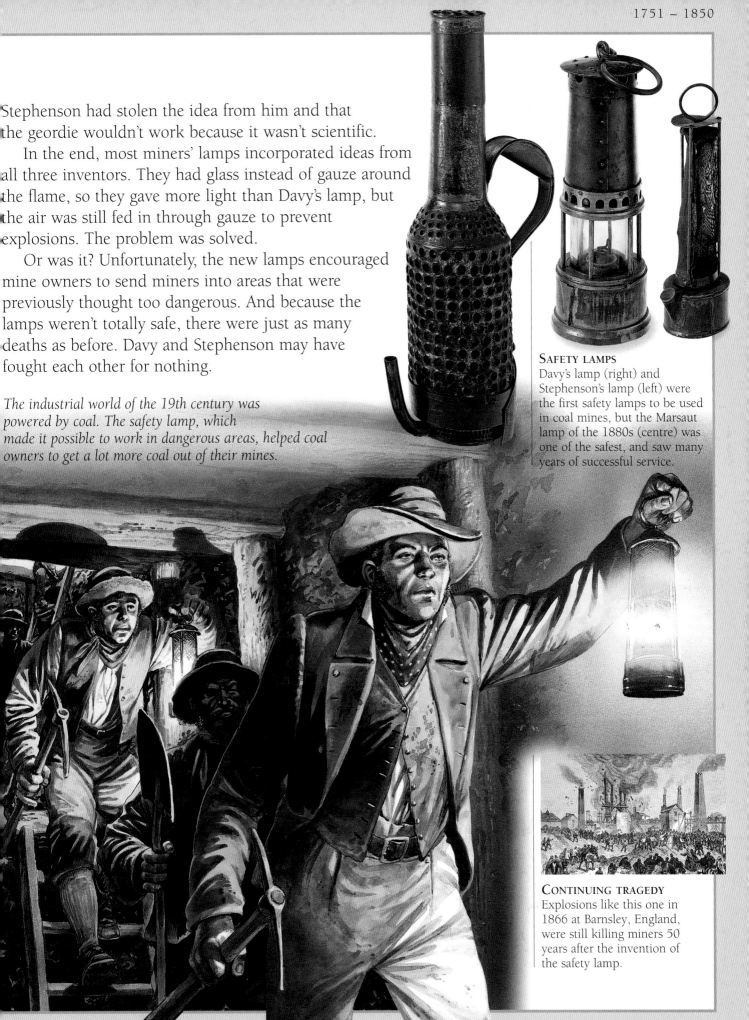

SAFETY LAMPS
Davy's lamp (right) and Stephenson's lamp (left) were the first safety lamps to be used in coal mines, but the Marsaut lamp of the 1880s (centre) was one of the safest, and saw many years of successful service.

CONTINUING TRAGEDY
Explosions like this one in 1866 at Barnsley, England, were still killing miners 50 years after the invention of the safety lamp.

121

Helmet made of copper and brass

Face plate

Stirling engine
1816

Robert Stirling

Exploding boilers upset Scottish clergyman Robert Stirling, so he invented an engine that didn't need steam. Patented in 1816, it works by compressing a cold gas then transferring it to a heated cylinder, where it expands against a piston to do work. It is then cooled again by a radiator. The Stirling engine is quiet, clean, and efficient, but its cost and bulk limit its use.

Superphosphate fertilizer
c1817

James Murray

Plants need phosphorus, and one source of this is fertilizer made of bones. In about 1817, Irish doctor James Murray discovered that treating bones with sulphuric acid made them soluble, so that plants got their phosphorus

DIVING SUIT *The heavy helmet of the 1830 Siebe suit gave a rather restricted view.*

more quickly. He called his product superphosphate. It didn't catch on, but became important in 1843 when British farmer John Lawes started making it on a larger scale.

Tunnelling shield
1818

Marc Brunel, Peter Barlow, James Greathead

Digging a tunnel under a river was impossible until French engineer Marc Brunel invented his shield in 1818. This supported the tunnel and stopped water rushing in. As the tunnel grew, workers moved the shield forwards and built a lining behind it. Brunel created the first river tunnel in 1843. Later, Peter Barlow developed a circular shield that allowed

precast tunnel rings to be inserted. South African-born civil engineer James Greathead improved this in the 1860s.

Diving suit
1819

Augustus Siebe

The first practical diving suit was invented in 1819 by German engineer Augustus Siebe. Until then, underwater workers sat in a diving bell – an open-bottomed air chamber. Siebe's first suit was a jacket with an airtight helmet into which air was pumped from the surface. By 1830, he had created a totally enclosed suit.

Stethoscope
1819

René Laënnec

French doctor René Laënnec wanted to listen to his patients' lungs and hearts, but

was perhaps shy of putting his ear to their chests. Instead, he listened through a wooden tube and found that this *cylindre* transmitted body sounds that he could relate to various medical conditions. After he published his findings in 1819, other doctors improved on his instrument, eventually creating the device seen today.

Adding machine
1820

Thomas de Colmar

The first calculating machine that really worked was the arithmometer, patented by French insurance agent Thomas de Colmar in 1820. Although it could add, subtract, multiply, and divide, it was at first a failure, mostly because its inventor was not an engineer. By the 1850s, an improved version was beginning to be noticed, and by 1880 hundreds were in use – particularly in the insurance industry.

1816 In Rome, the opera *The Barber of Seville* by Italian composer Gioacchino Rossini has its first performance. Based on an earlier comedy by the French writer Pierre de Beaumarchais, it will become one of Rossini's most popular operas.

1818 The first science-fiction novel, *Frankenstein*, is published. It was written two years earlier by Mary Shelley while she was staying in Switzerland with the poet Byron. She was one of several guests he challenged to write a ghost story.

Electromagnetism
1820

Hans Christian Ørsted

Until Danish physicist Hans Christian Ørsted's crucial experiment of 1820, electricity and magnetism were seen as two separate subjects. The experiment was made possible by the battery, which Volta invented in 1800 (✳ see page 116). Ørsted put a compass needle near a wire, then connected the wire to the terminals of a battery. The needle set itself at right angles to the wire, showing that electricity could create magnetism. The two subjects were really one.

Quinine
1820

Pierre Pelletier, Joseph Caventou

Quinine is the active substance in a tree-bark extract that helps patients with malaria, a disease caused by a parasite in the blood. It was isolated in 1820 by French chemists Pierre Pelletier and Joseph Caventou, and marked the start of a shift from the use of whole plant extracts towards chemically pure drugs for treating disease. The same pair of men also isolated several other well known natural chemicals, including chlorophyll.

Fourier analysis
1822

Joseph Fourier

Engineers and scientists often have to deal with waves, and these can have an infinite variety of shapes. Thanks to the work of French mathematician Joseph Fourier, engineers don't actually have to deal with every possible wave shape. In 1822, in a book about heat flow, he showed that a wave of any shape can be broken down into simpler waves known as sine waves. Fourier analysis, and a related mathematical technique called the Fourier transform, now help with the design of electronic communications systems and much else.

Non-Euclidean geometry
1823

János Bolyai, Nikolay Lobachevsky

School geometry includes Euclid's (✳ see page 45) statement that there can be only one line that passes through a given point and lies parallel to a given line. In 1823, Hungarian mathematician János Bolyai discovered that he could forget this idea and create a "non-Euclidean" geometry that made sense. Russian mathematician Nikolay Lobachevsky published the same discovery in 1829. Euclidean geometry describes the small spaces we are used to but may not be true for space as a whole. In the 1850s, German mathematician Bernhard Riemann extended non-Euclidean geometry, providing a basis for Einstein's view of gravity (✳ see pages 178–179).

Waterproof cloth
1823

Charles Macintosh

Charles Macintosh, working in rainy Glasgow, Scotland, found a way to make the first waterproof cloth. He discovered that rubber would dissolve in naphtha, a petrol-like liquid produced in the making of coal gas. In 1823, he stuck two layers of fabric together with his rubber solution. Although at first there were problems with leaking seams and softening rubber, a "macintosh" soon became the only thing to wear in the rain.

ADDING MACHINE *Arithmometers were made by several different companies. This wood-cased brass machine dates from about 1870.*

Digits of result appeared in windows

ADD\(^{ON}\) ET MULT\(^{ON}\)

SOUST\(^{ON}\) ET DIVIS\(^{ON}\)

Handle turned to calculate

1819 British administrator Sir Stamford Raffles founds a colonial settlement on the island of Singapore. Ideally positioned between the Indian Ocean and the South China Sea, the island will become a highly successful country.

1822 Ancient Egyptian hieroglyphs are deciphered thanks to the Rosetta Stone. Found by French troops in 1799, this has the same text in hieroglyphs and Greek, allowing French scholar Jean François Champollion to crack the code.

Maximum efficiency of a heat engine

1824

Sadi Carnot

A heat engine, such as a steam engine, turns heat, a form of energy, into mechanical work, another form of energy. The percentage of heat that gets turned into work is known today as the engine's thermal efficiency. It is never anywhere near 100 per cent. In 1824, French scientist Sadi Carnot discovered what limits the maximum power ouput of any given engine. It is simply the temperature difference between the engine's hottest and coldest parts: the larger the difference, the greater the power output.

Portland cement

1824

Joseph Aspdin

Portland cement is ordinary building cement. It has nothing to do with Portland, in the south of England; it was invented in the north of the country by a Yorkshire builder, Joseph Aspdin, in 1824. He burned a mixture of clay and limestone until it became so hot that it partly turned into glass. Aspdin thought his material was just as good as the fine stone quarried at Portland, hence the name.

Self-trimming candle wick

1824

J. J. Cambacères

To burn properly, a candle needs just the right length of wick. Before 1824, wicks had to be trimmed by hand, because the wax burned down but the wick didn't. French inventor Cambacères found out that if the wick is plaited instead of twisted, it flops over and sticks out through the flame, constantly burning away and trimming itself. All candles are now made this way.

Aluminium

1825

Hans Christian Ørsted

Although aluminium is the most common metal on Earth, nobody had seen any until Danish chemist Hans Christian Ørsted extracted some from aluminium chloride in 1825. It had already been named by Humphry Davy, who identified it in alum, used in dyeing. He called it alumium, then aluminum (now its name in North America), and finally aluminium to match names like sodium. Whatever the name, it is one of the world's most useful metals.

Public steam railway

1825

George Stephenson

George Stephenson was already building industrial locomotives when he became engineer of a proposed public tramway from Darlington to Stockton in north-east England. He thought that steam locomotives and iron rails would be better than the proposed horses and wooden rails. On 27 September 1825, a steam train ran from Darlington to Stockton. The world's first public steam railway had opened. Both passengers and freight travelled in open trucks – except the railway's directors who had a covered coach. (✳ *See also* **Railway mania**.)

Amalgam filling

c1826

August Taveau, Thomas Bell

Having teeth filled is no fun, but it used to be much worse. The first metal fillings had to be heated to boiling point before going into the tooth. In about 1826, August Taveau in France and Thomas Bell in Britain found that a mixture of mercury and silver formed a paste that could be inserted cold and would harden rapidly. They had invented the amalgam filling, which is still used today.

PUBLIC STEAM RAILWAY *Stephenson's* Locomotion No 1, *seen here as a model, provided the power for the first public steam railway.*

Water tank was carried in a truck behind the locomotive

LOCOMOTION 1825.

1824 The great German composer Ludwig van Beethoven, now totally deaf, composes his ninth symphony. Written for a large choir as well as full orchestra, its last movement contains a setting of Schiller's "Ode to Joy".

1825 The Bolshoi (Great) Theatre opens in Moscow, Russia. Taking over the dancers of its predecessor, the Petrovsky Theatre, it renames the company the Bolshoi Ballet. It will become one of the world's finest ballet companies.

RAILWAY MANIA

RAILWAYS STARTED AS WOODEN TRACKS for horse-drawn traffic, but once Stephenson had proved what steam could do, steam railways spread across Britain and the continents of Europe and America with astonishing speed. Money, both public and private, poured into the new technology. By 1850, Britain had more than 10,000 km (6250 miles) of track, while pioneers in the USA had opened up the West with 14,500 km (9000 miles) of railroads.

BRING YOUR OWN TRAIN

In Britain, the Surrey Iron Railway opened in 1803 and ran from Wandsworth on the Thames to Merstham, south of London. It was the first to be open to everyone, but carriers had to provide their own wagons and horses.

Horses walked between the wooden tracks

A simple horse-drawn railway speeded production at Ralph Allen's quarry near Bath, in about 1730.

THE RAILWAY AGE BEGINS

At the opening of the Stockton & Darlington Railway, crowds fought to experience the new thrill of rail travel. A total of 600 people piled into the wagons, some even clinging to the outside.

GOING LIKE A ROCKET

The first all-steam railway with its own rolling stock ran between Liverpool and Manchester. It opened on 15 September 1830 with a train hauled by Stephenson's *Rocket*, the clear winner of competitive trials held in 1829.

This 1949 painting by Terence Cuneo vividly captures the excitement surrounding the opening of the Stockton & Darlington Railway.

Interchangeable parts

1826

John Hall

Most products today are assembled from mass-produced parts. In the 18th century, nobody could make parts accurately enough to guarantee that they would fit together, but the US government needed guns with interchangeable parts so that weapons could be repaired quickly. In 1826, US gunmaker John Hall succeeded in making exactly what they wanted. He'd had to invent a new set of tools and techniques, but in doing so had perfected an essential ingredient of mass production.

Reaping machine

1826

Patrick Bell, Cyrus McCormick

Without mechanical help, harvesting demands fields full of people. The first successful reaper was designed in 1826 by Scottish farmer Patrick Bell, who encouraged other farmers to copy it. A few years later, in the USA, Cyrus McCormick invented a similar machine, which, like Bell's, had a revolving reel for drawing the corn into the cutter. McCormick's production models went on sale in 1840, and competed successfully with a factory-built version of the Bell reaper. McCormick sold his reapers by the thousand. His company continued until 1902, when it merged with four others to form the International Harvester Company.

Mammals from eggs

1827

Karl von Baer

Most people know that birds come from eggs, but it's not so obvious that mammals do too. This fact was published in 1827 by Estonian naturalist Karl von Baer. A professor at Konigsburg University (now Kaliningrad in Russia), he found out more about how animals develop, and created the science called comparative embryology.

1826 Japanese artist Katsushika Hokusai starts publishing a series of prints entitled *Thirty-six Views of Mount Fuji*. The series includes *The Breaking Wave off Kanagawa*, which will become the best known Japanese print of its time.

1827 The first volume of US bird artist John Audubon's *Birds of America* is published by London engraver Robert Havell. The complete book contains 435 magnificent hand-coloured illustrations, and makes Audubon famous.

Greenhouse effect

1827

Joseph Fourier

The greenhouse effect is in the news as cars and power stations pump carbon dioxide into the atmosphere. Natural greenhouse effects would keep Earth at a comfortable temperature, but the polluting gases produced by humans trap too much heat and make Earth warmer. The existence of the effect, and its similarity to how a greenhouse works, were first suggested by the French mathematician Joseph Fourier in 1827. He didn't know how much people would worry about it 175 years later.

Match

1827

John Walker

As chemical knowledge increased, inventors began to apply it in the search for a better light. A few burned their fingers with creations like chemical-tipped wood dipped in sulphuric acid, then, in 1827, British chemist John Walker produced the first practical match. His "Friction Lights" lit up when rubbed on sandpaper, just like some matches today.

MATCH
Early matches lit as soon as they were warmed by friction, so were supplied in a fireproof box in case they lit by accident. Modern matches are safer to carry.

Macadamized road

1827

John McAdam

Scottish engineer John McAdam realized that the best base for a road was dry soil. In 1827, he started building roads made from compacted soil with stones on top. Iron-tyred cartwheels broke the stones into smaller pieces, which filled any gaps and made the surface waterproof. "Macadamized" roads were used everywhere until cars, whose pneumatic tyres damaged them by sucking out the smallest stones, demanded a road surface made with tar or bitumen.

Multiple fire tube boiler

1827

Marc Séguin, George Stephenson

The first steam boilers were tanks on top of a fire. This was inefficient because little of the water was in contact with the fire. In 1827, French engineer Marc Séguin invented a boiler with tubes going through the water, and hot gases from a fire going through the tubes. It heated water quickly and wasted less

heat. George Stephenson used the same idea in *Rocket*, the first locomotive to run on an all-steam railway.

Ohm's law

1827

Georg Ohm

Ohm's law is fundamental to electrical and electronic engineering. It says that electric current = voltage ÷ resistance. So when you connect a wire across a battery, if you double the length of the wire, and therefore the resistance, you will halve the current. George Ohm's scientific colleagues in Germany thought that the law was nonsense when he published it in 1827, but Ohm had the last laugh. In 1841, the Royal Society gave him a medal, and his name lives on as the unit of resistance.

Water turbine

1827

Claude Burdin, Benoît Fourneyron

French engineer Claude Burdin coined the word "turbine" from the Latin *turbo*, meaning "spinning top". One of his students at the St Étienne Technical School, Benoît Fourneyron, built a working water turbine in 1827.

Thin wooden spill burned easily

Water fell on to a horizontal rotor and rushed through curved blades, making the rotor spin and producing as much power as six horses. He was soon building turbines that spun at 2000 rpm (revolutions per minute) to produce 40 kW of power – ideal for generating electricity. In 1895, Fourneyron turbines were installed for this purpose at Niagara Falls on the Canada/USA border.

Handles for pushing the machine

BUDDING

Clutch lever

Differential gear

1827

Onésiphore Pecqueur

A vehicle with both back wheels on one axle will have trouble getting around corners. This is because the wheel on the outside of the curve has to travel further, and therefore turn faster, than the wheel on the inside. This is impossible if both wheels are fixed to the same shaft. Modern rear-wheel drive cars avoid this problem by having

Head tipped with mixture containing phosphorus

1828 William Burke and William Hare, criminals who murdered at least 16 people and sold their bodies to an Edinburgh medical school, kill their last victim on 31 October. Hare gives evidence against Burke, who is hanged.

1829 Following a campaign by religious reformer Ram Mohan Roy, the rite in which a widow throws herself on her husband's funeral pyre is outlawed by the British authorities who control parts of India at this time.

each rear wheel on a separate axle, driven from the engine through an arrangement called a differential gear. This contains several gearwheels, which allow the two rear wheels to rotate at different speeds where necessary. It was invented by French engineer Onésiphore Pecquer in 1827, long before cars were thought of, for use on steam vehicles.

Braille
1829
Louis Braille

Louis Braille was blinded in an accident at the age of three. When he was ten, he went to Paris, where he was shown a way of writing messages with raised dots, designed for soldiers to use at night. Braille simplified and improved this system, and in 1829 and 1837 published his own six-dot code for blind people. It's difficult to learn, but is still in use today.

Lawnmower
1830
Edwin Budding

Lawns were possible before lawnmowers, but only for people with gardeners or sheep to keep them trimmed. Edwin Budding's cylinder mower, patented in 1830, made tidy green squares available to far more people. Largely displaced by other machines for small lawns, Budding's mechanism lives on in tractor-pulled mowers for large areas of grass.

Electromagnetic induction
1831
Michael Faraday, Joseph Henry

When Hans Christian Ørsted discovered that electricity could produce magnetism (✳ see page 123),

ELECTROMAGNETIC INDUCTION *Faraday's ring looks quite like some modern transformers.*

British scientist Michael Faraday guessed that magnetism might produce electricity. In 1831, he showed that it could. Plunging a magnet into a coil of wire produced a surge of current – the principle of the electric generator. Faraday also found that if two coils were wound on an iron ring, connecting or disconnecting one coil to or from a battery produced a current in the other – the principle of the transformer,

which is used to change electric voltages. US scientist Joseph Henry discovered electromagnetic induction at about the same time, but Faraday published his findings first.

Cell nucleus
1831
Robert Brown

Most living cells keep their genes in a nucleus, a distinct blob in their centre. This structure was first noticed and named by Scottish botanist Robert Brown in 1831, while he was investigating orchids. Although Brown didn't understand what the nucleus did, his discovery was part of a growing realization that plant cells, far from being empty, were full of life.

LAWNMOWER *Budding based his grass-cutting machine on the rotary cutter used for trimming the surface of woollen cloth in textile mills. Early Budding mowers were large machines for professional gardeners – this one was made by Ransomes of Ipswich, England – but the principle was later applied to domestic models.*

Gears turned the cutting cylinder

Handle for a second person to help with the machine

Cutting cylinder

Roller for adjusting the height of the cut

Main roller provided drive

1830 A group of British travellers, the Raleigh Travellers' Club, forms the Geographical Society of London. It supports explorations in Africa, the Arctic, and other areas, and in 1859 will become the Royal Geographical Society.

1831 Inspired by love for Irish actress Harriet Smithson, French composer Hector Berlioz writes his highly romantic *Symphonie Fantastique*. He fashions the huge orchestral work as a musical drama that ends with its hero's death.

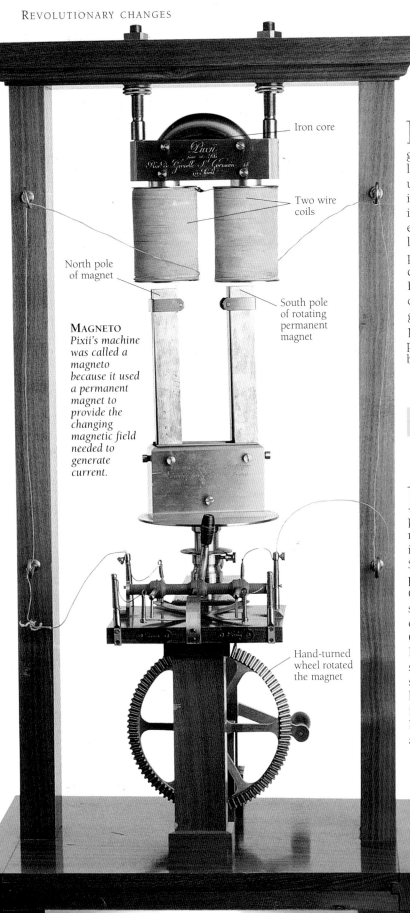

Iron core

Two wire coils

North pole of magnet

South pole of rotating permanent magnet

MAGNETO
Pixii's machine was called a magneto because it used a permanent magnet to provide the changing magnetic field needed to generate current.

Hand-turned wheel rotated the magnet

Safety fuse
1831

William Bickford

Blasting out rock from mines and quarries with gunpowder is a good idea as long as nobody gets blown up. Until William Bickford's invention of the safety fuse in 1831, miners set off explosions with gunpowder laid on the ground or packed into reeds or goose quills – all highly dangerous. Bickford made his fuse from cloth wrapped around gunpowder. It burned at a predictable rate, allowing people to get away to safety before the big bang.

Steam bus
1831

Goldsworthy Gurney, Walter Hancock

Buses existed before 1831, but they were pulled by horses. The first mechanical buses appeared in Britain. Inspired by Stephenson's *Rocket* (❋ *see page 125*), English inventor Goldsworthy Gurney built several steam coaches that operated between Cheltenham and Gloucester. In London, Walter Hancock set up a steam omnibus service. Opposition from horse-coach owners soon forced Gurney off the road, but Hancock's service was able to survive for five years.

Magneto
1832

Hippolyte Pixii

Soon after Michael Faraday discovered that relative motion between a magnet and a wire produces electric current, a young Frenchman devised the first practical electric generator. Hippolyte Pixii was the son of a Paris instrument maker. His machine, built in 1832, rotated a magnet near a coil of wire, generating alternating current. Later, at the suggestion of physicist André Ampère, he added a switch that broke the circuit for half of each rotation, creating pulsed direct current for experiments in electrolysis.

Electric motor
1832

William Sturgeon, Thomas Davenport

It wasn't easy to develop a useful motor from Hans Christian Ørsted's discovery that electricity could move a magnet (❋ *see page 123*). The vital component was the commutator, a switch that continually reverses the current to keep the motor rotating. Practical commutators were invented in 1832 by British engineer William Sturgeon and in 1834 by US blacksmith Thomas Davenport. Davenport used his motor to drive several machines, including a car.

Inductance
1832

Joseph Henry

In 1832, US scientist Joseph Henry discovered self-inductance, often called simply inductance. In this, the magnetism created by an electric current tends to maintain that current when conditions change. The effect is shown clearly when a wire is coiled up to create a stronger magnetic field. Joseph Henry discovered it when he disconnected an electromagnet and saw big sparks as the current carried on through the air instead of stopping.

1833 Britain's first Factory Act is passed after a campaign by Lord Anthony Ashley Cooper, later Earl of Shaftesbury. It limits the working hours of children in textile mills and ensures that they receive some education.

1835 Fourteen years after his death, one of Napoleon's pet projects, the Arc de Triomphe, is completed at the top of the Champs Élysées in Paris. Built by Jean Chalgrin and Jean Raymond, it celebrates past French victories.

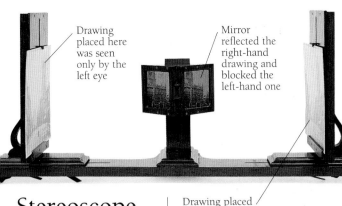

Drawing placed here was seen only by the left eye

Mirror reflected the right-hand drawing and blocked the left-hand one

STEREOSCOPE *Wheatstone's original device was cumbersome, but useful for investigating stereoscopic vision. Brewster redesigned it without the mirrors.*

Drawing placed here was seen only by the right eye

Pivoted magnetic needles

Letters engraved on the face

TELEGRAPH *The five-needle telegraph was easy to use but needed a six-wire connection. Pairs of needles swung left or right to point to the letters on the face.*

Terminals used to connect wires

Keys pressed in pairs to send letters

Stereoscope
1832

Charles Wheatstone

A stereoscope combines two slightly different pictures, one for each eye, into a three-dimensional image. The pictures are normally photographs, but British physicist Charles Wheatstone invented the stereoscope before photography existed. His invention was little used until David Brewster showed a simplified version at London's Great Exhibition in 1851. Queen Victoria was entranced, and stereoscopy soon became a popular craze.

Horse-drawn tram service
1832

John Stephenson, G. F. Train

The idea of using tracks for vehicles eventually spread from mines and railways to the streets. Trams were at first drawn by horses. Probably the earliest tram builder was the Irish-US inventor John Stephenson. His trams started running on the New York and Harlem Railroad in 1832, and his company later built trams for services all over the world. The US entrepreneur G. F. Train also brought the tram to many cities. In 1860, he installed a tramway in Birkenhead, near Liverpool – the first in Britain.

Telegraph
1837

William Cooke, Charles Wheatstone

Hans Christian Ørsted's discovery that a compass needle responds to electric current suggested a way of making an effective electric telegraph. In 1837, ex-soldier William Cooke and physicist Charles Wheatstone patented the first telegraph to send useful messages. Its five needles, operated by six wires, could point to 20 letters of the alphabet. By 1839, it was installed on the Great Western Railway in England and was sending the first public telegrams.

Reflex
1837

Marshall Hall

When someone pulls their finger away from a hot iron, they're using a reflex, a response that bypasses the brain for maximum speed. British physiologist Marshall Hall, seeing a headless newt respond to a pin-prick, was the first to realize that nerves from the spinal cord can act independently to receive sensations and make suitable responses. British colleagues ridiculed Hall's ideas, but European scientists discovered that he was right.

Morse code
1837

Samuel Morse, Alfred Vail

See **pages 130–131** for the story of how Morse and Vail invented a new way to communicate.

1836 During its fight for independence from Mexico, the state of Texas is hit hard when the Mexicans, under Santa Anna, wipe out everyone in the fort called the Alamo. Santa Anna is later defeated by Texans shouting "Remember the Alamo!"

1837 In the United Kingdom, King William IV dies without an heir. On Tuesday 20 June, his niece Victoria, aged only 18, becomes Queen. She will become one of the most important figures in British history.

WIRING THE WORLD

Samuel Morse and Alfred Vail invent a new way to communicate

MORSE'S FIRST TELEGRAPH
The first telegraph Morse built was more elaborate than the final version re-engineered by Vail. Its operator did not tap out messages directly, but assembled shaped pieces of metal in a holder, which moved through a switch mechanism to turn the current on and off.

The Reverend Jedidiah Morse did not want his son to be an artist, but he felt it was better than having him waste time with electricity. So, after tuition in England, Samuel Morse became a painter, one of the USA's best.

In 1832, on a ship home from Europe, Samuel heard about the newly invented electromagnet, and his interest in electricity was rekindled. With his artist's imagination, he could see it sending messages around the world.

By 1835, Morse had built an electric telegraph, using odds and ends that included one of his wooden frames for stretching artists' canvas. But how was he to convey thousands of different words along its single wire?

His first idea was to make a numbered list of words, then send the numbers, switching the current once for one, twice for two, and so on. It was terribly slow, even with an

This unlikely contraption was Morse's first receiver.

Morse's telegraph needed only one wire, which made it easy to construct. To make the single wire work, Morse and Vail invented a code based on patterns of pulses – an idea now used for all kinds of telecommunications.

automatic switch and a better code that used short and long bursts of current – "dots" and "dashes". His home-made telegraph proved to be unreliable, too.

That might have been the end of it, but in 1837, at an unsuccessful demonstration of the telegraph in New York, Morse met the young engineer Alfred Vail. Vail took one look at Morse's amateurish efforts and offered to redesign the whole thing. He strengthened the electromagnet and replaced Morse's complicated switch with a simple, hand-operated key. He threw out Morse's word list and devised a dot-and-dash code for each letter of the alphabet. The telegraph was beginning to take shape.

In 1843, after several successful demonstrations and some political wrangling, the US government gave Morse $30,000 to build a telegraph line between Baltimore and Washington, DC. There were quite a few technical problems, because nobody had ever laid 65 kilometres (40 miles) of wire before. But by 24 May, 1844, everything was ready.

With Vail in Baltimore tending a stack of batteries, and Morse in Washington looking after the politicians, the new line delivered its first message: "WHAT HATH GOD WROUGHT". Within a year, it was open to the public. Within another 30 years, telegraphs covered the globe. Thanks to Vail the engineer, the vision of Morse the artist had become a reality.

ALFRED VAIL
Vail met Morse soon after graduating from university. He agreed to help Morse and pay for getting patents as long as he could share in any profits. He got his father to help Morse as well.

A Morse key for sending messages

This receiver embossed dots and dashes on paper tape.

THE FINAL SYSTEM
By about 1870, many refinements had been made to the telegraph. Operators could decode a message just by listening to the clicking of a sounder, leaving them free to write it down. Punched tape allowed messages to be stored, and a version of Morse code had been developed for use with underwater cables.

NOT VERY PRIVATE
A picture from a songsheet of 1860 illustrates one problem with the telegraph: every message had to be read by the operator. This could cause embarrassment, as here, with messages of an intimate nature.

Ship's propeller
1839

John Ericsson, Francis Smith

Early steam ships had paddlewheels, but these did not work well in high seas. Engineers John Ericsson of Sweden and Francis Smith (later Sir Francis) of Britain both invented underwater propellers. Smith's looked like a screw, while Ericsson's was more like a fan. The British navy wasn't interested in either, but a small ship fitted with Ericsson's propeller was demonstrated to the US Navy. In 1839, both propellers were fitted to larger ships, and trials confirmed the effectiveness of this new form of propulsion.

SHIP'S PROPELLER *This is a model of SS* Francis Smith, *which was fitted with Smith's propeller. Modern ships have their propeller further back.*

Photography
c 1839

Louis Daguerre, William Fox Talbot

In 1826, French inventor Nicéphore Niepce coated a sheet of metal with tar, put it in a box with a lens, and pointed it out of the window. Eight hours later, he had a permanent photograph. By 1839, his colleague Louis Daguerre was taking pictures in 20 minutes. A year later, William Fox Talbot announced a rival system. It allowed shorter exposures and could produce multiple prints. (✴ *See also* **Photo pioneers.**)

Cell as the basic unit of living things
1839

Matthias Schleiden, Theodor Schwann

German lawyer Matthias Schleiden turned his hobby of botany into a full-time job and studied plants under the microscope. In 1838 he concluded that all plants are made of tiny building blocks, or cells, and they grow as the cells divide. A year later, his friend Theodor Schwann found that the same applied to animals, establishing one of the basics of biology.

Vulcanized rubber
1839

Charles Goodyear

Raw rubber gets weak and sticky when warm. In the USA, rubber worker Nathaniel Hayward discovered that sulphur reduced the stickiness. Businessman Charles Goodyear, who had himself been trying to improve rubber, bought Hayward's invention. In 1839, after a series of experiments, he discovered a chemical reaction with sulphur that made the rubber harder and stronger. This way of hardening rubber is called vulcanization, and it is essential today for car tyres and many other rubber items.

VULCANIZED RUBBER *By 1923, when this advertisement appeared, cars had become more common and rubber tyres were big business.*

1838 US lion tamer Isaac van Amburgh comes to England and amazes Queen Victoria by putting his head in a lion's mouth. She asks artist Edwin Landseer to paint the American's portrait, complete with lions.

1839 The Grand Liverpool Steeplechase, the horse race now called the Grand National, is run for the first time at Aintree, Liverpool, in England. The winner is Lottery, a nine-year-old owned by John Elmore and ridden by Jem Mason.

PHOTO PIONEERS

MANY EARLY 19TH-CENTURY artists and scientists wanted to capture the lifelike images they saw in the camera obscura (✳ *see page 81*), a common drawing aid at that time. Silver salts darkened on exposure to light, but they were not really sensitive enough. Worse still, they kept what sensitivity they had after the picture was taken, so the image was soon destroyed. Daguerre and Fox Talbot both solved these problems, but in completely different ways.

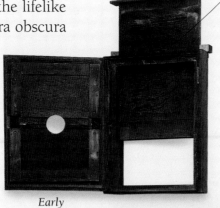
Plate holder

Early daguerreotype camera

Daguerreotype images

Aperture rings

Lens and attachments

A daguerreotype camera of the 1840s

DAGUERREOTYPES

Daguerre's pictures were taken with silver iodide, formed by iodine acting on a silvered copper plate. Sitters had to be clamped in place for the extremely long exposure. After treatment with mercury vapour and fixing with salt, the delicate, silvery image was framed under glass to protect it.

CALOTYPES

When daguerreotypes appeared, Fox Talbot hastened to perfect his calotype process. It used paper soaked in silver salts. He discovered that before these darkened visibly they formed a hidden image, which a developing solution could reveal, allowing shorter exposures. After fixing with a sodium salt, he used his paper negatives to make positive prints.

Calotype made by Fox Talbot at his home, Lacock Abbey, England, in about 1843

Fuel cell
1839
William Grove

Unlike ordinary electric batteries, fuel cells never run down – as long as they've got something to burn. A Welsh judge, William Grove, made the first one in 1839. Knowing that electricity splits water into hydrogen and oxygen, he simply reversed the process. His cell burned hydrogen in oxygen to produce water and electricity. Today, fuel cells are used in space and may soon appear in electric cars.

Polystyrene
1839
Eduard Simon

The clear plastic of CD cases is polystyrene. It is also made into a lightweight packaging material. It consists of molecules of a carbon-based chemical, styrene, linked to form chains. It was first made in 1839 by German chemist Eduard Simon, but was not used because impurities made it brittle. In 1937, US chemist Robert Dreisbach made purer styrene, and within a year polystyrene was on the market.

Babbitt metal
1839
Isaac Babbitt

Rotating machinery needs bearings – holes lined with metal that can stand up to the constant rubbing of a shaft. One of the best materials for lining plain bearings is babbitt metal. It is an alloy of two soft metals, tin and lead, and two harder ones, antimony and copper. It takes oil well, will not seize up if it runs dry, and lasts a long time. It was invented by US goldsmith Isaac Babbitt in 1839.

Electroplating
c 1840
George Elkington, Auguste de La Rive

Electroplating uses electricity to coat surfaces with a layer of metal. It can make brass look like gold. The process was invented independently in about 1840 by British industrialist George Elkington and Swiss physicist Auguste de La Rive. It was Elkington who made it a success. He invented a plating bath, then bought up all the rival processes so that people had to use his system.

1840 Britain gains control of New Zealand as 45 Maori chiefs sign the Treaty of Waitangi. The treaty aims to give Maoris British citizenship and protect their land, but its terms are not clear and will later lead to conflict.

1840 Canadian Samuel Cunard starts the first regular Atlantic steamship service when RMS *Britannia* sails from Liverpool to Boston. Cunard will continue to lead the way across the Atlantic with larger ships, such as *Queen Elizabeth*.

Ozone
1840

Christian Schönbein

Ozone in the stratosphere protects us from radiation, but ozone from a photocopier can be dangerous. It's a highly reactive form of oxygen, with three atoms per molecule instead of two. Ozone can be made by passing air through an electrical discharge – as in a photocopier. Discovered and named in 1840 by German chemist Christian Schönbein, many uses have since been found for it, from purifying water to bleaching food.

Postage stamp
1840

Rowland Hill

Rowland Hill believed in democracy. When he discovered that post office procedures made letters too expensive for ordinary people, he pointed out the folly of charges that were based on distance and collected on delivery. A fixed charge, he said, prepaid with a sticky stamp, would slash costs by 75 per cent. People listened in the end, and in 1840 Britain introduced the penny post. With it came the first postage stamp, the famous penny black.

Steam hammer
1840

James Nasmyth

In 1839, British engineer Isambard Kingdom Brunel started work on his ship *Great Britain*. He soon discovered that hammering out the giant shafts for its paddlewheels was beyond human ability. Scottish engineer James Nasmyth came up with the idea of a steam hammer and designed one that would hit harder than a whole gang of people. He made the first one in 1840 and patented it in 1842. By then, though, Brunel had changed his mind about his ship, deciding to use the more modern propellers instead of paddlewheels.

Dinosaurs
1841

Richard Owen

People had been finding fossilized dinosaur bones all over the place, but they didn't know what they were. Then British surgeon Richard Owen recognized that they belonged to an extinct group of reptiles unlike any now living. He named them "Dinosauria", meaning "terrible lizards", in 1841. Owen later became famous for opposing Darwin's theory of evolution and for getting the details of the earliest fossil bird completely wrong.

STEAM HAMMER *A gang of workers feeds a red-hot piece of iron through a hammer which slowly pounds it into shape.*

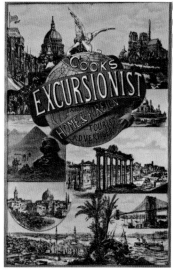

PACKAGE HOLIDAY *By the 1870s, Cook's brochure offered package holidays to wonders of the world both ancient and modern.*

Package holiday
1841

Thomas Cook

A British missionary, Thomas Cook, organized the first holiday package in 1841. It was only a train trip from Leicester to Loughborough, but it proved there was a demand. In 1855, Cook organized trips to France, and then tours of Europe. His firm is now famous worldwide.

Doppler effect
1842

Christian Doppler

The sound of a speeding car falls to a lower pitch as the car passes. Austrian physicist Christian Doppler explained this change in sound in 1842. As a sound source approaches, the waves reaching our ears are bunched up, but as it recedes they are stretched out. The same thing happens with light, so astronomers can tell how fast stars are approaching or receding, and with radio, enabling police radar to check the speed of cars.

1840 Snowshoe racing becomes an organized sport in Canada with the formation of the Montreal Snowshoe Club. Racers strap broad, flat frames to their feet to stop them from sinking, and run races of up to 1.6 km (1 mile).

1841 In London, Regent's Park is opened to all after being a private recreation space for kings and aristocrats. Once used by King Henry VIII for hunting, the 197 hectare (487 acre) park was restyled by John Nash in about 1815.

Conservation of energy

1842

Julius von Mayer

As early as 1806, a British doctor, Thomas Young, was using the word "energy" in its modern sense: the capacity to do work. In 1842, another doctor, Julius von Mayer of Germany, stated that energy cannot be created or destroyed. Mayer did not have much supporting evidence, and at the time few people understood what he was saying, but this principle of conservation of energy has since become central to science. The principle was discovered independently by at least three others with more influence: William Grove in 1846, and James Joule and Hermann von Helmholtz in 1847.

Christmas card

1843

John Horsley

The first Christmas card was designed by British painter John Horsley for Henry Cole, later a founder of the Victoria & Albert Museum in London. Showing people enjoying a Christmas party, it went on sale in London in 1843.

Fax principle

1843

Alexander Bain

Surprisingly, faxes were invented before phones. Scottish mechanic Alexander Bain patented his "electric printing and signal telegraph" in 1843, more than 30 years before the first phone. Bain proposed scanning printers' type to create a telegraph signal, with pendulums synchronizing transmitter and receiver. Bain never built his machine, but Giovanni Caselli used much the same principle for a fax service between Paris and Lyon in 1863.

River tunnel

1843

Marc Brunel, Isambard Brunel

The first underwater tunnel was dug under the River Thames in London, from Rotherhithe to Wapping. It was started in 1825 but didn't open until 1843. Even using Marc Brunel's tunnelling shield (✳ *see* **page 122**), water poured in several times during construction, once injuring Brunel's son Isambard so

CHRISTMAS CARD *John Horsley's card combined religion, good cheer, and rustic decoration.*

seriously that work stopped for several years. London Underground trains now rattle through the tunnel every day.

Sunspot cycle

1843

Samuel Schwabe

Amateurs can contribute a lot to astronomy by making regular observations. In Germany, Samuel Schwabe kept watch on the Sun for 17 years, hoping to find a planet closer to the Sun than Mercury. Instead, he found that the spottiness of the Sun increased and decreased in an 11-year cycle. He announced the fact in 1843. It's of great importance on Earth, because sunspots can ruin radio communication.

1842 China surrenders the island of Hong Kong to Great Britain as part of the Treaty of Nanking, which ends the First Opium War. Another island will be added in 1860, and in 1898 more territory will be leased for 99 years.

1843 A new dance sensation hits Paris in the shape of the polka, a step-and-hop dance from Bohemia with a lively 2–4 rhythm. In no time at all, people in the USA, Latin America, and Scandinavia will be polka-crazy too.

Type-rotating printing press
1845

Richard Hoe

The first printing press produced a couple of sheets a minute. Modern presses print ten whole newspapers every second, mainly because they go round and round instead of up and down. The first totally rotary press was built by US engineer Richard Hoe in 1845. It could print two sheets a second, but had one snag: if all the bits of type on its revolving cylinder were not locked in tightly, they shot out like bullets when the press started.

Anaesthetic
1846

William Morton

Anaesthetics were first used by two US dentists, Horace Wells and William Morton. Wells tried using laughing gas (✴ *see* **page 115**), unsuccessfully, in 1845 and had also tried ether as a local anaesthetic. Morton thought that he would try to get his patients to inhale ether, and he used it in a successful demonstration of anaesthetic surgery in 1846. A year later, Scottish surgeon James Simpson started using chloroform to help women through the pain of childbirth.

Lock-stitch sewing machine
1846

Walter Hunt, Elias Howe, Isaac Singer

Inventors struggled for years to mechanize sewing. The solution was to use two threads. An eye-pointed needle pushed one thread through the cloth from above while a shuttle whizzing to and fro below looped another thread through it. Walter Hunt invented this in the USA in about 1843, and Elias Howe patented the same idea in 1846, but we really owe the sewing machine to US inventor Isaac Singer. He added his own ideas to Howe's and turned a raw invention into a mass-market product.

Neptune
1846

Urbain Le Verrier, Johann Galle

The discovery of the planet Neptune proved the power of physics. Astronomers knew that Uranus had an irregular orbit, and the only explanation was that it must be attracted by another planet. French astronomer Urbain Le Verrier calculated where this planet must be. When German astronomer Johann Galle looked there on 23 September 1846, he found the planet within an hour. A British mathematician, John Adams, had already done the same calculation in 1844, but British astronomers did not take this seriously.

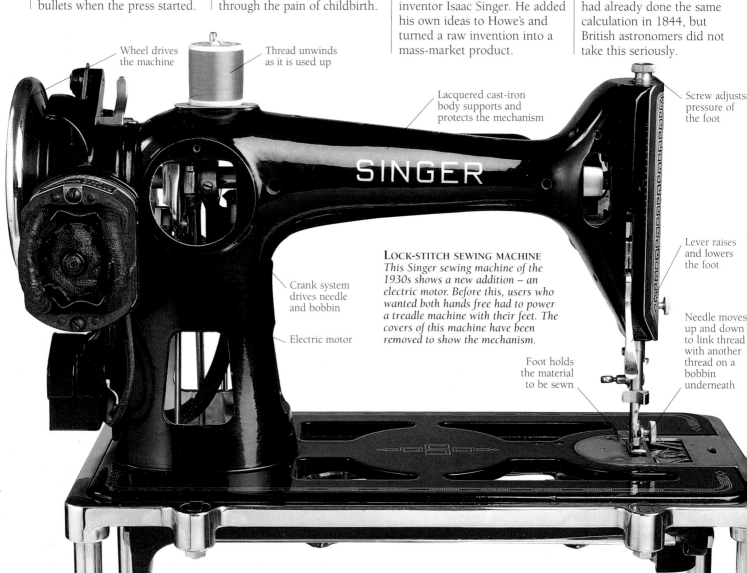

Wheel drives the machine

Thread unwinds as it is used up

Lacquered cast-iron body supports and protects the mechanism

Screw adjusts pressure of the foot

Crank system drives needle and bobbin

Electric motor

LOCK-STITCH SEWING MACHINE
This Singer sewing machine of the 1930s shows a new addition – an electric motor. Before this, users who wanted both hands free had to power a treadle machine with their feet. The covers of this machine have been removed to show the mechanism.

Lever raises and lowers the foot

Needle moves up and down to link thread with another thread on a bobbin underneath

Foot holds the material to be sewn

1846 The British government, under Robert Peel, repeals the Corn Laws, designed to keep grain prices high. His action follows famine in Ireland and a campaign by the Anti-Corn-Law League. It splits the Conservative party.

1847 Charlotte Brontë, one of three literary sisters living in Yorkshire, writes *Jane Eyre*. This powerful novel, with its self-willed heroine and emphasis on social psychology, will become one of the most famous in English literature.

Nitroglycerine
1846
Ascanio Sobrero

Until 1846, the only widely used explosive was gunpowder. Then Italian chemist Ascanio Sobrero discovered nitroglycerine, the first "high explosive". Much more powerful than gunpowder, it is also extremely dangerous: just dropping a container of the chemical on the floor can cause a devastating explosion. Despite this problem, nitroglycerine was used in mining even before a way was found to make it safe.

ALBUMEN PRINT *Lewis Carroll, the author of* Alice, *made this albumen print of two of his aunts in about 1858.*

Albumen print
c 1850
Louis Blanquart-Évrard

Those very old, brown family photos that you may have seen could have been printed on albumen paper. It was a breakthrough in its time. Before French photographer Louis Blanquart-Évrard invented it in about 1850, prints were made by Fox Talbot's original process (✷ *see* **page 132**). The new paper, with its glossy coating of egg white, gave much richer, sharper results.

ELECTRICAL NATURE OF NERVE IMPULSES *Emil Du Bois-Reymond invented this "frog pistol". He put a frog's leg inside the tube and formed a contact with the nerve ends, which made the leg muscles contract.*

Keys used to make a contact with the nerve ends in the frog's leg

Electrical nature of nerve impulses
1849
Emil Du Bois-Reymond

German physiologist Emil Du Bois-Reymond knew there was something electrical about animals when a fish gave him an electric shock. In 1849, he discovered that when nerves were stimulated electrical waves travelled along them. Du Bois-Reymond realized that far from being channels for "animal spirits", as some people had thought, nerves were more like telegraph wires delivering messages around the body.

Laws of thermodynamics
1849
William Thomson, Rudolf Clausius

The first law of thermodynamics is just conservation of energy (✷ *see* **page 135**). The second is: heat energy flows only from hot to cold. The consequences are surprising. For example, a glass of cold water contains more heat than a teaspoonful of boiling water (even though the boiling water has a higher temperature) because there is more of it. But the second law prevents this heat from doing any work. Several scientists worked on this idea from 1824 onwards. William Thomson coined the term "thermodynamics" in 1849 and Rudolf Clausius published the laws in 1850. Since then, two more have been added.

Mechanical equivalent of heat
1849
James Joule

Steam engines showed that heat could turn into work. Could the opposite be true? When British physicist James Joule announced in 1847 that he had warmed water simply by stirring it, nobody believed him. After a further two years' work, Joule submitted a paper to the Royal Society called *On the Mechanical Equivalent of Heat*, which was accepted. It stated exactly how much heat was produced by a given amount of work. The unit of energy now bears his name.

Speed of nerve impulses
1850
Hermann von Helmholtz

By 1849, scientists knew that nerve impulses were electrical, making it possible to measure their speed. The German scientist Hermann von Helmholtz quickly invented the necessary equipment. In 1850, his new "myograph" showed that nerves were quicker than most other things biological. He saw impulses zipping along at about 100 km/h (60 mph).

1848 Revolution sweeps Europe as French, Germans, Italians, Poles, Czechs, Slovaks, Hungarians, Danes, and Transylvanians demand greater political rights, better government, and, where necessary, national independence.

1849 The British writer Charles Dickens starts serial publication of what he considers his best novel, *David Copperfield*. The story of a young man betrayed by his stepfather earns Dickens the amazing sum of £7000.

SCIENCE TAKES
CONTROL

THE LATE 19TH CENTURY saw the rise of totally new industries that could not have existed without science. Plastics, synthetic fabrics, electric light, telephones, sound recording, popular photography, cars, and radio were just a few of the inventions that would eventually transform people's lives.

Mechanism of the inner ear
1851

Alfonso Corti

Buried deep inside the ear is the organ of Corti, a delicate mechanism that turns sound into nerve impulses. It was first described in 1851 by Italian anatomist Alfonso Corti. It contains thousands of tiny hairs, which brush against a membrane suspended in fluid. When sound waves shake the fluid, the membrane ripples against the hairs, making nerve cells attached to them send signals to the brain.

Prefabricated building
1851

Joseph Paxton

In 1851, British gardener Joseph Paxton created the first large building made from prefabricated components. The Crystal Palace was built to house the Great Exhibition in London. The spectacular glass and iron structure was 563 m (1848 ft) long, 33 m (108 ft) high and 124 m (408 ft) at its widest point. It went up in just six months. Paxton's secret was the repeated use of basic parts that slotted together like a construction kit.

Foucault's pendulum
1851

Jean Foucault

Although early 19th-century scientists knew that Earth must rotate on its axis, they had no direct proof. Then, in 1851, French physicist Jean Foucault hung a heavy ball on a 67 m (220 ft) wire inside a tall building in Paris, forming a large pendulum. As it swung back and forth, it appeared to be turning gradually, but it was actually Earth turning beneath it. Foucault's pendulum is a popular science exhibit today.

WET-PLATE PHOTOGRAPHY *Roving photographers had to carry all these bottles of chemicals – and a darkroom.*

REFRIGERATOR *The US General Electric "monitor top" refrigerator of 1934 had its compressor mounted on top.*

Refrigerator
1851

John Gorrie, Ferdinand Carré

Gases get hot when they are compressed and cool down when they expand. So one way to refrigerate is to compress a gas, let it cool, then lower its pressure to cool it still more. The cold gas can then cool other objects. US doctor John Gorrie found that he could produce cold air to cool feverish patients in this way, and patented a refrigerator based on this principle in 1851. Eight years later, French inventor Ferdinand Carré developed a refrigerator more like those we use today. These use a working fluid that changes from liquid to gas when it expands. This makes it absorb even more heat from inside the fridge.

Wet-plate photography
1851

Frederick Archer

Although calotypes could be reprinted, their paper negatives were grainy (✳ *see* page 133). In 1851, British sculptor Frederick Archer made the first transparent negatives by coating glass with a light-sensitive cellulose solution. The new plates produced clearer pictures than their predecessors, and needed shorter exposures, but they had to be exposed while wet and developed immediately. The results were so good that photographers did not mind, and "wet plates" quickly replaced the earlier processes.

Airship
1852

Henri Giffard

French engineer Henri Giffard's airship was the first successful powered flying machine. As in all airships, lift came from a light gas, in this case hydrogen, so its three-horsepower steam engine had only to push it along. Choosing a dead calm day, Giffard piloted the 44 m (144 ft) cigar-shaped craft over Paris at a speed of 10 km/h (6 mph) for 30 km (20 miles). It would be years before airships could cope with windy conditions.

1851 At La Fenice Theatre in Venice, Italian composer Guiseppe Verdi sees the first performance of *Rigoletto*, his 17th opera. It is a big step forward in the development of opera, with music and storytelling cleverly intertwined.

1852 One of Europe's most common birds, the house sparrow, is introduced into the USA. Arriving in Brooklyn, New York, and fed partly by grain spilled by horses, the newcomer will cover the continent within a century.

Gyroscope

1852

Jean Foucault

A wheel that is spinning resists changes in the direction of its axis. Jean Foucault used this fact to confirm his earlier observation of Earth rotating beneath a swinging pendulum (✳ *see* **page 139**). In 1852, he mounted a wheel so that its axis was free to point in any direction. He set it spinning and watched as it kept its position while Earth turned beneath it. He called this arrangement a gyroscope, meaning "something that makes rotation visible".

Bloomers

c1853

Amelia Bloomer

Trousers for women were thought outrageous in the 19th century, which may have been why US reformer Amelia Bloomer liked them. She advocated long, baggy trousers gathered at the ankle as part of a new costume that she hoped would liberate women. When she appeared in her trousers in about 1853, there was more laughter than liberation. But within 35 years, a new invention made "bloomers" seem like a good idea: they were ideal for women who wanted to ride a bike.

Glider

1853

George Cayley, Otto Lillienthal

Attempts to soar like a bird came to nothing until British aristocrat George Cayley abandoned flapping wings. He worked out what was needed to lift, stabilize, and control a fixed-wing machine. Realizing that no existing engine could power an aeroplane, he stuck to gliders. His coachman tested the first in 1853 with a 500 m (1650 ft) flight. Later, a young German named Otto Lilienthal built a series of small gliders and succeeded in making regular controlled flights in them. Cayley's and Lilienthal's work established the basics of aircraft design.

BLOOMERS *The new fashion, also known as Turkish trousers, was worn as early as 1849 by the actor Fanny Kemble and others, but it was Amelia Bloomer who gave it publicity, hence the name.*

Plunger with screw thread

HYPODERMIC SYRINGE *This fearsome syringe of the Pravaz type was made in France.*

Hollow needle

Hypodermic syringe

1853

Charles Pravaz, Alexander Wood

The two parts of the hypodermic syringe – the needle and the plunger – were invented in 1853 by two different people in two different countries. In France, surgeon Charles Pravaz invented a gadget for injecting fluid into veins through a tube with a blade inside it. In Scotland, physician Alexander Wood invented the hollow needle and adapted Pravaz's device to go with it, forming the first hypodermic syringe.

Safety lift

1853

Elisha Otis

Elisha Otis was working as a master mechanic in a US bed factory when he invented something to diminish a recurring nightmare. Knowing that people were scared of lifts, he invented a safety hoist with arms that shot out and grabbed the sides of the lift shaft if the supporting cable broke. He sold the first safety hoist, for goods only, in 1853. Later, in New York City, he demonstrated its effectiveness by having the cable cut while he was in it. He installed his first passenger safety lift in 1857 in a New York store. After his death, his sons, Charles and Norton, continued the business, and the name Otis can still be seen on lifts and escalators everywhere.

Boolean algebra

1854

George Boole

Today's computers owe a lot to someone whose only maths teaching came from a shoe repairer – his father. George Boole had to learn the rest himself, but by the age of 24 he was submitting work to serious mathematical journals. He thought that logic should be part of maths, and in 1854 he published *An Investigation into the Laws of Thought*. It described what is now called Boolean algebra. This allows complicated logical statements to be simplified, and underlies the design of much digital hardware and software.

Can-opener

1855

Robert Yeates

A hammer and chisel for getting into cans were essential kitchen tools until British inventor Robert Yeates invented his can-opener in 1855. It wasn't very convenient – just a sharp blade that had to be stuck into the can top and worked around the rim. But the design became popular in the USA when a canned-beef company gave it a cast-iron bull's head and issued it free of charge with their cans.

Printing telegraph

1855

David Hughes

The first electric telegraphs allowed messages to be sent along a wire (✳ *see* **page 129**). The message was given to a clerk, who tapped it out in Morse code. At the other end, another clerk translated the

1854 Florence Nightingale arrives at a British army hospital in Turkey, where more soldiers are dying from disease than from bullets in the war they are fighting. Her nursing services will make her famous throughout Europe.

1855 While exploring the Zambesi river in Africa, Scottish missionary David Livingstone discovers an enormous waterfall 108 m (355 ft) high and nearly 1.6 km (1 mile) wide. He loyally names it after Queen Victoria.

dots and dashes into words. Many inventors tried to bypass this with "printing telegraphs" that sent written messages directly. The first successful system was invented in 1855 by David Hughes, who taught music in the USA. Its keyboard, which looked a bit like a piano, sent out signals that were automatically translated and printed at the receiving end.

Condensed milk

c1856

Gail Borden

In 1851, US inventor Gail Borden was distressed to see children made ill by infected milk. By 1856, he had patented a process of boiling milk under vacuum, which sterilized it without spoiling its flavour. He called it condensed milk because, knowing nothing of bacteria, he thought that it was the removal of water that made it safer to drink.

Aniline dye

1856

William Perkin

Until 1856, natural plant extracts dominated the dye industry. This changed when a young British chemistry student, William Perkin, had a go at making the drug quinine and produced an intense violet dye instead. Mauve was soon in great demand by fashionable Victorians. Many more dyes of the same type, known as aniline dyes, were to come out of different labs as Perkin's little error turned into an industry.

Transatlantic telegraph

1858

Cyrus Field, Charles Bright, William Thomson

By the 1850s, there were several short underwater telegraph lines. US financier Cyrus Field wanted to go further and link the USA and Britain with a cable across the Atlantic. He recruited several brilliant engineers and scientists, including Charles Bright and William Thomson. After heroic efforts, a cable was laid in 1858 to great rejoicing on both sides. There were problems, including poor insulation, which made the cable fail within weeks, but it proved that the idea worked. A permanent link between the two countries was finally established in 1866.

Each key sent out a different letter of the alphabet

The message was recorded on paper tape

Chain and pulley drove the rotating mechanism

Heavy weight attached to the pulley descended to power the machine

PRINTING TELEGRAPH
Hughes' "piano" keyboard would have seemed quite natural in an age without typewriters. Each key sent a differently timed pulse to a printer at the other end of the line. Good operators could send 30 words a minute.

1858 In Australia, voting slips and ballot boxes appear as the first secret ballots are held in Victoria and South Australia. The system will be adopted in Britain in 1872 and in the USA after the 1884 presidential elections.

1858 A 14-year-old girl sees visions of the Virgin Mary at Lourdes, France. The Virgin, she says, revealed a spring whose water can cure the sick. Lourdes will become a place of pilgrimage and the girl will become St Bernadette.

Evolution by natural selection

1859

Charles Darwin

In 1859, Charles Darwin, the son of a doctor, published a book that shook the world. *On the Origin of Species* presented evidence that animals and plants were not created as we see them today, but evolved from earlier forms and are still evolving. Darwin's theory was based on what he called natural selection. Every member of a species is slightly different. Darwin said that the members with differences that make them more able to compete are more likely to survive and pass on these useful differences to their offspring. (✳ *See also* **Arguing about apes.**)

Although Lenoir's engines did not produce much power, he sold hundreds of them in France and Britain.

Lead–acid battery

1859

Gaston Planté

Even the latest cars rely on a very old type of battery. French physicist Gaston Planté knew that electrodes of lead and lead oxide immersed in sulphuric acid formed a rechargeable cell. Realizing that this would deliver more current than existing cells, he developed it into a practical battery in 1859. Commercial versions were ready just in time for the first cars.

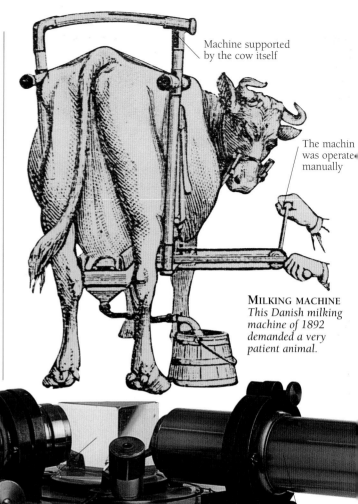

Machine supported by the cow itself

The machin was operate manually

MILKING MACHINE
This Danish milking machine of 1892 demanded a very patient animal.

Light from source enters here

Parallel beam of light produced in here

Prism separates light into its spectrum

Telescope to view the spectrum

Gas engine

1859

Étienne Lenoir

Burning an engine's fuel inside it rather than in a boiler promised a smaller, more efficient machine. But the first successful engine of this type was not particularly small and certainly not very efficient. Invented by French engineer Étienne Lenoir in 1859, it was basically a steam engine converted to run on gas. Its single piston sucked a mixture of gas and air into a cylinder. A spark then lit the mixture to push the piston out again.

Oil well

1859

Edwin Drake, George Bissell

People originally used petroleum only for lighting and medicinal purposes. They collected it as it oozed out of a soft rock called shale. One of the best places for this was Titusville, Pennsylvania, in the USA. There, in 1859, Edwin Drake persuaded landowner George Bissell to let him try drilling for oil instead of just waiting for it to emerge. Only 21 m (69 ft) down he struck lucky, creating the world's first oil well and the industry that would make the USA rich.

Spectroscope

1859

Robert Bunsen, Gustav Kirchhoff

Each element, when made hot enough, gives out light at wavelengths that identify it like a fingerprint identifies a person. The spectroscope reveals these as lines that can be photographed and measured. It was invented in 1859 by German chemist Robert

SPECTROSCOPE *This 19th-century instrument, based on Bunsen's and Kirchoff's design, used a prism to split light into its colours.*

1859 A clock with a huge bell known as Big Ben is installed in St Stephen's tower at London's Houses of Parliament. The sound of Big Ben will become known all around the world when the BBC begins to broadcast it 65 years later.

1859 Rights such as self-expression, privacy, and the rights of minorities, which future generations will take for granted, are defended by British philosopher John Stuart Mill in his essay *On Liberty*. It will influence many people.

Bunsen and physicist Gustav Kirchhoff. The two scientists used their new instrument to compare lines from the Sun with those from elements on Earth, giving the first analysis of the Sun's atmosphere.

Milking machine
1860

L. O. Colvin

The first successful milking machine was patented by US engineer L. O. Colvin in 1860. Its big disadvantage was that it applied a constant vacuum to suck out the milk, which could damage the cow's udder. It was 1889 before Scottish engineer Alexander Shields introduced the modern type of machine, which sucks intermittently like a calf.

Open-hearth process for making steel
1861

William Siemens, Pierre Martin

The open-hearth process was once the most important way of making steel. It was invented by German-British engineer William Siemens in 1861 and perfected by French engineer Pierre Martin. It works by blowing a very hot flame on to a mixture of steel scrap and molten iron from a blast furnace, held in a shallow, brick-lined bath. This melts the steel and burns out excess carbon from the iron. The hot gases from the hearth are used to heat brick-lined

chambers. Air to feed the flame is drawn through these chambers to preheat it. This saves fuel and also allows the flame to be made hot enough to melt steel.

Linoleum
c1861

Frederick Walton

Linoleum, invented by British rubber manufacturer Frederick Walton, in about 1861, was the first successful smooth floor covering. Walton originally made it by coating cloth with layers of a substance containing linseed oil and other ingredients. This slowly reacted with air to form a thick, resilient coating. Lino is still used in areas that get heavy wear.

Speech centre in the brain
1861

Paul Broca

Whenever we talk, certain parts of our brain, mostly on the left side, go into action. One of them is Broca's area, which helps us to find the right words. It was identified by French surgeon and anthropologist Paul Broca in 1861. He studied people with injuries that made them speak hesitantly, but did not stop them understanding what people said. He usually found damage to an area in the front left of the brain. It was the first time that anyone had identified a part of the brain with a particular job. Other scientists, notably the German neurologist Carl Wernicke, later found areas near Broca's that were associated with other aspects of speech and language.

ARGUING ABOUT APES

ALTHOUGH MOST SCIENTISTS accepted Darwin's theory, the public and most of the Church were not so happy. As well as contradicting the Bible, the theory implied that living creatures were ruled entirely by physical laws. Worse still, it seemed to treat people, made in God's image, as animals descended from apes. Fortunately for Darwin, who was a shy man, his friend, the naturalist Thomas Huxley, positively enjoyed speaking up for him in the great debate.

LIFE BEFORE DARWIN
Most people thought species were fixed, or replaced occasionally by God. Some scientists had proposed theories of evolution: Jean Lamarck thought that animals could pass on changes that happened to them during their lives.

HOW DARWIN GOT HIS IDEAS
Darwin saw that finches on various Pacific islands were different. He also looked at the fossil record. The idea of natural selection came to him after he read an essay by the naturalist Thomas Malthus. Malthus said that animals compete to survive, and Darwin realized that competition could explain why animals change.

In 1874, when this cartoon was published, the idea of people having apes for ancestors still seemed strange.

NEW FORMS OF DARWINISM
Darwin's theory fits well with modern genetics, but not all scientists accept it completely. The renowned US geologist Stephen Jay Gould says that it fails to explain the way species have evolved in jumps, rather than smoothly.

1861 The tiny principality of Monaco, just east of Nice in the south of France, regains its independence after 46 years of rule by Sardinia. Its only city, Monte Carlo, opens what will rapidly become the world's best known casino.

1861 On 17 March, after years of struggle, the Kingdom of Italy, with Victor Emmanuel II as its king, is proclaimed by a parliament assembled in Turin. Rome and Venice, still occupied by foreign troops, are not part of it.

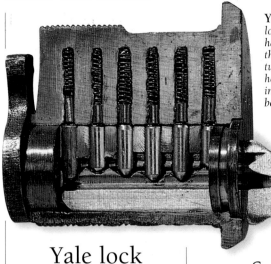

YALE LOCK *This lock has been cut in half to show how the key moves the tumblers to the right height so that the inner cylinder can be turned.*

Yale lock
1861
Linus Yale

The Yale is probably the most widely used type of lock. It was invented in the USA in 1861, and is based on a principle known to the ancient Egyptians: several pins stop the lock moving until the right key pushes them all into the right positions. Linus Yale's father had designed a lock using this "pin tumbler" idea in 1848, but it was Linus Yale Jr who perfected the compact revolving barrel and flat key that is used today.

Parkesine
1862
Alexander Parkes

The first plastic was based on the natural substance cellulose. British chemist Alexander Parkes discovered that if he treated cellulose with nitric acid, dissolved it in alcohol and ether, and mixed it with pigments, it formed a dough that he could mould into small articles. He won a medal for his discovery in 1862, and in 1866 the Parkesine Company went into business. It failed within two years, possibly because Parkes was too stingy to make his new material properly.

Solar hydrogen
1862
Anders Ångström

The Swedish physicist Anders Ångström was a pioneer of spectroscopy, a way of discovering the composition of things by studying the light they give out when hot. One of the things he studied was very hot indeed – the Sun. By comparing its light with light given out by hydrogen in his laboratory, he was able to show in 1862 that the Sun's atmosphere contains hydrogen.

Roller-skates
1863
Joseph Merlin, James Plimpton

The first person to skate without ice may have been Joseph Merlin, who lived in the 18th century in what is now Belgium. But his skates seem to have been more like Rollerblades than roller-skates. Four-wheeled skates were invented in 1863 by an American, James Plimpton. He started a US and British craze for roller-skating, which is still popular today.

Underground railway
1863
John Fowler

Traffic threatened mid-19th-century cities with death by choking. London fought back in 1863 with the world's first underground railway. It wasn't very far underground: just a deep trench dug down the centre of the street and roofed over so that traffic could run above it. Despite fumes from its steam locomotives, the Metropolitan Railway, engineered by John Fowler, was a great success. Electrified in 1906, the line is still in use today.

Plaque

Dish

Medallions

Female head

Head of Jesus

Female head

PARKESINE *The first plastic did not melt like most modern plastics, but was shaped by being squeezed into a mould while soft. It was not very strong, so was used only for small decorative items.*

Seal

Flat disc

Box

1863 In the American Civil War, President Abraham Lincoln issues a proclamation that slaves in the southern states are "forever free". His aim is to weaken the power of these rebellious states. After the war, all slaves will be freed.

1863 In October, soccer's governing body, the Football Association, is founded at a meeting in London. It will standardize the rules of the game and, within eight years, organize the English championship, which will be known as the FA Cup.

Antiseptics
1865

*Ignaz Semmelweis,
Joseph Lister*

Hungarian doctor Ignaz Semmelweis upset his boss by telling medical students at Vienna's maternity hospital to disinfect their hands. Although he proved that this made giving birth less dangerous, he was sacked in 1849. Even after 1864, when Louis Pasteur's germ theory was accepted in France, most surgeons still did not even put on clean clothes before an operation. In 1865, Scottish surgeon Joseph Lister sprayed carbolic acid, a powerful germ killer, around his operating theatre and on to dressings, and things began to change. Lister's ideas led in the end to modern, sterile surgery.

Mercury vacuum pump
1865

Hermann Sprengel

Early-19th-century vacuum pumps moved air with pistons. But, as the pressure dropped, the pistons and valves began to leak and contamination of the vacuum by lubricants became a problem. A German glassblower, Heinrich Geissler, found a solution in 1855 when he made use of the vacuum that appears above the mercury in a barometer. Then in 1865, Hermann Sprengel used falling mercury to sweep out gas molecules, producing a high-vacuum pump, which led to many further inventions, including the cathode-ray tube.

Pullman sleeping car
1865

George Pullman, Ben Field

Before air travel, it could take days to travel between cities in the USA, and people usually had nowhere to sleep but in their seat on the train. Builder George Pullman realized that there was a market for something more civilized than this. Working with his friend Ben Field, he introduced the first railway carriage with comfortable beds, the *Pioneer*, in 1865. The beds were arranged like bunks, with the lower bed doubling as a seat for daytime. Pullman was soon running a big organization with its own town, Pullman, to house its workers.

Clinical thermometer
1866

Thomas Allbutt

Nineteenth-century doctors knew that a patient's temperature was a good guide to their health, but until British physician Thomas Allbutt invented the clinical thermometer, there was no convenient way of measuring it. The only thermometers available could take 20 minutes to give a reading, and some of them were 30 cm (12 in) long. Allbutt reduced them to a pocket-sized instrument, which was not only more convenient to handle but also worked much faster. He usually put his thermometer under a patient's arm, not in their mouth.

SOLD BY S. MAW, SON, AND THOMPSON, LONDON.
Dr. Clifford Allbutt's Short Clinical Thermometer (Self-registering).

Hair slides

Flat discs

CLINICAL THERMOMETER *This Allbutt-type thermometer of about 1880 looks very like those used a century later. It was designed to hold its reading after removal from the patient.*

Pasteurization
1865

Louis Pasteur

Pasteurization gets its name from the great French scientist Louis Pasteur, who was the first person to show that invisible organisms can spoil food and cause disease. He invented the process in 1865. It makes liquids hot enough to kill any harmful organisms without destroying their food value. For example, milk can be pasteurized by being heated to 63°C (145°F) for 30 minutes, then quickly chilled for storage. Although pasteurization increases food safety, some people prefer untreated dairy products from disease-free cows.

Laws of heredity
1866

Gregor Mendel

A man and a woman, both with brown eyes, could have a one-in-four chance of producing a child with blue eyes. Basic genetic facts like this go back to the work of an Austrian monk, Gregor Mendel. By crossing different strains of peas, he discovered that organisms inherit their characteristics in a way governed by mathematical laws. He published his results in 1866, but it was only in 1900 that Dutch botanist Hugo De Vries realized their importance to modern biology.

1865 On Friday, 14 April, just days after the end of the American Civil War, President Abraham Lincoln, whose views remain unpopular in the defeated South, is shot while at a theatre in Washington DC. He dies the next day.

1865 Writing as Lewis Carroll, British mathematician Charles Dodgson publishes *Alice in Wonderland*. Based on stories written for a child called Alice Liddell, and illustrated by John Tenniel, the book is an immediate success.

LECLANCHÉ CELL *Liquid-filled glass cells just like this one remained in use well into the 20th century. They were ideal for powering electric door bells.*

Germs

1867

Louis Pasteur

In the mid 19th century, some natural processes were still a mystery. What turned grape juice into wine, for example? Why did it sometimes go sour? French chemist Louis Pasteur proved that invisible organisms were responsible. He also proved that diseases were transmitted by micro-organisms, rather than polluted air. The Academy of Sciences officially accepted his conclusions in 1864, and Pasteur was given his own laboratory at France's École Supérieure in 1867. His "germ" theory then began to be more widely accepted. By establishing the reality of germs, Pasteur revolutionized medicine and the food industry. (✳ *See also* **The bug hunters.**)

Leclanché cell

1866

Georges Leclanché

Modern batteries started as the Leclanché cell, invented in 1866 by French engineer Georges Leclanché. The cell's negative terminal was a glass jar containing a zinc rod in a solution of ammonium chloride. A smaller pot inside the jar contained manganese dioxide and a carbon rod, forming the positive terminal. It eventually developed into today's smaller, dryer battery.

THE BUG HUNTERS

OTHERS BEFORE PASTEUR had thought that invasion by invisible organisms might be responsible for decay and disease. But they had not been able to prove it, so most people believed that decaying matter created life by "spontaneous generation". Even after Pasteur, many people found it hard to believe in the invisible killers. Those who did, such as Scottish surgeon Joseph Lister and German doctor Robert Koch, made great progress.

GERMS BEFORE PASTEUR

In 100 BC, a Roman writer declared that disease was caused by an invisible invasion. Much later, in 1684, Francesco Redi wrote that spontaneous generation could not occur because "only life produces life". In the 19th century, Italian scientist Agostino Bassi showed that a disease of silkworms was caused by infection with invisible fungus spores.

PASTEUR'S LEGACY

German doctor Robert Koch showed that bacteria could be bred in the laboratory, and established many of the techniques of bacteriology. By 1883, he had isolated the organisms that cause cholera and tuberculosis. Scientists now know that not all bacteria are bad: we depend on many micro-organisms inside our bodies to keep them working properly.

Compound microscopes

Glass flask

Silkworm cocoons

GERMS *This selection of equipment from Pasteur's laboratory shows both his tools for studying germs and one of his major concerns – the health of silkworms.*

Bronze ink stand and ink wells

Pipette

Culture slide

1866 The world's first ski-jumping competition is held in Telemark, Norway. It is won by Sondre Nordheim, who made the sport possible by inventing ski bindings. He will later ski the 322 km (200 miles) from Telemark to Oslo.

1867 Russia sells Alaska to the USA, prompted by a fall in demand for furs from the region and the threat of British invasion. Many Americans think the price of $7.2 million is too high, but Alaska will prove to be rich in oil.

146

Dynamite
1867
Alfred Nobel

The dangers of nitroglycerine were brought home to Swedish chemist Alfred Nobel in 1864 when his nitroglycerine factory blew up, killing his younger brother. Determined to tame this otherwise useful explosive, he mixed it with an absorbent material, kieselguhr, converting the dangerous liquid into a safe solid, which he patented in 1867 as dynamite. Ironically, it made him rich enough to set up the foundation that awards the Nobel peace prize.

Paper boat
1867
Elisha Waters, George Waters

In 1867, US carton maker Elisha Waters and his son George started making rowing boats out of paper. They glued paper over a wooden former, let it dry, then varnished it. The keel and other main members were made of wood. The light, stiff boats were ideal for sport: during 1876, US crews rowing Waters boats won no fewer than 12 major races. The Waters construction technique has since been reinvented in the modern fibreglass boat.

Helium in the Sun
1868
Pierre Janssen, Norman Lockyer

The gas helium gets its name from *helios*, the Greek for "Sun", because that's where it was first detected. In 1868, French astronomer Pierre Janssen saw a dark line in the yellow region of the Sun's spectrum. He thought it came from sodium, but British astronomer Norman Lockyer declared that it indicated an unknown element. He named it with the help of chemist Edward Frankland.

Möbius strip
1868
August Möbius

German mathematician August Möbius died without revealing his best-known discovery, the Möbius strip. It was found among his papers after his death in 1868. It is a simple strip of paper given a half-twist and then glued to form a loop, and it has weird properties. For example, it has only one edge and it is impossible to make each side of it a different colour because it has only one side. When cut down the centre, it opens out into a single loop twice the size with a double half-twist. Two Mobiüs strips zipped together form what is called a Klein bottle, which has no edges and only one surface.

Margarine
1869
Hippolyte Mège-Mouriés

Many people today prefer margarine to butter, but it's hard to believe that anybody preferred the first margarine, a mixture of beef fat, skimmed milk, cow's udder, and pig's stomach. When French inventor Hippolyte Mège-Mouriés concocted it in 1869, Napoleon III awarded him a prize for producing the first alternative to butter. It soon improved, and by 1885 it was enough of a threat to the dairy industry for the British government to stop the use of its original name, "Butterine".

CHEWING GUM *Early competition produced some unlikely advertising, such as this suggestion that gum chewing was the height of fashion.*

Air brake
1869
George Westinghouse

To stop a long train, the brakes must be applied to all the wheels, but how? US inventor George Westinghouse found the answer in 1869 – use air. Unlike a mechanical linkage, air can be taken from coach to coach easily. Westinghouse's system also had an important safety feature. The brakes were held in the off position by air pressure and applied by releasing it, so any leaks automatically put them on.

Chewing gum
1869
Thomas Adams

The main ingredient of chewing gum is chicle, a rubbery substance from a Central American tree. Many 19th-century inventors tried to use it like rubber. One of them was US photographer Thomas Adams, who bought some from a Mexican. He failed to make rubber, but he noticed that the Mexican liked chewing chicle. In 1869, he boiled up some with flavourings and offered it to a store. Customers loved it.

1867 The British North America Act creates the Dominion of Canada from New Brunswick, Nova Scotia, and what will be Quebec and Ontario. Its government is based on British practice and its sovereign is the British monarch.

1869 In the Australian state of Victoria, John Deason and Richard Oates dig up Australia's largest gold nugget, weighing more than 71 kg (56 lb). They get £9534 for the find, which becomes known as the "Welcome Stranger" nugget.

Synthetic alizarin

1869

*Heinrich Caro,
William Perkin*

In 1869, Heinrich Caro in Germany and William Perkin in Britain demonstrated the power of chemistry by wiping out an entire industry. They both found a way to make alizarin, the active component of a natural red dye. It was one of the few red dyes available at the time, and thousands of people earned their living producing the natural substance – until the chemists got to work. Caro beat Perkin to the patent by one day, but Perkin still made the dye in Britain, using a cheaper method.

CELLULOID *Basically colourless, celluloid could be made in a variety of forms, from fake ivory to mock tortoiseshell.*

Periodic table

1869

Dmitry Mendeleyev

In 1866, Russian chemist Dmitry Mendeleyev listed the elements by atomic weight. He found that the list showed a pattern, with similar elements appearing at regular intervals, or periods. He published his periodic table in 1869, and in 1871 produced a version with gaps where there were breaks in the pattern. He said that the gaps represented undiscovered elements, but most chemists did not see the importance of this until at least 20 years later.

Dynamo

1870

Zénobe Gramme

Electric generators were not very effective until Belgian engineer Zénobe Gramme built his dynamo in 1870. It used an electromagnet powered by the generator itself. German electrical engineer Werner von Siemens had invented a dynamo in 1866, but Gramme's version went further. It had a highly efficient design and a new way of connecting its generating coils. Gramme's dynamo gave a strong, steady output, making it a much better generator.

Celluloid

1870

John Hyatt

Celluloid was the first truly successful plastic. Like its unsuccessful predecessor Parkesine (✳ *see page 144*), it was based on cellulose. Its US inventor, John Hyatt, created the first clear, flexible material, making possible both popular photography and motion pictures. Patented in 1870, celluloid was also used for everything from dolls to shirt cuffs. Unfortunately, it was extremely flammable and caused many accidents, so it is rarely used today.

Penny-farthing bicycle

1870

*James Starley,
William Hillman*

Bizarre though it looks, with its huge front wheel and tiny rear wheel, the penny-farthing was a serious invention by leading bicycle pioneers. British engineers James Starley and William Hillman created it in 1870 as a lighter alternative to existing velocipedes. The big front wheel did the same job as modern gears, enabling the rider to power the bike efficiently. It worked: on one long trip, a group of penny-farthing riders averaged 74 km (46 miles) a day.

"Ivory" box

"Mother of pearl" cigarette case

"Ivory" hairpin box

"Ivory" evening handbag

"Tortoiseshell" haircombs

Marble-effect handbag

"Ivory" hand mirror

1869 On 17 November, after 15 years' hard negotiating and harder digging, the Suez canal is opened. Designed by French diplomat Ferdinand de Lesseps, it provides a short cut from the Indian Ocean to the Mediterranean Sea.

1870 German archaeologist Heinrich Schliemann discovers the city of Troy, long thought to be just the stuff of ancient Greek legends. He finds battlements, walls, and gold treasure on a mound called Hissarlik in Turkey.

Modern microscope condenser

c1870

Ernst Abbe

The image-forming lenses of a microscope are important, but until about 1870, nobody had thought much about the optics that simply illuminate the object – the condenser. Early microscopists used condensers, but German physicist Ernst Abbe's was the first scientific design. Most microscopes now have Abbe condensers.

Dry photographic plate

1871

Richard Maddox

Although wet plates produced excellent photographs (❋ *see* **page 139**), they were not exactly convenient. Photographers searched everywhere for the magic ingredient that would allow them to make dry plates. They eventually found it in the kitchen cupboard: gelatine. In

"Ivory" hairbrush

"Ivory" clothes-brush

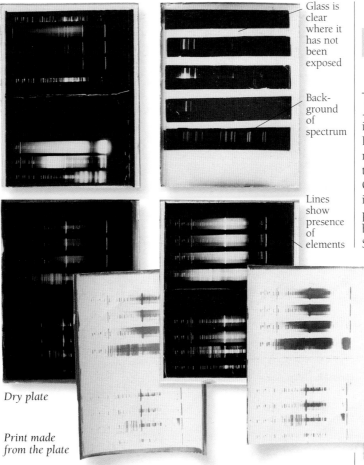

Dry plate

Print made from the plate

1871, British doctor Richard Maddox mixed some gelatine with silver bromide and spread it on glass. When it was dry, the new coating stayed sensitive, could be developed easily, and needed shorter exposure times. Modern photography had arrived.

Cable car

1873

Andrew Hallidie

Andrew Hallidie, a wire-rope maker in the USA, was shocked to see five horses killed as a horse-drawn bus slid down one of San Francisco's steep hills. So he used his ropes to create the world's first cable car. It opened in 1873 and is still running today. Cars are pulled along by a constantly moving rope running in a slot in the road.

Glass is clear where it has not been exposed

Background of spectrum

Lines show presence of elements

DRY PHOTOGRAPHIC PLATE *Dry plates were useful to scientists. These show spark spectra (c 1915).*

To move, the cars grab the rope; to stop, they let go and apply their brakes.

Jeans

1873

Jacob Davis, Levi Strauss

In the 1850s, the USA's gold rush attracted people from everywhere. Levi Strauss had a business that supplied them with everything they needed, including trousers. Tailor Jacob Davis started making denim trousers with riveted pockets, and suggested to Strauss that they could make lots of money. So Strauss provided cash to get started, Davis supplied the know-how, and in 1873 they got the first patent for jeans.

Barbed wire

1874

Joseph Glidden

How an invention is made can matter more than what it is. Barbed wire is an example. Early types cost so much to make that few people used them. US farmer Joseph Glidden saw some barbed wire in 1873, and the following year patented a new type that could be made cheaply by machine. Soon his Barb Fence Company was turning out miles of cattle-controlling wire and helping to make the USA's Great Plains into great farming country.

LEVI STRAUSS & CO.'s
COPPER RIVETED
Overalls.

JEANS *What we call jeans did not get their name for years. This 1910 advertisement calls them overalls.*

DNA

1874

Johann Miescher

DNA, the key to genetics and life, may seem like the latest thing, but it was discovered in 1874. Swiss scientist Johann Miescher was a student when he found a new substance, which he called nuclein, in the nucleus of white blood cells. He later realized that it was actually two substances. Separating out the acid part, he called it nucleic acid. It is now known as deoxyribonucleic acid, or DNA.

1872 In the USA, the world's first national park is opened. The president, Ulysses S. Grant, signs a bill that preserves Yellowstone, an 8983 sq km (3468 sq mile) area in the Rocky Mountains, as a permanent wilderness.

1873 Canada forms a new police force to combat smuggling, horse theft, and banditry. The Northwest Mounted Police, later the Royal Canadian Mounted Police, will become famous as the Mounties, who "always get their man".

TYPEWRITER *This 1875 Sholes and Glidden machine typed in capital letters only.*

Paper wrapped around a cylindrical patten

Type bars hit the paper from below

QWERTY keyboard

Handle for turning the cylinder

Telephone
1876

Alexander Graham Bell

See **pages 152–153** for the story of how Bell invented the telephone.

Sound recording
1877

Thomas Edison

In 1877, US inventor Thomas Edison was working on a recorder for telegraph signals. He noticed that paper indented with the signals made sounds when pulled under a needle. So he made a machine with tinfoil wrapped around a revolving cylinder and a needle connected to a thin metal disc. When he spoke, the disc vibrated and the needle indented waves on the tinfoil. Turning the cylinder again, Edison heard his own voice. He had invented sound recording. (✳ *See also* **Recording pioneers.**)

SOUND RECORDING *A phonograph from about 1885 shows recording at its simplest.*

Needle touches the cylinder here

Typewriter
1874

Christopher Sholes, Carlos Glidden, Samuel Soulé

As an ex-newspaper editor, Christopher Sholes knew exactly what a typewriter had to do: write faster than a pen. Many people had tried and failed to produce such a machine, but Sholes, helped by fellow US inventors Carlos Glidden and Samuel Soulé, succeeded. In 1873, he sold the idea to Remington, a firm of gunmakers. They launched the world's first real typewriter in 1874, after which their gun business took a back seat. The layout of the keyboard was developed to stop fast typists jamming the keys, and is still used today.

Four-stroke engine
1876

Alphonse Beau de Rochas, Nikolaus Otto

Most petrol and diesel engines use the four-stroke cycle. Fuel and air are drawn into a cylinder, compressed, burned, and the burned gases pumped out. The first person to think of it was French engineer Alphonse Beau de Rochas in 1862. His work was forgotten and reinvented by German engineer Nikolaus Otto in 1876. Despite de Rochas' earlier work, the cycle is still known today as the Otto cycle.

1874 A group of artists including Monet, Pisarro, and Renoir, rejected by the French Academy, hold their own show. Journalist Louis Leroy, shocked by pictures that capture real light and colour, dubs them the Impressionists.

1875 On Wednesday 25 August, British merchant navy captain Matthew Webb becomes the first person to swim the English Channel without any buoyancy aid. He completes the 34 km (21 mile) crossing in 21 hours 45 minutes.

Photographic motion capture
1877

Eadweard Muybridge

Eadweard Muybridge was born in Britain but worked in the USA. He was the first person to record live motion photographically. A racehorse owner had asked him to settle an argument: did a galloping horse ever lift all its hooves off the ground at once? In 1877, Muybridge set up a row of cameras along a racetrack. As a horse galloped by, it tripped their shutters, making each camera record a different part of the movement. The answer to the question was "yes".

Cream separator
1878

Gustav de Laval

Skimmed milk isn't skimmed – it's spun like clothes in a washing machine. The first cream separator using this principle was invented in 1878 by Swedish engineer Gustav de Laval. In its final form, his machine poured milk on to a set of spinning discs, which forced the watery part to the

outside and left the cream in the centre. By 1883, Laval had built a steam-powered separator, 40 times faster than a modern washing machine.

Light bulb
1878

Thomas Edison, Joseph Swan

In 1878, both Thomas Edison in the USA and the chemist Joseph Swan in Britain made light bulbs. Both of them had trouble finding a filament that would last long. Edison tried platinum, but soon switched to carbon, which Swan had first tried 20 years earlier. By 1880, both inventors had produced good light bulbs, which they showed off at the 1881 Paris Electrical Exhibition. From then on, their lamps began to be used everywhere.

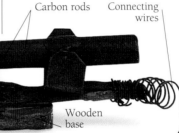

MICROPHONE *Two carbon rods touch to form one type of Hughes microphone.*

Microphone
1878

David Hughes

Returning to London after making a fortune in the USA, David Hughes set up as a full-time inventor. In 1878, he discovered that loose electrical contacts were sensitive to sound. Two barely touching carbon rods placed on a table and connected to a battery and telephone earpiece could reveal sounds as quiet as the tramp of a fly's feet. These sounds were so tiny that Hughes called his invention a microphone. Its real future was as part of a better telephone.

Carbon rods   Connecting wires

Wooden base

Two-stroke engine
1879

Dugald Clerk

A two-stroke engine uses more fuel than a four-stroke engine of the same power, but it also weighs less. Its mechanism is simpler, and each of its cylinders delivers power on every revolution, not every other revolution, as in a four-stroke. The first effective two-stroke engine was invented by Scottish engineer Dugald Clerk in 1879 and patented in 1881. It was designed to run on coal gas to power workshop machinery. Two-stroke engines are now used for things like scooters and lawnmowers, where lightness matters more than efficiency.

Early 20th-century gramophone

RECORDING PIONEERS

THE EARLY RECORDING industry solved its problems step by step. Tinfoil was not a good recording medium. It was soon replaced by wax. Edison produced cylindrical records on his phonograph, but they were slow and expensive to copy. Flat discs, which could be stamped out by the thousand, dealt with that. But the problem of how to make sounds louder was not solved until the arrival of electronics in the 1920s.

Threaded drive axle moves the tinfoil beneath the needle

Brass cylinder – tinfoil is wrapped around this

THE PHONOGRAPH
Edison developed his invention into a sophisticated home entertainment device that could produce surprisingly good sound. He eventually solved the problem of copying cylindrical recordings, but failed to sign up many good musicians.

THE GRAPHOPHONE
Recordings on wax were first made by US inventors Chichester Bell and Charles Tainter. Their machine recorded on cylinders that were wax-coated. Although used mainly for dictation, it could produce excellent recordings.

THE GRAMOPHONE
Flat disc records were invented in 1887 by a German engineer, Emil Berliner, working in the USA. Because of their shape, they were easily mass-produced. And when renowned musicians started recording on them, their future was assured.

1876 Financed by wealthy widow Nadezhda von Meck, Russian composer Peter Tchaikowsky writes the ballet *Swan Lake*. In 1877, it is danced, with little success, by the Bolshoi Ballet under choreographer Wenzel Reisinger.

1877 In March, cricket's first Test Match is played in Melbourne, Australia. The Australian opener, Charles Bannerman, scores a century (100 runs), and Australia wins by 45 runs. England's leading player, W. G. Grace, does not play.

151

DOING AWAY WITH DISTANCE

*Helped by Thomas Watson,
Alexander Graham Bell invents the telephone*

Bell's box telephone incorporated a larger magnet than others, which made it more sensitive.

Bell demonstrated this telephone to Queen Victoria.

PUBLICITY MACHINE
Bell was an expert at publicity. His crude laboratory instruments became fine objects of polished brass, rich wood, and ivory when they were to be demonstrated to someone as important as Queen Victoria. Bell made a good impression on the Queen when they met in 1878, despite making the mistake of touching her arm without permission to attract her attention to an incoming call.

It was St Valentine's day, 1876. A good day to tell the world about an invention that would help people communicate. It's lucky Alexander Graham Bell didn't leave it any longer. Two hours after he'd deposited papers describing his telephone to people at the US Patent Office, his rival, Elisha Gray, warned them he was about to do the same. But Bell was first.

It was hard on Gray. Both men had similar ideas but Bell had an advantage: he knew more about speech and hearing. Bell's father was a speech teacher and had invented a way to help deaf people speak. His grandfather had given speech lessons, so as Alexander grew up in Edinburgh, Scotland, he was surrounded by ideas about speech and hearing. He even got his dog to talk by making it growl, then moving its mouth with his hands!

The family emigrated to Canada in 1870. Bell went to Boston, USA, where he opened a school for teachers of deaf people. He also experimented with a harmonic telegraph, which sent messages as musical notes. Bell noticed that a strip of iron near an electromagnet mimicked the vibrations of a similar strip and electromagnet connected to it by wires. He thought he might use this to transmit speech.

With mechanic Thomas Watson, he tried hard to make electric currents imitate sound

Early telephone cable

WIRED FOR SOUND
As telephones became more popular, cities got choked with overhead wires, so some lines went underground. Early phone cables contained many paper-insulated wires in a lead sheath.

waves. The original arrangement wasn't sensitive enough, so Bell tried a needle dipping into acid. The needle was attached to a sheet of parchment stretched on a frame, with a horn to concentrate sound on to it. Sound shook the parchment, which varied the resistance of the needle's contact with the acid, which, in turn, varied the current.

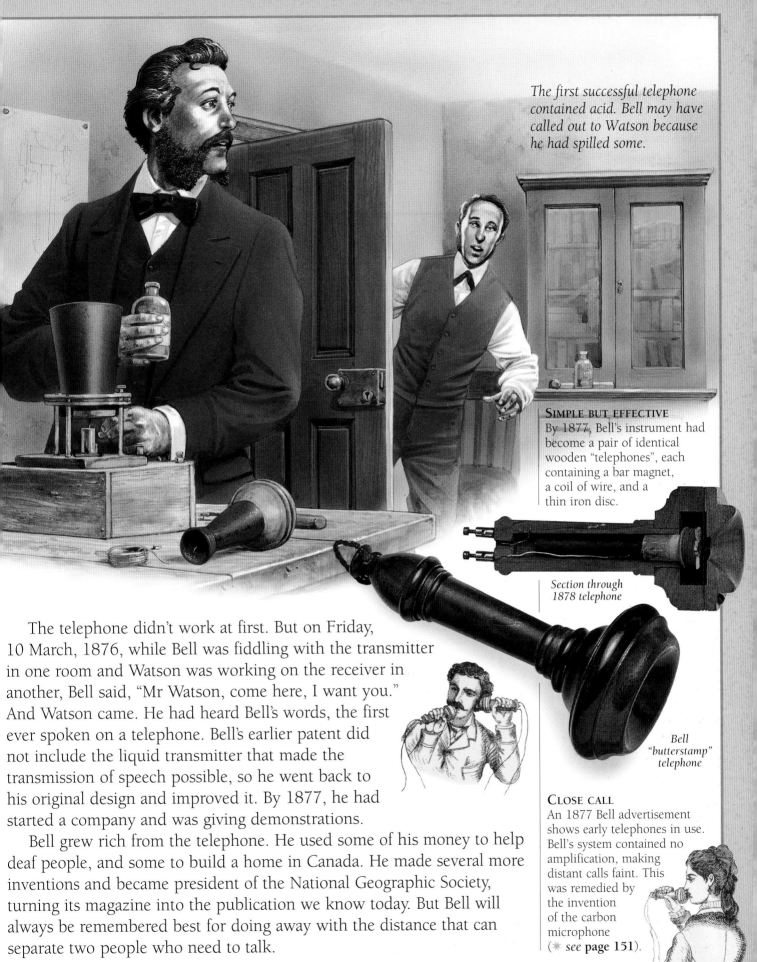

The first successful telephone contained acid. Bell may have called out to Watson because he had spilled some.

SIMPLE BUT EFFECTIVE

By 1877, Bell's instrument had become a pair of identical wooden "telephones", each containing a bar magnet, a coil of wire, and a thin iron disc.

Section through 1878 telephone

Bell "butterstamp" telephone

The telephone didn't work at first. But on Friday, 10 March, 1876, while Bell was fiddling with the transmitter in one room and Watson was working on the receiver in another, Bell said, "Mr Watson, come here, I want you." And Watson came. He had heard Bell's words, the first ever spoken on a telephone. Bell's earlier patent did not include the liquid transmitter that made the transmission of speech possible, so he went back to his original design and improved it. By 1877, he had started a company and was giving demonstrations.

Bell grew rich from the telephone. He used some of his money to help deaf people, and some to build a home in Canada. He made several more inventions and became president of the National Geographic Society, turning its magazine into the publication we know today. But Bell will always be remembered best for doing away with the distance that can separate two people who need to talk.

CLOSE CALL

An 1877 Bell advertisement shows early telephones in use. Bell's system contained no amplification, making distant calls faint. This was remedied by the invention of the carbon microphone (✳ see **page 151**).

Cash register
1879
James Ritty, John Patterson

A cash register records every sale, preventing shop assistants from putting money into their own pockets. The first one was invented by US tavern keeper James Ritty in 1879. It displayed the money paid on a dial, and recorded it by punching a paper roll. It wasn't easy to use, and cash registers caught on only after coal merchant John Patterson bought the idea. As well as improving it, he set up the world's first professional sales force to sell it.

CASH REGISTER *Many early cash registers, like this one from 1935, had dials rather than keys.*

Electric train
1879
Werner von Siemens

A s soon as good electric motors were available they were used in trains. The first electric train was exhibited in Berlin, Germany, in 1879. Built by German engineer Werner von Siemens, it ran in a circle, took only 30 people, and went no faster than 6 km/h (4 mph). Within five years, real electric trains and trams were running in Germany, USA, and Britain.

Saccharin
1879
Ira Remsen, Constantin Fahlberg

S accharin is very much sweeter than sugar and does not make people fat, so it is used a lot in food and drink, despite its disagreeable aftertaste. US chemist Ira Remsen and his student Constantin Fahlberg discovered it by accident in 1879. They noticed that after one session in the lab everything they touched tasted sweet. They soon tracked down the chemical responsible for this and turned it into a commercial product.

Venn diagram
1880
John Venn

V enn diagrams help with logic. They were invented in 1880 by a Cambridge University lecturer, John Venn, and use circles to stand for different things. For example, suppose there is one circle representing cats, another black things, and a third green things. The cat circle would be drawn to overlap the black circle, but not the green circle, to show that some cats are black but no cats are green. The idea can be extended to much more complicated statements.

Public electricity supply
1882
Thomas Edison

E lectric light bulbs were not much use without electricity. One of their inventors, Thomas Edison, knew this very well, so he built the first public electricity supply system. It opened in

New York in September 1882, a year after Edison had demonstrated the idea in London. Edison's system provided brighter, safer lighting than gas, but it used direct current, which made changing voltage difficult. Because of this, it lost out to alternating current in the end.

Trolley bus
1882
Werner von Siemens, Leo Daft

A trolley bus has an electric motor and takes its electricity from overhead wires. The first was a converted horse cab, which German engineer Werner von Siemens demonstrated in 1882. A few years later, US engineer Leo Daft gave the vehicle its name and built the first real trolley bus systems. Most trolley buses stopped running in the 1960s, but because they are clean and green they could yet make a comeback in some towns.

Function of thyroid gland
1883
Victor Horsley

T he thyroid gland lies in the neck, wrapped around the voice box. In 1883, Victor Horsley (later Sir Victor) proved that the gland's job is to control how fast the body burns food – called its metabolic rate. He did this by removing the thyroid glands from monkeys. We now know that the thyroid gland makes a hormone that speeds up the body's cells.

Electric tram
1883
Magnus Volk

A tram is an electric bus that runs on rails in the road. Many inventors created trams in the early 1880s. The German firm Siemens and Halske was operating trams between Frankfurt and Offenbach

ELECTRIC TRAM *This is a model of a double-decker tramcar that operated in London in about 1915. Trams were a feature of many large cities by 1900. Some places abandoned them; others kept them. Now some cities are bringing back this low-pollution form of transport.*

1879
In Boston, USA, religious leader Mary Baker Eddy founds the First Church of Christ, Scientist. Christian Scientists believe that human beings are spiritual, not material, and value prayer above conventional medicine.

1880
Australia's most famous outlaw, or bushranger, Ned Kelly, is hanged on 11 November after a career in which his gang killed several policemen, robbed a bank, and had a final gun battle in which they wore home-made armour.

In 1884, but the first tramway to take paying passengers was probably one built in 1883 by British engineer Magnus Volk. Running on narrow-gauge tracks along the sea front at Brighton, England, it is still in service.

Wires collect electricity from overhead cables to power the tramcar

Induction motor
1883

Nikola Tesla

An induction motor is an electric motor that has no electrical connections to the part that rotates. This makes it more reliable, because there are no sliding contacts. It was invented in 1883 by Serbian-US engineer Nikola Tesla.

He worked out how to create a rotating magnetic field using stationary electrical windings.

INDUCTION MOTOR
Tesla's original motor did not look much like the machines of today, but its operating principle was the same.

Windings

Rotor

Placed in this rotating field, a conducting rotor will spin. This is because the field induces currents in the rotor, turning it into a magnet, which is pushed around as the field rotates. Induction motors now power most of the world's electrically driven machinery.

Three-phase electricity supply
1883

Nikola Tesla, George Westinghouse

A three-phase electricity supply uses three wires instead of two. It gives two different voltages from one set of wires, and can create the rotating magnetic field needed in an induction motor. The idea occurred to Nikola Tesla in 1883. US engineer George Westinghouse, looking for something better than Edison's supply system, bought Tesla's idea in 1888. Today nearly all mains electricity is delivered by three-phase systems.

Car has controls at both ends so it does not have to turn round

Metal wheels ran along rails

1882 Judo begins in Japan when Kano Jigoro learns about a samurai form of fighting called jujitsu and founds his Kodokan School. Fighters in this unarmed combat sport try to master their opponent by turning their own force against them.

1883 The volcanic island of Krakatau in Indonesia destroys itself in one of the world's biggest eruptions. The explosion is heard 5000 km (3000 miles) away. Thousands are killed and dust pollutes the atmosphere for years.

Artificial silk

1884

Hilaire Chardonnet, Joseph Swan

Artificial silk was the first synthetic fibre. In about 1880 both Hilaire Chardonnet in France and Joseph Swan in Britain made "silk" by squirting cellulose nitrate solution through a nozzle. The product was highly flammable, but both inventors found a way of converting it back into safer cellulose. Chardonnet got a patent for his process in 1884, and by 1891 had set up a factory at Besançon to make artificial silk commercially.

Motorcycle

1884

Edward Butler, Gottlieb Daimler

The first motorcycle had three wheels. It was designed by British engineer Edward Butler in 1884, although he didn't build it until 1887. Its engine was at the back and drove a single rear wheel. In 1885, German engineer Gottlieb Daimler designed the first two-wheeled motorcycle. He built it purely because he wanted to test a new high-speed petrol

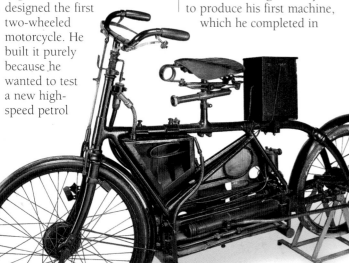

MOTOR CYCLE *The Holden motor cycle, patented in 1897, had four cylinders driving the back wheel directly.*

engine that he had designed (✻ *see page 157*). It got its first outing on 10 November, 1886.

Multi-stage steam turbine

1884

Charles Parsons

A steam turbine is like a fan in reverse. Steam rushes through blades, making them spin. If there were only one set of blades, most of the steam's energy would be wasted, but in 1884 British engineer Charles (later Sir Charles) Parsons invented a turbine with many sets of blades on one shaft. These were graded in size to capture most of the steam's energy. Turbines like this are now used everywhere to power ships and electric generators.

Adder-lister

1885

William Burroughs

The first adding machine that printed its calculations was created by a US inventor who left school at 15. It took William Burroughs four years to produce his first machine, which he completed in

ADDER-LISTER *The Burroughs machine had an intricate mechanism.*

1885. It had more than 80 keys, arranged in columns of nine, and a handle to operate the printer. The following year Burroughs formed the American Arithmometer Company. He continued to develop his machine, but it was 1892 before it was good enough to sell.

Bicycle

1885

John Starley

Many inventors worked on bicycles in the 1870s and 80s. But the first design that looked like a modern bike was made by British engineer John Starley in 1885. Several makers had already produced chain-driven "safety bicycles", but Starley was the first to make both wheels about the same size, put them in a diamond-shaped frame, and slope the front forks to the correct angle to make the wheel go in a straight line. His machine's name, the Rover, lives on in the Range Rover and Land Rover.

BICYCLE *The Rover in this 1888 advertisement has all the essential features of a modern bike.*

Bicycle hub gear

1885

W. T. Shaw

Cycling uphill is easier if you can change into a lower gear. British engineer W. T. Shaw was one of the first people to help cyclists, with his "crypto-dynamic" gearing of 1885. Then, in 1902, British engineers Henry Sturmey and James Archer both invented similar gears. These were brought together by bicycle maker Frank (later Sir Frank) Bowden. Like earlier designs, the Sturmey-Archer gear fitted inside the bike's rear hub.

1884 The first women's singles tennis championship is held at the All England Croquet and Lawn Tennis Club, Wimbledon, which was founded in 1877. Maud Watson claimed the title from Lilian Watson 6-8, 6-3, 6-3.

1884 US writer Mark Twain writes his most popular book, *Huckleberry Finn*. This children's novel, a sequel to his highly successful *The Adventures of Tom Sawyer*, uses vivid language and humour to deal with violence and racism.

Gas mantle
1885

Carl Auer von Welsbach

In the late 19th century, many people used gas lamps. Electric lighting could have swept these away, but in 1885, Austrian chemist Carl Auer von Welsbach discovered how to get more light from gas. He found that salts of thorium and cerium gave out an intense light when deposited on asbestos fibres and heated. By the 1890s, gas lamps were wearing little knitted covers known as mantles over their flames. When a lamp was lit, the metals in its mantle gave out enough light to rival an electric bulb.

Car
1885

Karl Benz, Gottlieb Daimler, Émile Levassor

The first car, the Motorwagen, was built in 1885 by German engineer Karl Benz. It was a three-wheeler with a single-cylinder engine. Soon Benz and others were making four-wheeled cars. In 1889, Gottlieb Daimler produced one with four gears. But it was French engineer Émile Levassor who produced the first car with its engine at the front, driving the rear wheels through a clutch and gearbox. His 1891 model was the forerunner of the cars we drive today.

Monotype typesetting system
1885

Tolbert Lanston

One of the slowest operations in traditional printing was setting up type. By the 1880s several inventors were trying to mechanize the process. First to succeed was US inventor Tolbert Lanston. His Monotype system of 1885 had a keyboard and a machine for casting type from molten metal. The caster followed instructions created by the keyboard, delivering type almost ready to print. Monotype dominated book printing for more than 70 years.

Petrol engine
1885

Gottlieb Daimler, Wilhelm Maybach

The petrol engine evolved from engines that ran on gas. These could not run on liquid fuel, so the carburettor, which turns petrol into a mist and mixes it with air, was an essential component of a petrol engine. By 1885, German engineers Gottlieb Daimler and Wilhelm Maybach had designed an effective carburettor. They used it in a new high-speed engine, which was the first true petrol engine and the forerunner of those that power most cars today.

Rabies vaccine
1885

Louis Pasteur

Rabies is an infection of the nervous system, which people can catch from animal bites, and usually kills if not caught in time. The French biologist Louis Pasteur developed the first vaccine against rabies by heating tissue from infected animals to create a weakened virus. On 6 July, 1885, he gave a dramatic demonstration of its power by vaccinating a boy who had been bitten by a dog with rabies. The boy lived.

Steering column and indicator

Chain drive to the wheels

CAR *This Benz car, made in 1888, was sold by Emile Roger, Benz's agent in Paris. It had a tubular metal frame, like a bicycle, and bodywork based on horse-drawn vehicles. The engine was at the rear, below the driver's seat.*

1884 The London Society for the Prevention of Cruelty to Children is founded following the passing of a cruelty law. Later, it will link with other societies to form the National Society for the Prevention of Cruelty to Children (NSPCC).

1884 The world system of standard time zones is established. Delegates from 27 nations meet in Washington D.C. to consider proposals about time zones made in the 1870s by Canadian railway planner and engineer Sir Sandford Fleming.

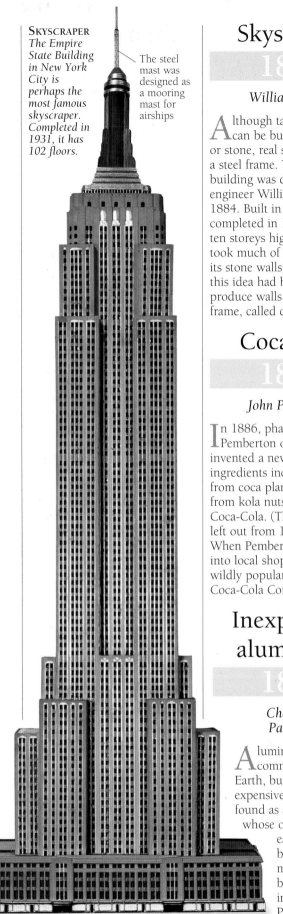

Skyscraper
1885

William Jenney

Although tall buildings can be built with brick or stone, real skyscrapers need a steel frame. The first such building was designed by US engineer William Jenney in 1884. Built in Chicago, it was completed in 1885 and was ten storeys high. Its steel frame took much of the weight of its stone walls. By the 1930s, this idea had been extended to produce walls hung from the frame, called curtain walls.

Coca-Cola
1886

John Pemberton

In 1886, pharmacist John Pemberton of Atlanta, USA, invented a new drink. Its ingredients included cocaine from coca plants and caffeine from kola nuts, so he called it Coca-Cola. (The cocaine was left out from 1903 onwards.) When Pemberton put the drink into local shops, it became wildly popular. By 1892 the Coca-Cola Company was born.

Inexpensive aluminium
1886

Charles Hall, Paul Héroult

Aluminium is the most common metal on Earth, but was once too expensive to use. It is found as aluminium oxide, whose oxygen cannot easily be removed by chemical means. In 1886, both Charles Hall in the USA and Paul Héroult in France dissolved aluminium oxide in molten cryolite (sodium aluminium fluoride) and used electricity to drag the aluminium and oxygen apart. The Hall-Héroult process has transformed aluminium from an exotic curiosity to the stuff of jumbo jets.

Recording on wax
1886

Chichester Bell, Charles Tainter

The first sound recordings were made on foil wrapped around a grooved cylinder. A needle, moving up and down, created "hills and dales" in the shape of the sound waves. These recordings were fragile and inaccurate. In 1886, US inventors Chichester Bell and Charles Tainter patented a machine called the Graphophone, which recorded on waxed cardboard cylinders. The wax, together with a recording stylus that made a v-shaped groove, gave better sound. They were soon in use for all recordings.

Function of the ear's semicircular canals
1886

Marie Flourens, Yves Delage

The semicircular canals of the inner ear are three fluid-filled tubes joined together at right angles. In 1824, French biologist Marie Flourens noticed that pigeons moved strangely after a tube was cut. In 1886, another French biologist, Yves Delage, realized what was happening. Moving the head moves the tubes, but the liquid inside lags behind. Hairs in the tubes detect the relative movement and tell the brain which way the head is moving.

Linotype typesetting machine
1886

Ottmar Mergenthaler

Until the 1970s, most newspapers were set in type using a machine invented by German-US engineer Ottmar Mergenthaler in 1886. The Linotype machine used molten metal, but instead of making individual letters like the Monotype machine (✳ *see* **page 157**), it produced whole lines of type – hence the name. Newspaper printers liked it because it was quick to use and needed only one operator.

Steam sterilization of surgical instruments
1886

Ernst von Bergmann

Once surgeons realized that infections were caused by germs (✳ *see* **page 146**), they had to decide what to do about them. Should they kill them with antiseptics or try to keep them out of the operating theatre from the start? Today, the second approach is normal practice. It was pioneered by German surgeon Ernst von Bergmann in 1886. He was the first person to sterilize instruments and dressings with steam. He later made everything else used in operations as germ-free as possible.

1886 French sculptor Auguste Rodin creates the first version of what will be one of his best known works, *The Kiss*. Originally placed in a set of doors called *The Gates of Hell*, it is based on a scene from Dante's *Divine Comedy*.

1886 US president Grover Cleveland accepts one of the world's most famous symbols, the Statue of Liberty, as a gift from the people of France. Marking the centenary of US independence, it stands 93.5 m (306 ft 8 in) high.

Comptometer
1887

Dorr E. Felt

The Comptometer was one of two calculating machines used in accounting offices from the late 19th to the mid 20th century. While its rival, the Burroughs machine (✳ *see* **page 156**), could produce a printed record, the Comptometer was faster. Invented by US engineer Dorr E. Felt, it was first used in 1887. As with the Burroughs machine, numbers were entered using columns of keys – one for units, one for tens, and so on. The result was displayed in a set of windows for clerks to copy out by hand.

Esperanto
1887

Ludwik Zamenhof

International cooperation is hampered by the fact that people in different countries speak different languages. Many people have tried to solve this problem by inventing a universal language. The only one that has had any success is Esperanto, invented in 1887 by Polish oculist Ludwik Zamenhof. Based on European languages, it has simple, regular rules. Some of these seem strange to English-speakers: plural nouns demand plural adjectives, for instance. Despite this, more than 100,000 people can speak it.

Fractal curve
1887

Giuseppe Peano

A fractal curve is a wiggly line that looks the same however much it is magnified. An example is the coast of a country, which looks just as wiggly on a small-scale map as on the actual shore where sand meets sea. The first fractal curves were described by Italian mathematician Giuseppe Peano, in 1887. They were viewed as a mere curiosity until the 1970s, when Polish mathematician Benoit Mandelbrot investigated them in more detail. He used them to create some stunning computer graphics.

Gramophone
1887

Emile Berliner

The first recording machines made cylindrical records. In 1887, German engineer Emile Berliner, working in the USA, came up with a better idea – discs. He coated metal with wax, recorded sound by cutting through the wax, then etched the metal to make a permanent record. The cutter moved from side to side, not up and down as in earlier machines. On playback, the needle followed this "lateral-cut" groove more faithfully, giving better reproduction. More importantly, discs could be stamped out by the thousand, making Berliner's Gramophone the best choice for music lovers.

Horn channelled the sounds from the disc

Handle was used to keep the turntable moving round

Disc was played on a turntable

Steel needle was lowered on to the disc

Drive belt

GRAMOPHONE *Early Berliner gramophones had no motor, so listeners had to turn a handle. The discs were the same size as a CD, but played for only about a minute.*

1886 Scottish writer Robert Louis Stevenson publishes *The Strange Case of Dr Jekyll and Mr Hyde*, about a doctor who can turn into a fiend. A "Jekyll and Hyde" will come to mean anyone with two sides to their character.

1887 Two more classic fictional characters are born when Scottish writer Sir Arthur Conan Doyle writes *A Study in Scarlet* featuring ace detective Sherlock Holmes and his friend Dr Watson. The story will be followed by many others.

MAIL ORDER *The Sears, Roebuck catalogue became a part of the American way of life, allowing people in rural areas to enjoy the fruits of the nation's prosperity.*

Mail order
1887

*Richard Sears,
Alvah Roebuck*

Richard Sears thought up mail order while working for a US railway company. Acquiring some unwanted watches, he sold them by post to other railway workers. He used the profits to set up a company, which by 1887 had produced the first mail-order catalogue. He later formed a new company with repairman Alvah Roebuck. By 1894, the Sears, Roebuck catalogue was 507 pages thick.

High-voltage power transmission
1887

Sebastian de Ferranti

In the 1880s there were many rival electricity systems. But British engineer Sebastian de Ferranti could see the future. Electricity would be generated in big power stations outside cities, not little ones inside them, and transmitted at high voltage. In 1887, he designed a giant power station at Deptford, just outside London, and cables that could take 10,000 volts. The station's directors pushed him out in 1891, and it was not completed to his plan. But Ferranti was right: high-voltage transmission is universal today.

Steam tricycle
1887

Leon Serpollet

At one time it looked as though steam, not petrol, might be best for motor vehicles. Several inventors designed steam tricycles in the 1880s. In 1887, French engineer Leon Serpollet overcame their chief problem with a boiler that produced instant steam. He built this into a tricycle, then showed it off by driving it 451 km (282 miles) from Paris to Lyon. Later, he built steam cars. In 1903, one reached 130 km/h (80 mph).

Pneumatic tyre
1888

*Robert Thomson,
John Dunlop*

British inventor Robert Thomson patented air-filled leather tyres in 1845, but these were never as popular as solid rubber ones. The first successful pneumatic tyre was patented in 1888 by Scottish vet John Dunlop, after he experimented with rubber tubing on the wheels of his son's tricycle. The finished product was protected by a canvas cover. Dunlop's tyre was ideal for bicycles, and later became essential for cars.

Kodak camera
1888

George Eastman

Until 1888, photography was difficult. Cameras were complicated, and users had to process their own pictures. US businessman George Eastman changed that with his Kodak camera. It was simple to use and came ready loaded with film. After use, the camera went back to Eastman, who returned it, reloaded, along with the pictures. With his slogan "You press the button, we do the rest", Eastman became a rich man.

Radio waves
1888

*James Clerk Maxwell,
Heinrich Hertz*

In 1864, Scottish physicist James Clerk Maxwell predicted the existence of electromagnetic waves moving at the speed of light. German physicist Heinrich Hertz wanted to generate such waves electrically and see if they

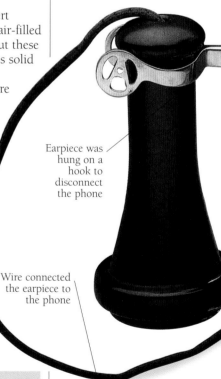

Earpiece was hung on a hook to disconnect the phone

Wire connected the earpiece to the phone

AUTOMATIC TELEPHONE EXCHANGE *This 1905 phone was designed for use with a Strowger exchange. Automatic dialling was available for local calls only.*

1888 Dutch painter Vincent van Gogh cracks under the strain of living with French painter Paul Gauguin in the south of France. He cuts off part of his left ear and later paints a portrait of himself with his head bandaged.

1889 A baby is born in the town of Branau, 50 km (30 miles) north of Salzburg, Austria. His father's surname, earlier changed from Schicklgruber, is Hitler. The baby is named Adolf. Fifty years on, he will plunge the world into war.

behaved like light, to find out if light itself was electromagnetic. He found that electrical sparks produced waves that could be focused on to a distant loop of wire, producing more sparks. He had discovered radio waves. Further experiments showed that they did behave like light. Satisfied with these discoveries, complete by 1888, Hertz made no further use of them.

Automatic telephone exchange
1889
Almon B. Strowger

Telephone exchanges are needed to connect phones to each other. At first, connections were made by operators pushing plugs into sockets. Then, in 1889, Kansas City funeral director Almon B. Strowger, fed up with his operator diverting calls to a rival, devised the first successful automatic telephone switch. Callers could control it from their own phone by sending groups of electrical pulses down the line. The first automatic exchange opened at La Porte, Indiana, in 1892. At first, callers generated the control pulses by repeatedly pushing a button. Later, the more convenient rotary dial mechanism made this process automatic too. (*See also* **Getting connected**.)

Tabulating machine
1889
Herman Hollerith

As the population of the USA grew, classifying the people took longer. Engineer Herman Hollerith decided to mechanize the 1890 census. Citizens were recorded as holes punched in a card. Hollerith's "tabulating" machines then sorted and counted the cards at speed.

GETTING CONNECTED

TELEPHONES WOULD NOT WORK without exchanges. Your phone would have to be permanently connected to every other phone in the world, just in case you wanted to call it. In reality, connections are set up only when they are needed, by routing a call through a number of switches that connect you first to the exchange that handles the phone you want, then to that particular phone.

An operator on a telephone exchange switchboard connects callers to the number they ask for.

CALLING THE OPERATOR
Before automatic exchanges, all calls were connected by operators. To make a call, you would lift the receiver and, on some systems, alert the operator by turning a handle. You would then ask for the number you wanted and the operator would make the connection by plugging your line into a switchboard.

STROWGER'S SYSTEM
Strowger's basic idea was a remote-controlled switch that could connect one phone to any of several others. It was operated by electric pulses from the user's telephone line. Electromagnets and ratchets moved a connector to one of ten rows of contacts, then along the selected row to reach the exact phone required.

1889 French engineer Gustave Eiffel builds a spectacular iron tower for the Paris World's Fair. It beats 100 other entries in a competition, pushing technology to its limits. Not everyone likes it, but it will become the emblem of Paris.

1889 In November, US investigative journalist Nellie Bly sets out to beat Jules Verne's fictional hero Phileas Fogg and travel around the world in less than 80 days. She does it in 72 days, 6 hours, 11 minutes, and 14 seconds.

Halftone screen
1890
Max Levy, Louis Levy

Black-and-white photos, with all their tones of grey, are printed by the halftone process. This turns them into dots – large ones in dark areas, small ones in paler areas. In the original process, the dots were made by copying the photo with a camera that had a screen carrying criss-cross lines just in front of the film. The first successful halftone screen was made in 1890 by US inventors Max and Louis Levy. They cemented together two sheets of glass, each ruled with straight lines. Screens like this were in use until the 1970s.

Tetanus immunization
1890
Emil Behring, Kitasato Shibasaburo

Tetanus, or lockjaw, is an infection caused by germs in soil. These can breed inside a cut, producing poisons that make muscles contract and may cause death. In 1890, German and Japanese bacteriologists Emil Behring and Kitasato Shibasaburo found they could protect animals from tetanus by injecting serum from another infected animal. Today, most people in the West receive

routine immunization with tetanus vaccine. If they suffer a deep, dirty cut, they will need only a booster dose to ensure continued protection.

TETANUS IMMUNIZATION *Tetanus vaccine, or toxoid, contains the poison produced by tetanus germs, made safe by heat or chemicals.*

Steam-powered aeroplane
1890
Clément Ader

French engineer Clément Ader was very nearly the first person to fly a plane. His steam-powered aircraft, the *Eole*, managed a longer flight than the more famous Wright brothers (✱ see **page 175**), but it didn't quite count. On 9 October, 1890, Ader managed a 50 m (160 ft) "flight" near Paris, but the machine wasn't really flying because it wasn't under control. The experiment proved that a steam engine was just too heavy for flight.

Surgical gloves
1890
William Halsted

By the 1880s, many surgeons were convinced that germs were a threat to their patients. Sterilization and antiseptics could help, but what about the surgeon's hands? They were a source of infection, even when scrubbed, but could not be replaced by instruments. US surgeon William Halsted found the answer in 1890: he invented the thin rubber gloves that all surgeons wear today.

Gaslight photographic paper
1891
Leo Baekeland

In the 1880s, photographers made prints by daylight. This restricted their hours of work. The first photographic paper that worked in artificial light – usually gaslight – was invented by Belgian-US chemist Leo Baekeland in 1891. He sold his Velox paper to George Eastman in 1898, helping to make photography affordable for all.

Long-distance telephone cable
1892
Oliver Heaviside, Michael Pupin

Early long-distance telephone calls suffered from blurring and distortion, an effect already noticed on telegraph cables. It could make it impossible to understand what someone was saying. Scientists were baffled until British telegraph engineer Oliver Heaviside invented a new mathematical method that showed where the problem lay. He published his results in 1892, and in 1900 US physicist Michael Pupin used them to improve long-distance lines by adding special coils at regular intervals.

Vacuum bottle
1892
James Dewar

Scottish physicist James (later Sir James) Dewar was one of the first to make oxygen so cold that it turned into a liquid. But he had storage problems, because at −183°C oxygen turns back to gas. So he invented a special bottle, the Dewar flask. It was made of two layers of glass, silvered like a mirror and with a vacuum between them. Infra-red radiation, or radiant heat, was reflected from the silvering, while the vacuum stopped heat being carried in through air currents.

Double walls greatly reduce heat transfer by air currents

VACUUM BOTTLE *Dewar flasks can be made of metal as well as glass. This model of a metal flask has been cut open to reveal its double wall. Metal flasks are not easy to make, but have the advantage of being stronger and safer than glass flasks.*

1890 Norwegian dramatist Henrik Ibsen challenges accepted attitudes to women with his realistic play *Hedda Gabler*. Ignoring the conventions of 19th-century drama, Ibsen creates a powerful new form of theatre.

1891 New York City opens a new concert hall, financed by industrialist Andrew Carnegie. Illustrious Russian composer Tchaikowsky is guest conductor during its first week. Carnegie Hall will still be there in the 21st century.

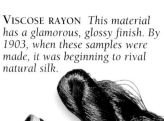

MOVING PICTURE *Using a Kinetoscope was nothing like going to the cinema. Peering through the eyepiece, the viewer saw a moving image that lasted about as long as a modern TV commercial.*

Viscose rayon
1892

Charles Cross, Edward Bevan, Clayton Beadle

The first artificial silk was expensive because it was made by a slow, dangerous method (✳ see **page 156**). In 1892, three British chemists, Charles Cross, Edward Bevan, and Clayton Beadle, invented the viscose process. Cellulose is converted into non-flammable cellulose xanthate, which is dissolved in caustic soda to form a yellow, treacly liquid. This is squirted through nozzles and reacts with other chemicals to make a silky artificial fibre called viscose rayon.

Viruses
1892

Dmitry Ivanovsky, Martinus Beijerinck

A virus is an infectious particle that can multiply only inside a living cell. It is basically just a set of genes wrapped in a protective coating. It takes over a plant or animal cell, forcing it to make copies of the invader. The first scientist to realize that bacteria were not the only infective agents was Russian micro-biologist Dmitry Ivanovsky. He published a paper on a virus infection of tobacco plants in 1892. Dutch botanist Martinus

Beijerinck did similar work in 1898. Both discovered that viruses were far smaller than bacteria and invisible under an ordinary microscope.

Moving picture
1893

William Dickson, Thomas Edison

It is not clear who invented movies. A young US engineer, William Dickson, who worked for Thomas Edison, has a good claim. Edison thought that phonograph listeners might like something to watch, and asked Dickson to provide it. Dickson devised a machine, the Kinetograph, which took 40 pictures each second on a long strip of film. The film was then viewed, by one person at a time, in another machine, the Kinetoscope. It held only 15 m (50 ft) of film, so a movie lasted only 20 seconds.

Film passed through in a continuous loop

1892 In the USA, a five-month struggle between a big trade union and bosses of the steel industry starts in Homestead, Pennsylvania, after workers' wages are cut. The strike ends violently with several deaths.

1893 Norwegian painter Edvard Munch produces *The Scream*, a painting that conveys intense feelings of anxiety and emotional torment. It will become one of the most famous examples of the style known as expressionism.

163

Zip fastener
1893

*Whitcomb Judson,
Gideon Sundback*

Chicago engineer Whitcomb Judson got tired of lacing up his boots, and invented a fastener that hooked them up with one pull. He patented it in 1893, but it tended to come unhooked. Swedish engineer Gideon Sundback realized that the hooks were the problem. By 1914 he had developed the modern fastener, with cups, not hooks, locking together. It was used in 1923 for a boot called the Zipper, and the name stuck.

Bubonic plague agent
1894

*Kitasato Shibasaburo,
Alexandre Yersin*

Bubonic plague is a deadly disease carried by rat fleas. It has killed millions in repeated epidemics. Thanks to the discoveries of Japanese and Swiss bacteriologists Kitasato Shibasaburo and Alexandre Yersin in 1894, we now know that it is caused by a type of germ known as a bacillus. It is usually called *Yersinia pestis* in honour of Yersin's contribution.

Phototypesetting
1894

Eugene Porzolt

Photography offers an alternative to metal type. Letters can be projected on to film. The first phototypesetting machine, designed in 1894 by Hungarian engineer Eugene Porzolt, was a failure. But from the 1960s, with computers controlling the process, phototypesetting became the way most words got printed. Computers now store letter shapes in digital form. So, like metal type, phototypesetting itself is now a thing of the past.

Radio communication
1894

Guglielmo Marconi

Italian inventor Guglielmo Marconi started experimenting with radio waves in 1894, when he was only 19. Others, such as the British and Russian physicists Oliver Lodge and Alexander Popov, did the same. But it was Marconi who really got radio going. Within a year he was sending signals 2 km (1.25 miles). By 1896 he was in Britain and had got the world's first radio patent. After much further development, it was Marconi's "wireless telegraph" that sent the distress signals from the sinking ship *Titanic* in 1912.

Argon
1894

*Lord Rayleigh,
William Ramsay*

Argon is known as an inert gas because it does not react chemically. It is used in light bulbs because it makes the filament last longer. It was discovered by British physicist Lord Rayleigh, who noticed that nitrogen from air was denser than nitrogen from chemicals. Both he and British chemist William (later Sir William) Ramsay thought that atmospheric nitrogen might be contaminated with an unknown, heavier gas. They both found it in 1894. Its name "argon" is Greek for "inactive".

Cinema
1895

*Auguste Lumière,
Louis Lumière*

Movies did not become a truly theatrical experience until French brothers Auguste and Louis Lumière invented the Cinématographe, the first system that could show an audience a moving picture that ran for several minutes. Their machine acted as both camera and projector. It gave its first public performance on 28 December, 1895, in Paris. The programme of 12 short films, including one showing Lumière factory workers, caused a sensation.

Helium on Earth
1895

William Ramsay

Helium, the gas that is used to fill party balloons, was first found on Earth by William Ramsay in 1895. He heated a mineral called cleveite, which contains uranium, and discovered that it gave off a gas. The gas's spectrum contained a yellow line matching that of helium in the Sun, which proved its identity. Swedish chemists Nils Langlet and Per Cleve also found the gas at about the same time. Later, Ramsay and British chemist Frederick Soddy discovered that helium is produced whenever radioactive elements decay.

1893 On 23 December, Richard Strauss conducts the first performance of German composer Engelbert

Humperdinck's tuneful opera *Hansel and Gretel*. The story, by Humperdinck's sister Adelheid, is based on a well known folk tale.

1894 London's Tower Bridge, started in 1886, finally opens. Built by Sir Horace Jones and Sir John Wolfe

Barry, and powered by steam, it is London's only moving bridge. Its twin towers will become a well known symbol of the city.

164

Liquid air

1895

Carl von Linde

If air is made cold enough, it turns into a liquid. The drop in temperature is produced by compressing air, letting it cool, then letting it expand so that it cools still further. The first to do this on a large scale was German engineer Carl von Linde.

His system, invented in 1895, produced a continuous stream of liquid air. He later distilled air to produce liquid nitrogen, used as a coolant, and liquid oxygen, used in steel making.

Wheel guided the film into the mechanism

Rotating shutter has red, green, and blue apertures to give the film colour

CINEMA *The early movie camera (left) was hand-cranked. The projector (right) could show films in colour.*

Lenses for red, green, and blue images

Handle was turned to show the film

Film wound on to a spool

X-rays

1895

Wilhelm Röntgen

German physicist Wilhelm Röntgen discovered X-rays in 1895 while he was investigating cathode rays (electrical discharges inside a tube containing very little air). He noticed that when the tube was working, some crystals lying nearby glowed, even though the tube was shielded so that no light could escape from it. He worked out that the cathode rays, hitting the glass of the tube, were producing other rays that made the crystals glow. He did some further experiments, which showed that the rays could pass through solid objects and affect photographic plates. This led him to make the first ever X-ray picture. Röntgen was at first not sure that he should announce his discovery. He was worried that other scientists might not believe him. But soon everyone was talking about the new rays that made hidden things visible.

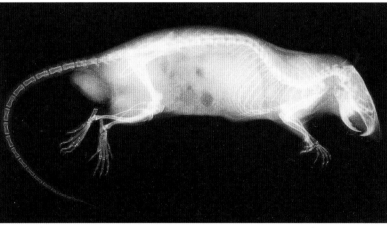

X-RAYS *Small animals like this rat made good subjects for early experimenters with X-rays. For the first time, their skeletons could be seen without dissection.*

Radiation from uranium

1896

Henri Becquerel

French physicist Henri Becquerel wanted to see if crystals that glowed after exposure to sunlight gave out X-rays. In 1896, he found that certain uranium salts affected a wrapped-up photographic plate when placed on it in sunlight. Becquerel thought that sunlight may have made the crystals produce X-rays, which went through the wrapping. Then he discovered that the experiment worked in the dark. The crystals gave out penetrating radiation all by themselves.

1895 In April, the song *Waltzing Matilda*, by "Banjo" Paterson, is performed in Winton, Queensland, Australia, for the first time. Its title means "carrying a bag of belongings, or swag", and it tells the story of a wandering labourer, or swagman.

1896 The ancient Greek Olympic Games are revived in Athens by Pierre Fredi, Baron de Coubertin. Fourteen nations take part in the all-male competition. It includes a new event, the marathon, which is won by a Greek shepherd.

Surgical mask

1896

Johannes von Mikulicz-Radecki

With sterilization of instruments, and surgical gloves in frequent use, one of the last sources of infection in the operating theatre was the surgeon's own breath. In 1896, a gifted Polish surgeon working in Germany, Johannes von Mikulicz-Radecki, blocked up this loophole by placing gauze over his mouth to form the first surgical mask.

Toothpaste in a tube

1896

William Colgate

Toothpaste existed in the 19th century, but was packaged in jars. The first person to put it in a tube was US dentist Washington Sheffield. His Creme Dentifrice of 1892 was not very popular and it was eclipsed four years later with the marketing of Colgate Ribbon Dental Cream by New York soap and candle maker William Colgate. He changed the shape of the tube nozzle, and described the result with the successful slogan "Comes out a ribbon, lies flat on the brush".

Sphygmomano-meter

1896

Scipione Riva-Rocci

The usual instrument for measuring blood pressure, the sphygmomanometer, was invented in 1896 by Scipione Riva-Rocci, an Italian children's doctor. A cuff around the arm is inflated until the blood stops flowing. The air pressure is then reduced until the flow just starts again, indicating the maximum blood pressure.

Doctors now listen to the flow with a stethoscope, a refinement added in 1905 by Russian surgeon N. S. Korotkoff. This allows them to measure the minimum pressure as well.

SPHYGMOMANO-METER *This 1905 instrument is quite like those used today. The rubber bulb pumps air into the arm cuff.*

Blood pressure reading taken from here

Cathode ray oscilloscope

1897

Ferdinand Braun

Electricity is invisible, so the cathode ray oscilloscope, which displays electrical signals on a screen, is a valuable tool. It was invented in 1897 by German physicist Ferdinand Braun. He took the still-experimental cathode ray tube (a glass tube containing very little air, in which a negative electrode, or cathode, gives off electrically charged "rays") and added magnetic coils to move the rays horizontally and vertically in response to signals. In this way Braun managed to get the rays to draw patterns on a screen inside the tube.

Exhaust casing received the spent steam

Diesel engine

1897

Rudolf Diesel

In 1892, German engineer Rudolf Diesel patented an engine that gave more power for less fuel. It compressed its fuel and air to a much higher pressure than a petrol engine, making it so hot that it burned without the aid of a spark. In 1897, he built a fully developed engine, which

TOOTHPASTE IN A TUBE *People who were accustomed to toothpaste from a jar seem to have had trouble with it when it came out of a tube, but Colgate's toothpaste behaved itself.*

1896
Popular British newspaper the *Daily Mail* is founded by media tycoon Alfred Harmsworth. It includes features such as a women's column, competitions, and stories, and will soon change the nature of newspaper publishing.

1897
Vampires get a boost from British writer Bram Stoker's horror novel *Dracula*. He bases it on the ancient Slavic religious belief that a buried body that does not decompose will leave its grave at night to drink human blood.

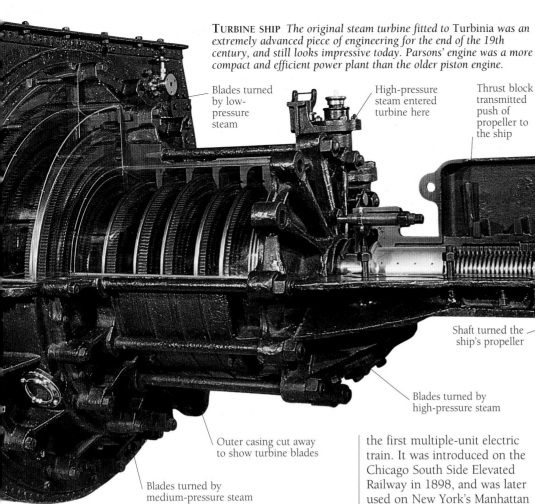

TURBINE SHIP *The original steam turbine fitted to* Turbinia *was an extremely advanced piece of engineering for the end of the 19th century, and still looks impressive today. Parsons' engine was a more compact and efficient power plant than the older piston engine.*

Blades turned by low-pressure steam

High-pressure steam entered turbine here

Thrust block transmitted push of propeller to the ship

Shaft turned the ship's propeller

Blades turned by high-pressure steam

Outer casing cut away to show turbine blades

Blades turned by medium-pressure steam

Turbine ship
1897
Charles Parsons

Steam ships changed for ever when British engineer Charles (later Sir Charles) Parsons launched *Turbinia*, the first ship powered by his steam turbine. In 1897, he demonstrated it to the Royal Navy near Portsmouth, England. Navy ships were powered by piston engines, and *Turbinia* made them look ridiculous as it darted among them at the record speed of 34 knots (69 km/h or 43 mph). Tests in other ships confirmed the turbine's superiority.

delivered 25 horsepower from a single cylinder. Diesel engines can be expensive, heavy, and noisy, but are unbeatable where fuel consumption really counts.

Electron
1897
J. J. Thomson

British physicist J. J. (later Sir J. J.) Thomson was the first person to show that atoms contain smaller particles. He studied cathode rays and, by subjecting the rays to electric and magnetic fields, he showed in 1897 that they consisted of negatively charged particles. Thomson discovered that it made no difference what materials he used, and he concluded that the particles existed in everything. He believed that they were lighter

and could move faster than any atom, and realized that he had found something new. We now call the particles electrons.

Multiple-unit electric train
1897
Frank Sprague

Instead of one powerful locomotive at the front, many electric trains have smaller driving motors at several points along their length. This gives better acceleration and more passenger space, but the motors have to work together so that all the coaches speed up and slow down at the same rate. In 1897, US engineer Frank Sprague managed to control separate motors in this way, and used them in

the first multiple-unit electric train. It was introduced on the Chicago South Side Elevated Railway in 1898, and was later used on New York's Manhattan Elevated Railway.

Transmission of malaria by mosquito
1897
Ronald Ross

Malaria is a disease caused by tiny parasites living in the blood. Patients suffer recurrent chills and sweats. Nobody knew how the parasites got there until British bacteriologist Ronald (later Sir Ronald) Ross studied infected birds in India. He proved in 1897 that the parasites are carried by mosquitoes and injected when they bite. A year later three Italian scientists showed that only one kind of mosquito, the *Anopheles*, gives malaria to humans.

Conditioned reflex
1898
Ivan Pavlov

A reflex is an automatic response, such as pulling a hand away from a hot object. In 1898, Russian scientist Ivan Pavlov started experiments that led him to discover a more complicated kind of reflex. When investigating digestion in dogs, he found that the sound of food being prepared made their mouths water. He later found he could train them to salivate whenever a bell was sounded. Pavlov called this kind of reflex conditional, because it only happened after learning, but it is now usually called a conditioned reflex.

1897 The world's first mass marathon is run in the USA from Hopkinton, Massachusetts, to Boston – just over 42 km (26 miles). It will be repeated every April, but women will not be allowed to compete for another 75 years.

1898 Canadian adventurer Joshua Slocum reaches Newport on the USA's north-east coast to become the first person to sail around the world single-handed. He set out from Boston in a 95-year-old boat more than three years earlier.

Magnetic recording
1898

Valdemar Poulsen

Danish telephone engineer Valdemar Poulsen was worried by one obvious defect of the telephone. Unlike the telegraph, it didn't work without someone there to answer it. So in 1898 he invented the first telephone answering machine, the Telegraphone. To do so, he had to invent a totally new technology – magnetic recording. His machine recorded telephone messages on a reel of thin steel wire, and could also be used for dictation. (✳ *See also* **Recording with magnetism**.)

Polonium
1898

Marie Curie, Pierre Curie

Polonium is a very rare element. Highly radioactive, it can be used to discharge unwanted static electricity. The best source is pitchblende, but 1000 tonnes of this yield only 40 mg of polonium. Polonium was the first element to be revealed by its radioactivity, and it was discovered by radioactivity pioneers Marie and Pierre Curie in 1898. They called it polonium after Marie's native country, Poland.

ASPIRIN *Soluble aspirin from Bayer is seen here in its original packaging.*

Radium
1898

Marie Curie, Pierre Curie

See **pages 170–171** for the story of how Marie and Pierre Curie discovered radium and made radiotherapy possible.

Paper-clip
1899

William Middlebrook

The most common kind of paper-clip seems to have come from nowhere. It is known as the Gem clip, and may have been made first by an English company called Gem. One inventor who was involved, US engineer William Middlebrook, patented a paper-clip-making machine in 1899. The patent drawings show it making a Gem.

Aspirin
1899

Felix Hoffman

Other drugs have partly replaced aspirin as a pain-killer, but it is still used for treating strokes and heart attacks. Chemically related to a plant extract, salicylic acid, it was first made by German chemist Felix Hoffman, whose father may have taken the acid for rheumatism. The compound was first marketed by the German company Bayer in 1899.

RIGID AIRSHIP *Airships like this were used by the Royal Naval Air Service in the First World War.*

Rudder steered the airship left or right

Cabin for the crew was called a gondola

Escalator
1900

George Wheeler, Charles Seeberger

The first escalator, invented by US engineer Jesse Reno, was just a sloping, moving walkway with a grooved tread to stop passengers slipping. It wasn't even called an escalator. This name was used by US engineer Charles Seeberger to describe a design with folding steps originally invented by George Wheeler. Seeberger joined the Otis Elevator Company, which exhibited the escalator at the 1900 Paris Exposition. Later, the company added the grooved tread from Reno's design to complete the escalator we know today.

Fingerprinting
1900

Francis Galton, Edward Henry

Fingerprints are a good way of tracking down criminals, but they only work because there is a way of classifying them. Without this, a new print could not be compared with those on record. British scientist Francis (later Sir Francis) Galton, having confirmed that every fingerprint is different, devised a basic classification. Police officer Edward (later Sir Edward) Henry developed this into the system widely used today. It was published in 1900. Two years later, fingerprints made their first appearance in court.

1899 What will become one of the most played piano pieces of all time, *Maple Leaf Rag*, is published in Missouri by US composer and pianist Scott Joplin. A later attempt by Joplin to break into opera will prove unsuccessful.

1899 Three years of war begin in South Africa when the Boers (descendants of the original Dutch settlers), led by Paul Kruger, start fighting with the British. Resentment had built up over the huge influx of Britons seeking gold there.

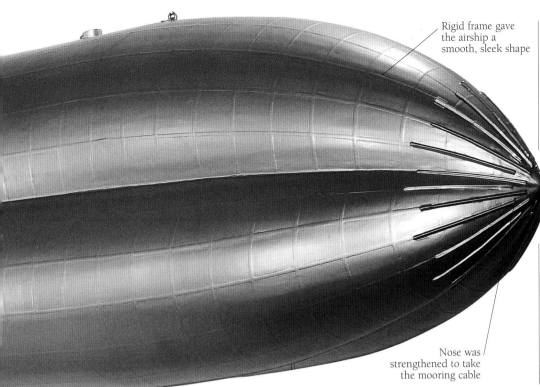

Rigid frame gave
the airship a
smooth, sleek shape

Nose was
strengthened to take
the mooring cable

Propellers
moved the
airship forwards

Rigid airship
1900

Ferdinand von Zeppelin

The first airships were just elongated balloons with an engine and passenger compartment. In 1900, German general Count Ferdinand von Zeppelin built the first airship with a rigid frame. Its lifting gas was held in separate gas bags inside the frame, allowing a more aerodynamic shape. Zeppelins, as they became known, were used as bombers in the First World War. After this they carried passengers, until public confidence was destroyed in 1937 when the *Hindenburg* caught fire in a dramatic accident, killing 35 passengers.

Quantum theory
1900

Max Planck

In 1900, physicists had some problems. One was that the light from red-hot objects was not of the expected colour. German physicist Max Planck found he could predict the colour correctly by assuming that energy was radiated only in multiples of a fixed amount, or quantum. This also explained why the energy of electrons ejected from metals by light depended on the colour, not the brightness, of the light. Over the next 30 years, quantum theory allowed Niels Bohr, Erwin Schrödinger, Werner Heisenberg, and others to develop a new view of the world in which matter and energy could be both waves and particles (❋ *see* **page 190**). This has transformed physics.

RECORDING WITH MAGNETISM

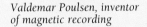

RECORDINGS ON WAX WERE FRAGILE and quickly wore out. The alternative, magnetic recording, also had problems, including noise and distortion. Both were eventually conquered. Even before this, magnetic recording proved ideal for recording computer data and television pictures. Its use with computers has more recently developed into digital magnetic recording, which produces the near-perfect tapes used to make CDs.

Valdemar Poulsen, inventor of magnetic recording

FROM METAL TO PLASTIC
Early magnetic recordings were made on steel wire or tape. During the Second World War, the first modern recorder, the Magnetophon, was developed by AEG and BASF in Germany. Like all later machines, it used coated plastic tape.

VIDEO RECORDING
Video signals contain very high frequencies. An ordinary recorder would need to run very fast to record these. Video recorders, invented in 1956, have a recording head that scans the tape at a high enough speed to record these frequencies.

Ampex VR1000 video recorder from about 1956

DIGITAL RECORDING
Since about 1950, computers have used magnetic recording for storing data. Unlike sound, data can be recorded without errors. Sound converted into digital form before recording gives a perfection unknown to the pioneers.

1900 China sees the end of a long campaign against foreigners in the country, led by a secret martial arts society known as the Boxers. After a year of terrorism, Western troops finally rescue besieged foreigners from Beijing.

1900 US tennis player Dwight F. Davis donates a cup to be awarded at an annual international lawn-tennis tournament for men. It will become known as the Davis Cup. Intended for amateurs, it will later become professional.

PARTNERS IN DISCOVERY

*Marie and Pierre Curie discover radium and
make radiotherapy possible*

HAPPY FAMILY
Marie and Pierre Curie were
devoted to each other and their
children as well as to science.
They are seen here in 1904,
two years before Pierre's
tragic death, with their
daughter Irene, who
was then aged seven.

*Quadrant
electrometer
built by
Pierre
Curie*

Ionization
chamber

*Glass flask used
by Marie Curie*

*Ionization
chamber made
by Pierre Curie*

MEASURING RADIATION
The Curies had to build most
of their research equipment
for themselves. Radiation can
make air conduct electricity,
and Pierre developed several
highly sensitive measuring
instruments that made use
of this effect.

In 1891, Marie Sklodowska arrived in Paris, aged 23. She had done well at school in Poland and now, after eight years as a governess, she had saved enough money for university. She registered at the Sorbonne, the university in Paris, and became a student, studying physical science and mathematics.

By 1894, Marie had her degree. Something else important happened that year, too. She met Professor Pierre Curie, and in 1895 they got married, forming one of science's most fruitful partnerships.

Marie decided to research the uranium radiation recently discovered by Henri Becquerel. She studied pitchblende, a mineral containing uranium, and found that it produced more radiation than the uranium alone could account for. It clearly contained something more "radioactive", as she called it, than uranium. With Pierre, she dissolved pitchblende in chemicals to produce compounds they could separate out. Work stopped briefly in 1897 for the birth of Marie's first daughter.

In the summer of 1898, the Curies found a new radioactive element, polonium, but there was more radiation still unaccounted for. Its source must be very radioactive indeed. Although they hadn't isolated it yet, they dubbed it radium, announcing their discovery in December.

After another four years' work, Marie had produced just one-tenth of a gram of pure radium chloride. She became a Doctor of Science – the first woman in Europe to do so – and in 1903 shared the Nobel prize for physics with Pierre and Becquerel. As the first woman to win a Nobel prize, Marie became famous. She and Pierre both got top jobs. In 1904, the Curies had another daughter. Then,

In 1906, tragedy struck. Pierre was hit by a speeding cart and was killed. Marie had to take over Pierre's professorship at the Sorbonne – another first for a woman – and carry on the research by herself. With the help of a colleague, she finally produced pure radium in 1910. The following year she received a second Nobel prize. This time, there was nobody for her to share it with.

During the First World War, Marie's research took a back seat. After the war she toured the world, using her fame to drum up support for a new use of her great discovery. Doctors had found that radium, the most powerful source of radiation then known, could treat cancer. Marie Curie had made radiotherapy possible. Although radium is now little used for this purpose, it remains to remind us of a remarkable woman.

LASTING FAME
By 1927, when this photograph was taken, Marie Curie had earned her place at the Solvay Congress, a meeting of top physicists held in Brussels, Belgium. She is sitting in the front row, third from the left. Other famous names in the group include Bohr, Bragg, Einstein, Heisenberg, Lorentz, Pauli, Planck, and Schrödinger.

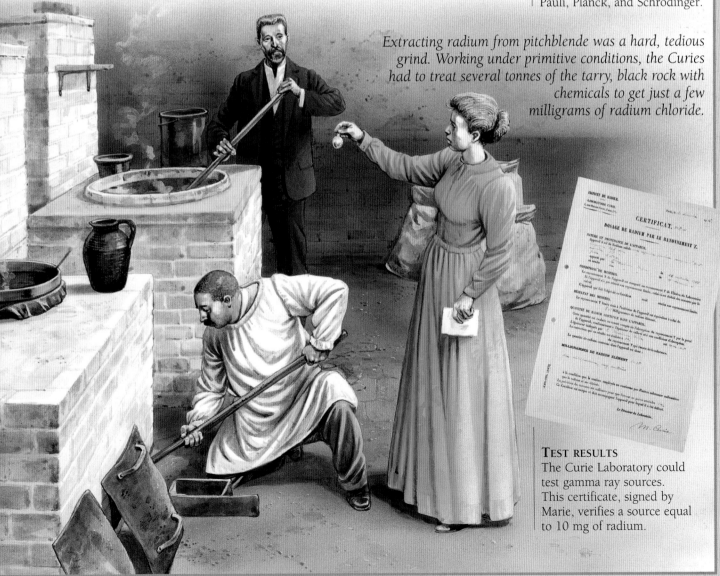

Extracting radium from pitchblende was a hard, tedious grind. Working under primitive conditions, the Curies had to treat several tonnes of the tarry, black rock with chemicals to get just a few milligrams of radium chloride.

TEST RESULTS
The Curie Laboratory could test gamma ray sources. This certificate, signed by Marie, verifies a source equal to 10 mg of radium.

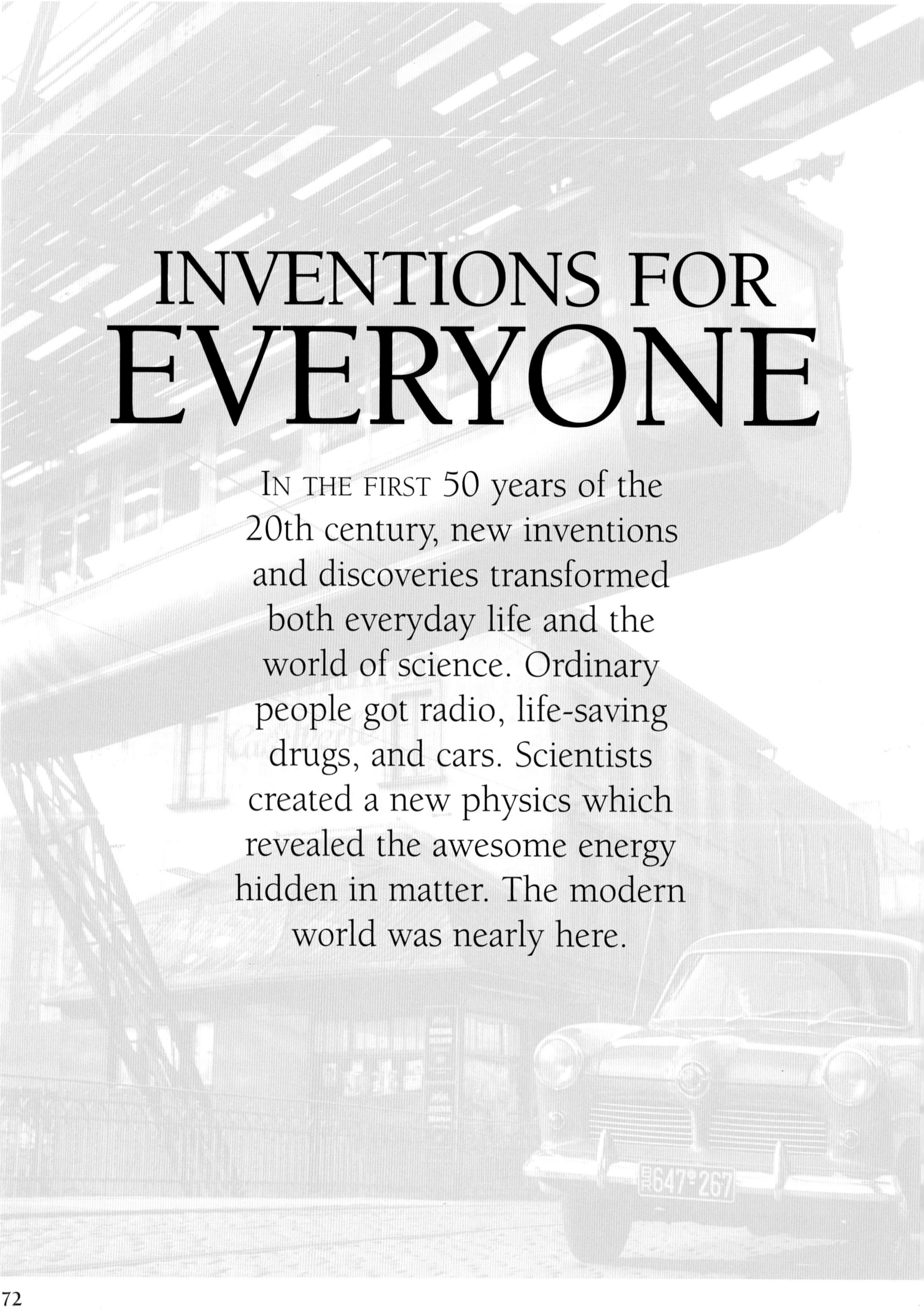

INVENTIONS FOR EVERYONE

IN THE FIRST 50 years of the 20th century, new inventions and discoveries transformed both everyday life and the world of science. Ordinary people got radio, life-saving drugs, and cars. Scientists created a new physics which revealed the awesome energy hidden in matter. The modern world was nearly here.

Blood groups
1901

Karl Landsteiner

Early attempts at blood transfusion often killed the patient. In 1901, Karl Landsteiner, an Austrian pathologist (someone who studies the effects of disease on body tissues), showed why. Unless carefully matched, the red cells in one person's blood can destroy those of another. He discovered three groups of human blood, which he called A, B, and O. Only bloods of the same group could be safely mixed. He later found a fourth group, AB, and other groups have been discovered since. As well as ensuring safe transfusions, blood grouping can help eliminate suspects in murder cases.

Monorail
1901

Eugen Langen

Monorails are railways with a single rail. The earliest was built in 1880, and had its rail underneath the cars. The more interesting suspended type, sometimes seen in theme parks, has also been used for serious transport. The earliest successful example, which still survives, is the monorail that runs along the River Wupper at Wuppertal in north-west Germany. It was designed in 1901 by Eugen Langen, a German engineer better known for his work on the internal combustion engine.

DISC BRAKE *This Lockheed disc brake was made in about 1970.*

Brake disc "caliper" housing pads

Safety razor
1901

King C. Gillette

King C. Gillette changed the life of men the world over when he followed the advice of a colleague and invented "something that would be used and thrown away". It was the disposable razor blade, which fitted into a new safety razor. Men may not have liked having to buy new blades all the time (by 1904 Gillette had sold more than 12 million) but they did appreciate a razor that was safer and quicker to use than the old, open-bladed "cut-throat" razor.

Disc brake
1902

Frederick Lanchester

Most modern cars have disc brakes. A steel disc is gripped between a pair of pads when braking is needed. The system was patented in 1902 by British car pioneer Frederick Lanchester, who, in 1896, also built the first all-British four-wheeled car. Lanchester's brake must have been rather noisy, because the pads were lined with copper. Another British engineer, Herbert Frood, substituted quieter, asbestos-lined pads in 1907.

Air conditioning
1902

Willis Carrier

A combination of high temperature and high humidity is uncomfortable. When air is saturated with water vapour, sweat cannot evaporate. US engineer Willis Carrier realized in 1902 that refrigeration could deal with both heat and humidity. He designed an "apparatus for treating air", in which air was cooled to the temperature at which moisture condenses out of it. The water was then drained away, producing pleasantly cool, dry air.

BLUE Gillette BLADE
REGD. TRADE MARK
King C. Gillette
REGD. TRADE MARK

REGISTERED TRADE MARK
Gillette
MADE IN ENGLAND

SAFETY RAZOR *An otherwise well-shaved King C. Gillette sports a moustache on this 1930s packaging.*

1901 On New Year's Day, the six separate colonies of Australia become states in a new federation, the Commonwealth of Australia. It has an independent government, but it is still ruled by Britain's Queen Victoria.

1902 Britain's most exclusive club is formed as Edward VII founds the Order of Merit, an honour given for services to science or art. Only 24 people can hold it at any one time. The first female OM will be Florence Nightingale.

Hormones
1902

*William Bayliss,
Ernest Starling*

Hormones are chemicals that control the body, such as adrenaline, which makes the heart pound in times of stress. The first hormone was discovered in 1902 by British physiologists (people who study how living things work) William (later Sir William) Bayliss and Ernest Starling. They found that the gut puts a chemical into the bloodstream when food reaches it, making the pancreas secrete digestive juice. They called the chemical secretin. Starling later coined the word "hormone" from the Greek for "setting in motion".

Tea-making alarm clock
1902

Frank Clarke

Although the British love their early morning tea, few can have risked

Frank Clarke's 1902 automatic tea maker to get it. It was perhaps a little ahead of the technology. While you dozed, clockwork struck a match that lit a flame under a kettle. When the water boiled, the steam operated a mechanism that tipped the kettle to pour water into the pot, and sounded an alarm – as if you'd need one!

Copper kettle

Methylated-spirit stove

TEA-MAKING ALARM CLOCK
Clarke's tea maker was mechanical because in 1902 few homes had electricity.

Spark plug
1902

Robert Bosch, G. Honold

A common problem with early internal combustion engines was how to ignite the fuel. One way was with sparks made by passing electricity through moving contacts inside the cylinder. In 1902, a German engineer, G. Honold, who worked for electrical engineer Robert Bosch, invented a better method. He applied

a much higher voltage to contacts with a fixed gap between them – a spark plug. Ignition was now controlled electrically. At the right moment, the high voltage caused a spark to jump the gap, igniting the fuel.

Teddy bear
1902

*Morris Mitchtom,
Margarete Steiff*

Popular US president Theodore "Teddy" Roosevelt became even more popular in 1902 when he went on a hunting expedition but refused to shoot a defenceless bear cub.

Cotton fabric stretched tightly over the framework of the wing

Propellers to push the plane through the air

Two wings linked by struts braced to combine their strength

Cashing in on this, New York retailer Morris Michtom began selling plush-covered bears with boot-button eyes and jointed limbs, calling them "Teddy's Bears". They were a huge success, and their name soon became "teddy bears". At about the same time, German designer Margarete Steiff started making similar bears. Although not technically teddies, Steiff bears became the number one bestsellers.

Vacuum cleaner
1902

Hubert Booth

Early gadgets for removing dust just tried to blow it away. When British engineer Hubert Booth put a

1902 In April, French composer Claude Debussy's only opera, *Pelléas et Mélisande*, receives its first performance. Scottish soprano Mary Garden becomes famous for her interpretation of the female lead, Mélisande.

1902 British empire builder Cecil Rhodes dies. His will creates a new scholarship to Oxford University (for men only) meant to promote unity among English-speaking nations. Rhodes Scholarships will later be open to women.

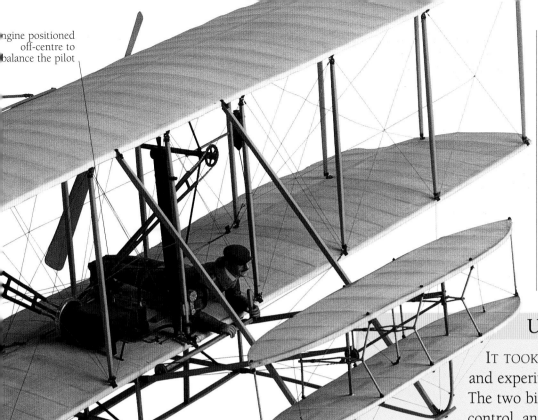

Engine positioned off-centre to balance the pilot

Take-off and landing skid

Multi-stage rocket
1903
Konstantin Tsiolkovsky

Russian scientist Konstantin Tsiolkovsky was thinking about interplanetary flight as long ago as 1895. In 1903, he suggested a way of getting large objects into space, using rockets with several stages that would be jettisoned as their fuel was used up. All major rockets are now built this way.

UP AND AWAY

It took a century of thought and experiment to conquer the air. The two big problems were lift and control, and the obvious masters of both were birds. One breakthrough came with the observation that a bird's tail is as important as its wings. The early pioneers also realized that flapping wings were not essential, which led to a practical aeroplane driven by a propeller.

GEORGE CAYLEY
A wealthy aristocrat, Cayley had established the basic shape of the aeroplane by 1799. It had a fuselage carrying fixed wings and a tail. After much research, he launched the first human-carrying glider in 1853.

OTTO LILIENTHAL
Lilienthal, a German engineer, studied the flight of birds before going on to develop effective fixed-wing gliders. In 1896, after thousands of experimental flights, he died in a crash.

OCTAVE CHANUTE
French-US engineer Chanute was in his 60s before he got interested in flying. During the 1890s, he made thousands of successful glider flights, accumulating data that he passed on to the Wright brothers.

Lilienthal glider built in about 1891, seen here from underneath

AEROPLANE *Striking features of the 1903 Wright Flyer included pusher propellers at the back, and no cockpit. The plane was controlled by wires that warped the wings.*

handkerchief over his mouth and sucked the upholstery of a chair, the filth he collected convinced him that vacuum cleaning would be much better. His company, started in 1902, made cleaners, but they were so big they had to be parked outside the houses they cleaned.

Electrocardiogram
1903
Willem Einthoven

Doctors routinely check a patient's heart by making a record of its electrical activity, called an electrocardiogram, or ECG. The first person to measure the heart's electrical signals was Dutch physiologist Willem Einthoven. Using a sensitive instrument that he built in 1903, he set about finding out how a normal heart behaved. By 1913 he had identified the points that doctors should look for.

Aeroplane
1903
Orville Wright, Wilbur Wright

Although people had been going up in balloons since 1783, they were not satisfied. They wanted to fly like birds, not just drift with the wind. The first real flight was made in North Carolina, USA, on 17 December, 1903. Watched by his brother Wilbur, US bicycle mechanic Orville Wright kept their fragile plane airborne for 12 seconds. The Wright brothers had at last solved the two great problems of flight: getting a machine to take off and controlling it in the air. (✳ *See also* **Up and away**.)

1903 Emmeline Pankhurst founds the Women's Social and Political Union to campaign for votes for British women. Ignored at first, the "suffragettes", as they are called, are driven to violent methods, such as burning empty buildings.

1903 The Tour de France bike race is started by French journalist Henri Desgrange to provide a source of exciting stories for his paper. Out of 60 riders, only 21 finish. Maurice Garin wins after nearly 95 hours in the saddle.

Lie detector
1904
*Max Wertheimer,
John Larson*

Czech psychologist Max Wertheimer developed the first so-called lie detector in 1904, while he was still a student. In California, another medical student, John Larson, worked with police to build a better one in 1921. Known as a polygraph, it monitored blood pressure, pulse, and breathing, because these can change when people lie. They sometimes change when people are telling the truth, too, so not all courts accept lie detector tests.

Thermos flask
1904
Rheinhold Burger

James Dewar's vacuum bottle (✳ *see* **page 162**), was far too delicate to take on a picnic. One of Dewar's students, Rheinhold Burger, saw how to make it more useful. He enclosed the glass bottle in a metal case with protective rubber mountings and a screw cap. Burger sold the idea to a German company and, after a competition to find a name, it was launched in 1904 as the Thermos flask.

Theory of relativity
1905
Albert Einstein

See **pages 178–179** for the story of how Einstein's theories of relativity shed light on Newton's universe.

Function of chromosomes
1905
*Nettie Stevens,
Edmund Wilson*

US biologist Nettie Stevens was the first to link cell structures with genetics. In 1905, while experimenting with beetles, she discovered that two structures, the X and Y chromosomes, determine whether an animal is male or female. Another American, Edmund Wilson, discovered the same thing independently. He suggested that chromosomes were an essential part of the mechanism of inheritance. He was right.

CAT'S WHISKER *Crystal sets were popular in the 1920s. Placed in contact with a metal whisker, a crystal such as galena (lead sulphide) could turn radio waves into sound signals – but only if the whisker was touching one of the crystal's sensitive spots.*

Headphones convert varying electric currents into sound waves

Wire connecting the crystal set to the headphones

TRIODE VALVE *The De Forest Audion of 1907 was based on a light bulb. The screw cap connects to the hot cathode; the wires go to the other electrodes.*

"Cat's whisker"

Crystal

Laminated glass
1905
Édouard Bénédictus

The first cars had ordinary glass windscreens, which could slice people to ribbons in a crash. French artist Édouard Bénédictus came up with an answer in 1905: two sheets of glass with plastic glued between them. If the glass broke, the plastic held the fragments in place. With better filling, laminated glass is still in use today.

Cat's whisker
1906
Greenleaf Pickard

In the 1920s, listening to the radio often meant fiddling with a "cat's whisker". The whisker – a short piece of wire – tickled the surface of a crystal and enabled radio waves to work headphones. German physicist Karl Braun had discovered this effect in about 1900, but it was US engineer Greenleaf Pickard who patented the arrangement in 1906. His device gave rise to one of the most important inventions of the 20th century, the transistor.

Triode valve
1906
Lee De Forest

Electronics started in 1904, when British scientist John Fleming found that a vacuum tube containing two electrodes, one of them heated, passed

1904 The first of London's famous black taxis hits the streets. The new cabs quickly displace their horse-drawn predecessors. Tight regulations on the size of their turning circle will be responsible for their odd, upright shape.

1905 Chicago lawyer Paul P. Harris founds Rotary International, a worldwide group of business and professional people dedicated to higher ethical standards in their work. Meetings "rotate" from office to office, hence the name.

176

current in one direction only. In 1906, US inventor Lee De Forest added a third electrode. By varying its voltage, he could control the current between the other two. De Forest called his device the Audion. We would now call it a triode. He used it first to detect radio waves, but was soon using it to amplify and generate them as well.

Sound radio
1906

Reginald Fessenden

Marconi got the first radio patent in 1896 (✳ *see* **page 164**) but it took ten years for radio to get a voice. Early stations could send out radio waves only in short bursts, but to transmit sound, continuous waves are needed. In 1906, Canadian-US engineer Reginald Fessenden invented an electric generator that worked at 1000 times the frequency of an ordinary power outlet, creating continuous radio waves that could carry sound. His first broadcast, on Christmas Eve, 1906, was a programme of speech and music.

Colour photography
1907

Auguste Lumière, Louis Lumière

Before French inventors Auguste and Louis Lumière introduced their Autochrome process in 1907, photographers had to take three photographs to get one colour picture. The Lumière brothers coated glass with red, green, and blue starch grains, filled the gaps between them with black, then added a coating that was sensitive to all colours. The starch acted as filters, giving three images in one shot. These combined to form a pleasing colour picture.

Vitamins
1907

Frederick Hopkins, Casimir Funk

We all need carbohydrates, proteins, minerals, and fats, but these alone are not enough. British biochemist Frederick (later Sir Frederick) Hopkins found that rats died when fed on artificial milk with only these ingredients but thrived if real milk was added. He concluded in 1907 that the rats needed "accessory factors" in their diet. In 1912, Polish biochemist Casimir Funk

COLOUR PHOTOGRAPHY
Autochromes needed long exposures so most were of tranquil scenes.

identified one of these in rice. Finding that it was a chemical called an amine, he proposed the name "vitamine". Not all vitamins are amines, but the name, minus its "e", has stuck.

1907 Irish people wanting independence for their country are outraged by the portrayal of Irish peasants in the first performance of J. M. Synge's *Playboy of the Western World* at the Abbey Theatre, Dublin. They will later admire the play.

1907 Italian educator Maria Montessori begins teaching children in Rome with the system that will become known by her name. The Montessori method is based on children's ability to learn by themselves, with guidance.

RIDDLES OF SPACE AND TIME

Albert Einstein publishes his Theories of Relativity and sheds light on Newton's universe

Train is travelling at nearly the speed of light

The time it takes a beam of light to travel up to a mirror and down represents one tick of a clock

Man on the train sees a short "tick"

Train in starting position

Woman on the platform sees a long "tick"

Train has moved forwards by the time the light beam hits the mirror

Train has moved further by the time the light beam reaches the detector

RUNNING LATE
Because relative motion cannot alter the speed of light, it must make moving clocks slow down.

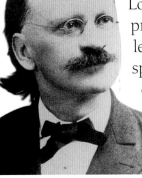

German-US physicist Albert Michelson

FAILED EXPERIMENT
Michelson and Morley used a turntable with two light beams crossing it. Mirrors combined the beams into a pattern that would show up any difference in the speed of light in the two directions. But, whichever way they turned their table, they found no change.

US physicist Edward Morley

When Albert Einstein was a small boy in Germany, he saw his first pocket compass. It made a great impression on him. Whichever way he turned it, its needle always pointed the same way. Some outside force was controlling it. The incident helped set him searching for the truth about the universe.

For a while, Einstein couldn't get a job because he had upset some important people. When he did get work in 1902, in Bern, Switzerland, it was only as a clerk in the Patent Office. But in his spare time he began to develop a revolutionary theory.

In 1887, US scientists Albert Michelson and Edward Morley thought they would use light to measure the speed of Earth in its orbit. According to Isaac Newton, light travelling in the same direction as Earth would slow down, just as a car looks slower when seen from the car behind. But the speed of light didn't change. Something was wrong with Newton's world.

Einstein's Special Theory of Relativity, published in 1905, rescued physics from this embarrassment. It reconciled the behaviour of light with the mechanical forces known to Newton. With the help of ideas from Dutch physicist Hendrik Lorentz, Einstein modified Newton's laws to make them predict a constant speed for light. The modifications leave Newton's laws almost unchanged at ordinary speeds, but at speeds approaching the speed of light, strange things happen to moving objects. As seen by someone moving at a different speed, their length in their direction of motion decreases, their mass increases, and any processes within them slow down.

At its simplest, the Special Theory says that the mass of an object depends on its speed. If a force acts on an object, it accelerates, but as it speeds up, more energy goes into increasing its mass and less into increasing its speed. This prevents it from reaching the speed of light. One consequence is the equation $E = mc^2$, which says that mass and energy are interchangeable.

Although revolutionary, the Special Theory was incomplete. It did not deal with gravity. Einstein put this right in 1915 with his General Theory of Relativity. Replacing Newton's space and time with a unified space-time, it proposed that gravity was a property of space, not a force between bodies. It led to amazing predictions, such as the bending of light by gravity and the existence of black holes, both of which have since been confirmed.

ORIGINAL GENIUS
Albert Einstein was a highly original thinker who gave us a new view of the world. As well as creating the Special and General Theories of Relativity, he contributed greatly to the quantum theory of matter.

BLACK HOLE
Gravity, a warping of space and time, affects everything – even light. Black holes create gravity so intense that light is trapped, but they can be detected by their effects. In this picture, matter is being pulled away from a giant star.

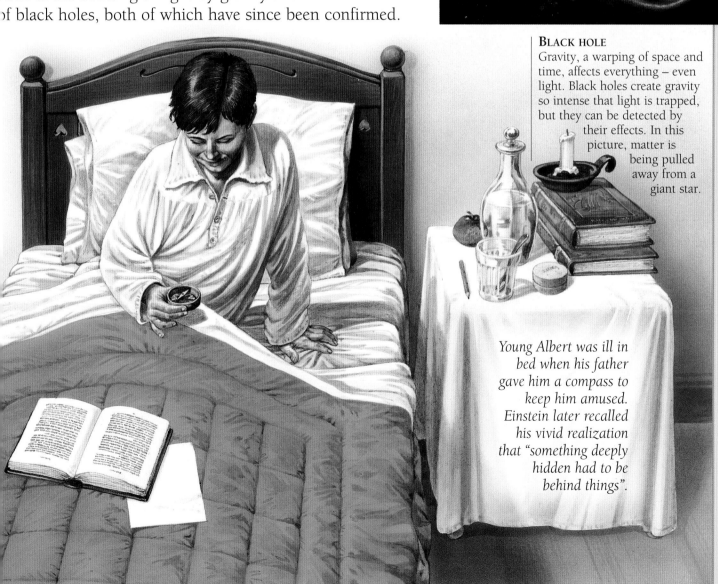

Young Albert was ill in bed when his father gave him a compass to keep him amused. Einstein later recalled his vivid realization that "something deeply hidden had to be behind things".

Handle to engage the mangle drive

Mangle for squeezing water out of the washing

1919 advertisement for an early washing machine

Electric washing machine

Alva Fisher

Inventors tried for years to find a way of reducing the hours spent over a steaming washtub, but only electric power could offer real labour saving. The first electric washing machine, the Thor, was designed in 1907 by US engineer Alva Fisher. It had a drum that turned back and forth to tumble clothes clean. Its motor was simply bolted on to the outside, so it wasn't all that safe with water splashing around.

Paper cup

1908

Hugh Moore

Nobody today would think of sharing an unwashed cup with strangers, but water in places such as railway stations once came from a tap with a shared tin cup attached. In 1908, US inventor Hugh Moore designed a vending machine to deliver water in individual paper cups. He soon realized that selling cups was more profitable than selling water, and set up a company to make them. He chose the name Dixie in 1919. By the 1920s, paper "Dixies" were holding ice cream as well as drinks.

Tea bag

c1908

Thomas Sullivan

Tea bags seem to have been invented by accident. A likely date is 1908. The story is that New York tea merchant Thomas Sullivan started

Lifting the lid automatically disconnected the motor

Long drive belt

Wooden tub

ELECTRIC WASHING MACHINE *Early washing machines were often just hand-operated models with an electric motor bolted on. Even in 1920, Beatty Brothers of Canada, a pioneer of washing machines, was still making this wooden-tub machine with its alarmingly exposed motor.*

Tap for letting out the water

Electric motor mounted under the tub

Wheels allowed the machine to be moved around easily

Tub was supported on a four-legged "dolly"

1909 Italian writer Filippo Marinetti starts a disturbing new movement with his *Manifesto of Futurism*. Rejecting women, existing institutions, and conventional morality, *Futurism* glorifies war, danger, and masculine energy.

1910 Cinema newsreels begin as French film magnate Charles Pathé's company, Pathé Frères, releases the first of a weekly news compilation called *Pathé Journal*. The crowing cockerel of Pathé News will be known worldwide.

sending out tea samples stitched into cloth bags. Rather than open these, people just poured boiling water over them, and Sullivan was soon getting orders for more. By 1920, proper tea bags were being used in the USA, mainly large ones for the catering trade. Teabags were introduced to Britain by Joseph Tetley & Company in 1953.

Neon sign

1910

Georges Claude

Several 19th-century inventors experimented with tubes containing gas at low pressure, and found that electricity could make the gas light up. In 1910, French

Electric starter

1912

Charles Kettering

In early cars, the driver had to turn a handle at the front to start the engine. The handle could kick dangerously. Henry Leland, head of Cadillac Motors, found this unacceptable, and

Stainless steel

1913

Harry Brearley

British metallurgist Harry Brearley hit on stainless steel by accident while trying to make a steel that would resist the heat inside a gun. He was in charge of the Firth Brown Laboratories in Sheffield, England, an important steel making centre. In 1913, after a series of experiments, he made some steel containing about 13 per cent chromium. He found that it was of little use for guns, but realized that it was resistant to corrosion. Unlike other scientists, who had made similar steels, Brearley saw its potential for cutlery. It was a local Sheffield cutler who suggested the name that we now use for it.

NEON SIGN *New techinques had to be invented before neon signs could be widely used for advertising.*

Fertilizer from the air

1909

Fritz Haber, Carl Bosch

Plants need nitrogen. Although air is four-fifths nitrogen, plants cannot absorb it directly. Nitrogen-rich fertilizers are one answer, but by 1900, natural supplies, such as bird droppings, were beginning to run out. In 1909, German chemist Fritz Haber succeeded in capturing nitrogen from the air. He used heat and high pressure to make it react with hydrogen, forming ammonia, which could be made into fertilizers and other products. By 1914, another German chemist, Carl Bosch, had found a way to increase the yield of ammonia, and developed Haber's method for large-scale use. The Haber-Bosch process is now essential to agriculture and much else.

physicist Georges Claude tried the gas neon, and found that it produced an intense orange-red glow. This was of little use for lighting, but after the new tubes had been used at the Paris Motor Show, an advertising agency suggested that they could be made into signs. By 1912, the first neon sign was in place over a Montmartre barber's shop.

Continental drift

1912

Alfred Wegener

If you look at an atlas of the world, you will see that South America and Africa would fit together like jigsaw-puzzle pieces. In 1912, German meteorologist Alfred Wegener said that this was not a coincidence. He said that all the continents had once been joined together as a continent he called Pangaea, which began to drift apart millions of years ago. His ideas were forgotten, but in the 1960s, scientists realized that he had been right.

asked US engineer Charles Kettering to create a self-starter. Kettering succeeded where earlier inventors had failed, and the 1912 Cadillac was the first car that could be started from the driver's seat.

Cosmic rays

1913

Victor Hess

The pioneers of radioactivity found their instruments responding to radiation from outside their labs. Its origin was a mystery until US physicist Victor Hess sent balloons carrying measuring instruments high into the atmosphere. By 1913, he had found that the radiation became stronger as the balloons went higher, suggesting that the "rays" came from beyond Earth. US physicist Robert Millikan confirmed this, and in 1925 coined the term "cosmic rays" for this radiation from the depths of the universe.

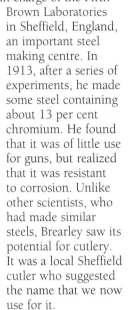

Mark of stainless steel makers Butler of Sheffield

Bone handle

STAINLESS STEEL *This tea knife of 1915 was one of the first that did not need cleaning with an abrasive after a meal.*

Assembly line

1913

Henry Ford

See **pages 182–183** for the story of how Henry Ford adopted the assembly line to mass produce the world's most successful car.

1911 On 14 December, Norwegian explorer Roald Amundsen and his team become the first people to reach the South Pole. Powered only by dogs, they beat the motorized expedition led by Robert Scott, which sadly never returns.

1912 On the night of Sunday, 14 April, the supposedly unsinkable *Titanic* hits an iceberg on its maiden voyage. By the next morning it is on the bottom of the Atlantic Ocean. More than 1500 people die, but about 700 are saved.

A MOTOR FOR THE MULTITUDE

Henry Ford adopts the assembly line to mass produce the world's most successful car

MAN OF VISION
Henry Ford looked to a future in which efficient production methods would make everyone rich. His factory eventually had raw materials going in at one end and finished cars coming out at the other.

TIN LIZZIE
Between 1908 and 1927, one of every two cars built in the world was a Model T. With its rugged construction and low price, it was ideal for the still rural USA.

MORE MOTORS
The Ford story does not, of course, end with the Model T. Later designs included the sleek Edsel, the sporty Mustang, and the GT40, designed in Britain and built for serious racing.

In 1891, when the first modern car was built, Henry Ford was a young engineer working in Detroit, USA, not far from the farm where he had been born. Most people still worked on the land. Ford would be one of the people who helped to change this, transforming the USA into an industrial nation.

By 1896, Ford had built his first car. In 1903, he set up the Ford Motor Company. At that time, cars were individually built and very expensive, so they were strictly for the rich. Ford realized he could keep costs down by producing just one type of car, and in 1908 he launched "a motor car for the great multitude" – the Model T.

Demand for the "Tin Lizzie", as it was nicknamed, was soon running ahead of supply, and Ford moved to a new factory at Highland Park, just outside Detroit. Even here, people still had to walk from car to car to work on each one – and when they were walking they were not working.

Ford wanted to find a faster, less expensive production method. In the US meat industry, workers stood still while carcasses were moved slowly past them. In 1913, Ford experimented with this "assembly line" idea for making part of the Model T. Output of the part went up by 300 per cent, so he decided to make the whole car on an assembly line.

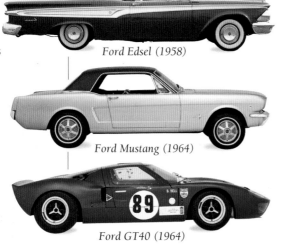

Model T Tourer (1916)

Ford Edsel (1958)

Ford Mustang (1964)

Ford GT40 (1964)

Ford succeeded in his mission to bring motoring to the multitude, and in doing so changed the American way of life. As well as providing pleasure on picnics, low-cost vehicles made every industry more efficient.

Now, instead of wandering about the factory, workers spent all their time adding parts to cars as they passed by. Each worker did only one operation, and their pace was set by the moving line. By April 1914, Ford had cut the time it took to make a car from 12 man-hours to one and a half. Soon the factory was turning out a car every 24 seconds. The Model T became the world's most successful car, with total sales reaching more than 15 million.

The assembly line did have its disadvantages. Working in this way was stressful, so workers often left. Ford solved this problem by doubling his workers' pay and reducing the hours they had to work. It seemed crazy, but it was just good business. Ford realized that his employees had a private life and didn't just make cars. Thanks to his new methods, they would soon be buying them, too.

MODERN MANUFACTURE

The first cars had their bodies bolted on to a separate chassis, but today's car body is a single, self-supporting steel shell. For many years, the shell was hand-welded together by skilled workers, but such heavy, repetitive tasks are now done by robots, like these at Ford's plant in Ontario, Canada.

Structure of the atom

1913

Niels Bohr

British physicist Ernest Rutherford pictured the hydrogen atom as a heavy nucleus with an electron orbiting around it. But classical physics said this could not be right because the electron would radiate energy and stop orbiting. Danish physicist Niels Bohr saved the situation in 1913 by showing that electrons could radiate energy only when jumping from a higher to a lower orbit. The radiation would appear as light whose frequency depended on the size of the jump.

Bra

1914

Mary Jacob

Although a "breast supporter" was patented in 1893, the idea didn't catch on until New York partygoer Mary Jacob realized that whalebone corsets and her new, slinky dress just didn't go together. She sewed together a couple of handkerchiefs and some ribbon and wore that instead of the whalebone. In 1914, she changed her name to Caresse Crosby, patented the brassière, and started selling it. Although she was not very successful in this, she did manage to sell the idea to a big corset company, and by the 1920s women everywhere were wearing bras.

Lipstick

1915

Maurice Levy

Lipstick has been with us for centuries, but without a convenient package, women couldn't carry it around. In 1915, US inventor Maurice Levy attached a solid lipstick to a sliding carrier inside a metal tube with a lid. The lipstick could be slid out for use, then put back safely inside its container to protect handbags and pockets. Lipstick soon became more widely used.

LIPSTICK *As this early print shows, lip colour became popular when presented in convenient, solid form.*

Black hole

1916

Karl Schwarzschild

German astronomer Karl Schwarzschild published his first scientific paper while still a schoolboy. In 1916, the year of his death, he published a more important one. Using Einstein's General Theory of Relativity (✴ see **pages 178–179**), he worked out what happens near a massive star that has collapsed to a single point. Its gravity becomes so intense that within a certain distance (now called the Schwarzschild radius), even light cannot escape. Black holes, as they are now known, emit no light but can be detected by the effect of their gravity on nearby stars.

Intelligence test

1916

Lewis Terman

Although nobody seems to know whether intelligence can really be measured, intelligence tests are still in use. Their results are expressed as an "intelligence quotient", or IQ, with an IQ of 100 representing average intelligence. The first widely used test, the Stanford-Binet, was published in 1916 by US psychologist Lewis Terman. A professor at Stanford University, Terman based his test on earlier ones devised by French psychologists Alfred Binet and Theodore Simon.

Domestic food mixer

1919

Herbert Johnson

Bakers had been mixing dough by electricity for years before an effective mixer reached the

DOMESTIC FOOD MIXER *By the 1930s, when many homes had electricity, appliances like food mixers were beginning to be more widely used.*

1914 Archduke Ferdinand, heir to the Austrian and Hungarian thrones, is assassinated on 28 June. The resulting conflict escalates to involve 32 countries. It will end in 1918, after 47 million people have been killed.

1916 A work that will become a favourite of concert goers and science-fiction producers alike, *The Planets*, is published by British composer Gustav Holst. His orchestral suite portrays the planets' astrological characters.

kitchen. Early domestic mixers were little more than motorized egg-whisks, but the Troy Metal Products H-5, introduced in 1919 and later called the Kitchen Aid, was based on a professional mixer designed by US engineer Herbert Johnson. Its built-in bowl revolved in the opposite direction to the beaters, and this "planetary" action is now used in most mixers.

Wall-fixing plug
1919

John Rawlings

British builder John Rawlings didn't like the way other builders fixed things to walls. They just chiselled out a large hole, rammed in a lump of wood and put a screw in it. The fixing was weak, and it messed up the wall. Rawlings realized that screws would grip small, drilled holes if they were surrounded by something that expanded as they went in. After trying brass, he devised a plug made of fibre. Once he had convinced people that such a

neat device could do the job, the Rawlplug became everyone's favourite fixing.

Public broadcasting service
1920

David Sarnoff, Guglielmo Marconi

Although US engineer Reginald Fessenden broadcast speech and music in 1906, and US radio executive David Sarnoff proposed a "radio music box" in 1915, real public broadcasting only began in the 1920s. By this time, electronics had developed greatly, allowing big transmitters to be built. The first regular service was started in Britain by Guglielmo Marconi in February 1920. In November 1920, US station KDKA began broadcasting from Philadelphia. Governments in both countries later stepped in to regulate the new medium. (✳ *See also* **Birth of broadcasting**.)

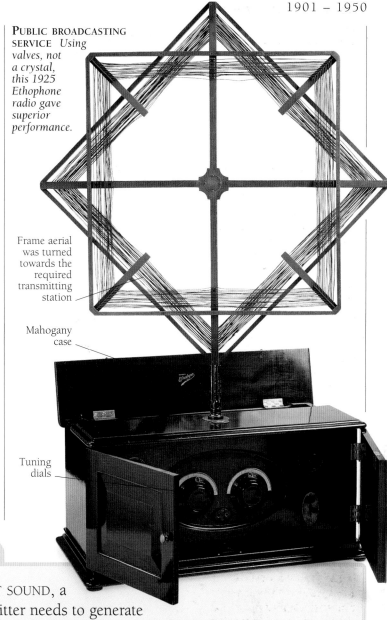

PUBLIC BROADCASTING SERVICE *Using valves, not a crystal, this 1925 Ethophone radio gave superior performance.*

Frame aerial was turned towards the required transmitting station

Mahogany case

Tuning dials

BIRTH OF BROADCASTING

Listening to radio on a train in 1930

TO TRANSMIT SOUND, a radio transmitter needs to generate powerful, continuous, high-frequency waves. Reginald Fessenden pioneered these with high-speed electric generators, but it was the development of large electronic valves during the First World War that really made broadcasting possible. The first listeners had to build their own receivers because the lack of regular broadcasts meant there was no market for ready-made radios.

BROADCASTING IN BRITAIN
Marconi's early radio broadcasts were banned, but after public pressure, his company was allowed to broadcast for 15 minutes a week from a hut near Chelmsford, starting in February 1922. In May, the station moved to London, and October saw the birth of the British Broadcasting Company. In 1927, this became a public corporation, the BBC.

BROADCASTING IN THE USA
Unhampered by red tape, and led by visionaries such as David Sarnoff of the Radio Corporation of America, US broadcasting grew rapidly. By 1922, the USA had 600 stations, mainly financed by advertising, while Britain still had only one. But competition threatened chaos, so in 1927 the industry finally came under government regulation.

1917 The Union of Soviet Socialist Republics, the USSR, is formed following the Russian revolution. The Congress of Soviets, controlled by the Bolsheviks under their leader Vladimir Lenin, takes over the former Russian Empire.

1920 Two Australian flying veterans and a cattle farmer found Queensland and Northern Territory Aerial Services. At first they offer only an airborne taxi service and the odd joyride, but their company will later become Qantas.

Self-adhesive dressing
1920

Earle Dickson

Before ready-made dressings, cuts were covered with gauze stuck down with tape. Earle Dickson, of US surgical dressing manufacturer Johnson & Johnson, changed this in 1920. Working in his kitchen, he took a strip of adhesive tape, laid down squares of gauze on it, covered it with fabric and rolled it up for future use. His invention was soon on sale as Band-Aid. In 1928, T. J. Smith & Nephew introduced the similar Elastoplast to Britain.

Tube connects the pump to a needle

Dials for setting the amount of insulin to be injected

Theremin
1920

Leon Theremin

The theremin was the first successful electronic musical instrument. Still played today, it produces those spooky wailing sounds popular in science-fiction films. It was invented in 1920 by Russian scientist Leon Theremin, who originally called it the etherophone. It is one of the few instruments played by hands being waved near it, not by being touched. The distance of the hands affects its tuning, giving total control over its unearthly notes.

Insulin
1921

Frederick Banting, Charles Best

Insulin is a hormone that tells the liver to remove glucose from the blood. People whose bodies cannot make enough insulin suffer from diabetes, in which blood glucose may reach dangerous levels. It was known that insulin came from a gland called the pancreas, but efforts to extract it from the pancreas of certain animals failed. The gland's digestive juices were also released and digested the insulin before it could be extracted. Then, in 1921, Canadian doctor Frederick (later Sir Frederick) Banting, assisted by a student, Charles Best, worked out a way to stop the pancreatic juices destroying the hormone. Thanks to their work, insulin is now available for controlling diabetes.

Leaded petrol
1921

Thomas Midgley Jr

In a properly adjusted car engine, the fuel and air burn smoothly rather than exploding. When engineers made car engines more powerful by increasing the pressure inside them, they found that destructive explosions, or "knocking", became a problem. In 1921, US engineer Thomas Midgley Jr discovered that adding lead compounds to the fuel could restore smooth running. Most cars used leaded petrol until the 1980s, when concerns about pollution caused a switch to fuels that didn't need lead to stop the knock.

Ice lolly
1923

Frank Epperson

Refreshing, flavoured ice on a stick was patented by US salesman Frank Epperson in 1924, but its US brand name, Popsicle, was registered a year earlier. The legend is that Epperson invented the ice lolly by accident in 1905, when he was a boy, by leaving a drink with a stirrer in it out on a cold night. His patent describes cylindrical lollies made in ordinary test tubes.

Traffic signal
1923

Garrett Morgan

A traffic signal was installed in London in 1868, but a more widely used signal was patented by US inventor

INSULIN *This modern electric pump gives someone with diabetes a convenient way to inject themselves with insulin, slowly and continuously.*

Viewfinder

35MM CAMERA *The Leica was not a single-lens reflex, as most 35mm cameras are today, but gave good results.*

1921 Nine years after the death of Emperor Meiji, who helped Japan become a modern industrial nation, a shrine to his memory is built in Tokyo. Its traditional wooden buildings will be destroyed in an air raid 24 years later.

1922 British archaeologist Howard Carter discovers the treasure-filled tomb of the Egyptian pharaoh Tutankhamen in the Valley of the Kings. Unlike most tombs, this one has not been looted, making it important to Egyptology.

Garrett Morgan in 1923. It had three movable arms with STOP and GO written on them, mounted on a pole. Signals were given by raising, lowering, and swivelling the arms to show or hide these words. The signal also had a position that stopped all traffic, to allow an orderly switch from one direction to another.

Frozen food

1924

Clarence Birdseye

US naturalist Clarence Birdseye got the idea for frozen foods on a trip to Newfoundland, Canada, in 1912. It's very cold there, and Birdseye saw people leaving freshly caught fish outside to freeze. He invented a machine that froze fish between refrigerated metal plates, and in 1924 helped found the General Seafoods Corporation. He was soon selling quick-frozen fruit and vegetables as well as fish. His name lives on as the familiar brand name Birds Eye.

35mm camera

1924

Oskar Barnack

The first precision miniature camera was the Leica, designed by German mechanic Oskar Barnack. It went into production in 1924. Barnack had started working on it much earlier, but was delayed by the First World War. To make the Leica, he adapted an instrument for testing 35mm movie film, made by the company he worked for, Ernst Leitz. He created the now standard frame size, 24 × 36 mm, simply by doubling the size of a movie frame.

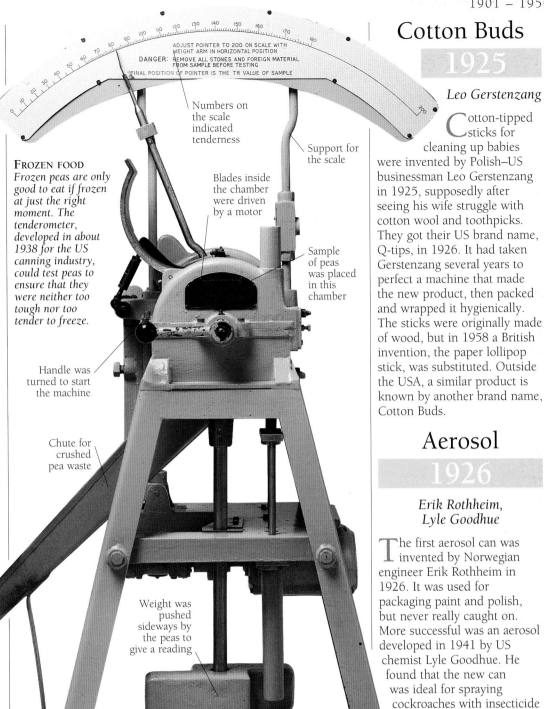

ADJUST POINTER TO 200 ON SCALE WITH WEIGHT ARM IN HORIZONTAL POSITION
DANGER: REMOVE ALL STONES AND FOREIGN MATERIAL FROM SAMPLE BEFORE TESTING
FINAL POSITION OF POINTER IS THE TR VALUE OF SAMPLE

Numbers on the scale indicated tenderness

FROZEN FOOD
Frozen peas are only good to eat if frozen at just the right moment. The tenderometer, developed in about 1938 for the US canning industry, could test peas to ensure that they were neither too tough nor too tender to freeze.

Support for the scale

Blades inside the chamber were driven by a motor

Sample of peas was placed in this chamber

Handle was turned to start the machine

Chute for crushed pea waste

Weight was pushed sideways by the peas to give a reading

Cotton Buds

1925

Leo Gerstenzang

Cotton-tipped sticks for cleaning up babies were invented by Polish–US businessman Leo Gerstenzang in 1925, supposedly after seeing his wife struggle with cotton wool and toothpicks. They got their US brand name, Q-tips, in 1926. It had taken Gerstenzang several years to perfect a machine that made the new product, then packed and wrapped it hygienically. The sticks were originally made of wood, but in 1958 a British invention, the paper lollipop stick, was substituted. Outside the USA, a similar product is known by another brand name, Cotton Buds.

Aerosol

1926

Erik Rothheim, Lyle Goodhue

The first aerosol can was invented by Norwegian engineer Erik Rothheim in 1926. It was used for packaging paint and polish, but never really caught on. More successful was an aerosol developed in 1941 by US chemist Lyle Goodhue. He found that the new can was ideal for spraying cockroaches with insecticide to kill them. Millions of these "bug bombs" were supplied to US troops in the Second World War, and by 1946 aerosols were in production for domestic use. Fifty years later, world production was numbered in billions.

1925 One of the first films to use the technique of "montage" – telling a story by rapid cutting between shots – is made in Russia by Sergei Eisenstein. His *Battleship Potemkin* will become a model for many other film makers.

1926 The first woman to swim the English Channel unaided, US Olympic swimmer Gertrude Ederle, knocks two hours off the record as she makes it from Cap Gris-Nez in northern France to Kingsdown, Kent, in 14 hours, 31 minutes.

Film soundtrack
1926
Lee De Forest

Sound for the first films was supplied by live musicians. The only recordings available were gramophone discs, and it was difficult to keep these in step with the film. The obvious place for the recording was on the film itself. The first person to succeed in putting it there was US inventor Lee De Forest. His Phonofilm system of 1926 produced the first sound track – a narrow stripe down the side of the film, recording sound waves as a varying shade of grey. It was the forerunner of the later, more successful Movietone system.

Liquid-fuelled rocket
1926
Robert Goddard

The first rockets used solid fuel. They were really just big fireworks. Modern rockets use liquid fuel, which allows much more controllable motors to be built. The first liquid-fuelled rocket was launched by US physicist Robert Goddard. Burning petrol and liquid oxygen, it lifted off briefly from his Aunt Effie's farm in Auburn, Massachusetts, on 16 March, 1926. It was another 15 years before the same idea was used in Adolf Hitler's deadly flying bombs during the Second World War.

LIQUID-FUELLED ROCKET
A Titan II rocket lifts off in January 1965 carrying an unmanned Gemini spacecraft. The 30 m- (100 ft-) long rocket was powered by the liquid fuel hydrazine.

Combustion tank where fuel mixed with oxidiser burned

Plant growth hormones
1926
Friedrich Went

The life of plants is controlled by a number of different hormones. The first to be discovered was a group known as auxins. Dutch botanist Friedrich Went, a professor at the University of Utrecht, found them in 1926 while studying how plants grow. He discovered that auxins were not only responsible for stimulating plant growth, but were also involved in the one-sided growth that makes plants bend towards the light.

Pop-up toaster
1926
Charles Strite

Burnt toast was normal with early electric toasters. They just kept toasting until someone turned them off. The first that turned off and popped the toast out automatically was patented in 1919 by US inventor Charles Strite. It was designed for caterers. The toaster as we know it, based on Strite's design, did not reach the breakfast table until 1926, when the Waters Genter Company, later known as McGraw Electric, marketed the first Toastmaster.

Expanding universe
1927
Edwin Hubble

Until US astronomer Edwin Hubble started studying the sky in the 1920s, nobody suspected that there were countless galaxies beyond our own Milky Way. Having proved the existence of such galaxies, Hubble discovered in 1927 that

1926 The Showa (bright peace) period begins in Japan with the enthronement of Emperor Hirohito. He is content to leave government to others until August 1945, when he ends the Second World War by insisting that Japan surrenders.

1927 Indian lawyer Bhimrao Ranji Ambedkar begins a campaign of direct action aimed at improving the social status of the Dalits, or "Untouchables". He will urge the Dalits, traditionally given the worst jobs, to take up Buddhism.

Biological clock

1927

Curt Richter

Anyone who has had jet-lag knows that we have a built-in clock that tells us when to be active and when to sleep. The first scientist to study this was US biologist Curt Richter, head of the psychiatric clinic at Johns Hopkins University in the USA. In 1927, he published the results of research into the biorhythms, or internal cycles, that govern animal behaviour. We now know that they apply to humans too.

POP-UP TOASTER *By the 1960s, toasters were looking smarter, but their simple principle – releasing the toast after a set time – was the same.*

they were rushing away from us, with speeds that increased the further away they were. The universe, far from being changeless, was expanding. Cosmologists now accept this as evidence for the Big Bang that started it all.

Chainsaw

1927

Emil Lerp, Andreas Stihl

The world's first petrol-engined chainsaw let rip on Mount Dolmar, Germany, in 1927. German engineer Emil Lerp's new, "portable" sawing machine had a moving chain like a modern saw, but was too heavy for one person to pick up. A chainsaw light enough for one person to wield didn't appear until 1950, made by a company founded by Lerp's rival, Andreas Stihl.

Big Bang theory

1927

Georges Lemaître, George Gamow

In 1927, Edwin Hubble discovered that the universe is expanding. In the same year, Belgian astronomer Georges Lemaître proposed a simple, but radical explanation: everything had originally been squeezed into an incredibly dense "primeval atom" that had exploded to create the universe we know. In 1948, Russian physicist George Gamow revived Lemaître's idea in an attempt to explain how the chemical elements were formed. British astronomer Fred Hoyle scornfully dubbed this the Big Bang theory, and the name stuck. (✳ *See also* **Starting with a bang**.)

BIG BANG THEORY *It is impossible to know what the Big Bang was like, but this is an artist's impression.*

STARTING WITH A BANG

WHEN ALBERT EINSTEIN HEARD Georges Lemaître's Big Bang theory, he exclaimed "This is the most beautiful and satisfactory explanation of creation to which I have ever listened." Although it doesn't explain where the "primeval atom" came from, an explosion about 15 billion years ago does account for the universe we see today. Backed up by recent evidence, the Big Bang is now the preferred picture of the beginning of time.

George Gamow (right) with Swiss-US physicist Wolfgang Pauli

EVIDENCE FOR THE BIG BANG

The strongest evidence for the Big Bang is the expansion discovered by Hubble. The theory also predicts that the universe should be filled with low-level microwave radiation, and this was found in 1965. Finally, about a quarter of the universe (by mass) is made of helium. Stars alone could not have produced this amount, but the first fireball could.

STEADY STATE THEORY

In the same year that George Gamow revived the Big Bang theory, British astronomers Hermann Bondi, Thomas Gold, and Fred Hoyle proposed that the universe had always existed in a "steady state". They suggested that as the universe expanded, new matter filled the gaps to keep everything looking the same. Recent discoveries have made this theory seem unlikely.

1927 Australia's parliament moves from Melbourne to Canberra, a new city designed by US architect Walter Griffin. Building work had started in 1913. The name derives from an Aboriginal word meaning "meeting place".

1927 Intrepid US aviator Charles Lindbergh lands safely at Le Bourget airport, near Paris, after crossing the Atlantic single-handed in his plane *The Spirit of St Louis*. The flight from Roosevelt Field, Long Island, USA, makes him a star.

Bubble gum
1928
Walter Diemer

Walter Diemer, a young accountant working for the Fleer Chewing Gum Company in Philadelphia, USA, thought he could improve on the company's product. In 1928 he produced a gum that was so stretchy he could blow bubbles with it. He had created bubble gum. His company started selling it as Dubble Bubble. Once Diemer had taught the sales force how to blow the perfect bubble, the new gum became a favourite worldwide.

Penicillin
1928

Alexander Fleming, Ernst Chain, Howard Florey

See **pages 192–193** for the story of how Ernst Chain and Howard Florey built on Alexander Fleming's lucky find.

Electric razor
1928

Jacob Schick

Attempts to do away with wet shaving go back to 1908 or earlier, but the first

BUBBLE GUM *This Dubble Bubble advertisement from the 1940s is obviously aimed at children. Unlike chewing gum, bubble gum has always been seen as mainly a product for children and younger adults.*

Uncertainty principle
1927
Werner Heisenberg

Elementary particles, such as electrons, are described by the branch of physics called quantum mechanics (✳ *see* **page 169**). This says that a particle is not only a particle, but also a wave. One consequence of this is that nobody can know both the momentum (mass × velocity) and position of a particle at the same time. Momentum comes from a spread-out wave, while position comes from a concentrated wave, and you can't have both at once. German physicist Werner Heisenberg announced this "uncertainty principle" in 1927.

Chloro-fluorocarbons
1928

Thomas Midgley Jr, Albert Henne

Early refrigerators used chemicals like ammonia, which is extremely smelly and poisonous. In 1928, it took US scientists Thomas Midgley Jr and Albert Henne just two days to find something better: chlorofluorocarbons, or CFCs. These compounds of chlorine, fluorine, and carbon had already been produced by Belgian chemist Frederic Swarts in the 1890s, but Midgley and Henne found a better way of making them. Unfortunately, they have a devastating effect on Earth's protective ozone layer, so they have not been made since the late 1990s.

ELECTRIC RAZOR *Razors like this 1934 Schick allowed men to shave anywhere there was a power point.*

Spare cutter

Electric lead

1927 Thin meets fat as two stars, Stan Laurel from Britain and Oliver Hardy from the USA, team up at Hal Roach's Hollywood Studio for their first film, *Putting Pants on Philip*. The comic duo will make many more films together.

1928 British women finally get the same voting rights as men, after ten years in which they could vote only if they owned a house, were married to a man who owned a house, or had a university degree and were over 30.

Electrodes on scalp

inventor to tackle the problem successfully was Lieutenant-Colonel Jacob Schick of the US Army. In 1928 he used the profits from an earlier invention, a razor that stored blades in its handle, to finance his new electric razor. Despite the Great Depression that hit the USA in the following year, Schick's dry shaver was soon selling well.

Cinemascope

1928

*Henri Chrétien,
Claude Autant-Lara*

Cinemascope squeezes a wide image on to normal movie film by distorting it with a special lens. A similar lens on the projector distorts the image back again to produce a wide-screen picture. French physicist Henri Chrétien invented the lens in the late 1920s, and experimental films were made in 1928 by French film director Claude Autant-Lara. But Cinemascope really hit the screens in the 1950s, as cinemas struggled to tempt audiences away from television.

Sliced bread

1928

Otto Rohwedder

Devising a machine that sliced bread can't have been that difficult, but US inventor Otto Rohwedder took 16 years to do it. One reason was that in 1917, after five years' work, he lost everything in a fire. More important was

the fact that sliced bread quickly went stale. By 1928, Rohwedder had perfected a machine that not only sliced, but also wrapped the bread into a handy, long-lasting package. Within five years, most bread in the USA came sliced.

Pre-stressed concrete

1928

Eugène Freyssinet

Ordinary concrete tends to crack under loads that stretch it. One elegant solution was invented in 1928 by French civil engineer Eugène Freyssinet. He put stretched steel wires into concrete while it was wet. When it had set, he released the wires so that they squeezed the concrete together, cancelling out the forces that would otherwise make it crack. Pre-stressed concrete is now used to produce light, strong structures of all kinds.

Electro-encephalograph

1929

Hans Berger

Electrodes placed on someone's head can reveal the electrical activity of their brain. This helps doctors to diagnose disorders such as epilepsy. An electroencephalograph, or EEG, machine, records the activity as a set of squiggly lines. The first machine was built by German physiologist Hans Berger in 1929, after five years' work with dogs and humans. No-one showed much interest in Berger's work at first, but a local optical company, Carl Zeiss, was impressed by his device and helped him to build a better one.

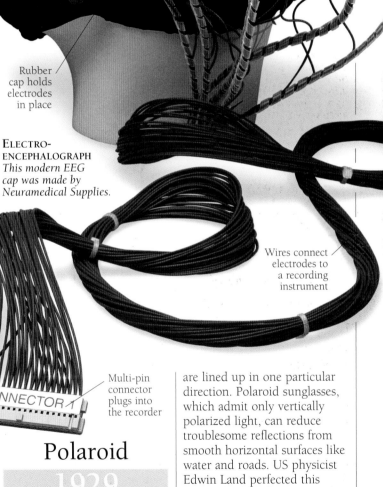

Rubber cap holds electrodes in place

ELECTRO-ENCEPHALOGRAPH
This modern EEG cap was made by Neuramedical Supplies.

CONNECTOR 1

Multi-pin connector plugs into the recorder

Wires connect electrodes to a recording instrument

Polaroid

1929

Edwin Land

Polaroid polarizes light. That is, it blocks all light waves except those whose vibrations are lined up in one particular direction. Polaroid sunglasses, which admit only vertically polarized light, can reduce troublesome reflections from smooth horizontal surfaces like water and roads. US physicist Edwin Land perfected this material, which has many other uses, in 1929. The thin plastic sheet, treated with optically active crystals, quickly replaced the bulkier polarizers that had been used earlier.

1928 A ground-breaking new dictionary of the English language, *A New English Dictionary on Historical Principles*, is published after years of work by James Murray and others. It will be better known as the *Oxford English Dictionary*.

1929 In October, prices on the New York stock exchange collapse, ruining thousands of people who had poured money into the market. The crash triggers a depression that lasts for years and makes millions of people jobless.

THE ANTIBIOTIC MIRACLE

*Howard Florey and Ernst Chain build on
Alexander Fleming's find to develop a life saver*

It was September 1928. Scottish bacteriologist Alexander Fleming was showing a friend some plates he used for growing bacteria. Suddenly he stopped. The plate in his hand was covered with bacteria, but there was also a patch of mould, and around the mould there were no bacteria.

Fleming worked at Sir Almroth Wright's vaccine laboratories in St Mary's Hospital, London. There, he grew more mould and made an extract he called penicillin. He tested it, used it to cure an eye infection, and wrote about it, but pursued it no further. He was more interested in vaccines. Penicillin, he thought, would be best used in laboratories.

Alexander Fleming working in his lab at St Mary's Hospital, Paddington, London

Ten years later, German biochemist Ernst Chain, working at the Sir William Dunn School of Pathology in Oxford, England, suggested to his boss, Australian pathologist Howard Florey, that they should investigate penicillin. Florey decided to see if it would affect bacteria inside animals – something Fleming hadn't tried. Chain's job would be to isolate the active agent from the mould.

In May 1940, Florey injected eight mice with lethal bacteria. Then he injected four of them with penicillin. Next day, the untreated mice were dead, but the rest were fine. Florey phoned a colleague. "It's a miracle," he told her.

Culture dish showing the effect of penicillin on bacteria

HAPPY ACCIDENT
Bacteria can be grown in dishes filled with nutrient jelly. Fleming had piles of these lying around, which led to his lucky find.

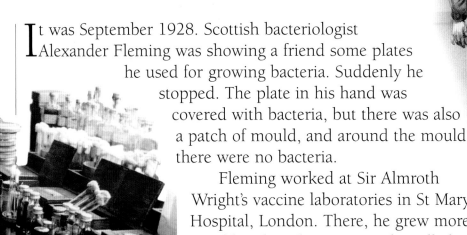

ANIMAL MAGIC
Fleming thought that penicillin would be good for getting rid of unwanted bacteria in the laboratory. But Florey and Chain saw its potential for curing disease, and were the first to try it on mice.

Florey wanted to test penicillin on human patients, but to produce enough he had to turn his lab into a factory. Soon it was filled with piping and chemical fumes. By February 1941, he had enough penicillin for the first human trial.

Policeman Albert Alexander was gravely ill with a serious infection. On 12 February, 1941, he started receiving penicillin. The effect was spectacular. He almost recovered, but Florey didn't have enough penicillin to keep the treatment going, and Alexander died. Later, five

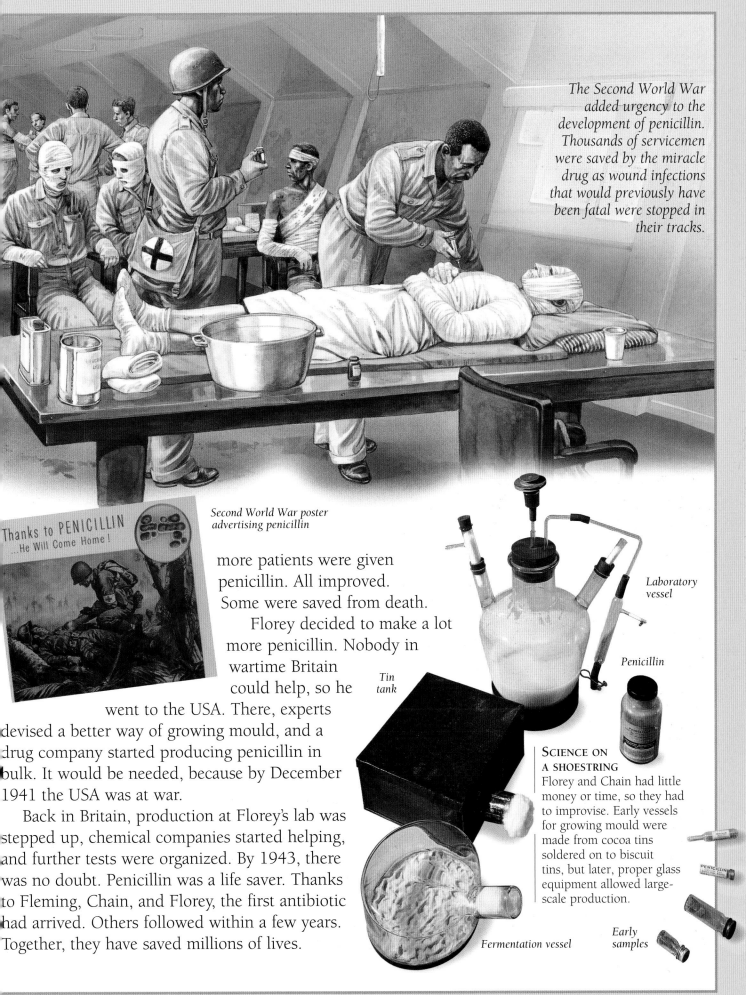

The Second World War added urgency to the development of penicillin. Thousands of servicemen were saved by the miracle drug as wound infections that would previously have been fatal were stopped in their tracks.

Second World War poster advertising penicillin

Thanks to PENICILLIN *...He Will Come Home!*

more patients were given penicillin. All improved. Some were saved from death.

Florey decided to make a lot more penicillin. Nobody in wartime Britain could help, so he went to the USA. There, experts devised a better way of growing mould, and a drug company started producing penicillin in bulk. It would be needed, because by December 1941 the USA was at war.

Back in Britain, production at Florey's lab was stepped up, chemical companies started helping, and further tests were organized. By 1943, there was no doubt. Penicillin was a life saver. Thanks to Fleming, Chain, and Florey, the first antibiotic had arrived. Others followed within a few years. Together, they have saved millions of lives.

Laboratory vessel

Penicillin

Tin tank

SCIENCE ON A SHOESTRING

Florey and Chain had little money or time, so they had to improvise. Early vessels for growing mould were made from cocoa tins soldered on to biscuit tins, but later, proper glass equipment allowed large-scale production.

Fermentation vessel

Early samples

Synthetic rubber tyres

1929

*Walter Bock,
Eduard Tschunkur*

By the 1880s, scientists had some idea of the chemical composition of rubber, but their attempts to copy it failed. They had more success when they tried imitating its properties rather than its chemistry. In 1929, German chemists Walter Bock and Eduard Tschunkur made a synthetic rubber good enough for tyres. This was important in the Second World War, when Germany's natural rubber supplies were cut off.

Supermarket

1930

Michael Cullen

The first essential of a supermarket is self-service. This was invented in 1916 by US grocer Clarence Saunders. His Piggly Wiggly store in Memphis, Tennessee, cut costs by letting customers take their purchases straight off the shelves, something unheard of at the time. The other vital ingredients, bulk buying and quick turnover, were added in 1930 when another US grocer, Michael Cullen, opened his King Kullen store in an old garage in Long Island, New York. Customers flocked to this, the first true supermarket.

Jet engine

1930

*Frank Whittle,
Hans von Ohain*

The jet engine was patented in 1930 by a young British Royal Air Force pilot, Frank (later Sir Frank) Whittle. He had great difficulty convincing anyone that it would be useful. Things were different in Germany. When Hans von Ohain thought up a similar engine, it was immediately taken up by a major plane company. The first jet plane, a Heinkel HE-178, flew from a German airfield in 1939, two years before the first British jet flight.

Clear adhesive tape

1930

Richard Drew

Cellophane appeared in the late 1920s. One of its main uses was for wrapping items like flowers and fruit to make them look attractive, so it demanded a clear sealing tape to go with it. First to solve the problem was US engineer Richard Drew of the Minnesota Mining and Manufacturing Company, now known as 3M. Having invented masking tape – a sticky tape made from paper – in 1925, he coated Cellophane with a similar adhesive to produce Scotch Tape in 1930. Seven years later, Colin Kininmonth and George Gray produced Sellotape, a British competitor.

Radio astronomy

1931

Karl Jansky, Grote Reber

Radio astronomy started at Bell Telephone Labs in the USA, where engineer Karl Jansky was tracking down radio interference. One source of interference eluded him until, in 1931, after months of frustration, he pointed his antenna upwards. The mysterious interference was coming from the stars. Another US radio engineer Grote Reber built the first radio telescope, a 9.5 m (31 ft) dish, in 1937. By 1942 he had made the first radio map of the sky.

Electronic flash

1931

Harold Edgerton

The flash in most of today's cameras took 50 years to perfect. It started as a bulky device used when taking research photographs

JET ENGINE *The Gloster E28/39 was the first plane to be fitted with the jet engine designed by Frank Whittle. It took to the skies in April 1941, four years after Whittle's first engine was started up, and two years after the first successful German jet flight.*

Undercarriage retracts during flight

Wings designed for subsonic flight

1930 After 19 days' solo flying in her converted De Havilland Moth, British aviator Amy Johnson reaches Darwin, Australia, from England. The feat, achieved after only 50 hours' flying experience, wins Johnson a £10,000 prize.

1930 After the formation of the football organization FIFA in 1904, the World Cup finally kicks off in Montevideo, Uruguay. Only 13 teams compete, which do not include any from Britain. Uruguay takes the cup.

of high-speed objects, such as bullets. US engineer Harold Edgerton realized as early as 1926 that a high voltage applied to a tube containing xenon gas could produce very brief but intense pulses of light. By 1931 he had devised a practical flash.

Scrabble

1931

Alfred Butts

The world's best known word game was invented in 1931 by an unemployed New York architect, Alfred Butts.

He called it Criss-Cross. Nobody wanted to make the game, so Butts went into partnership with a retired government official, James Brunot, who started making it in his garage. Renamed Lexico, the game went on sale in 1946. Within two years, games makers Selchow & Righter had snapped it up and were selling it under yet another name – Scrabble. The letter values were fixed by counting the number of times each letter appeared on a page of the *New York Times*.

SCRABBLE *The Scrabble board contains 225 squares, of which 81 are "premium" squares that increase a player's score.*

because it contains a heavier form of hydrogen, called deuterium. US chemist Harold Urey discovered deuterium in 1931. He then realized that electrolysis of water releases more hydrogen than deuterium, leaving behind water enriched with deuterium. Using this process, he and fellow chemist Edward Washburn created the first heavy water. They published their discovery in 1932.

Button-through shirt

1932

Cecil Gee

British tailor Cecil Gee opened his first shop in 1929 in London. His customers didn't want fussy shirts that had to be pulled on over their head. Nor did they like separate collars attached with fiddly studs. So in 1932 Gee designed a shirt with buttons all the way down, which could be slipped on like a jacket, and also had its collar sewn in place. After years of resistance by traditionalists, Gee's design became the standard men's shirt.

Ailerons control banking and turning

High-speed jet of hot gases from the engine pushes the plane along

Heavy water

1932

Harold Urey, Edward Washburn

Heavy water has the same chemical properties as ordinary water, but is nearly 11 per cent heavier. This is

Full-colour movie

1932

Herbert Kalmus

Several colour movie processes were invented in the early 20th century, but most used only two colours, giving unrealistic results. One of these two-colour processes

FULL-COLOUR MOVIE *The Technicolor camera was really three cameras in one. After processing, its three films were printed on to a single film for projection.*

was Technicolor, invented by US engineer Herbert Kalmus. In 1932, it was redesigned to work with three colours. The first full-colour movies had arrived. Although hampered by a huge camera taking three reels of film at once, Technicolor was used for many classics, including *The Wizard of Oz*.

1931 The Empire State Building, the world's tallest skyscraper, is completed in New York. It will eventually be outdone by taller buildings, but with 102 storeys, and a starring role in the film *King Kong*, it will remain a tourist attraction.

1932 Britain has its first and only brush with organized fascism, as aristocrat Sir Oswald Mosley founds the British Union of Fascists. Preaching racism, he recruits gullible young men and gets them to march in black shirts.

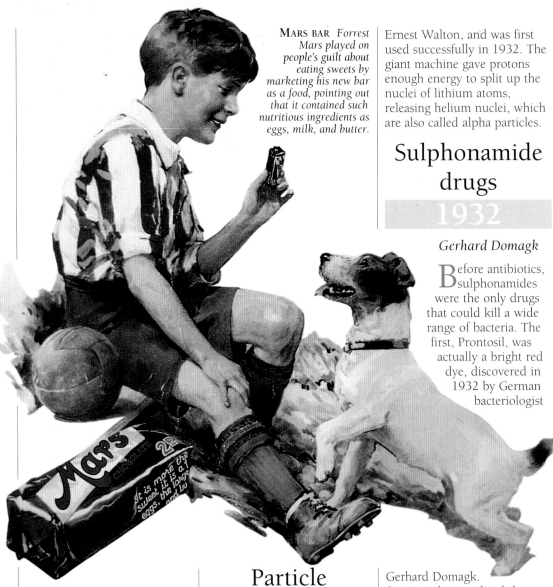

MARS BAR *Forrest Mars played on people's guilt about eating sweets by marketing his new bar as a food, pointing out that it contained such nutritious ingredients as eggs, milk, and butter.*

Ernest Walton, and was first used successfully in 1932. The giant machine gave protons enough energy to split up the nuclei of lithium atoms, releasing helium nuclei, which are also called alpha particles.

Sulphonamide drugs

1932

Gerhard Domagk

Before antibiotics, sulphonamides were the only drugs that could kill a wide range of bacteria. The first, Prontosil, was actually a bright red dye, discovered in 1932 by German bacteriologist Gerhard Domagk. Scientists later realized that this broke down in the body to give a more potent drug, sulphanilamide. From 1936 onwards, after clinical trials by British doctor Leonard Colebrook, this and other related "sulpha" drugs began to save thousands of lives. They are still used today when antibiotics fail.

Electron microscope

1933

Ernst Ruska

An image cannot contain detail smaller than the waves used to form it. Because of this, ordinary light microscopes cannot reveal really tiny objects. In 1933, German engineer Ernst Ruska invented a microscope that worked with much smaller waves. The waves were electrons. Although these were once regarded as particles, quantum physics (✳ *see* **page 169**) shows that they are also waves. Using them, electron microscopes can now reveal objects as small as molecules.

Stereophonic sound

1933

Alan Blumlein, Harvey Fletcher

Stereophonic sound was developed independently on both sides of the Atlantic. In Britain, engineer Alan Blumlein, seeking realistic sound for large-screen films, obtained a patent covering the fundamental principles of stereophony in 1933. He also developed a microphone technique for stereo recording and developed the basic system that is used to make stereophonic discs. In the USA, physicist Harvey Fletcher of Bell Telephone Laboratories gave his first public demonstration in 1934, in New York City.

FM radio

1934

Edwin Armstrong

The letters FM on a radio station stand for "frequency modulation". This means that the transmitted frequency goes up and down slightly with the ups and downs of the sound wave it is carrying. It's more complicated than the earlier "amplitude modulation", or AM, system, but resists interference better. FM

Mars bar

1932

Forrest Mars

The Mars bar started with the idea of turning malted milk into confectionery. In 1922, Forrest Mars suggested this to his father, US candy maker Frank Mars, who created a chocolate-covered nougat and caramel bar called Milky Way. After a row with his father, Forrest left for England in 1932. He set up his own company in Slough, near London, where he perfected the Mars bar, a version of his father's product cleverly adapted to British tastes.

Particle accelerator

1932

John Cockcroft, Ernest Walton

Nuclear physicists can study the structure of matter by firing sub-atomic particles such as protons and alpha particles (helium nuclei) at other atoms to smash them up and see what comes out. At first, the physicists had to use particles emitted naturally by radioactive materials like radium. Today, they nearly always use particle accelerators, which produce energetic particles artificially. The first was built by British physicists John Cockcroft and

1932 Sydney Harbour Bridge, designed by John Bradfield, is officially opened by the New South Wales Premier, Jack Lang. Before he can cut the ribbon, fascist agitator Francis de Groot slashes it. He is arrested and fined.

1933 Adolf Hitler is appointed Chancellor in Germany. He uses his position to establish the absolute rule of the National Socialist (Nazi) Party. Violently suppressing all opposition, he establishes himself as a dictator.

...was perfected in 1934 by US engineer Edwin Armstrong, who first demonstrated it using a transmitter on top of the Empire State Building.

Front-wheel drive car

1934

Andrè Citröen, André Lefèbvre

Many modern cars have their engine connected to the front wheels, avoiding lengthy transmission systems and giving them better grip. A lot of inventors tried this in the early 20th century, but the first to succeed in a big way was French car maker Andrè Citröen, whose chief engineer was André Lefèbvre. Their "traction avant" system appeared in 1934, and car manufacturers Citröen have been making front-wheel drive cars ever since.

HAMMOND ORGAN *One of the Hammond's great advantages was that it was much smaller than a traditional pipe organ. It could compete with the piano as an instrument for the home.*

Perspex

1934

Rowland Hill, John Crawford

The first thick, clear plastic available in large sheets was Plexiglas. Developed by German chemist Otto Röhm, it was introduced by the Röhm & Haas companies in Germany and the USA in 1931. The following year two British chemists, Rowland Hill and John Crawford, discovered how to make sheets of a related, but more glass-like material, polymethyl methacrylate. Produced by chemical company ICI, it went on sale in 1934 under the more user-friendly name of Perspex.

Hammond organ

1934

Laurens Hammond

The sound of the Hammond organ comes from lots of spinning magnetic wheels, one

Dual keyboard allows a different sound for each hand

Swell pedal controls the volume of sound

Gauge indicates gas pressure

for each note. Teeth on the wheels create pulsating currents in magnetic coils, and these are mixed and amplified to produce the final sound. US engineer Laurens Hammond built his first organ in 1934, using a constant-speed motor he had invented earlier. Each wheel could have only a whole number of teeth, so the scales he got were slightly out of tune. His solution was to add a wobble to every note, covering up the errors while creating the unique Hammond sound.

Cat's-eyes

1935

Percy Shaw

Cat's-eyes are the little reflectors set in the road which make driving at night safer. Possibly inspired by real cats' eyes, British engineer

Percy Shaw invented them in 1934, but they were not used until the following year. Their secret was in the rubber that housed the reflectors. Whenever a car ran over a cat's-eye, a flexible "eyelid" wiped the reflectors clean, ready for the next driver. Shaw became a millionaire, but never left his home town in Yorkshire.

Polyethylene

1935

Eric Fawcett, Reginald Gibson

Chemists Eric Fawcett and Reginald Gibson were part of a team at British chemical company ICI. They were investigating the reactions of the gas ethylene at high pressure. In 1935, they found a white, waxy solid in one of their reaction vessels. It was a new plastic, polyethylene. It was an excellent insulator and easy to mould. ICI marketed the new material in 1939 as Alkathene.

POLYETHYLENE *Chemists Fawcett and Gibson used this apparatus in their discovery of polyethylene.*

1934 "Bollywood", the Indian version of Hollywood, gets started with the opening of a major film studio, Bombay Talkies, in Mumbai. It is the brainchild of Indian producer Himansu Rai and a London-based Indian playwright, Niranjan Pal.

1934 In October, 100,000 Chinese communists are driven out of Jiangxi Province by Guomindang leader Chiang Kai-shek. They begin a 9600 km (6000 mile) "long march" to safety in Shaanxi. It will take a year – and only 8000 will arrive.

MONOPOLY
THE NEW GAME
AND THE
RAGE OF AMERICA
MILLIONS NOW PLAYING IT

MADE BY JOHN WADDINGTON LTD.
MAKERS OF LEXICON,
OBTAINABLE FROM ALL STATIONERS, STORES & TOY DEALERS.

MONOPOLY *The British version of Monopoly, with London street names, appeared in 1936. Its advertising traded on its success in the USA.*

Monopoly
1935
Charles Darrow

This popular board game was invented by US heating engineer Charles Darrow. He based it on a less successful game invented in 1924 by Elizabeth Phillips. His first board featured streets in Atlantic City, a favourite holiday spot. The tokens – dog, hat, and so on – were copies of charms on his wife's bracelet. Manufacturers rejected the game at first, but it finally appeared in time for Christmas 1935.

Radar
1935
Robert Watson-Watt

In 1935, the British government, fearing war, asked Scottish engineer Robert Watson-Watt if he could produce a radio "death ray". Watson-Watt knew that radio could not destroy enemy aircraft, but thought it might be able to detect them. On 26 February, using signals from a BBC transmitter, he detected a distant bomber. After this, he supervised the construction of radar stations along the English coast. These started working just as the war with Germany began in 1939. They helped the Royal Air Force win the Battle of Britain. (✳ *See also* **Seeing by radio**.)

RADAR *One detection system helps another: radar used to aim a searchlight in 1945.*

Colour film
1935
*Leopold Mannes,
Leopold Godowsky*

Colour film was invented by two US classical musicians, Leopold Mannes and Leopold Godowsky. Their film had three separate light-sensitive layers. Each layer formed an image in one of the three primary colours. Although its processing was complicated, the pictures it produced were so good that, in 1930, Kodak invited Mannes and Godowsky to work in its research laboratories. The result, Kodachrome, was launched on 15 April, 1935.

1935 US composer George Gershwin writes his folk opera *Porgy and Bess,* a unique blend of jazz, pop, and opera that will come to be thought of as his greatest work. Its lyrics are written by his elder brother, Ira.

1936 On 11 December, Britain's King Edward VIII tells the nation that he must leave his throne for love of the woman he has been forbidden to marry, Mrs Wallis Simpson. He settles in France and marries her the next year.

SEEING BY RADIO

"RADAR" GETS ITS NAME from "radio detection and ranging". It detects objects and measures their distance, or range, by sending out short pulses of radio waves and showing if anything reflects them back. The time between sending a pulse and getting it back shows the distance of the reflecting object. Its direction is found by using a steerable antenna.

EARLY RADAR

The discoverer of radio waves, Heinrich Hertz, showed that they were reflected from metallic surfaces, and several early radio experimenters thought that they might be used to detect objects. German engineer Christian Hülsmeyer patented a detection system in 1904, and a crude form of ranging with radio pulses was achieved in 1925.

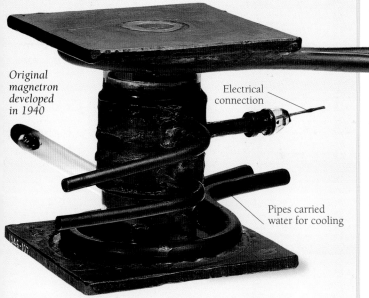

Original magnetron developed in 1940

Electrical connection

Pipes carried water for cooling

LATER DEVELOPMENTS

The first radar stations worked with quite large wavelengths. This made their measurements rather imprecise, and also meant that the stations had to be big. In 1940, the invention of the magnetron, which could produce much shorter waves called microwaves, allowed compact, precise radars to be installed in aircraft. Radar is now essential to aviation.

HELICOPTER *The Fw 61 looked more like a wingless plane than a helicopter. Its rotors spun in opposite directions to make it fly straight.*

Richter scale
1935

Charles Richter, Beno Gutenberg

News reports usually rate earthquakes on the Richter scale. Devised in 1935 by US seismologists Charles Richter and Beno Gutenberg, the scale relates to the energy released by an earthquake at its centre, with each step representing ten times the energy of the previous one. So an earthquake measuring 8 on the Richter scale, which would usually be catastrophic, releases a million times as much energy as one rated at 2, which wouldn't be noticed.

Snorkel
1936

Jan Wichers

Snorkels allow swimmers to breathe underwater, but they were originally used on submarines, allowing them to run their engines while submerged. The first modern snorkel was a tower on top of a submarine. It let fresh air in and exhaust gases out, and was designed by Lieutenant Jan Wichers of the Royal Netherlands Navy in 1936. After the Netherlands was invaded by Germany in 1940, the Wichers snorkel idea was applied to German submarines. By 1944, these could cruise for hours just below the surface, invisible to radar.

Helicopter
1936

Heinrich Focke

It took a long time to develop a really usable rotating-wing aircraft. Early helicopters had little lift, and because the way the rotor worked was not fully understood, they tended to flip over sideways. The French Breguet-Dorand gyroplane of 1935 solved most of these problems, but the first helicopter to develop into a practical production machine was the Focke-Wulf Fw 61. Designed by German engineer Heinrich Focke, the machine had two rotors and took to the air in 1936.

Suntan lotion
1936

Eugène Schueller

The first mass-market suntan lotion was produced in 1936, after Paris designer Coco Chanel acquired a house in the south of France and made tanning fashionable. The perfumed, golden oil that helped to prevent the skin from burning was created by a small company founded by French chemist Eugène Schueller. Today, his company, L'Oréal, is much larger, and the name of his oil, Ambre Solaire, is known worldwide.

Parking meter
1935

Carlton Magee

The hated parking meter first appeared in 1935, on the streets of Oklahoma City, USA. It was invented by Oklahoma businessman Carlton Magee, who wanted to stop all-day parkers clogging the streets. He also thought it might make a little money for his city. The Park-O-Meter, as Magee called it, was remarkably similar in appearance to the meters used today. Much to the annoyance of inconsiderate parkers, Magee's idea has proved a hit with city authorities everywhere.

1936 Adolf Hitler fails to demonstrate white racial superiority at the carefully stage-managed Olympic Games in Berlin, when black US athlete Jesse Owens wins four gold medals. Hitler simply refuses to acknowledge the fact.

1936 After years of strife between Nationalists and Republicans, the Spanish Civil War starts on 17 July. People from many nations join in. After three years and 100,000 deaths, Nationalist general Franco will control Spain.

Television
1936

Vladimir Zworykin, Isaac Shoenberg

See **pages 202–203** for the story of how Vladimir Zworykin and Isaac Schoenberg perfected all-electronic television.

Pulse code modulation
1937

Alec Reeves

In 1937, British engineer Alec Reeves came up with a new way to reduce interference on telephone calls: convert them into code, like telegraph messages. The code would resist interference during transmission, and could be converted back into speech once received. Reeves called his idea pulse code modulation. With the electronics of his day, it was too expensive to use widely, but it is central to the digital communications revolution of today.

Trampoline
1937

George Nissen

As a child, US businessman George Nissen loved to watch trapeze artists bouncing on their safety nets. So he later designed his own, more effective bouncing rig. In 1937, he learned that the Spanish for springboard was "*trampolín*". This, in English form, would become the trademark of his new product. Children loved the Trampoline, and when war came Nissen sold lots to the US air force to help pilots with fitness training. The first world trampolining championship was held in 1964.

Epoxy resin
1937

Henry Moss

Epoxy resins are found in glues that come in two tubes. One tube contains resin, the other a hardener. When the two are mixed, they set hard because the hardener contains chemical groups that link the resin molecules together. British chemist Henry Moss made the first epoxy resins in 1937, and a two-part glue was marketed in 1946. Its Swiss makers, Ciba (now Ciba-Geigy) named their new product Araldite.

Superfluidity
1937

Peter Kapitsa, John Allen

It normally takes an effort to make a fluid flow. But at really low temperatures things can be very different. In 1937, Russian physicist Peter Kapitsa discovered that below about -271°C (-456°F) liquid helium loses its resistance to flow, and also develops strange habits, such as climbing up the walls of its container as a thin film. Kapitsa published his findings in 1938, as did Canadian physicist John Allen, who discoverered it independently.

Supermarket trolley
1937

Sylvan Goldman

US retailer Sylvan Goldman noticed that people in his Humpty Dumpty supermarkets never bought more than they could carry. He reasoned that if they could carry more they would buy more. So, in 1937, he got a local odd-job man to weld wheels and baskets to metal folding chairs. Customers resisted the strange-looking contraptions at first, so Goldman hired people to push his first crude trolleys around the store until everyone got the idea and started to use them.

Pressurized aircraft cabin
1937

Lockheed Corporation

Aircraft fly more smoothly and use less fuel at high altitudes. But the low pressure at these heights does not agree with people, so passenger cabins have to be pressurized. The first fully pressurized aircraft was the experimental US Lockheed XC-35, which was based on an existing Lockheed plane, the Electra. Built in 1937, the modified plane's reinforced fuselage had few windows, causing pilots to dub it the "Can't see-35".

Espresso coffee
1938

Achille Gaggia

When Italian engineer Achille Gaggia wanted coffee, he wanted it fast. So he invented a pump that forced nearly boiling water through finely ground coffee. Because the water moved so quickly, there wasn't time for bitter flavours to develop. A cup of espresso took only the pull of a lever, so it soon became popular with café owners. Gaggia patented his invention in 1938, and his name is now likely to be seen wherever coffee lovers gather.

Chamber into which hot water was forced

Holder for ground coffee

Cup was placed here to catch the coffee

ESPRESSO COFFEE
Small espresso machines, like this one from about 1950, use steam pressure to force water through the coffee.

1937 San Francisco's elegant Golden Gate Bridge opens to traffic, after heroic struggles with rock and water by engineer Joseph Strauss. For another 27 years its 1280 m (4200 ft) main span will be the longest in the world.

1937 On 7 July, a misunderstanding between Chinese and Japanese soldiers near Beijing escalates into war. The local problem is cleared up, but Chinese leader Chiang Kai-shek later attacks Japanese troops in Shanghai.

Nylon

1938

Wallace Carothers

Nylon was launched by US chemical company DuPont in 1938. Its inventor, US chemist Wallace Carothers, specialized in polymers – molecules made by joining lots of identical molecules together. He was trying to imitate silk, which is a protein, so he tried joining molecules with a linkage found in proteins, called the amide bond. In 1934, he succeeded so well that he could pull a continuous strand of "polyamide", or nylon, straight out of a laboratory beaker. The first nylon stockings went on display, to wild acclaim, in 1939.

Ballpoint pen

1938

Ladislao Biró, Georg Biró

Hungarian artist Ladislao Biró and his brother Georg, a chemist, thought they were making a totally new writing instrument. In fact, US inventor John Loud had invented something similar in 1888. New or not, Ladislao's ball-tip rolled on, lubricated by Georg's greasy, smudge-proof ink. The Biro pen was patented in 1938.

Later, the brothers met British entrepreneur Henry Martin. He noticed that ballpoints didn't leak at high altitude, and sold them to the Royal Air Force. Biros reached British shops in 1945 – in time for Christmas.

BALLPOINT PEN *The original Biro pen of the 1940s, made by the Miles Martin Pen Company, was a luxury product, which cost more than an ordinary fountain pen.*

NYLON *After being knitted, stockings are shaped to ensure a wrinkle-free fit by pulling them over dummy legs, a process known as boarding. It is seen here in a factory of 1946.*

Worker checks for flaws in the stocking while she boards it

Dummy legs made of metal

Teflon

1938

Roy Plunkett

The slippery, heat-resistant plastic used for coating pans was discovered by accident. On 6 April, 1938, Roy Plunkett, a research chemist for US chemical company DuPont, was testing the refrigeration gas tetrafluoroethylene. He had some in a cylinder, but it wouldn't come out. When he investigated, he found that it had turned into a white powder. The gas molecules had joined together to form polytetrafluoroethylene. Its more familiar trademark, Teflon, was registered in 1945. In the 1960s, researchers found a way to make the non-stick plastic stick to metal.

1938 The world's first large oceanarium, Marineland, in Florida, USA, opens to the public. Visitors are thrilled by fish such as sharks and rays, normally seen only in the open sea. Later, they will get soaked as dolphins do tricks.

1938 On 13 March, the Nazi chancellor of Austria, brutally installed by Hitler, asks in German troops to suppress disorder. Next day, Hitler and troops are in Vienna, declaring *Anschluss* (union) – just what Hitler always wanted.

MAKING THE DREAM COME TRUE

Vladimir Zworykin and Isaac Shoenberg work to perfect all-electronic television.

Saturday 30 January, 1937, was a sad day for Scottish television pioneer John Logie Baird. That was when the British Broadcasting Corporation (BBC) finally abandoned his mechanical television system, with its whirring wheels and messy chemicals. He had come a long way since his first experiments with television in 1923, but it wasn't far enough. His dream was over. The future was electronic.

Three months earlier, on 2 November, 1936, the BBC had started the world's first regular, high-definition, public television broadcasting service. In alternate weeks it used two different sets of equipment. The idea was to test two rival systems. One was Baird's; the other had been created by a team at Electrical and Musical Industries (EMI) led by Russian-born engineer Isaac Shoenberg. The all-electronic EMI system won easily. Its pictures were sharper, its cameras were more mobile, it was more reliable, and it cost less. In all but detail, it was the system we use today.

Shoenberg's team had been formed five years earlier. They had worked with remarkable speed, but they weren't the first to research into all-electronic television. On the other side of the Atlantic, a lone pioneer, Philo T. Farnsworth, had started work on his electronic "image dissector" in 1926. He gave the first demonstration of all-electronic television in 1934. Unfortunately, his cameras needed too much light, and his work came to a dead end.

ELECTRONIC EYE

The strange shape of the Emitron camera reflected the shape of the image tube inside it. The drooping nose held the tube's electron gun. Above this were two lenses, one of which was a viewfinder.

PICTURES FROM A SPINNING DISC

Baird did much to create interest in television. He used a rotating disc to sweep a spotlight over the subject to be televised, with a matching disc in the receiver. This mechanical system could not make pictures good enough to compete with electronics.

John Logie Baird

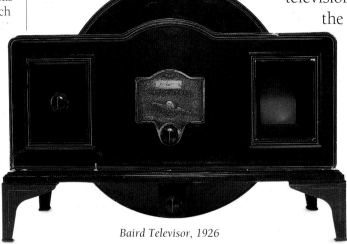

Baird Televisor, 1926

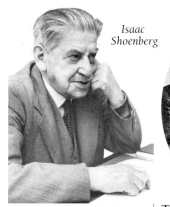

Isaac Shoenberg

Vladimir Zworykin

Modern television owes far more to another US engineer, Russian-born Vladimir Zworykin. He was the first to take up the suggestion, made in 1908 by Scottish engineer Alan Campbell Swinton, that a cathode ray tube could create as well as display pictures. In 1929, Zworykin took charge of

TV PIONEERS
The two main pioneers of all-electronic television were both born in Russia. Shoenberg was born in 1880, and Zworykin in 1889. Shoenberg emigrated to Britain in 1914, and Zworykin to the USA in 1919. It was Zworykin who developed the first successful camera tube. It scanned the image with a beam of electrons. Tubes of this type were highly sensitive and could show fine detail.

Britain's first television receivers were very expensive, worked only in London, and offered only a single channel. But they were the start of something big.

television development at the Radio Corporation of America. By 1931, he and his team had created the first successful electronic camera tube, the Iconoscope. Shoenberg's team later used Zworykin's basic idea to develop their own Emitron tube, which formed the heart of the cameras they designed for the BBC.

On 1 September, 1939, as war gripped Europe, the BBC television service was closed down. Just four months earlier, the USA's first regular television service had started, when the National Broadcasting Company (NBC) broadcast the opening of the New York World's Fair. Zworykin, Shoenberg, and a host of other engineers and enthusiasts had finally made the dream of television come true.

TELEVISION IN THE USA
Regular television broadcasts began later in the USA than in Britain, but the system there expanded more quickly. This National Broadcasting Company studio, equipped by the Radio Corporation of America, is seen in 1939, carrying on where war had forced the BBC to stop.

XEROGRAPHY *Chester Carlson did much of the basic research into dry photocopying in his kitchen.*

Xerography
1938

Chester Carlson

US physicist Chester Carlson wanted to make office work easier. He studied various methods of copying documents, then, in 1938, produced his first xerographic copy, using a zinc plate coated with sulphur. The original was on a microscope slide, and the copy was formed from moss spores stuck to waxed paper. (✳ *See also* **Making copies**.)

DDT
1939

Paul Müller

The chlorine-based chemical DDT had been known for years before Swiss chemist Paul Müller discovered, in 1939, that it made a good insecticide. It kills insects but has little effect on warm-blooded animals. In the Second World War, DDT was used to protect troops from insect-borne diseases. Later, it was used to kill insects that attack crops. Because DDT tends to persist in the environment and can find its way into food, it is now little used.

MAKING COPIES

XEROGRAPHY GETS ITS NAME from the Greek "*xeros*" meaning "dry". A lens projects an image on to a drum, the surface of which conducts electricity when exposed to light. Where the image is bright, the drum becomes more conductive and the electricity leaks away. Powdered resin dusted on the drum is attracted to the bits that are still electrified. The resin is transferred to paper and heated until it melts to form a permanent copy.

Early xerographic copiers were big and slow. This is part of one from 1960.

XEROGRAPHY AT WORK
Carlson's process has transformed office work. Machines that make 60 copies a minute are now commonplace. Xerography is also used in laser printers, which produce documents directly from digital data, rather than from other documents. Colour copiers, basically three machines in one box, now offer excellent quality.

LIFE WITHOUT XEROGRAPHY

Copying documents used to be difficult. They could be photographed with a special camera, but this was expensive and too big for an office. Or they could be made by the diffusion-transfer process, invented in 1939. This made copies in the office, but used wet chemicals and was very slow.

Nuclear fission
1939

Lise Meitner, Otto Frisch

When uranium is bombarded with neutrons, the nuclei of its atoms can split, forming lighter elements. This was discovered by German chemists Otto Hahn and Fritz Strassmann in 1938, but it was Austrian physicists Lise Meitner and Otto Frisch, her nephew, who explained the details and coined the term "nuclear fission". Realizing that it could be used to make a bomb, they quickly alerted other physicists and, through them, the US president.

Single-rotor helicopter
1940

Igor Sikorsky

The first successful helicopter, made in 1936, had two rotors that went round

1939 On 1 September, German troops invade Poland. Two days later, Britain and France declare war on Germany. The French rely on their heavily fortified "Maginot Line" along the German border. Britain prepares for all-out war.

1940 US writer Ernest Hemingway writes his novel *For Whom the Bell Tolls*, based on his experiences in the Spanish Civil War. Its main idea is that everyone, wherever they live, should be concerned by oppression occurring anywhere.

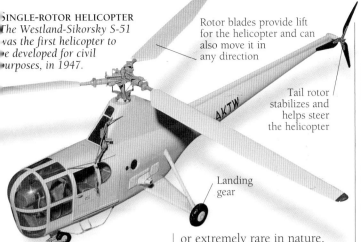

SINGLE-ROTOR HELICOPTER
The Westland-Sikorsky S-51 was the first helicopter to be developed for civil purposes, in 1947.

Rotor blades provide lift for the helicopter and can also move it in any direction

Tail rotor stabilizes and helps steer the helicopter

Landing gear

n opposite directions. This stopped the machine from spinning around. By 1940, the Russian-born US engineer Igor Sikorsky had flown a single-rotor helicopter. He stopped the spin with a small tail rotor that pushed sideways. It could also be used to help the helicopter turn left or right.

Digital logic design
1940

Claude Shannon

Digital logic circuits operate machines from computers to dishwashers. They would be almost impossible to design without US engineer Claude Shannon's thesis of 1940. He said that the work of British mathematician George Boole (✳ *see page* **140**) could be used to simplify the design of electrical circuits that worked out what a machine should do next. To prove it, he built a robot mouse that could find its way around a maze.

Plutonium
1940

Glenn Seaborg

Plutonium is one of several elements, all heavier than uranium, that are non-existent

or extremely rare in nature, but can be made in artificial nuclear reactions. US chemist Glenn Seaborg and his colleagues discovered ten of these between 1940 and 1955. Plutonium is the most important because of the special properties of one form called plutonium-239. This highly toxic material, which is produced in some types of nuclear reactors, can be used to make atomic weapons.

Binary electronic computing
1940

John Atanasoff, Clifford Berry

Early computing machines used the decimal system to represent numbers. This is not a good way of using electronic circuits. US mathematician John Atanasoff and his student Clifford Berry realized this as early as 1940. Their unsuccessful attempt at a computer, the ABC, used the binary system, which works with the base 2 instead of 10. It was more efficient because logic circuits work best when switching between just two voltages. Although the ABC was little known at the time, it may have influenced EDVAC, the first modern computer design (✳ *see page* **208**).

Anti-g flying suit
1941

Frederick Banting, Wilbur Franks

A fighter plane making a tight turn acts like a spin-dryer. The so-called "g" force drains blood out of the pilot's brain, possibly

ANTI-G FLYING SUIT *By the 1950s, suits like this one by Dunlop were filled with air, not water.*

causing a blackout. When a team under Sir Frederick Banting, better known for his work on insulin (✳ *see* **page 186**), discovered this, US scientist Wilbur Franks started work on an anti-g suit. The design his team produced was made from two layers of rubber with water in between them. When the suit was laced tightly around the pilot, it kept the blood in place, allowing tighter turns. The Franks Flying Suit Mk II was ready by 1941. Sadly, on his way to Britain to demonstrate it, Banting died in an air crash.

Suit covers the legs and abdomen

1941 On 7 December, the USA wakes up to the reality of world war as Japanese submarines and carrier-based planes attack the US Pacific fleet based at Pearl Harbor. Eight battleships and ten other vessels are sunk or damaged.

1941 US sculptor Gutzon Borglum completes his giant heads of presidents George Washington, Thomas Jefferson, Abraham Lincoln, and Theodore Roosevelt carved into the granite of Mount Rushmore, South Dakota, USA.

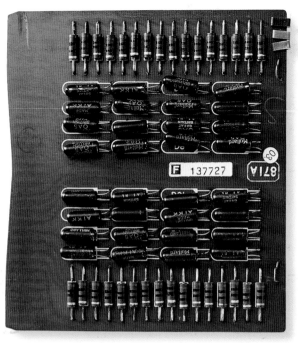

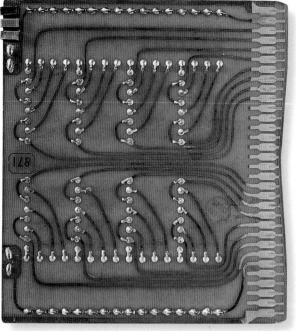

engineer Wernher von Braun and first launched in October 1942. It carried 725 kg (1600 lb) of explosive 80 km (50 miles) above Earth to drop on London as the most feared weapon of the Second World War.

Scanning electron microscope

1942

Vladimir Zworykin, Dennis McMullan

Scanning electron microscopes, or SEMs, combine high magnification with great depth of focus to produce vivid pictures of tiny three-dimensional objects. They work by scanning objects with a beam of electrons. The first SEM was built by Russian-born US physicist Vladimir Zworykin and others in 1942. It didn't seem as good as existing electron microscopes (* *see* **page 196**), so it was

SCANNING ELECTRON MICROSCOPE *The picture from a SEM is viewed on a screen, not through an eyepiece.*

Electro-mechanical computer

1941

Konrad Zuse

The first true computer was built in 1941 by German engineer Konrad Zuse. It was controlled by a program, and represented numbers in binary form, but it was not electronic. It used relays – switches operated by electromagnets. As these have actual moving contacts, they are extremely slow compared with electronic switches. So Zuse's Z3 computer was really the last of the mechanical computers, not the first of those we use today.

Printed circuit board

1941

Paul Eisler

Until Austrian engineer Paul Eisler invented the printed circuit board, or PCB, all electronic equipment was laboriously wired by hand. In 1941, Eisler printed wiring patterns on to copper foil stuck to plastic sheet, then placed this in an etching bath to remove the copper not protected by printing. After cleaning, and drilling holes for wires, the board was ready to receive components. The first PCBs were fitted inside anti-aircraft shells.

Polyethylene terephthalate

1941

Rex Whinfield, James Dickson

Clothes, duvet filling, bottles, and photographic film can all be made from polyethylene terephthalate, better known as PET. It was invented in 1941 by British chemists Rex Whinfield and James Dickson. Because Britain was at war, it was not until 1954 that the new material went into production there, as Terylene. By then, the US DuPont company had already developed and launched their own version of the material, which they called Dacron.

Silicon solar cell

1941

Russell Ohl

Solar cells convert sunlight into electricity. Modern cells can convert about one-third of the sunlight that falls on them, but the very first devices, made from about 1890, converted less than one-hundredth. The breakthrough came with a cell invented in 1941 by US scientist Russell Ohl. He used two types of impure silicon, rather than pure silicon and a metal. When brought together and exposed to light, current flowed from one to the other.

Ballistic missile

1942

Wernher von Braun

A ballistic missile is a rocket with a warhead that flies high into the sky and then falls on to its target. The development of such weapons has now led to the design of large rockets for peaceful purposes. The first effective ballistic missile was the V-2, designed for Hitler by German

1942 The elegant French luxury liner *Normandie*, holder of the Blue Riband for the fastest Atlantic crossing – which it won with a time of 3 days, 22 hours, and 7 minutes – catches fire in New York harbour and is destroyed.

1942 In Oxford, England, an organization called Oxfam is created to raise money for hungry children in Greece, which is ravaged by war. It will continue after the war to provide aid for refugees and for poorer parts of the world.

dropped. Later, British engineer Charles Oatley got his student Dennis McMullan to try again, and by 1951 he had built a working instrument. The first commercial SEM, producing the striking images familiar today, was launched in 1965.

Nuclear reactor
1942

Enrico Fermi

When a uranium-235 nucleus splits under bombardment by neutrons, it gives out further neutrons. These can split other nuclei, which release yet more neutrons. This process was first kept going in a controlled "chain reaction" by a team led by Italian-born US physicist Enrico Fermi. Their nuclear reactor, built in a squash court at Chicago University, was used for research that helped build the first atomic bomb. The reactor was working by December 1942.

Aqua-Lung
1943

Jacques Cousteau, Émile Gagnan

Before French explorer Jacques Cousteau and engineer Émile Gagnan thought up the Aqua-Lung in 1943, divers got air through pipes, used a snorkel, or just held their breath. They could not swim freely well below the surface. The Aqua-Lung had compressed air cylinders worn on the body and connected to the diver's mouthpiece through an automatic pressure regulator. It changed our view of the oceans and created the popular sport of scuba diving.

AQUA-LUNG *Scuba divers, like this one exploring Red Sea corals, take their own air with them, which gives them greater freedom.*

Silicones
1943

Frederic Kipping, Eugene Rochow

Silicones are oily or rubbery compounds. They are used as lubricants and sealants for waterproofing and in surgical implants. Their molecules are chains of units that have a core of silicon and oxygen atoms with carbon-based groups attached. Silicones were studied by British chemist Frederic Kipping from about 1900 onwards, but it was not until 1943 that US chemist Eugene Rochow developed an economic process for making them.

Function of DNA
1944

Oswald Avery

The first step towards unlocking the mechanism of genetic inheritance was taken in 1944 by Canadian-born US bacteriologist Oswald Avery, who explained an observation made by British researcher Fred Griffith in 1928. Griffith found that pneumonia bacteria were either rough or smooth, and that an extract of the smooth bacteria could make the rough ones smooth. More important, all their descendants inherited this characteristic. In a long series of experiments, Avery showed that the substance responsible was not a protein, as expected, but a nucleic acid, DNA (✳ *see* **page 149**).

see **page 149**

1943 The Rodgers and Hammerstein musical *Oklahoma!* opens on Broadway, New York, to wild acclaim. Including songs such as *Surrey with the Fringe on Top*, it will win a Pulitzer prize and continue for 2248 performances.

1944 Kiri Te Kanawa is born in Gisborne, New Zealand, to an Irish mother and an aristocratic Maori father. After success as a soprano in her own country, she will study singing in London and eventually become an international star.

Only part of Charles Babbage's Analytical Engine was completed before Babbage's death in 1871. This is part of the "mill" or processor of the machine, with its printing mechanism.

Artificial kidney

1944

Willem Kolff

When kidneys fail, a machine can take over their job. Artificial kidneys clean up blood by passing it through a membrane that lets out unwanted chemicals but keeps in the rest. The first practical machine was invented in 1944 by Dutch doctor Willem Kolff. It passed the blood through artificial sausage skin, which has microscopic pores. The skin was wrapped around a slatted drum immersed in a special fluid. Kolff later pioneered better machines and techniques that have now made kidney dialysis a routine procedure.

Electronic computer

1945

John Mauchly, John Presper Eckert

Mechanical computers were in use by the 1930s, but electronics promised much faster computation. The first

ARTIFICIAL KIDNEY *Home dialysis machines appeared in the 1960s. This machine, discreetly disguised as furniture, was used by one of the first home patients.*

all-electronic computer was developed by US engineers John Mauchly and John Presper Eckert of the Moore School of Electrical Engineering at the University of Pennsylvania. ENIAC was a huge machine containing 18,000 electronic tubes. Programmed by plugging in wires, it performed 5000 operations per second. It went to work in 1945, but was soon replaced by machines of a completely different design.

Modern computer architecture

1945

John von Neumann

Most modern computers keep their programs, and the data on which they work, in one and the same memory. This makes them more flexible. It is not clear who invented the idea, but the best candidate is Hungarian-born US

mathematician John von Neumann, who was heavily involved in designing the "stored program" computer EDVAC. This design appeared in 1945, but the concept was first proved by an experimental computer in Manchester, England, in 1948. (✳ *See also* **Computer pioneers**.)

Atomic bomb

1945

Robert Oppenheimer

Most people would prefer that the atomic bomb had not been invented. But in 1940, with Germany at war

Little Boy, dropped on Hiroshima

ATOMIC BOMB *The Manhattan project produced two types of bomb. Little Boy was a plutonium bomb and Fat Man was a uranium bomb.*

Fat Man, dropped on Nagasaki

with the world and possibly working on a bomb of its own, the development of an atomic weapon seemed essential. US physicist Robert Oppenheimer took charge of the Manhattan project, which developed the technology needed to purify the right kind of uranium or plutonium and make it explode. After a test in July 1945, the first atom bomb used in war was dropped on 6 August, destroying the Japanese city of Hiroshima and most of its inhabitants.

Bikini

1946

Jacques Heim, Louis Réard

Skimpy two-piece swimsuits get their name from Bikini Atoll in the South Pacific. French fashion designer Louis Réard chose the name to upstage rival designer Jacques Heim who, in 1946, had started selling a two-piece called the Atome. On 5 July, four days after the USA tested an atomic bomb over Bikini, Réard launched his explosively small creation under the suddenly well known name.

1944 US composer Aaron Copland writes *Appalachian Spring* for US ballet dancer Martha Graham. The music from the ballet perfectly expresses the open-air, pioneering spirit of the USA, and will become a concert classic.

1945 On 8 May, the end of war in Europe is formally declared. On 14 August, after atom bombs have flattened the cities of Hiroshima and Nagasaki, the Japanese surrender to the USA and Allies. The Second World War is over.

COMPUTER PIONEERS

THE COMPUTER ARCHITECTURE pioneered by John von Neumann is basically simple. A single memory stores data coming from outside and from the arithmetic unit that does the computing. Instructions and data are retrieved from the same memory by the control unit – which sequences and decodes instructions – and by output devices such as displays. Earlier computers used several different architectures, and often worked with inefficient decimal arithmetic.

BEFORE ELECTRONICS
The idea of a programmable computer goes back to British mathematician Charles Babbage's Analytical Engine, conceived in 1834 but never built. The first working, non-electronic computer was built in 1941 by German engineer Konrad Zuse.

EARLY ELECTRONIC COMPUTERS
The first all-electronic computer, ENIAC, was huge and slow. Better architecture and use of the binary system gradually improved things. The first practical stored-program machine, EDSAC, started working in Cambridge, England, in 1949.

MODERN COMPUTERS
The arrival of integrated circuits (ICs) transformed computers from the early 1960s onwards. Computers had already been shrunk by transistors, but ICs made them even smaller and could also form compact, high-speed memories.

Microwave oven
1946
Percy Spencer

When US engineer Percy Spencer was working on radar for the Raytheon Company in 1945, he noticed that the powerful microwaves had melted some sweets in his pocket. After experimenting with popcorn and eggs, Spencer built the first, crude microwave oven. In 1946, Raytheon took out a patent, and in 1947 the Radar Range went on sale at $5000.

Tupperware
c1946
Earl Tupper

Plastic fridge boxes were invented by US plastics manufacturer Earl Tupper, in about 1946. He found the right plastic and designed an airtight seal, but people did not seem to want the boxes. In 1948, after meeting ace saleswoman Brownie Wise, Tupper hit on a new sales technique. Hostesses invited their friends round, then demonstrated and sold the boxes to them. These Tupperware parties did the trick.

Motor scooter
1946
Corradino d'Ascanio

The shape of the modern motor scooter was determined in 1946 by Italian engineer Corradino d'Ascanio.

His boss, Enrico Piaggio, wanted something to get him around the aircraft engine works he owned. D'Ascanio soon came up with the basic design: U-shaped body, two-stroke engine under the seat, and small, easy-to-change wheels. Cheap to make and fun to ride, the Vespa (Italian for wasp) was named after the sound its engine made, and it became an engineering classic.

Grip was twisted to control the throttle

MOTOR SCOOTER *This Vespa 125 is the 1951 version of the first 125, which was introduced by Piaggio in 1948.*

Engine and gearbox directly connected to the rear wheel

Easily changed wheels

1946 A new name enters the airline industry when Tata Airlines, founded in 1932, becomes Air-India Limited. Two years later, sister company Air-India International is flying to Europe. Nationalized in 1953, by 1962 it will be renamed Air India.

1946 Perhaps the most widely read book about babies, *Common Sense Book of Baby and Child Care*, written by US paediatrician Benjamin Spock, is published. It will be blamed for many things, including the youth culture of the 1960s.

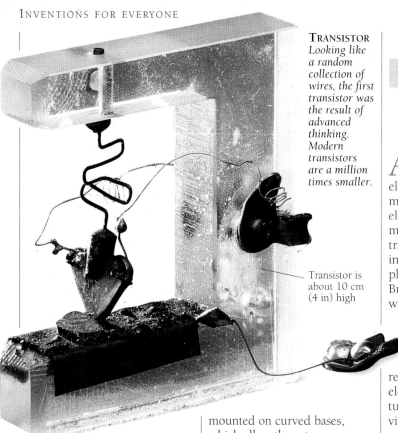

TRANSISTOR *Looking like a random collection of wires, the first transistor was the result of advanced thinking. Modern transistors are a million times smaller.*

— Transistor is about 10 cm (4 in) high

Transistor

1947

John Bardeen, Walter Brattain, William Shockley

A transistor is a tiny piece of silicon within which electricity controls electricity, making the whole of modern electronics possible. There are many different types of transistor. The first one, invented in 1947 by US physicists John Bardeen, Walter Brattain, and William Shockley, was made of germanium, not silicon, and worked on a different principle from those in modern computer chips. But it started a revolution. Within 25 years, electronics based on vacuum tubes (✳ *see* **page 176**) was virtually dead.

Holography

1948

Dennis Gabor

Unlike an ordinary photograph, a hologram captures every detail of the light waves reflected by an object. This makes objects appear with startling realism: in a hologram viewed at an angle, objects look just as they would from that angle. The technique was invented in 1948 by Hungarian-born British engineer Dennis Gabor. It works by recording the interference pattern created when light reflected from an object mixes with unreflected light. The best light source is a laser. As this was not invented in 1948, Gabor had to make do with ordinary light shining through a small hole.

Long-playing record

1948

Peter Goldmark

Before 1948, a 30 cm (12 in) record played for only four minutes each side, produced poor sound, and broke easily. So a disc that

LONG-PLAYING RECORD *By 1967, when The Beatles released the record* Sgt Pepper's Lonely Hearts Club Band, *LP sleeve design had become high art.*

Carbon dating

1947

Willard Libby

Carbon dating enables archaeologists to estimate the age of organic materials. It was developed by US chemist Willard Libby in 1947. He showed that Earth's atmosphere contains a tiny proportion of a radioactive form of carbon, carbon-14, and that living organisms take up both this and ordinary carbon. After the death of an organism, its carbon-14 starts to decay, so the smaller the proportion of carbon-14, the older the sample must be.

Subbuteo

1947

Peter Adolph

Subbuteo is a popular table-top football game played with model footballers mounted on curved bases, which allow them to move without falling over. Players flick their chosen footballers at an oversized ball. The game was invented in 1947 by British birdwatcher Peter Adolph. He named it using the Latin name of a bird called the hobby, *Falco subbuteo*. When its current makers, Hasbro, said in 2000 that production would have to stop, there was an international outcry. They relented and the game lives on.

False eyelashes

1947

David Aylott, Eric Aylott

The first convincing false eyelashes were made for the film industry. In 1947, British studio make-up artists David and Eric Aylott created strips of false eyelashes that were easy to apply and could stand the scrutiny of a close-up. The Aylotts later developed lashes for everyday use under the name Eyelure. By the 1960s, Eyelure was selling eight million pairs a year.

1947 To the joy of miners, Britain's coal mines are at last nationalized as the National Coal Board comes into being on New Year's Day. The Labour government pays out £165 million for property that includes about 1650 mines.

1948 The General Assembly of the United Nations adopts the Universal Declaration of Human Rights at a session in Paris on 10 December. The vote is carried unopposed, but eight members, including the USSR, abstain.

offered 25 minutes of pure sound per side, and was made of bendy vinyl, created a sensation. It was developed by Hungarian-born US engineer Peter Goldmark for Columbia Records. Rival company RCA-Victor soon brought out a record that played for the same time as the old "12-incher" – ideal for a single song – but was only 18 cm (7 in) across. Both were highly successful.

Polaroid camera
1948
Edwin Land

US inventor Edwin Land had a successful company making Polaroid material. When his daughter asked to see a picture he had just taken of her he asked himself "Why not?" In 1948, after a few years' work, he launched the Polaroid Land camera. The secret was in the film, which contained its own developing system and could produce a brown and white print 60 seconds after the picture was taken.

Trainers
1949
Adolf Dassler

Trainers can be traced back to a design that German sports shoe manufacturer Adolf "Adi" Dasler registered in 1949 – a year after he split with his brother Rudolf to found the company Adidas. Dasler's shoes were worn by some notable athletes, including the American Jesse Owens, who won four gold medals in the 1936 Olympics. The new shoes had three stripes down each side, which gave extra support. The stripes were probably the start of the elaborate decoration seen on trainers today. Adi's brother later created the rival Puma brand.

Cling film
1949
Dow Chemical Company

Traditional cling film is a plastic called PVDC. It is related to PVC, a material used for window frames and electrical insulation. Cling film was supposedly discovered in 1933 by accident, as an indestructible sticky residue on laboratory glassware. It was first marketed in the US by the Dow Chemical Company in 1949. The first users were professional caterers, but a domestic version, Saran Wrap, appeared in 1953.

Error-correcting code
1950
Richard Hamming

Today, much information comes in the form of digital codes. Mobile phones and CDs, for example, use digital codes. Unfortunately, the media that transmit or store these codes are not perfect, and errors occur. If these were not corrected, many systems would not work. US mathematician Richard Hamming solved this problem as early as 1950. He devised codes that showed when an error had been made, and also how to correct it.

Lens panel was folded flat for carrying

Cable release could be attached here

Front moved on rails for focusing

POLAROID CAMERA *The first Polaroid Land camera looked much like the roll-film cameras many photographers were using at the time.*

1949 On 1 October, China becomes a communist country as Mao Zedong, having defeated Nationalist opposition, proclaims that the government of the People's Republic of China is now established in Beijing.

1950 US scientist and science-fiction writer Isaac Asimov publishes a collection of short stories entitled *I, Robot*. It includes his three laws of robotics, a moral system that should be built into all robots to stop them hurting humans.

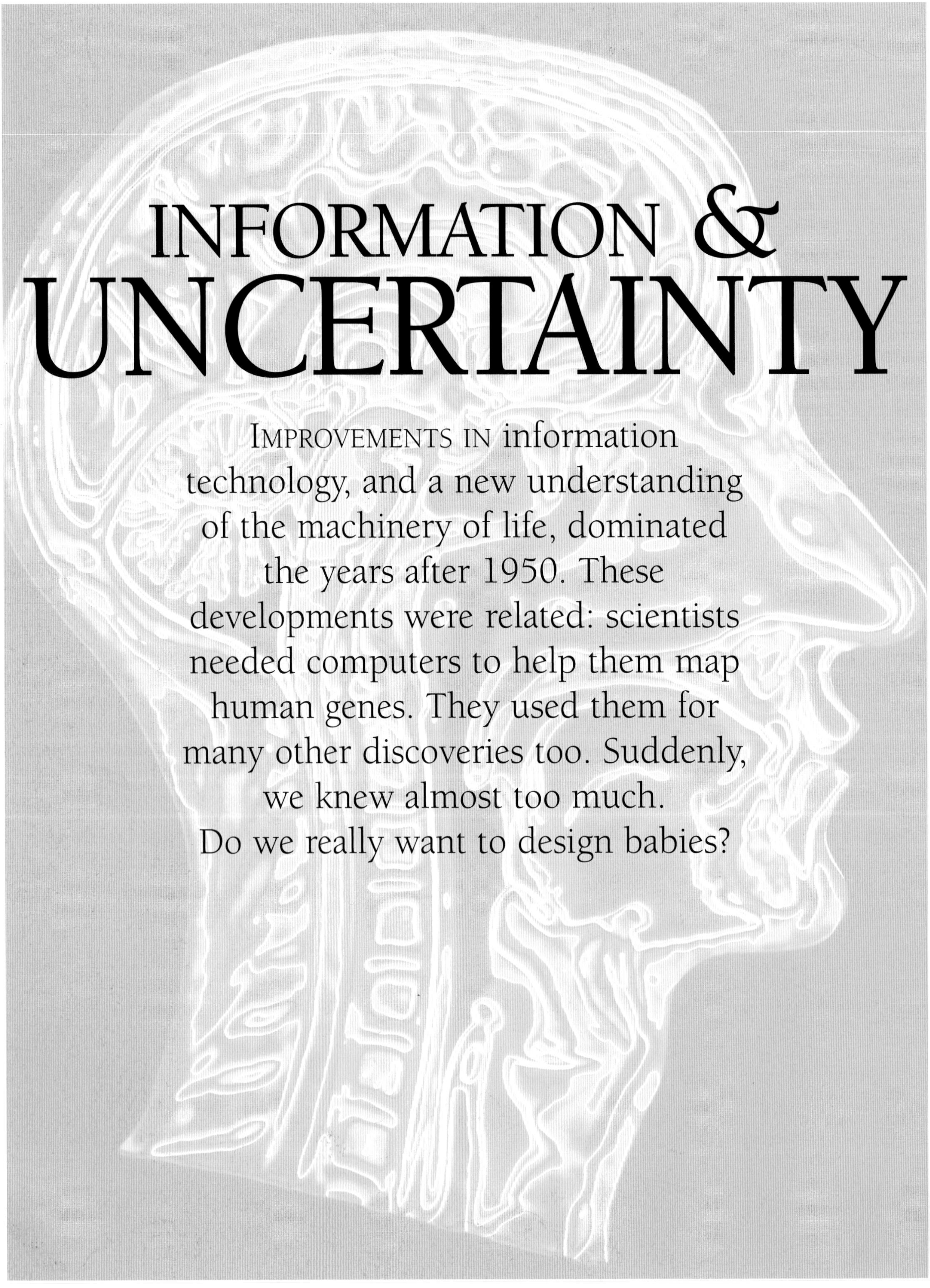

INFORMATION & UNCERTAINTY

IMPROVEMENTS IN information technology, and a new understanding of the machinery of life, dominated the years after 1950. These developments were related: scientists needed computers to help them map human genes. They used them for many other discoveries too. Suddenly, we knew almost too much. Do we really want to design babies?

Airbag
1952
John Hetrick

The first airbag was patented in 1952 by US inventor John Hetrick. But it was not until 1973, when the rising death toll on US roads began to cause concern, that General Motors developed a practical airbag and offered it as an option. In spite of consumer resistance, and worries about deaths caused by early airbags, they were fitted to most US cars by 1988. European car makers followed suit later.

Cinerama
1952
Fred Waller

Movies that fill the whole field of vision make a big impact. US photographer Fred Waller created them with his Cinerama process in 1952. He bolted three cameras together then projected the resulting films on to a wide screen. Apart from fuzzy areas where the pictures joined, the result was sensational, particularly for scenes such as roller-coaster rides. But it wasn't so good for serious drama, and was not used after 1963.

Polio vaccine
1952
Jonas Salk, Albert Sabin

Poliomyelitis, or polio, is a viral infection that can cause paralysis. It posed a serious threat until US physician Jonas Salk developed a vaccine that could create resistance to the virus. It contained an inactive (dead) virus, and was first used in a successful trial in 1952. After further trials, the Salk vaccine was approved in 1955. Later, Polish–US physician Albert Sabin developed the vaccine more widely used today, which is taken by mouth. This contains weakened polio virus, which creates immunity without causing harm.

COLOUR TELEVISION *The Sony Trinitron, introduced in 1968, was a descendant of the tubes first developed to show colour pictures in the NTSC system. It was based on the same principle, but it had a much simpler design and gave brighter, more stable pictures.*

Colour television
1953
National Television Systems Committee

It was hard to make television show colour without making existing black-and-white receivers useless. The US National Television Systems Committee (NTSC) provided the solution in 1953. Their system splits pictures into brightness variations, which can be displayed on a normal black-and-white set, and colour information, which colour receivers use to add colour to the picture. Later variants of NTSC that transmit colours more accurately are now in use.

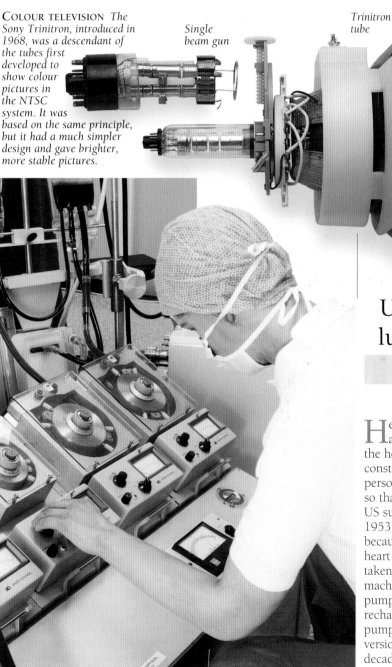

Single beam gun

Trinitron tube

USE OF HEART–LUNG MACHINE *This reconstruction of a 1980 operating theatre shows a heart–lung machine in use. The circular devices in the centre pump blood.*

Use of heart–lung machine
1953
John Gibbon, Jr

Heart surgery was once almost impossible, because the heart is full of blood and constantly moving. The first person to drain a human heart so that he could work on it was US surgeon John Gibbon, Jr in 1953. He was able to do this because the job of the patient's heart had been temporarily taken over by a heart–lung machine. This continually pumped blood out of the body, recharged it with oxygen, and pumped it back. Modern versions are the result of decades of development by experimenters. Their use in heart surgery is now routine.

1952
In Kenya, the British declare a state of emergency and arrest Jomo Kenyatta, leader of the Kenya African Union, in an effort to crush the Mau Mau – armed members of the Kikuyu tribe rebelling against British rule.

1953
Nepalese Sherpa Tenzing Norgay and New Zealand mountaineer Edmund Hillary reach the top of Mount Everest, on 29 May. They are the first people who can prove they have climbed to the summit. Hillary is later knighted.

Structure of DNA
1953

Francis Crick, James Watson

See **pages 216–217** for the story of how Francis Crick and James Watson raced to find the structure of DNA.

Breathalyzer
1954

Robert Borkenstein

The difficulty of proving a driver had been drinking led US policeman Robert Borkenstein to invent the Breathalyzer in 1954. Alcohol

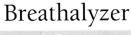

BREATHALYZER *A police officer would fit a fresh sample tube into this 1979 Breathalyzer before asking a driver to blow into the bag.*

US psychologist James Olds and physiologist Peter Milner found a part of the rat's brain that they could stimulate electrically to give a reward greater than any food. By wiring this "pleasure centre" to a lever, they could get the rat to push it thousands of times an hour. The centre is now thought to be involved in human behaviours such as drug addiction.

Bag inflated to measure breath

Nuclear power station
1954

Institute of Physics and Power Engineering

The first operational nuclear power station was built at Obninsk, near Moscow. It started working in June 1954. The station was designed by the USSR's Institute of Physics and Power Engineering, which started work on it in 1951. It was small and simple, and had a power output of only 5 megawatts (MW), as compared with 1000 MW for a modern reactor, but it was still a triumph for the USSR.

Polypropylene
1954

Karl Ziegler, Giulio Natta

In 1953, Italian chemist Karl Ziegler discovered a catalyst (a substance that speeds up a chemical reaction) that allowed polythene to be made from the gas ethylene more easily. In 1954, Italian chemist Giulio Natta discovered that Ziegler's catalyst also worked with the related gas propylene. The result was polypropylene, the tough, flexible plastic now used for everything from dustbins to carpets. Commercial production began in 1957.

Turboprop airliner
1953

Vickers Armstrong Aircraft

The turboprop led the way towards today's mass air travel. Basically a jet engine driving a propeller, it gave higher speeds and a smoother flight than a piston engine. The first turboprop airliner was the British Vickers Viscount. It carried its first paying passengers in 1953. The makers liked to boast that it was so smooth you could balance a coin on the arm of your seat – on its edge.

in the bloodstream passes into the breath, so the more alcohol there is in a driver's blood, the more there will be in their breath. The Breathalyzer has a glass tube containing chemicals that change from orange to green as they react with alcohol. Drivers blow into a bag to give a measured quantity of breath. If the green goes too far along the tube, they are over the limit.

Pleasure centre in the brain
1954

James Olds, Peter Milner

Laboratory rats can be trained to work a lever in return for food. But in 1954,

Kidney transplant
1954

Joseph Murray

All early attempts to transplant organs failed. Scientists eventually realized that rejection was caused by the body's immune system. US surgeon Joseph Murray confirmed this when he tried to graft skin on to wounded soldiers. He noticed that the only successful grafts came from an identical twin. In 1954, he and several colleagues tried transplanting a kidney from one twin to another. The twin given the new kidney survived for years. In the 1960s, after drugs to suppress the immune system were developed, Murray made successful kidney transplants from unrelated donors.

Atomic clock
1955

Louis Essen, Jack Parry

In 1955, working at the National Physical Laboratory with his colleague Jack Parry, British physicist Louis Essen made a clock that would gain or lose less than one second in 300 years. It worked by electrically sensing a natural vibration of caesium atoms.

1954 British medical student Roger (later Sir Roger) Bannister runs a mile in less than four minutes, breaking both a record and a psychological barrier. Bannister's time will be beaten seven weeks later by Australian John Landy.

1954 Japanese director Akira Kurosawa blends Japanese tradition with western technique in *The Seven Samurai*, perhaps the best ever film about the Samurai, a powerful warrior caste. It wins silver at the Venice Film Festival.

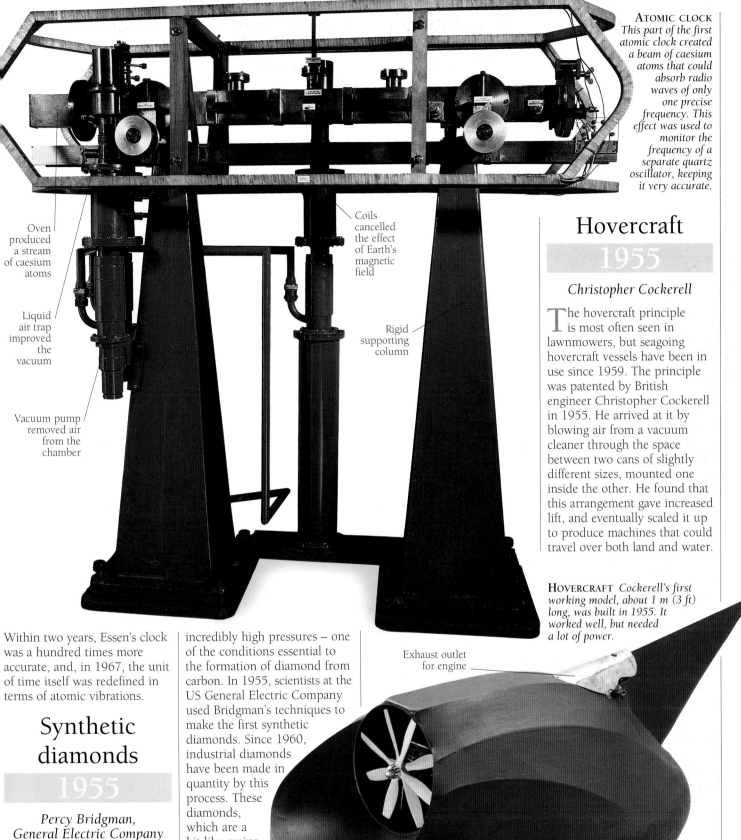

ATOMIC CLOCK *This part of the first atomic clock created a beam of caesium atoms that could absorb radio waves of only one precise frequency. This effect was used to monitor the frequency of a separate quartz oscillator, keeping it very accurate.*

Oven produced a stream of caesium atoms

Liquid air trap improved the vacuum

Vacuum pump removed air from the chamber

Coils cancelled the effect of Earth's magnetic field

Rigid supporting column

Hovercraft

1955

Christopher Cockerell

The hovercraft principle is most often seen in lawnmowers, but seagoing hovercraft vessels have been in use since 1959. The principle was patented by British engineer Christopher Cockerell in 1955. He arrived at it by blowing air from a vacuum cleaner through the space between two cans of slightly different sizes, mounted one inside the other. He found that this arrangement gave increased lift, and eventually scaled it up to produce machines that could travel over both land and water.

HOVERCRAFT *Cockerell's first working model, about 1 m (3 ft) long, was built in 1955. It worked well, but needed a lot of power.*

Exhaust outlet for engine

Smooth skin reduced drag

Within two years, Essen's clock was a hundred times more accurate, and, in 1967, the unit of time itself was redefined in terms of atomic vibrations.

Synthetic diamonds

1955

Percy Bridgman, General Electric Company

US physicist Percy Bridgman never made diamonds himself, but he did develop ways of subjecting materials to incredibly high pressures – one of the conditions essential to the formation of diamond from carbon. In 1955, scientists at the US General Electric Company used Bridgman's techniques to make the first synthetic diamonds. Since 1960, industrial diamonds have been made in quantity by this process. These diamonds, which are a bit like grains of sand, are used to add bite to cutting tools like saw blades and drill bits.

1954 British writer William (later Sir William) Golding publishes his first and best known novel, *Lord of the Flies*. Schoolboys stranded on an island descend to savagery as they struggle to survive. It will be filmed in 1963 and 1990.

1955 Rock 'n' roll gets its first wide airing as US band Bill Haley and the Comets shoot to the top of the charts with *Rock Around the Clock*. Its blues-based harmony and strong back-beat enrage the old and enchant the young.

THE SECRET OF LIFE

Francis Crick and James Watson race to find the chemical structure of DNA

CRICK AND WATSON
The Second World War interrupted Francis Crick's studies, so he was still working for a higher degree when biologist James Watson arrived at the Cavendish. Crick's official work was soon put aside as he took up the challenge of DNA.

Francis Crick

James Watson

In February 1953, two men rushed into the Eagle, a pub in Cambridge, England. The English one, Francis Crick, said that they had found the secret of life. The American, James Watson, wondered if they really had.

The race to find the structure of DNA began in 1944, when US immunologist Oswald Avery showed that bacteria inherited their characteristics through DNA. This has four key components – A, T, G, and C for short. In 1949, Austrian biochemist Erwin Chargaff noticed that the amount of A is always the same as the amount of T, and likewise for G and C.

This was all that was known about DNA when biologist James Watson arrived at Cambridge's Cavendish Laboratory in 1951. The Cavendish specialized in X-ray analysis of molecular structures, and physicist Francis Crick was an expert there. Watson was convinced that unravelling DNA

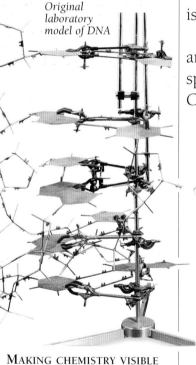

Original laboratory model of DNA

MAKING CHEMISTRY VISIBLE
The ways that atoms fit with each other follow known rules. Before computers, it was hard to see the effect of these rules without building a physical model. This double helix was assembled by James Watson using metal plates shaped to represent the chemical groups he knew were present in DNA.

would be the breakthrough of the century. He needed Crick's help because in the USA, the great chemist Linus Pauling was already hot on the trail.

At King's College, London, physicist Maurice Wilkins and his assistant, Rosalind Franklin, were using X-rays on DNA. Crick and Watson decided to do something different. They used Franklin's X-rays to help them build models. The first attempt looked like three spiral staircases. Wilkins and Franklin said that Crick and Watson had to think again. All the time, Pauling was breathing down their necks. Crick and Watson eventually saw a draft diagram of his proposed structure, but they knew it was wrong.

Watson studied Franklin's latest X-ray picture and became convinced that a DNA molecule was spiral, or helical, in shape. He wondered whether it could be a double helix, rather than the triple helix they

ROSALIND FRANKLIN
Using X-rays alone, Rosalind Franklin nearly found the structure of DNA. Her work was vital to Crick and Watson. She died in 1958, four years before they and Wilkins got their Nobel prize.

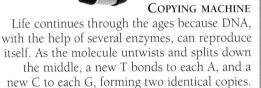

COPYING MACHINE
Life continues through the ages because DNA, with the help of several enzymes, can reproduce itself. As the molecule untwists and splits down the middle, a new T bonds to each A, and a new C to each G, forming two identical copies.

had considered, because important biological objects come in pairs. Then Franklin suggested that DNA's "backbone" was on the outside. Suddenly, Watson saw that T fitted with A, and C with G, like rungs between the uprights of a twisted ladder. It explained Chargaff's observation and, more importantly, how DNA was copied. He told Crick, and that was when they rushed to the Eagle.

Watson and Crick were worried in case they were mistaken, so they raced to build an accurate model. There was nothing wrong with it. It was definitely the structure of DNA. Later, even Pauling was delighted to agree that Crick and Watson had indeed found the secret of life.

Thymine *Adenine*

Cytosine *Guanine*

PAIRING OFF
In DNA, atoms forming a type of sugar are linked by groups containing phosphorus. Between these, hydrogen atoms link thymine (T) to adenine (A), and cytosine (C) to guanine (G). This model is diagrammatic only.

VIDEO RECORDER *Video cameras of the early 1970s needed a heavy box like this to make the actual recording on a reel of wide tape.*

The problem was solved by US engineers Charles Ginsburg and Ray Dolby in 1956. They used a wide tape running horizontally at low speed while a rotating head scanned it vertically at high speed, effectively folding up a long, fast tape into a short, slow one. Domestic video recorders, such as VHS, use a related principle.

Field ion microscope
1956

Erwin Müller

The first microscope to reveal individual atoms, the field ion microscope, was invented in 1956. (Ions are atoms or groups of atoms that have lost or gained one or more electrons to become electrically charged.) Working in the USA, German physicist Erwin Müller put an extremely sharp metal point inside a cathode ray tube (✳ *see* **page 166**) containing helium at low pressure, and subjected it to an electric field. Helium around the tip was ionized by the stronger field that developed at the boundaries between atoms. The ions flew towards the screen of the tube, spreading out to give an image ten million times bigger than the metal point and revealing its atomic structure.

Video recorder
1956

Charles Ginsburg, Ray Dolby

Television signals contain much higher frequencies than those recorded on audio tape (✳ *see* **page 169**). Capturing them by running the tape faster is not practical.

Velcro
1956

George de Mestral

The name Velcro comes from the French for velvet (*velours*) and hook (*crochet*). It is actually two materials: one covered in tiny hooks, the other in tiny loops. Placed in contact, the hooks catch in the loops and the surfaces cling together to fasten clothes and much else. Swiss inventor George de Mestral got the idea in 1941 by noticing plant burrs clinging to his dog. It took 15 years of research to copy the burrs' hooked surface in a fabric.

Artificial satellite
1957

Valentin Glushko, Sergey Korolyov

The first artificial Earth satellite was Sputnik I, launched on 4 October, 1957.

It weighed only 84 kg (184 lb) and went only 942 km (584 miles) into space, but proved that the USSR was well ahead in space technology. The engineers responsible, Valentin Glushko and Sergey Korolyov, received many honours. The USA responded by creating the National Aeronautics and Space Administration (NASA) in July 1958. The space race was on.

Chemical mechanism of nerves
1957

John Eccles, Alan Hodgkin, Andrew Huxley

Nineteenth-century scientists knew that nerves worked electrically. By 1957, the exact mechanism had been unravelled by Australian physiologist John Eccles and British physiologists Alan Hodgkin and Andrew Huxley (all later knighted). They found that an excited nerve releases a substance that opens pores in the outer membrane of the next nerve cell. Sodium ions then flow in, making the cell electrically positive and also making more pores open. The process continues, causing an electrical wave to travel down the nerve.

Rotary internal combustion engine
1957

Felix Wankel

Car engines go round and round, but their pistons go up and down. German engineer Felix Wankel thought this was bad. By 1957, he had built and tested an engine without pistons. The Wankel engine has a rotor that spins inside a fixed

Engine is mounted in the rear compartment

Car body is basically the Bertone-styled Sportprinz

ROTARY INTERNAL COMBUSTION ENGINE
The first production car with a Wankel engine was the German NSU Spider, a sports car launched in 1963. It won the German GT Rally Championship in 1966 and all classes of the German Hill Climb Championship in 1967.

1956 Soviet writer Boris Pasternak's only novel, *Dr Zhivago*, is published in the West. Because it describes an individual's struggle for identity within the USSR, it is considered subversive and not published there until 1987.

1956 Egyptian president Gamal Abdel-Nasser nationalizes the Suez Canal. France and Britain, fearing he will close it to vital oil shipments, launch an invasion of the area, with Israel as an ally, but pull out under international pressure.

chamber to carry out the various stages of combustion. Although it has been used in cars, it has proved difficult to maintain a gas-tight seal between rotor and chamber. So the piston engine, in spite of needing more parts than the Wankel, still rules the road.

FORTRAN
1957

John Backus

Early computer programmers had to write thousands of virtually unreadable coded instructions to make their machines work. US researcher John Backus changed this with the first successful high-level programming language, which could translate English-like statements into machine

code. FORTRAN, released by IBM in 1957, produced results nearly as good as those achieved by hand coding, but in a fraction of the time.

Penrose triangle
1958

Lionel Penrose, Roger Penrose

Many drawings by the Dutch artist M. C. Escher show "impossible worlds" that include baffling tricks

of perspective. Inspired by these, British geneticist Lionel Penrose and his physicist son Roger invented the Penrose triangle in 1958. It looks like a triangle until you realize that it contains three right-angle joints, so could not be made. Escher was in turn inspired by the Penroses' work to draw some more impossible worlds.

In reality, the sides of the triangle do not meet

The impossible looks possible from this angle

PENROSE TRIANGLE *A real Penrose triangle is impossible, but this object looks like one when viewed from the correct angle.*

Wearable pacemaker
1958

Earl Bakken

Pacemakers keep faulty hearts going with electrical impulses. US heart specialist Paul Zoll invented one in 1952, but it was too big to wear. US surgeon Walton Lillehei wanted a pacemaker that could be strapped to the body, allowing children to move around, and would also keep going during power failures. In 1957, US engineer Earl Bakken produced a battery-powered pacemaker, which was small enough to wear. He marketed his invention the following year as the Meditronic 5800.

Superglue
1958

Harry Coover, Fred Joyner

Superglue bonds surfaces carrying any trace of water. The water triggers a reaction that turns the liquid glue into strong plastic. The chemical involved – cyanoacrylate – was discovered in 1942, but it was 1951 before US researchers Harry Coover and Fred Joyner realized its potential. Superglue became a product in 1958, and Coover demonstrated it on television by using just one drop to lift the presenter right off the floor. Many careless people have since confirmed how well it sticks to skin.

Flap conceals the fuel filler cap

Radiator and fan at the front

1957 Chinese communist leader Mao Zedong launches his "Great Leap Forward", a programme that diverts farm labour to industry. Agriculture is affected so badly that 20 million people starve to death over the next four years.

1958 Top British football team Manchester United is virtually wiped out when their plane crashes as it takes off in snow at Munich airport, Germany. Eight players die, but manager Matt Busby survives to rebuild the team.

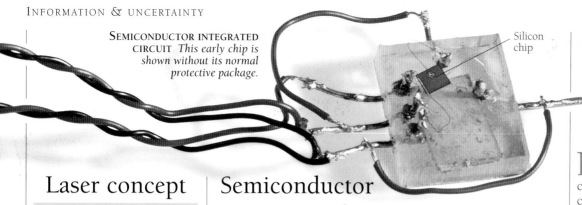

SEMICONDUCTOR INTEGRATED CIRCUIT *This early chip is shown without its normal protective package.*

Silicon chip

Laser concept

1958

Charles Townes, Arthur Schawlow

The laser started out in 1953 as a type of amplifier for microwaves called a maser (from Microwave Amplification by Stimulated Emission of Radiation). One of its inventors, US physicist Charles Townes, and another US physicist, Arthur Schawlow, later showed that the same principle could apply to light. Changing the initial M to L for light gave the name laser. Most lasers are, however, used not as light amplifiers but as light sources with very special properties. (✴ *See also* **Masers and lasers**.)

Lego

1958

Godtfred Christiansen

Lego bricks existed in 1949, but were re-invented in their modern form in 1958 by Godtfred Christiansen. He was the son of a Danish carpenter, Ole Christiansen, who, in 1932, founded a company making wooden products, including toys. By 1934, the toys were taking over, and the company was renamed Lego, from the Danish *"led godt"* meaning "play well". Godtfred, who joined the company when only 12, was also the force behind the creation of Legoland.

Semiconductor integrated circuit

1958

Jack Kilby, Robert Noyce

Modern electronic devices, such as laptop computers, pack a lot into a small space. They do this with integrated circuits – silicon chips containing thousands or millions of transistors and other components connected to form a complex circuit. The first of these, made in 1958 by US engineer Jack Kilby, contained only a few components, but demonstrated the principle. The following year, another US engineer, Robert Noyce, invented a better way of making integrated circuits. He used a film of metal to connect up transistors buried beneath the surface of a silicon chip. With many improvements, this process is still used today.

Van Allen radiation belts

1958

James Van Allen

Earth is surrounded by deadly atomic particles that come from the Sun and are captured by Earth's magnetic field. They gather in two doughnut-shaped belts around the equator. The inside of the inner belt is about 1000 km (600 miles) above Earth's surface, while the outside of the outer belt is about 25,000 km (15,000 miles) up. These dangerous regions are called the Van Allen belts, after US physicist James Van Allen, who discovered them in 1958 by studying cosmic-ray data gathered by equipment on board the Explorer 1 satellite.

A mould can produce 2880 bricks an hour

Shape of brick

LEGO *Massive, accurate moulds like these are needed to make bricks that will always snap together.*

1959 Twelve nations sign the Antarctic Treaty. Its aim is to keep the world's last wilderness free of military operations, including nuclear weapons, and make it somewhere science can flourish in a spirit of international cooperation.

1959 After an unsuccessful rebellion by the people of Tibet against Chinese rule, their spiritual leader, the Dalai Lama, flees to India with 100,000 followers. He sets up a government in exile at Dharmsala, in the Himalayas.

MASERS AND LASERS

WHEN ATOMS OR MOLECULES absorb energy, they become "excited". If they are then struck by radiation of a suitable frequency, they release their energy as a wave exactly in step with that radiation. This "stimulated emission" was predicted by Albert Einstein in 1917. In a laser, the new radiation strikes other excited atoms, which then emit further light. This chain reaction produces high-intensity radiation with all the waves in step with each other.

LASER LIGHT

Laser light is pure, that is it consists of waves of a single frequency, all in step. This makes it useful where a light bulb's jumbled waves of many frequencies would not do. It can be very intense, allowing industrial lasers to cut through metal, and can also be formed into a much narrower beam than ordinary light.

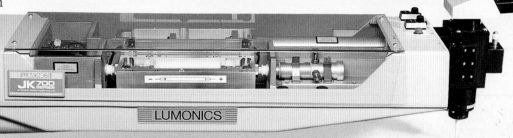

Lasers in machines like this cut metal without distorting it.

This enlarged view of the music layer of an audio CD shows fine depressions that a laser can read.

LASERS IN ACTION

Lasers are ideal for measurement. Their narrow beam is used in surveying to bounce off distant reflectors and give pinpoint positioning. Tiny, low-powered infra-red lasers detect the microscopic messages written on CDs. Lasers are essential for making holograms (✳ *see* **page 210**), as well as great for putting on light shows.

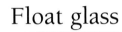

Float glass
1959
Alastair Pilkington

Nearly all window glass is made by the float glass process. A ribbon of molten glass is poured on to the mirror-like surface of a pool of molten tin. The tin smooths the underside of the glass while flames play on the top to smooth this. Alastair Pilkington of British glass company Pilkington thought up the idea in 1952. After seven years' development, it was ready to use.

Seat-belt
1959
Nils Bohlin

When a car stops suddenly, as in a crash, Newton's first law (✳ *see* **page 96**) says that its occupants will carry on at their original speed. This means that they will hit the inside of the now stationary car, and be injured. The way to prevent this is to anchor them to the car, so that they stop when it stops. Various seat-belts were tried before Swedish engineer Nils Bohlin came up with today's lap-and-diagonal design. His belts were first fitted inside a 1959 Volvo.

Cause of Down's syndrome
1959
Jérôme Lejeune

Human cells usually have 46 chromosomes containing their genes. But in 1959, French geneticist Jérôme Lejeune showed that the cells of people with Down's syndrome, a condition which can cause learning difficulties and medical problems, have an extra copy of one particular chromosome, known as chromosome 21, making 47 in all. As a result of later work, babies can now be checked for this and other gene problems before they are born.

Bubblewrap
1960
Alfred Fielding, Marc Chavannes

Bubblewrap consists of two layers of soft plastic with rows of bubbles trapped between them. Used to pack delicate articles, it is cleaner and more effective than materials like shredded paper. It appeared in its earliest form, AirCap cellular cushioning, in 1960. Its US inventors, Alfred Fielding and Marc Chavannes, were originally trying to make textured wall coverings, but soon realized that packaging offered a bigger market.

1960 In Sharpeville, South Africa, a crowd gathers in protest against laws that restrict the movement of black Africans. Police open fire; 67 people are killed. A state of emergency is declared, and black political groups are outlawed.

1960 One of the U-2 spy planes regularly flown over Soviet territory by the USA is shot down. Pilot Gary Powers parachutes to safety, but is put in gaol for ten years. The incident wrecks an East–West summit meeting in Paris.

Communications satellite

1960

John Pierce

Communications satellites are radio relay stations in space. They enable signals to reach places far away from the transmitter. In 1960, to convince people that this would work, US engineer John Pierce made use of the experimental satellite Echo 1. This giant aluminium-coated balloon made a good radio reflector, and Pierce showed that signals could be bounced off it over long distances. His work led to the launch of *Telstar*, the first satellite to relay television, in 1962.

Artificial neural network

1960

Frank Rosenblatt

An artificial neural network (ANN) is a lot of electronic "nerve cells" joined together. It processes information in a similar way to the brain. Electronic models of natural nerve cells were developed in the 1940s by US researchers Warren McCulloch and Walter Pitts to help them understand how the brain worked. Another US scientist, Frank Rosenblatt, put these cells together to form the first ANN, a pattern-recognizing network called the Perceptron, demonstrated in 1960. ANNs are used in deep learning – training computers on real-world data, such as for use in speech recognition.

SI units

1960

11th General Conference on Weights and Measures

Science and technology need consistent units of measurement for things like length, mass, force, and electric current. The Système International d'Unités, or SI, provides such units. Adopted in 1960, SI tidied up an older system called MKS (metre–kilogram–second) by defining six basic units (plus a seventh added in 1971) and deriving all the others from them. It also standardized the prefixes, such as kilo (a thousand), that are used to express measurements.

Synthetic ruby rod

Lamp lies next to the ruby rod when the unit is closed

Mirror-like surface ensures that the ruby is bombarded with as much light as possible

Synthetic ruby rod

Closed laser unit

RUBY LASER *Flash tubes pumped energy into the pale pink ruby rod of this 1960 laser. The inside of the casing was silvered to prevent energy being wasted. The ends of the rod had to be precisely parallel to get laser action.*

Quasar

1960

Allan Sandage, Maarten Schmidt

Quasars are star-like objects. They are found in some parts of the sky that also give out strong radio waves. US astronomer Allan Sandage found the first in 1960. Its spectrum was puzzling. In 1963 Dutch-born US astronomer Maarten Schmidt suggested that it was a normal spectrum shifted sideways by a huge amount. According to astronomical theory, this showed that the quasar was billions of light-years away and therefore must be fantastically bright. Further observations indicated that quasars are also quite small, suggesting that they are caused by black holes (✳ *see* **page 184**).

Ruby laser

1960

Theodore Maiman

A year after it was shown that lasers were possible (✳ *see* **page 220**), US physicist Theodore Maiman made one. He used a rod of synthetic ruby with aluminium-coated ends, surrounded by flash tubes. Light from the tubes excited atoms in the rod, making them give out light. Trapped between the reflecting ends, this stimulated further atoms, creating the first pulses of laser light.

Disposable nappy

1961

Vic Mills

From the mid 1940s onwards, many attempts were made to invent a

1961 Sheep lose their wool in record time as the first Golden Shears competition is held in Masterton, New Zealand. Sheep shearers from all over the country compete in the event, which will eventually become international.

1961 The Communist East Germany stems the flow of illegal emigrants by building a wall across Berlin to prevent them getting into West Germany. Temporary at first, it soon becomes 47 km (29 miles) of solid concrete.

disposable nappy. None were really successful until US engineer Vic Mills, fed up with the cloth nappies worn by his granddaughter, put the US company Procter & Gamble to work on the problem. After several years of tests, Pampers were launched in 1961.

Shape memory alloys
1961

William Buehler, David Muzzey

When strongly heated and then cooled, shape memory alloys (SMAs) "remember" the shape they had when hot. However much they are bent while cold, heating them restores their original shape. They are useful for making, among other things, sleeves to join metal tubes, and valves to control the rate of fluid flow. The first SMA was made from nickel and titanium by US researcher William Buehler. Another US scientist David Muzzey discovered its properties in 1961, supposedly by heating a bent metal strip with his lighter.

Industrial robot
1961

George Devol, Joseph Engelburger

Industrial robots are jointed arms controlled by computer. They can do complex jobs, such as welding and painting cars. They are also good at tedious jobs like unloading finished parts from a machine. The first working robot did this. It was developed by US engineer George Devol and installed in 1961. With businessman Joseph Engelburger, Devol went on to found the first industrial robotics company. (✳ *See also* **Willing slaves.**)

WILLING SLAVES

THE WORD "ROBOT" comes from the Czech word for forced labour. It first appeared in 1920, in the play *R.U.R.* by Karel Capek, but people have been making machines that imitate life for centuries. By the 18th century, clockwork dolls were serving tea in Japan, while French inventor Jacques de Vaucanson had made a realistic mechanical duck. But a self-sufficient, intelligent robot remains the stuff of science fiction.

A robot arm spot-welding the suspension unit of a car. Robots are ideal for dangerous, repetitive jobs like this.

WORKING TO RULE
Most modern robots have little intelligence or awareness of their surroundings. They have to be programmed in great detail to tell them what to do. Some robot arms can learn what movements to make by recording the actions of a human operator. They then simply play these back.

BREAKING FREE
More advanced robots have less need of humans. With sensors to detect obstacles, they can move around freely, while a computer gives them enough intelligence to do complex tasks like cleaning, cooperating with other robots, or even exploring Mars.

1961 US writer J. Heller invents a new phrase in *Catch-22*. To be grounded, airman Yossarian has to be crazy, and he must be crazy to be flying, but if he asks to be grounded he can't be crazy any more, so he has to keep flying. Catch 22!

1961 The USA starts something it will find hard to stop when it sends 400 military advisers into Saigon (now Ho Chi Minh City) to help South Vietnam combat the North. Within seven years, the USA will have half a million troops there.

Space flight

1961

Yuri Gagarin

The first person to fly through space was Yuri Gagarin, a major in the USSR's air force. He went into orbit around Earth in the spacecraft Vostok 1 on 12 April, 1961. Gagarin's flight lasted for 1 hour, 48 minutes. He reached a speed of 27,400 km/hr (17,000 mph) and a height of 327 km (203 miles). Gagarin was an international hero on his return. Sadly, he was killed seven years later, while he was testing a new plane.

Hip replacement

1962

John Charnley

As people grow older, their hips can wear out. The first successful hip replacements were largely the work of British surgeon John (later Sir John) Charnley in 1962. He fixed a metal ball into the top of a patient's thigh bone with a new kind of cement, and matched this with a cup made of tough polythene fitted to the pelvis. With improvements, this became the method now used for millions of people every year.

HIP REPLACEMENT *Many designs of artificial hip have been tried since Charnley's work in the 1960s. This "Exeter" joint, made in 1985, uses stainless steel for its metal part.*

SPACE FLIGHT *This poster was produced in 1973 to commemorate Russian cosmonaut Yuri Gagarin's space flight. It reads, "Cosmonaut Day USSR 12 IV 1961".*

Re-sealable plastic bag

1962

Steven Ausnit, Kakuji Naito

Plastic bags with little toothless zips built in were conceived by Danish inventor Borgda Madsen in the 1940s. Romanian engineer Steven Ausnit, working in the USA, produced the first practical versions of these about 10 years later. His zips were formed separately and then welded on to the bags. In 1962, Japanese inventor Kakuji Naito created even better bags by forming bag and zip from the same piece of plastic.

Carbon fibre

1963

Leslie Phillips

Fibres of carbon, made by stretching synthetic fibre then toasting it to blackness, are twice as stiff as the same weight of steel. Plastics reinforced with them are both stiff and light, making them ideal for critical structures in advanced aircraft and for high-performance sports equipment. Carbon fibre technology was pioneered in 1963 by British engineer Leslie Phillips at the Royal Aircraft Establishment. It is now used throughout the aircraft industry.

Push-button phone

1963

AT&T

Phones with buttons began to replace phones with dials in 1963, when US phone company AT&T introduced their Touch-Tone system. Dial phones work by disconnecting the phone line once for 1, twice for 2, and so on. Push-button phones send musical tones down the line. There are four tones for the four rows of buttons, and three for the three columns. Pressing a button sends out the pair of tones corresponding to its row and column.

Polaroid colour photograph

1963

Edwin Land

Polacolor film, launched in 1963, has three layers, each sensitive to light of one colour – red, green, or blue. Each layer contains a dye that absorbs just the light to which the layer is sensitive. The blue-sensitive layer, for example, contains yellow dye, which absorbs only blue light. Pulling the film out of the camera activates it and squeezes it into contact with a white print sheet. As the layers

1962 War threatens as presidents Kennedy of the USA and Khrushchev of the USSR stage a stand-off over the installation of Soviet nuclear missiles in Cuba. After a tense few days, Khrushchev backs down and the missiles go home.

1962 After thousands of babies are born with abnormally short arms and legs, the sedative drug thalidomide, introduced in 1958, is finally withdrawn. Doctors had traced the malformations to mothers taking the drug while pregnant.

develop, their dyes are trapped in proportion to the exposure received, and the remaining dye moves into the print. Where the subject absorbs blue, for example, the blue layer receives less exposure, so more of its yellow dye reaches the final print, making it, too, absorb blue. The process takes just 60 seconds.

POLAROID COLOUR PHOTOGRAPH
In 1975, Polaroid launched a new camera, the Color Swinger. It was designed to encourage use of a new and improved Polacolor film introduced the same year.

Electronic music synthesizer
1964

Robert Moog

Several people had already attempted to produce electronic music before US inventor Robert Moog invented the Moog synthesizer in 1964. Unlike most of its earlier, less successful rivals, it could be played from a normal keyboard. It produced each of its different sounds by starting with a note that was rich in harmonics – multiples of the note's basic frequency – and

MINISKIRT *Ultra-short skirts and dresses were a symbol of the social upheaval of the 1960s. In Britain, they even created problems for the tax man, because their length allowed them to be classified as children's clothes, which were tax-free.*

passing it through filters that reduced the loudness of each harmonic by a different amount. This is known as subtractive synthesis. The Moog could also vary the way in which sounds started, continued, and stopped, giving effects that varied from plucked strings to organ notes.

Miniskirt
1964

André Courrèges

Miniskirts, shorter than any that women had worn before, first appeared in the collection of French fashion designer André Courrèges, who showed them in Paris in 1964. His models wore them with boots. By December 1965, the fashion had reached Britain, where London designer Mary Quant offered skirts that stopped more than 15 cm (6 in) short of the knee.

Quarks
1964

Murray Gell-Mann

In the early 1960s, nuclear physicists observed more and more new subatomic particles. It seemed that even protons and neutrons were made up of particles, which could combine in previously unseen ways. In 1964, US physicist Murray Gell-Mann, building on earlier work with Israeli physicist Yuval Ne'eman, proposed a set of truly basic particles that explained the new observations. He called them quarks. He and other scientists then developed an elaborate, and now accepted, theory of how they work.

Electronic telephone exchange
1965

AT&T

Old-fashioned automatic telephone exchanges (✳ *see* page **161**) were built from unreliable electro-mechanical switches in which electromagnets moved mechanical contacts. They were replaced in the 1960s by so-called "electronic" exchanges. Calls were actually switched by a new type of electromechanical switch, because purely electronic switching proved difficult to combine with the existing network. The first such exchange was the ESS No. 1. Developed by the US company AT&T, it went into service in 1965.

1963 On 22 November, US president John F. Kennedy is shot dead as he travels in an open car through Dallas, Texas. The alleged killer, Lee Harvey Oswald, is himself murdered by a nightclub owner before he can be tried.

1963 Comic art meets the serious sort when US artist Roy Lichtenstein paints *Whaam!*, a 4 m- (13 ft-) wide blow-up of a comic strip frame. His careful rendering of the comic's crude printing helps start the Pop Art movement.

Computer mouse
1965

Dois Engelbart

US engineer Doug Engelbart was leader of the Human Factors Research Center of the Stanford Research Institute in the USA. The computer mouse was one of several similar devices his team tried out in the 1960s. It was the clear winner. Despite its ease of use and friendly nickname, it was nearly 20 years before the mouse was introduced to the public with the launch of the Macintosh computer in 1984.

Minicomputer
1965

Kenneth Olsen

In the 1960s, computers were huge – and cost at least $1,000,000 apiece. US engineer Kenneth Olsen thought that smaller might be better. In 1965, he produced the PDP-8, one of the first computers to use integrated circuits (✳ see **page 220**). It was small (about the size of a two-drawer filing cabinet), powerful, and cost an affordable $18,000. Designed mainly for laboratory use, it was an instant success with scientists and engineers around the world.

Hypertext
1965

Vannevar Bush, Ted Nelson

Hypertext allows computer users to click on a word and jump to a related

Cable attaches to the computer

Transparent plastic matches modern Macs

Shape suits left- or right-handed users

COMPUTER MOUSE
The Apple Pro Mouse, introduced in 2001, uses optical tracking rather than the rolling ball of the conventional mouse. It also does away with a separate mouse button: users click by pushing its whole body.

document. The idea of a machine for instant cross-referencing dates back to 1945, when US engineer Vannevar Bush described an imaginary device, the Memex. US computer guru Ted Nelson, believing that computers should be simple to use, took up the idea and in 1965 coined the term hypertext. In the 1980s, British computer expert Tim Berners-Lee made

hypertext the basis of his program Enquire, which developed into the World Wide Web (✳ see **page 240**).

Ring-pull can
1966

Ermal Fraze

The first drinks cans had to be opened with a separate opener. If this got left behind on a picnic, everyone went thirsty. So, in 1965, US engineer Ermal Fraze patented a new kind of can with a ring-pull on the top. Pulling the ring peeled off a metal tab to open the can. Sharp-edged can tabs became a menace on streets and beaches, but in 1976, US engineer Daniel Cudzik saved the ring-pull by inventing the stay-on type used today.

Dolby noise reduction system
1966

Ray Dolby

Tape recordings were plagued by background hiss until US engineer Ray Dolby invented his noise reduction system. It works by boosting quiet, high-frequency sounds during recording. On playback, these sounds are reduced to their original volume. Since the hiss is a high-frequency sound, it gets reduced too. Dolby delivered his first batch of noise reduction units to the Decca Record Company in 1966.

Jump jet
1966

Hawker Siddeley Aviation

Most aircraft get lift from wings or rotors, but jump jets get off the ground by

JUMP JET *The Harrier GR1 showed its capabilities at Britain's Farnborough air display in 1968, and in a transatlantic air race. Powered by a Bristol (later Rolls-Royce) Pegasus Mk 101 engine, it entered service with the Royal Air Force in 1969.*

Cockpit holds single pilot

Air for engine is sucked in here

1965 US artist Andy Warhol achieves fame with his painting of a can of Campbell's tomato soup.

By choosing such an everyday object, he states that painters have no exclusive claim to call their work art.

1966 On St Valentine's Day, Australian currency goes decimal. The nation rejects the British pound

and its proposed replacement, the royal, and opts for the dollar. The switch goes smoothly and is completed in 1967.

226

directing the thrust of their jet engines downwards, giving them the versatility of a helicopter with the speed of a jet. Once the plane is airborne, the thrust is directed backwards for forward flight. The first operational "vectored thrust" aircraft was the Harrier, made in Britain by Hawker Siddeley Aviation. Based on the earlier, experimental Kestrel fighter, it jetted off the ground in August 1966. Needing no runway, it could be used to fly in and out of combat areas to support troops. The Harrier is now used by several air forces.

Heart transplant
1967

Christiaan Barnard

The world's first heart transplant was carried out by South African surgeon Christiaan Barnard in 1967. The patient survived for only 18 days, but he would have died anyway if he hadn't had the operation. During the following year, more than 100 heart transplants were attempted by Barnard and other surgeons around the world. Results continued to be poor at first, but new techniques and better drugs to prevent rejection have now made transplants an option where nothing else offers hope.

Pulsar
1967

Jocelyn Bell, Antony Hewish

In 1967, in Cambridge, England, a young astronomer, Jocelyn Bell, found a new kind of radio source that emitted short, closely spaced pulses. She and fellow astronomer Antony Hewish later realized that it was the spinning remnant of a supernova (✳ see **page 82**) sending out a rotating beam of radiation, like the lamp on a police car. Whenever the beam hit Earth, it created a pulse. Since then, more than 300 pulsars have been discovered.

Smoke alarm
1967

BRK Electronics

The shriek of a smoke alarm can wake the occupants of a burning building and give them time to escape. Smoke alarms use light or low-level radioactivity to detect the tiny smoke particles produced as a fire starts. The first domestic alarm was designed in 1967 by US company BRK Electronics, and received official approval in 1969. By the 1980s, intensive marketing and safety drives had helped to put smoke alarms in millions of homes.

Graphical user interface
1968

Doug Englebart, Alan Kay

Computer screens with a graphical user interface – windows, icons,

GRAPHICAL USER INTERFACE *The window-icon-menu idea is very adaptable. Here it is seen displaying a museum database.*

and menus – seem normal now. But when US engineer Doug Engelbart and his team showed the beginnings of such a system, the "electronic office", at the National Computer Conference in San Francisco in 1968, the audience were stunned. Among them was graduate student Alan Kay, who later developed the idea of the computer screen as a virtual desktop, complete with icons.

Movable nozzles direct thrust downwards for take-off

Main undercarriage with wheels for landing

Pylons for attachment of weapons

Outrigger wheels stabilize aircraft on the ground

1968 Black US civil rights leader Martin Luther King visits Memphis, Tennessee, in support of a strike by sanitation workers. While standing on his motel balcony, he is killed by a sniper. The gunman, James Earl Ray, gets 99 years in gaol.

1968 In May, increasingly rebellious French students bring turmoil to the streets of Paris with political protests and riots. The same year sees demonstrations worldwide against US involvement in the Vietnam war.

Sailboard
1968

Newman Darby, Jim Drake, Hoyle Schweitzer

Windsurfers get closer to the waves than do most other sailors. The idea started with US enthusiast Newman Darby, but the first people to get a patent were two Californian surfers, Jim Drake and Hoyle Schweitzer. Their 1968 Windsurfer was 3.5 m (12 ft) long and weighed 27 kg (60 lb). Modern boards are shorter and lighter, typically weighing only 12 kg (26 lb).

Workmate
1968

Ron Hickman

The Workmate is a folding workbench that also acts as a large vice. It was invented by British engineer Ron Hickman, who patented it as the Minibench in 1968. He failed to get support from manufacturers, so he started producing it himself. Eventually, his idea was taken up by tool makers Black & Decker, who began selling it as the Workmate in 1972. It reached the USA in 1975, and has sold millions worldwide.

Structure of insulin
1969

Fred Sanger, Dorothy Hodgkin

Insulin (✱ *see* **page 186**) is a hormone that is essential to health. The sequence of its 51 amino acids was determined by British biochemist Fred Sanger

in 1955, but the way its atoms are arranged in space – useful information for people trying to make a synthetic version – was finally worked out in 1969 by British crystallographer Dorothy Hodgkin. She analysed the structure of insulin crystals with X-rays, a technique pioneered by physicist Lawrence (later Sir Lawrence) Bragg in the early 20th century.

Floppy disk
1970

IBM

Floppy disks were originally 20 cm (8 in) across and held only 100 kilobytes of data. IBM engineers used them from about 1970 onwards to update programs on mainframe computers. By 1973, IBM had a disk drive that could accept input from users, but the disks were just as big. In 1980, small, 9 cm (3.5 in) floppy disks were introduced by the Sony Corporation. Today, disks are largely out of use as new media, such as online sharing and storage, have taken over.

Microprocessor
1971

Ted Hoff

The microprocessor, which made personal computers possible, was invented by accident. In 1969, Japanese calculator makers Busicom asked US microchip company

Intel to develop a new scientific calculator chip. Engineer Ted Hoff at Intel thought it would be much easier to design a programmable chip than to build in all the required functions. When Busicom went bust in 1970, Intel bought back the rights to the chip and, in 1971, launched it as "a micro-programmable computer on a chip", the Intel 4004. Although very slow by modern standards, it was the first in a series of devices that led to today's powerful microprocessors.

Microchip

MICROPROCESSOR *Two Intel 8008 processors, successors to the original 4004, are seen with their top covers removed to reveal the chip inside.*

Kevlar
1971

Stephanie Kwolek, Herbert Blades, Paul Morgan

Kevlar is a plastic that, weight for weight, is five times as strong as steel. It was developed in the USA by chemists Stephanie Kwolek, Herbert Blades, and Paul Morgan. Chemically, it is related to nylon, but the addition of an extra chemical group adds strength and stiffness. This makes it suitable for demanding applications such as radial tyres and bullet-proof vests. Kevlar is also used in fibre-reinforced panels for aircraft and boats, and in golf clubs and flameproof clothing. It can even stand the heat in brakes, replacing asbestos.

KEVLAR *This Kevlar-reinforced vest, made in 1996, was designed to resist both bullets and knives.*

1969 In September, Arab nationalist Captain Muammar al-Qaddafi seizes control of the government of Libya in a military coup that deposes King Idris. Al-Qaddafi later allegedly supports international terrorist groups.

1972 China and the USA creep towards a better relationship when Chinese premier Zhou Enlai and US president Richard Nixon sign the Shanghai Communiqué in March. Formal diplomatic relations will start in 1979.

Food processor

1971

Pierre Verdon

A food processor, unlike a food mixer (✳ *see* **page 184**) can chop and blend solid foods such as vegetables. Its electric motor can save hours of work with knife and whisk. The first domestic machine of this kind was the Magi-Mix, introduced in 1971 by French engineer Pierre Verdon, who based it on an earlier, professional machine of his called the Robot-Coupe. It now has many imitators.

Video game

1972

Nolan Bushnell

The first successful video game, Pong, was designed by US computer enthusiast

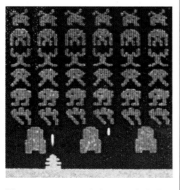

VIDEO GAME *Toshihiro Nishikado's classic game Space Invaders was written in 1978 and is still played.*

Nolan Bushnell in 1972. Although extremely simple – just two on-screen paddles that flipped a ball back and forth – it fascinated customers in bars and pubs, who had never seen anything like it before. The prototype, installed in Andy Capp's Tavern in Sunnyvale, California, quickly broke down as its makeshift coinbox filled up and jammed. Later adapted for a phone app, Pong can still be played today.

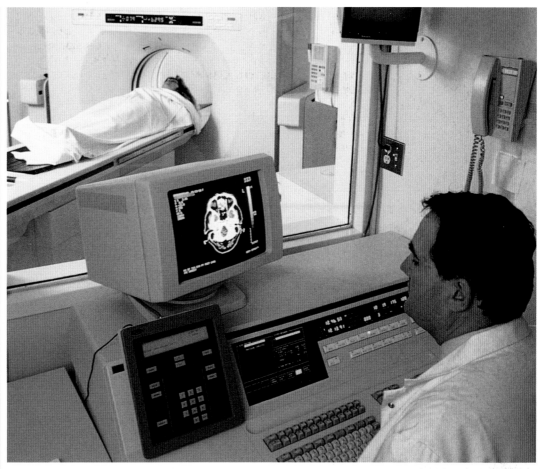

CAT SCANNER *With the patient's head inside an X-ray scanner, a radiographer builds up a picture of their brain, slice by slice.*

CAT scanner

1972

Godfrey Hounsfield, Allan Cormack

Normal X-ray pictures are taken from just one angle. By taking them from several angles, and doing some calculations, much more can be revealed. British engineer Godfrey (later Sir Godfrey) Hounsfield and US physicist Allan Cormack worked independently on this idea. Cormack developed much of the maths, while Hounsfield built the first practical machine. His computerized axial tomography (CAT) scanner used X-rays and a computer to produce images of successive slices across the long axis of the body. ("Tomography" comes from the Greek "*tomos*" a "slice".) When the scanner was tested in 1972, it gave doctors their first three-dimensional glimpse inside a living human body.

Pocket calculator

1972

Jack Kilby, Jerry Merryman, James van Tassel, Clive Sinclair

The earliest "pocket" calculator, the Canon Pocketronic, weighed 880 g (31 oz). Released in 1970, it was based on work by US engineers Jack Kilby, Jerry Merryman, and James Van Tassel at Texas Instruments. British inventor Clive (later Sir Clive) Sinclair developed his pocket calculator later, and benefited from advances in technology. His Executive calculator, launched in 1972, was only 1 cm (0.4 in) thick.

Genetic engineering

1972

Stanley Cohen, Herbert Boyer

An organism's genes are carried in its DNA. In 1969, US biochemists discovered how to snip DNA into smaller pieces. Then, in 1972, US biochemists Stanley Cohen and Herbert Boyer began work on altering organisms by cutting up the DNA of one organism and inserting genes from another. This is called genetic engineering. It has produced useful new bacteria and plants, but some people worry about its long-term effects.

1972 At the Munich Olympics in Germany, 22-year-old US swimmer Mark Spitz wins a record seven gold medals. He also sets a new world record in each of the seven events that bring him gold.

1972 The nuclear arms race slows down as the first series of Strategic Arms Limitation Talks (SALT 1) between the USA and the USSR finally bears fruit. The most important outcome is a treaty to limit deployment of missiles.

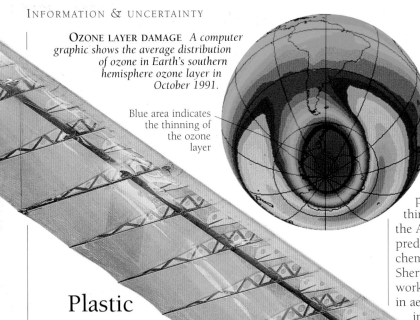

OZONE LAYER DAMAGE *A computer graphic shows the average distribution of ozone in Earth's southern hemisphere ozone layer in October 1991.*

Blue area indicates the thinning of the ozone layer

Plastic fizzy drink bottle
1973

Nathaniel Wyeth

Most plastics can't stand up to the pressure exerted by fizzy drinks, so for a long time bottle manufacturers stuck to glass. Then US engineer Nathaniel Wyeth worked out a way of using the plastic PET (✳ *see* **page 206**) to make a stronger bottle. Knowing that synthetic fibres were strengthened by being stretched during manufacture, he designed a tool that stretched PET in two dimensions as it was moulded. The result, patented in 1973, was the first fizz-proof bottle.

Space station
1973

NASA

A space station is a base in space with accommodation and laboratories for several people. The earliest attempt was Salyut 1, launched by the USSR in 1971, but this crashed back to Earth within six months. The first successful space station was the 75 tonne Skylab, launched by NASA in May 1973 and occupied until February 1974. It was used to observe the Sun and a comet, and to experiment with manufacturing in space. It survived until 1979.

Binary pulsar
1974

Joseph Taylor Jr, Russell Hulse

In 1974, US astronomer Joseph Taylor Jr and his student Russell Hulse discovered an unusual pulsar (✳ *see* **page 227**). The time between its pulses varied over an eight-hour period. Taylor and Hulse deduced that the pulsar was orbiting another, unseen star. The Doppler effect (✳ *see* **page 134**) squeezed the pulses together when the pulsar was approaching Earth, and stretched them apart when it was receding. The orbit seems to be shrinking gradually, suggesting that the system is radiating gravitational waves, as predicted by Einstein (✳ *see* **pages 178–179**).

Ozone layer damage
1974

Mario Molina, Sherwood Rowland

In the 1980s, scientists noticed that Earth's protective ozone layer had thinned dramatically over the Antarctic. This had been predicted. In 1974, US chemists Mario Molina and Sherwood Rowland had worked out that the gases used in aerosols would decompose in intense sunlight, releasing chlorine that destroyed ozone. Dutch chemist Paul Crutzen had earlier predicted a similar effect for nitrogen oxides from cars. Many governments had taken action to reduce these pollutants, but too late.

PET scanner
1974

Michael Phelps, Edward Hoffman

A PET (positron emission tomography) scanner can produce images that show events inside a living body, particularly the brain. It works by responding to the gamma rays produced when positrons meet electrons. A substance modified to make it emit positrons is tracked inside the body by combining information from several gamma ray detectors. The first PET scanner for human studies was built in 1974 by US chemist Michael Phelps, assisted by his student Edward Hoffman.

Supercomputer
1976

Seymour Cray

Even with the enormous power of today's computer chips, scientists with really serious calculations to do have to use supercomputers. These big machines crunch numbers at high speed by using several processors at once. The first was the Cray-1, produced by US engineer Seymour Cray in 1976. It could perform 240 million calculations a second, operating not just on pairs of numbers, like a normal computer, but on lists of pairs. By 1985, the Cray-2 was churning out more than a billion results per second.

Long, thin wings like a glider

Gossamer Albat

DUPONT

Modified bicycle in the cockpit powered the propeller

Conductive plastics
1977

*Alan Heeger,
Alan MacDiarmid,
Hideki Shirakawa*

Metals conduct electricity. Plastics don't. Unless they're conductive plastics, created in 1977 by US chemist Alan Heeger, New Zealand chemist Alan MacDiarmid, and Japanese chemist Hideki Shirakawa. They used iodine to free up the electrons in polyacetylene, creating a plastic a billion times less resistant to electricity. It can even, in some cases, emit light. The possibilities are endless.

inside a huge magnet, a picture of the inside of their body can be created. Magnetic resonance imaging (MRI) reveals chemical differences, so it can detect abnormal cells. US chemist Paul Lauterbur and US physician Raymond Damadian both contributed to its invention. Damadian produced the first human body image in 1977.

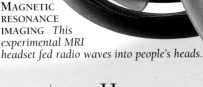

MAGNETIC RESONANCE IMAGING *This experimental MRI headset fed radio waves into people's heads.*

Magnetic resonance imaging
1977

*Paul Lauterbur,
Raymond Damadian*

Placed in a magnetic field, some atomic nuclei absorb radio waves. So, if someone is probed with radio waves while

Public-key cryptography
1977

*Whitfield Diffie,
Martin Hellman, Ron Rivest,
Adi Shamir, Leonard Adleman*

Public-key cryptography, conceived in 1975 by US cryptographers Whitfield Diffie and Martin Hellman, allows people to send electronic messages securely. The system was given practical form by US researchers Ron Rivest, Adi Shamir, and Leonard Adleman in 1977. People give out a public key that specifies how messages sent to them should be scrambled. Once in this form, messages can be read only by someone with the matching private key. A public key is a huge number containing hundreds of digits. It could take a powerful computer years to find the matching private key.

Human-powered aircraft
1977

*Paul MacCready,
Bryan Allen*

Dreams of human flight faded in the 17th century, when scientists realized the size of the wings and muscles required. Then, with the invention of modern plastics, long, light wings became possible. Using these, human leg muscles are just big enough for flight. US engineer Paul MacCready provided 29 m- (96 ft-) long wings with *Gossamer Condor*. Cyclist Bryan Allen provided muscles to drive a propeller. They achieved human-powered flight on 23 August, 1977. Two years later, Allen pedalled *Gossamer Albatross* across the English Channel.

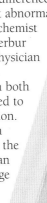

HUMAN-POWERED AIRCRAFT Gossamer Albatross *got its name from its structure – thin plastic stretched over a frame – and its huge wingspan.*

Polyester film covering

Wings could be removed for transport

Gene exons and introns
1977

*Phillip Sharp,
Richard Roberts*

When scientists discovered that DNA carries genes, they thought that these would be strung along the molecule one after the other. Then, in 1977, US biologist Phillip Sharp and British biologist Richard Roberts both discovered that genes are often separated or split by stretches of DNA that don't do anything. They called the active parts exons and the inactive parts introns. Before genes get to work, the cell makes a copy with the introns chopped out.

1975 Former Portuguese colony East Timor is taken over by Indonesia, despite protests from Portugal, who had granted it independence, and the UN. It will become an Indonesian province in 1976 and will suffer continuing unrest.

1976 Popular interest in black history is increased by the publication of US writer Alex Haley's book *Roots*. Built around the life story of an African slave, Kunta Kinte, it explores black identity while promoting racial understanding.

Personal computer

1977

Steve Jobs, Stephen Wozniak

The first three computers for personal use appeared in 1977. The Commodore PET and Tandy TRS-80 are now almost forgotten, but the third was the Apple II, a machine with its own monitor and plug-in expansion cards. The other machines were good, but the dedication of the Apple's promoter and designer, US computer enthusiasts Steve Jobs and Stephen Wozniak made all the difference. (✳ *See also* **Computers for all**.)

Global positioning system

1978

US Air Force

If you had a global positioning system (GPS) receiver you would never get lost. The present GPS began in 1978 with the launch by the US Air Force of the first two NavStar satellites.

MOBILE PHONE
The first mobiles were called "car phones" because they were too big to carry around.

Receivers now tune in to four out of 24 satellites, each of which carries a highly accurate atomic clock. By comparing the received times with the actual time and the known positions of the satellites at that time, the receiver can work out where it must be.

Test-tube baby

1978

Patrick Steptoe, Robert Edwards

Louise Brown, the world's first "test-tube" baby, was born in England on 25 July, 1978. British gynaecologist Patrick Steptoe took an egg from her mother. His colleague Robert Edwards added sperm from her father. The doctors placed the fertilized egg in her mother's womb, where it grew into a healthy baby. Twenty-one years later, Louise had a job in a nursery.

COMPUTERS FOR ALL

In 1975, ENCOURAGED by his friend Steve Jobs, US computer hobbyist Stephen Wozniak built and marketed the Apple I computer – a bare circuit board aimed at electronics hobbyists. Jobs saw that computers had a wider market, and got Wozniak to design a more complete, stylish-looking machine that simply plugged in and worked. Apple II transformed the computer industry, making even giants like IBM take notice.

Apple I computer

RISE OF THE HOBBYIST
The personal computer came out of the work of countless electronics hobbyists – some of them now big names – who, in the early 1970s, built and programmed their own crude machines in their bedrooms and garages.

THE ALTAIR 8800
The first kit computer appeared in 1975. The Altair 8800 had no screen, no keyboard, and hardly any memory, but its very simplicity made it ideal for computer pioneers to cut their teeth on.

Mobile phone

1979

Bell Labs

Mobile phones were pioneered in the USA by Bell Telephone Laboratories. After a trial in Chicago in 1979, the first public service opened in 1983. Meanwhile, Scandinavia had launched its own system in 1981. All mobiles use the same idea. There are relatively few radio frequencies, but millions of users, so the base stations that relay calls to the fixed phone network are given a limited range. Outside that range, frequencies can be re-used. As callers move, computers automatically retune their phones to a frequency in the new area. It nearly always works.

Word processor software

1979

Seymour Rubinstein

By the late 1970s, personal computers could display a page of text. With cheaper printers available, they looked set to replace typewriters. US software developer Seymour Rubinstein, seeing his chance, started writing word processor software. Unsuccessful at first, he launched a second attempt, WordStar, in 1979. This used short, easy-to-remember, non-printing codes typed into a document to specify its fonts and formatting. Although it cost $450 (about $1150 today), the program quickly took a two-thirds market share, selling nearly a million copies in five years. People were still using it in the late 1980s.

1979 Margaret Thatcher becomes Britain's first female prime minister after a decisive election victory for her Conservative party. Her time in office will bring more freedom for private companies and less for trade unions.

1979 The nuclear power industry reels when the "impossible" happens at the Three Mile Island nuclear power station in Pennsylvania, USA. An accidental meltdown damages the plant and dents public confidence in nuclear safety.

its launch in 1979 it was the Soundabout in the USA and Stowaway in Britain. Morita got his way in the end – it is now the Walkman everywhere.

Cellular address code
1980

Günter Blobel

Healthy people have all their different proteins in the right places, wherever they are needed. By 1980, German doctor Günter Blobel had discovered how this happens. He found that every protein carries a molecular code, a sequence of amino acids, which controls its movement through the body. Responding to the code, a cell membrane either blocks the protein or lets it through – unless it is needed by the membrane itself, in which case it hangs on to it.

Apple II computer

COMPUTER LIBERATION
In the early 1970s, some people, including Ted Nelson, son of a Hollywood actress, began to demand computing power for all. Personal computers and the Internet have given this to many in the West, but most of the world's population still has no access to computers.

Spreadsheet software
1979

Daniel Bricklin, Bob Frankson

A spreadsheet program displays a constantly updated table of related numbers. This simple idea has probably sold more personal computers than any other piece of software. When US student Daniel Bricklin and programmer Bob Frankson launched the first spreadsheet program, VisiCalc, in 1979, it was a revelation. People were amazed by the way they could make changes to one number and instantly see the effect on all the others. They had a new management tool.

Walkman
1979

Akio Morita

Akio Morita, co-founder of the Japanese firm Sony, invented a cassette player small enough for people to carry around. His name for it was Walkman. This was considered bad English, so at

WALKMAN *Sold in Britain as the Stereo Stowaway, this early Walkman had some facilities absent from later models, including provision for two sets of headphones.*

Transparent area allows tape to be seen

Adjustable headset

Lead plugs into the cassette player

Headphones allow the user to listen to music without disturbing other people nearby

1979 Soviet Union troops cross the border into Afghanistan to prop up the country's communist regime, which has been weakened by years of infighting between its leaders. Within days, the USSR has installed a new leader.

1980 Strikes over food prices in Gdansk, Poland, lead to workers getting the right to form free trade unions. Under their leader, Lech Walesa, they form the union Solidarity, which will later defeat the communist government.

Genetic control of embryonic development

1980

Edward Lewis, Christiane Nüsslein-Volhard, Eric Weischaus

The fruit fly breeds quickly and has large chromosomes (✳ see page 176), so is ideal for genetics research. In 1978, US geneticist Edward Lewis found that its genes are arranged along its chromosomes in the same order as the body parts they control. By 1980, German geneticist Christiane Nüsslein-Volhard and US geneticist Eric Weischaus had found that only 140 of the genes are essential during development. Some control the body plan, others create segments of the body, and others determine features within segments. Work like this helps scientists to understand development in humans.

G proteins

1980

Martin Rodbell, Alfred Gilman

Bodies wouldn't work if cells didn't respond to things. Heart cells respond to adrenaline (✳ see page 174) by pumping harder. Eye cells respond to light with nerve impulses. US pharmacologist Alfred Gilman used the work of US biochemist Martin Rodbell to help find the link between stimulus and response. By 1980, he had found G proteins. Activated by a stimulus, these make cells containing them respond. Gilman's finding has helped to explain some diseases, including cholera.

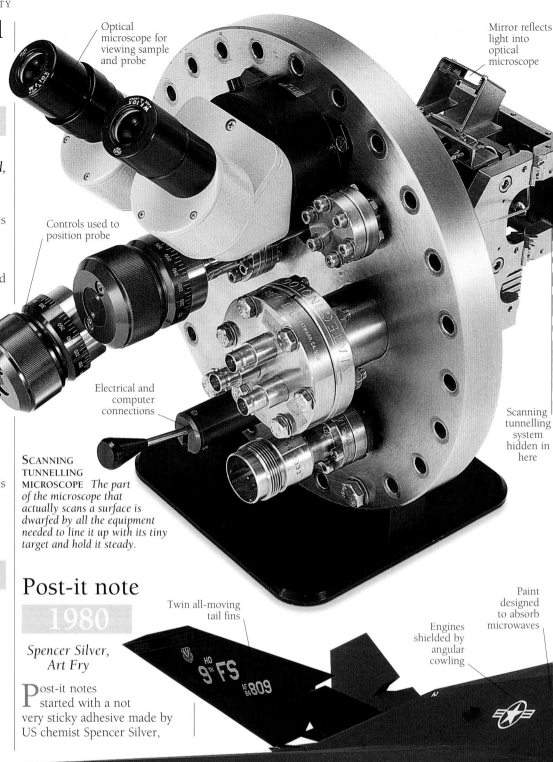

Optical microscope for viewing sample and probe

Mirror reflects light into optical microscope

Controls used to position probe

Electrical and computer connections

SCANNING TUNNELLING MICROSCOPE *The part of the microscope that actually scans a surface is dwarfed by all the equipment needed to line it up with its tiny target and hold it steady.*

Scanning tunnelling system hidden in here

Twin all-moving tail fins

Paint designed to absorb microwaves

Engines shielded by angular cowling

Post-it note

1980

Spencer Silver, Art Fry

Post-it notes started with a not very sticky adhesive made by US chemist Spencer Silver, who worked for US manufacturing company 3M. He had a feeling that the adhesive might be useful, but couldn't think of a use for it. Eventually, his colleague Art Fry found one. Art sang in a choir, and needed bookmarks that wouldn't fall out of his music. A strip of Silver's adhesive was the answer. After much development, and the realization that the peelable, sticky sheets had many other uses, 3M's Post-it notes were launched in 1980.

1982 In April, Canada gets total independence from the British parliament when Queen Elizabeth II signs the Constitution Act. Canada's new status is largely the result of a long campaign by its prime minister, Pierre Trudeau.

1982 Argentine troops invade the British-run Falkland Islands, off South America. Britain's prime minister, Margaret Thatcher, sends troops to defend the islands. Altogether, about 900 British and Argentine troops die. Argentina is defeated.

Scanning tunnelling microscope
1981

Gerd Binnig, Heinrich Rohrer

The scanning tunnelling microscope, invented by Swiss physicists Gerd Binnig and Heinrich Rohrer in 1981, reveals the three-dimensional reality of individual atoms. It scans a metal surface with a sharp probe that doesn't quite touch it. A small voltage makes electrons "tunnel" out of the metal, creating a current, and a control signal raises or lowers the probe to keep this current constant as the surface is scanned. Fluctuations in the control signal can then be converted into an amazingly detailed picture of the surface.

IBM PC
1981

William Lowe, Don Estridge

In 1980, US computer giant IBM saw the desktop computer as both a threat and an opportunity. One of its managers, William Lowe,

suggested that the company should develop a personal computer. A small company called Microsoft provided the operating system. By autumn, the design was ready, and another manager, Don Estridge, took over production. The IBM PC was launched in New York on 12 August, 1981. Within days, output had to be quadrupled as demand outstripped supply.

Space shuttle
1981

NASA

A space shuttle blasts into space, then glides home like a plane. Unlike a plane, it starts each journey attached to a huge fuel tank and boosters, the whole thing weighing 2000 tonnes. The tank is discarded, but the boosters are re-used. After trials in which shuttles were launched from jumbo jets, the shuttle *Columbia* lifted off from Cape Canaveral in Florida on 12 April, 1981. Its 54-hour mission, ending at Edwards Air Force Base in California, was the first of many.

Compact disc
1982

Philips Electronics, Sony Corporation

Competing companies Philips and Sony did not want a repeat of earlier mistakes, in which their rival video systems had both been beaten by the VHS recorder (✳ *see* **page 218**), so they worked together to invent the CD. The basics were agreed by 1980, and the two companies then started developing players and disc-making machinery. When commercial CD players appeared in 1982, the Philips player included a key component made by Sony.

Polymerase chain reaction
1983

Kary Mullis

Detectives and doctors can now use tiny amounts of DNA to find out about bodies, dead or alive. In just an hour or two, the polymerase chain reaction, invented in 1983 by US biochemist Kary Mullis, can turn a few DNA molecules

into enough to analyse. A machine repeatedly uses heat to split DNA into its two component strands, then uses the enzyme polymerase to make more DNA from these. The process is cheap enough to use routinely.

Stealth aircraft
1983

Lockheed Martin Corporation

Stealth technology tries to make planes invisible to radar (✳ *see* **page 198**). The idea is not new: in the Second World War, German submarine snorkels were coated with radar-absorbing material to reduce the risk of detection. Another technique is to shape objects so that they do not reflect radar waves back to where they came from. Both ideas were used in the first stealth aircraft, the US Lockheed F-117 fighter, which became operational in 1983. Despite its weird shape and special paint, one was shot down over Yugoslavia in 1999.

Cyclonic vacuum cleaner
1983

James Dyson

See **pages 238–239** for the story of how James Dyson took on the world with the first cyclonic vacuum cleaner.

STEALTH AIRCRAFT *The angular shape of the F-117A deflects radar pulses, while its special black paint absorbs them and also makes it less visible at night.*

Conventional wheels hidden during flight

Louvres hide hot engines from heat-seeking missiles

1983 On Wednesday 16 February, which will be known as "Ash Wednesday", Australia's worst ever bush fires kill 72 people, including 12 firefighters, and cause $400m of damage. Some fires are the work of arsonists.

1983 At Black Rock, Nevada, USA, British businessman Richard Noble makes land speed history in his jet car *Thrust 2*. His speed of 1019.467 km/h (633.468 mph), is 17.797 km/h (11.061 mph) faster than the world record.

Internet

1983

J. C. R. Licklider, Larry Roberts

US psychologist J. C. R. Licklider, head of Information Processing at the US Advanced Research Projects Agency (ARPA) started his Intergalactic Computer Network – officially known as Arpanet – in 1963. Its aim was to link research computers together. Network specialist Larry Roberts took over in 1966. By 1970, Arpanet was using packet switching, the transmission technique that makes the Internet possible. Procedures for transferring data were fixed by 1978, and became compulsory in 1983, effectively creating the modern Internet. (✳ *See also* **Network of networks**.)

Dust-free builder's chute

1984

G. H. Vlutters, A. J. Vlutters

Dutch building equipment suppliers G. H. and A. J. Vlutters invented their rubbish chute in 1984. Before then, builders made their own chutes from planks. Dust went everywhere, and large objects sometimes bounced out and fell. The Vlutters were inspired by a stack of disposable cups. If the cups had no bottoms, they would form a flexible tube. They made the cups bigger, added chains and a winch, and persuaded builders to buy them.

Sections link together to form the chute

DUST-FREE BUILDER'S CHUTE *A chute like this, erected in minutes, is safer than earlier chutes, which took hours to build.*

Top "cup" is attached to the building

3D graphics computer

1984

James Clark

Computer-generated images for films and advertising are made with specialized graphics computers. The first person to see the need for such computers was US engineer James Clark. He intended them for scientific and military work, but when his company, Silicon Graphics, gave one of its first workstations to *Star Wars* director George Lucas, in 1984, it opened up a new market. Today, digital actors can replace extras in a film and entire films are created without a single actor.

DNA fingerprinting

1984

Alec Jeffreys

Every person's DNA is unique. DNA fingerprinting compares DNA found after a crime with DNA from a suspect. It was invented in 1984 by British geneticist Alec (later Sir Alec) Jeffreys. The DNA is first split into fragments with an enzyme. Everyone's DNA will split differently. When drawn through jelly by electricity, some fragments move faster than others. The resulting pattern of spots is revealed by making radioactive DNA stick to the original DNA. It can be used as evidence in a trial. In 2013, advanced DNA sequencing techniques were developed that can distinguish between identical twins.

Figures' movements based on those of real actors

3D GRAPHICS COMPUTER *Graphic computers generated hundreds of "actors" for the film* Titanic.

1983 Germany's *Stern* magazine excites world interest with excerpts from what it says are Hitler's diaries. Despite the approval of British historian Hugh Trevor-Roper, they turn out to be the work of a forger called Konrad Kujau.

1984 In Bhopal, central India, a leak at an insecticide plant releases 45 tonnes of deadly gas into a populated area. About 2500 people are killed, 50,000 are temporarily disabled, and many more will claim lasting effects.

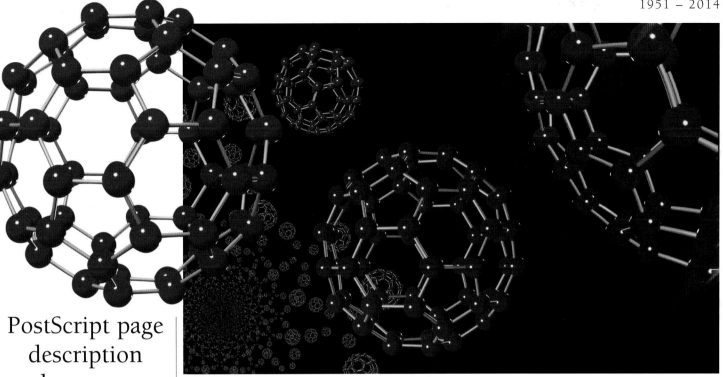

PostScript page description language

1984

John Warnock, Charles Geschke

PostScript is a language that describes printed pages. Any printer that understands PostScript can print a PostScript file. Because the language describes shapes, rather than issuing instructions, the result is limited only by the quality of the printer. PostScript was devised by US computer scientists John Warnock and Charles Geschke and released by their company, Adobe, in 1984. When Apple used it in their LaserWriter printer, and a third company, Aldus, added a layout program, PageMaker, desktop publishing was born.

Fullerenes

1985

Harry Kroto, Richard Smalley, Robert Curl

Scientists once knew only three forms of carbon – diamond, graphite, and amorphous. Then, in 1985,

FULLERENES *A buckminster-fullerene molecule is a semi-regular polyhedron. Buckminster Fuller based designs for huge domes on polyhedra of this kind.*

British chemist Harold (later Sir Harold) Kroto and US chemists Richard Smalley and Robert Curl vaporized graphite with a laser beam. This formed molecules containing 60 carbon atoms arranged as a hollow ball. They named the new form of carbon buckminsterfullerene, after a US architect famous for his domes. Other fullerenes have since been found.

Windows operating system

1985

Microsoft Corporation

The Apple Macintosh set a new standard. Its point-and-click interface made the IBM PC's text-based operating system, Microsoft's MS-DOS, look old-fashioned. In 1985,

Microsoft hit back with Windows, but because PC users wanted to keep their old programs, Windows operated through MS-DOS, making it slow. An improved

NETWORK OF NETWORKS

THERE ARE MANY INTERNETS but only one Internet with a capital "I". An internet is any network that interconnects several smaller networks. The Internet connects thousands of internets to form a vast global network. It consists of "backbones", such as NSFNET in the USA and EBONE in Europe, into which are plugged smaller regional and local networks. These connect to individual computers.

GETTING THE MESSAGE

A home computer connects to the Internet through a computer belonging to an Internet Service Provider (ISP). This computer is connected through the ISP's network to the Internet, and has a unique address. Data travels as independent "packets", which find their way with the help of special computers called routers.

EXCHANGING DATA

Computers using the Internet have to talk TCP/IP, its official "language". This is actually a pair of protocols, or standards. TCP is Transmission Control Protocol, responsible for the exchange of data between programs running on different computers. IP is Internet Protocol, which ensures that data can find its way around the Net.

version, so Mac-like that it provoked a lawsuit, appeared in 1987. Finally, Windows 3, launched in 1990, helped the PC dominate the computer it had once imitated.

1984 India's prime minister, Indira Gandhi, is killed by her Sikh bodyguards. It is the end of a conflict in which Sikh extremists in the Punjab violently sought independence, and resented the use of troops to clear the Sikh temple at Amritsar.

1985 Irish musician Bob Geldof organizes Live Aid, a 16-hour charity concert at London's Wembley Stadium, with further time at Philadelphia's JFK Stadium in the USA. World-class performers take part, and money rolls in for the world's poor.

TAMING THE WHIRLWIND

James Dyson takes on the world with the first vacuum cleaner that doesn't need a bag

EARLY VACUUM CLEANER
From their invention in about 1902 until Dyson applied the cyclonic principle, all vacuum cleaners sucked air through a bag. Some early models were powered by hand. Electricity made cleaning easier and a little more efficient.

Vacuum cleaner early 1900s

Dust collected in here

Dyson got the idea for his cleaner from the industrial cyclone, which is used to collect unwanted particles, such as the sawdust from a sawmill. His challenge was to get the principle to work on a much smaller scale inside a domestic machine.

It was late at night. An intruder was creeping about a factory yard. For a long time, he stared at and examined a giant metal cone sticking out of the factory roof. He made several sketches of the cone, then he was off into the darkness. James Dyson had just had his first encounter with an industrial cyclone, a device that removes dust from the air coming out of a factory. It was to change his life.

The next morning, Dyson built a copy of the cyclone in his own small factory, where he was making wheelbarrows. He wanted it to trap the paint powder that filled the air when his wheelbarrows were sprayed. There was already a fan in the factory that sucked air through a cloth filter, but the cloth needed cleaning hourly. In the cyclone system, the air whirled around inside a cone. The powder was flung out like water out of clothes in a spin dryer and deposited at the bottom of the cone.

Then Dyson thought of something else. At home, near Bath, England, he used a powerful vacuum cleaner. The design of vacuum cleaners hadn't changed much since they were invented. They worked well only with a new bag, because the dust they sucked up from the carpet quickly clogged the pores in the bag, reducing suction. The bag was like the cloth filter in Dyson's factory, which he had replaced with a cyclone, and he wondered if he could replace the bag with a cyclone system too.

Dyson rushed home and made a cardboard model of the industrial cyclone. He ripped the bag off an old vacuum cleaner and replaced it with his cardboard cone. To his delight, he found that the bagless vacuum cleaner worked well. He had made an important invention.

That was in 1978. It would be another 15 years before Dyson's Dual Cyclone cleaner was launched, although his first cyclonic cleaner, the G-Force, featured on the cover of *Design* magazine in 1983 and reached Japan in 1986. Those years were filled with intensive engineering, which he loved, and dealing with businessmen and lawyers, which he hated. In the end, he had to manufacture his invention himself. He didn't want his idea stolen or suppressed by jealous rivals.

When the Dual Cyclone was finally launched in 1993, the first reaction from customers was shock: it looked so different. Then sales grew. After two years, Dyson's invention was the number one vacuum cleaner in Britain and was generating worldwide sales of well over $1 million a day. The whirlwind was tamed.

Dyson G-Force cyclonic vacuum cleaner, sold in Japan from 1986

1940s advertisement for a Hoover vacuum cleaner

FORCE FOR CHANGE
Japanese customers loved the unusual pink of the G-Force, the first cyclonic cleaner to go into production. The colour was suggested by the early morning light in the fields of Provence in the South of France.

JAMES DYSON
The multi-cyclone cleaner seen here is just one of many ideas Dyson has produced. Training at the Royal College of Art, London, helped him to develop his creativity. Before the cyclonic cleaner, he had invented a new kind of boat, and a wheelbarrow with a ball-shaped wheel. Just as important as his creativity, though, was his determination to see things through.

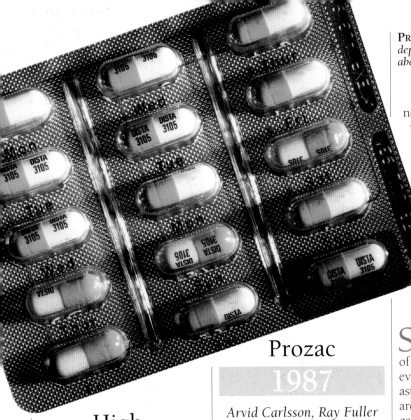

World Wide Web

1990

Tim Berners-Lee

The World Wide Web grew from the work of British physicist Tim Berners-Lee at the European Centre for Nuclear Research (CERN) in Switzerland. CERN's scientists needed to get at information scattered among computers worldwide. Berners-Lee's answer was the Web. In 1990, when he had written the software and defined the standards that would make it work, the Web became available to CERN scientists. The public saw it a year later.

Gene therapy

1990

French Anderson

Gene therapists attempt to restore health to people with genetic disorders by replacing faulty genes. The first person to receive officially approved gene therapy was a four-year-old girl who had inherited a defective immune system. In 1990, US geneticist French Anderson removed some white cells from her blood, inserted normal copies of a faulty gene, then replaced the cells. With regular follow-up treatments to maintain enough gene-corrected white cells, the girl became able to lead a normal life.

Digital mobile phone

1991

Groupe Spécial Mobile

The first mobile phones used a simple but insecure analogue radio system, in

---

neurologist Arvid Carlsson, who developed another anti-depressant, later withdrawn because of side effects.

Supermassive black hole

1987

John Kormendy, Alan Dressler, Douglas Richstone

Supermassive black holes have the mass of millions of Suns. They can destroy everything around them, but astronomers now believe they are involved in the creation of galaxies. They can be detected by the way nearby stars orbit them at colossal speeds. In 1987, a 30-million-Sun black hole was found independently by Canadian astronomer John Kormendy and US astronomers Alan Dressler and Douglas Richstone. Many more have been found since then.

Gene that causes cystic fibrosis

1989

Lap-Chee Tsui, Francis Collins

In cystic fibrosis (CF), thick, sticky mucus clogs the lungs and gut. A child can inherit the condition if both parents are carriers. The faulty gene that causes it was found in 1989 by Canadian geneticist Lap-Chee Tsui at the Hospital for Sick Children in Toronto, Canada, and US geneticist Francis Collins at the University of Michigan, USA. Their discovery makes it possible to detect CF carriers and may one day make the condition curable.

Prozac

1987

Arvid Carlsson, Ray Fuller

In 1972, a team led by US biochemist Ray Fuller synthesized the compound fluoxetine. Fifteen years later, it became the antidepressant Prozac. Fluoxetine reduces the rate at which serotonin, a nerve chemical, is reabsorbed. This makes more serotonin available, which eases depression. Fuller's work used some research by Swedish

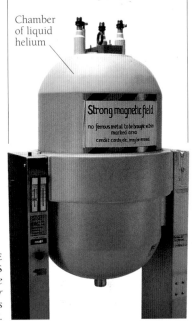

Chamber of liquid helium

High-temperature superconductors

1986

Georg Bednorz, Alex Müller

Superconductors, used in powerful electromagnets, show no resistance to electric current. But they work only at very low temperatures. In 1986, German physicist Georg Bednorz and Swiss physicist Alex Müller found a superconductor that worked at a higher temperature. Their new barium-lanthanum copper oxide sparked off a search for others. By 1988, researchers had found a similar oxide that was superconductive at -148°C (-234°F), which could be made to work by being cooled with cheap liquid nitrogen.

HIGH-TEMPERATURE SUPERCONDUCTORS *Electromagnets like this use superconductors to carry their huge currents. The magnet is enclosed in a cooling chamber.*

1986 Chernobyl power station in the USSR explodes, showering much of northern Europe with long-lasting radioactive fallout. Coming after several other nuclear disasters, this one finally shatters dented confidence in the industry.

1989 TV screens worldwide fill with scenes of jubilation as the Berlin Wall is torn down after 28 years. Berliners of all ages join in cracking up the concrete barrier between East and West. Bemused East German soldiers just watch.

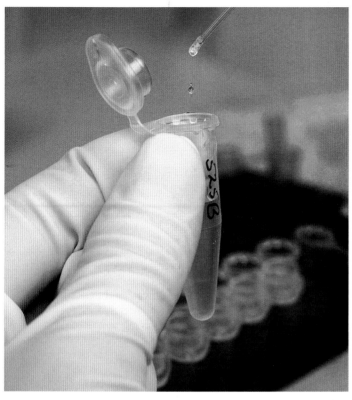

GENE THERAPY *A scientist pulls a thread of pure DNA out of solution to isolate it from an organism.*

which speech was converted more or less directly into radio waves. In 1982, the Groupe Spécial Mobile was formed to develop a digital system for Europe and beyond. Digital phones convert sound waves into numerical codes describing their shape, then send these codes by radio. By 1991, trial versions of the GSM system were ready, and the following year all major European operators began to use it. GSM now powers mobiles in 85 per cent of the world market.

Expressed sequence tags
1991

Craig Venter

A gene is a sequence of chemical units strung along a DNA molecule. Specific genes can be spotted by sifting through thousands of such units. Because nearly all the DNA is "junk", not genes, this takes a long time. US geneticist Craig Venter made use of the ability of living cells to remove the junk, leaving fragments of actual genes. He examined the resulting "expressed sequence tags" to find which fragments corresponded to anything interesting. This meant he could track down genes much more quickly. In 1991, he revealed more than 330 new genes – adding some 10 per cent to the then known total.

Disposable TV camera
1992

Smith & Nephew Dyonics

In surgery, the smaller the incision the better. So one essential tool of modern surgery is the endoscope, a fibre-optic device that lets surgeons peer through a "keyhole" incision. In 1992, US company Smith & Nephew Dyonics patented a more flexible alternative: a tiny camera that could be passed into the body. As it is difficult to sterilize, the camera is designed to be used only once, then thrown away.

Graphical Web browser
1993

Marc Andreessen

The first World Wide Web sites (✳ **see page 240**) were entirely text-based. The Web could deliver pictures, but not with text. This changed in 1993, when the US National Center for Supercomputing Applications released Mosaic, the first graphical Web browser. Developed by 21-year-old US student Marc Andreessen, it changed the way we use the Web. The richness and convenience of Mosaic's direct descendants, Netscape (by Andreessen) and Internet Explorer, are now taken for granted by Web users.

GRAPHICAL WEB BROWSER *Mozilla Firefox, released in 2002, is available in 75 languages and is used by more than 500 million people around the world.*

1990 After 27 years in gaol, South African anti-apartheid activist Nelson Mandela is released by President F. W. de Klerk. Mandela and de Klerk work to create a non-racial democracy. Mandela will win the first election open to all races.

1993 British artist Damien Hirst shocks conservative critics with *Mother and Child, Divided*, two tanks of preserving solution containing a cow and calf, each split down the middle, which he shows at the Venice Biennale exhibition.

COMET HALE-BOPP *When Hale-Bopp was at its closest to the Sun, in April 1997, its dust tail was longer than the distance from the Sun to Earth.*

Genetically modified food

1994

Calgene Inc.

Farmers and growers have been changing the genetic make-up of our food for centuries. The first genetically modified (GM) food produced by genetic engineering (✳ **see page 229**) and approved for sale was the Flavr Savr tomato, produced by US company Calgene. A modified gene made it firmer, allowing it to be picked later without its being too soft to transport. This meant it had more flavour. Other GM foods, such as soya beans, followed.

Flavr Savr tomatoes stayed firmer for longer

Comet Hale-Bopp

1995

Alan Hale, Thomas Bopp

In 1995, two US amateur astronomers, Alan Hale and Thomas Bopp, independently discovered a new comet. At seven times further away from Earth than the Sun, it was the most distant ever spotted by amateurs. The professionals found that it was a thousand times as bright as Halley's comet, with a nucleus about 50 km (30 miles) across. By 1997, it was much closer to the Sun, and was clearly visible to the naked eye. It has now retreated into space, and will not be seen from Earth for another 2400 years.

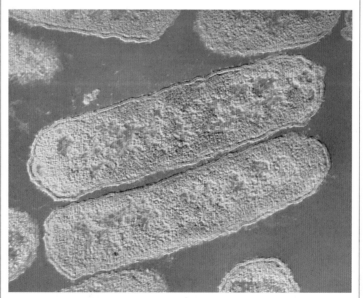

COMPLETE BACTERIAL DNA SEQUENCE *Haemophilus influenzae (above) was the first of several organisms to have its entire DNA sequenced by The Institute for Genomic Research in the mid-1990s.*

Complete bacterial DNA sequence

1995

Robert Fleischmann

An organism's complete set of genes – its genome – is hidden among the millions of chemical units making up its DNA (✳ **see pages 216–217**). To study a genome, scientists first have to list these units in the right sequence. The first free-living organism to have its entire DNA sequence revealed was a bacterium that can cause meningitis – Haemophilus influenzae. A team led by US geneticist Robert Fleischmann at The Institute for Genomic Research (TIGR) in California, USA, used the "shotgun" method. The team first broke the bacterium's DNA into thousands of random fragments then used a computer to put these into a complete sequence. The result was presented, to great acclaim, in May 1995.

1994 The dream of decades is realized when the Channel Tunnel, which runs under the English Channel to link Britain and France by rail, is opened. Construction of the tunnel has taken more than six years and cost £10.5bn.

1994 South Africa rejoins the Commonwealth after holding its first election open to people of all races. The clear winner is the African National Congress, led by Nelson Mandela, who becomes the country's first black president.

Internet retailing

1995

Jeff Bezos

While hundreds of Internet retailers crashed in 2001, the oldest of them all remained healthy. Amazon.com, the Internet bookstore (which now sells other things as well) was founded by US computer scientist Jeff Bezos in 1994. It sold its first book in July 1995. Following a great US tradition, business whizz Bezos started the website in his garage. He also wrote his own software for the site, which he named after the world's longest river.

Full-length computer-generated movie

1995

The Walt Disney Company

Making a full-length animated film is laborious and expensive. In the early 1990s, specialized graphics computers (✳ see page 236) became capable of doing most of the work. The first film that was made in this way was Disney's *Toy Story*, a tale of rivalry between a hand-crafted cowboy and a mass-produced space ranger. It was released in 1995. Its success led to the making of other computer-generated films, including *A Bug's Life* and *Monsters, Inc.*

Proof of Fermat's last theorem

1995

Andrew Wiles, Richard Taylor

The last unproved theorem of 17th-century French mathematician Pierre de Fermat stated that, for n greater than 2, there were no positive whole numbers x, y, and z such that $x^n + y^n = z^n$. Fermat said he had a proof, but never wrote it down. In 1993, British mathematician Andrew Wiles produced his own 200-page proof. Other mathematicians spotted some gaps, but by 1995, with the help of Richard Taylor, one of Wiles' former students, these were plugged and Fermat's last theorem was proved.

Life on Mars?

1996

David McKay

In August 1996, US geologist David McKay made an announcement about a meteorite. It contained evidence, he said, that there may once have been life on Mars. The 4.5 billion-year-old meteorite was found in Antarctica in 1984, but its Martian origin was not confirmed until 1994. Two years' work revealed organic chemicals within it that suggested the presence of living bacteria at some time in the past. The surface of the meteorite carried no such chemicals, ruling out Earth contamination. There were also inorganic compounds that are secreted by bacteria. Scientists regard the evidence as inconclusive.

INTERNET RETAILING
Amazon.com is the world's biggest Internet business. It has more than 80 giant warehouses worldwide.

Dolly the sheep

1997

Ian Wilmut, Keith Campbell

See **pages 244–245** for the story of how Ian Wilmut and Keith Campbell created Dolly the sheep.

Growth of new brain cells

1998

Fred Gage, Peter Eriksson

People used to think that once all our brain cells are in place, no more can grow. In 1998, neurologists Fred Gage in the USA and Peter Eriksson in Sweden showed this is not so. They labelled brain cells in terminally ill patients with a chemical that revealed cell division. On examining the brains after death, they found that they had been producing up to 1000 new cells every day.

MicroStar air reconnaissance vehicle

1998

Lockheed Martin Corporation

Small aircraft are harder to detect than large ones. In 1989, the US Lockheed Martin Corporation took this to an extreme with their military reconnaissance plane MicroStar. Its wingspan was 12 cm (5 in), and it weighed 85 g (3 oz). It carried a tiny television camera and transmitter. Designed to fly at a height of 60 m (200 ft), it could send vital spy pictures to people below.

1996 Afghan Islamic fundamentalists, the Taliban, capture the capital, Kabul, in the civil war that broke out in Afghanistan when Soviet troops left in 1989. They seize power and impose a strict rule based on Islamic law.

1997 Britain's lease on Hong Kong runs out after 100 years, and the area is handed back to China. Elaborate agreements are negotiated by the British in an attempt to ensure that Hong Kong citizens retain their full political rights.

CLONING AN ADULT MAMMAL

Ian Wilmut and Keith Campbell create Dolly, a perfect copy of a grown-up sheep

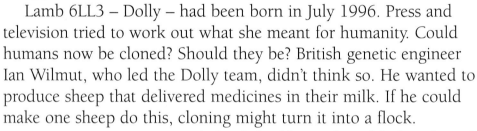

IAN WILMUT

Born in 1944, Ian Wilmut joined the Animal Breeding Research Station (now the Roslin Institute) near Edinburgh, Scotland, in 1974. There, with Keith Campbell, he developed a way of cloning animals from partly developed embryos. The results, two sheep called Megan and Morag, were born in 1995. They were forerunners of the first clone from an adult.

Harry Griffin picked up the phone. It was the evening of Saturday 22 February, 1997, and he was enjoying a break from the busy Roslin Institute, Scotland, where one of his jobs was to deal with journalists. The call shattered his weekend. Tomorrow, a Sunday newspaper was going to publish a story that was supposed to be kept secret until the following week. Scientists at the Institute, collaborating with the biotechnology company PPL Therapeutics, had created a sheep that was an exact copy – a clone – of an adult sheep.

Lamb 6LL3 – Dolly – had been born in July 1996. Press and television tried to work out what she meant for humanity. Could humans now be cloned? Should they be? British genetic engineer Ian Wilmut, who led the Dolly team, didn't think so. He wanted to produce sheep that delivered medicines in their milk. If he could make one sheep do this, cloning might turn it into a flock.

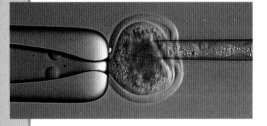

An egg cell has its nucleus removed.

HOW ANIMALS ARE CLONED

To create a copy of an animal, one of its cells is grown in a laboratory under special conditions then injected into a cell from which the nucleus has been removed. The fused cells are usually given a brief electric shock to activate them. Although the basic technique for moving genetic material from cell to cell dates from 1952, success rates for cloning are still low.

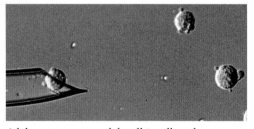

A laboratory-grown adult cell is collected.

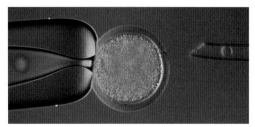

A pipette, on the left, holds the nucleus-free egg cell in place while the complete adult cell is pushed into it by the tube seen on the right.

Animals had been cloned before, but all from cells at an early stage of development. As an embryo grows, its cells become specialized. Some of them form nerves, some form muscles, and so on. The genes not needed in any particular type of cell are "turned off". It is this that allows many different types of cell to be created from just one set of genes. So although every adult cell contains every gene, none has all its genes available in working form.

In 1995, another scientist at the Roslin Institute, Keith Campbell, had found a way to turn back the clock and make an adult cell behave like an early embyronic cell.

The world's press converged on Dolly after Britain's Observer newspaper printed her story on Sunday 23 February, 1997.

He kept adult cells alive in culture dishes using a medium that contained very little "growth factor" – in effect putting them on a starvation diet. This starvation turned the genes that had been turned off during development back on again. A cell treated in this way, because it had a full set of genes available for work, could, when fused with an egg that had had its nucleus removed, form the starting point for a new animal.

Wilmut and his colleagues took an egg from a sheep and sucked out its genetic material with a tiny tube. Then they inserted a "starved" cell from the udder of a different sheep. A tiny electric shock started the egg dividing to produce an embryo. They implanted this in the womb of another sheep. They had to do this 277 times to get just one Dolly – the others all died at some stage.

When Dolly was born, she didn't look like the sheep that had carried her, or even like the sheep that had provided the egg. She looked exactly like the sheep that had provided the udder cell. Shaped by the genes from that cell, Dolly was that sheep's clone – a world first. A little ahead of schedule, Dolly was front-page news.

DOLLY BECOMES A MUM
On 13 April, 1998, Dolly proved that she was a fully functional sheep by giving birth to a healthy lamb named Bonnie. The following March, Dolly produced triplets, seen here with their mother. The lambs are completely normal, but Dolly seems to be older than her chronological age.

MP3 compression standard

1998

Fraunhofer Institut, Moving Picture Experts Group

Downloading music from the Internet would take forever without compression to remove unnecessary information. This could reduce quality, but MP3 (or MPEG Layer-3) ensures that the effects of compression are masked by louder sounds. It was developed by the Fraunhofer Institut in Germany, and released by the Moving Picture Experts Group (MPEG) in 1998. Although its use on the Internet created some copyright problems, a little MP3 player is a really neat way to carry music around.

SATELLITE MOBILE PHONE *Ordinary satellite phones use satellites in high orbits. They are not truly mobile because they have to be carefully aimed at the chosen satellite before use.*

Satellite mobile phone

1998

Iridium Satellite LLC

Mobile phones will not work in remote areas where there are no base stations. Phones working through satellites in high Earth orbits have been available since 1982, but the mobile network Iridium, which went live in 1998, uses 66 satellites in much lower orbits.

At first, demand fell short of expectations, and Iridium had to close down, but it is now back in business.

Carbon nanotube "muscle"

1999

Ray Baughman

Better robots came closer in 1999 with the demonstration of "muscles" made from fullerenes (✳ **see page 237**). Robots are normally operated by electric or pneumatic actuators. These are slow and heavy, but an actuator made from "buckypaper" – a sheet containing billions of tubular carbon molecules – promises superior performance. Developed by an international team led by US scientist Ray Baughman, the muscle flexes when a low voltage is applied. The movement is small, but the force is greater than with human muscle. With the right leverage, it could work a robot.

Biological molecular motor

1999

Carlo Montemagno

Molecular motors are so small that they contain only a few molecules. In 1999, researchers led by US engineer Carlo Montemagno demonstrated a motor whose shaft, 12-millionths of a millimetre in diameter, and made from a protein molecule, rotated at 200 revolutions per minute. The movement was created by a reaction between the protein and the enzyme ATPase.

It occurred when the motor was immersed in a solution of the energy-rich molecule ATP. Such motors may one day power invisible pumps inside human bodies.

Home-grown replacement organ

1999

Anthony Atala

Rejection problems and lack of donors make replacing human organs difficult. In 1999, US doctor Anthony Atala showed that an entire new organ could be made from just a few cells of the old one. He took muscle and lining cells from the bladders of dogs, and grew them around plastic balls to form new bladders.

When he replaced the dogs' bladders with the artificial ones, they worked perfectly.

1999 South African novelist J. M. Coetzee becomes the first author to win the prestigious Booker Prize twice. Having won it in 1983, with his novel *The Life and Times of Michael K*, he completes the double with *Disgrace*.

2000 The century's most feared "insect", the millennium bug, bites only mildly, as computer clocks flip from 1999 to 2000. Although some older chips think it is now 1900, the worldwide chaos predicted by doomsters fails to materialize.

Leech neuron computer

1999

Bill Ditto

In 1999, US physicist Bill Ditto demonstrated the first computer made by connecting living nerve cells together. His "leech-ulator" could do only simple operations, and needed an ordinary computer to help it display the results, but it worked. Ditto's aim was to develop a computer that could "think" without detailed programming.

Gene targeted sheep

2000

Kenneth McCreath

Gene targeting is inserting a new gene at a specific point in an organism's genome (✳ see **page 242**), rather than adding it at random. It allows the gene to work properly and be inherited by offspring. The first person to target genes in a large animal was Scottish geneticist Kenneth McCreath. He put the gene for an enzyme into the DNA of sheep cells, moved the nuclei to egg cells, and grew these into sheep. The enzyme appeared in their milk.

Growing bone outside the body

2000

Julia Polak

In 2000, Julia Polak and her team at the Chelsea and Westminster Hospital in Britain discovered that human bone cells could be made to grow outside the body. The cells were helped to bond together using Bioglass, a ceramic material containing silicon, calcium, and phosphorus. This had been developed in the 1960s by British researcher Larry Hench. It is now hoped that it will be possible to inject liquid Bioglass enriched with bone cells into patients to aid the healing of broken bones or to treat brittle bones in older people.

Human genome

2000

Francis Collins, Craig Venter

The human genome – a human being's complete set of genes – is contained within a long sequence of chemical units (A, T, G, or C) that is unique to human DNA (✳ see **pages 216–217**). A draft of the sequence was announced on 26 June 2000, by two rivals, the public Human Genome Project (HGP), led by Francis Collins, and the private Celera Genomics, led by Craig Venter. Neither genome was actually complete. Celera had done more, but charged people to see theirs, while HGP's less-complete genome was free. Both organizations published more complete information in February 2001. (✳ See also **Start of something big**.)

Cloned endangered animal

2001

Philip Damiani

The gaur, an ox found in Asia, is on the list of endangered species. In January 2001, a baby gaur called Noah was born to a domestic cow in Iowa, USA. Researcher Philip Damiani cloned it (✳ see **pages 244–245**) from skin cells

START OF SOMETHING BIG

THE HUMAN GENOME is only the start of a project that could last another century. Scientists will use it, among other things, to find connections between genes and diseases. There will be several areas of study. Important among these will be functional genomics, which is about what genes do, and structural genomics, which deals with the shape of the proteins that enable them to do it.

Dr Craig Venter, former president of Celera Genomics

HUMAN GENOME PROJECT
This international project was started in 1990, with the aim of completing it by 2005. This was later brought forward to 2003. There are four major participants in the USA and one in Britain, with research centres in at least 18 other countries making contributions. Its results are freely published.

CELERA GENOMICS
Celera was founded in 1998 by the PE Corporation, a US biological laboratory equipment company, and Craig Venter. It operates the world's largest genomic production plant and makes extensive use of supercomputers. Academic and commercial organizations pay a subscription to make use of the company's genomic information.

CLONED ENDANGERED ANIMAL
The gaur is found in forests in Asia. It eats grass and bamboo shoots.

from a dead gaur, frozen eight years earlier. He fused these with cow eggs whose genes had been removed, producing embryos that he implanted into cows. Noah was the only calf to come through alive, but he later died from an infection.

2000 It's "Happy Birthday" to Queen Elizabeth the Queen Mother, affectionately known as the Queen Mum, as she reaches 100 on Friday 4 August. Crowds see her on the balcony of Buckingham Palace with three generations of royal children.

2001 On 11 September, two Boeing 767s, hijacked by terrorists on their flights from Boston to Los Angeles, plough into the towers of the World Trade Center in New York. Thousands die. The USA is at war – but with whom?

Self-cleaning glass

2001

Kevin Sanderson

Window cleaning may soon be a thing of the past. In 2001, Britain's Pilkington glass company announced the invention of self-cleaning glass, developed by a team under chemist Kevin Sanderson. Its secret lies in a special coating, which makes rain run off the glass, taking dirt with it. The coating, which is extremely thin, also acts as a catalyst, allowing ultraviolet light and oxygen to unstick any dirt that might be left behind.

iPod

2001

Steve Jobs, Lee Black

Apple launched its now-famous music player, the first pocket device able to hold 1000 songs, in 2001. Early models used the MP3 music compression system (✳ *see* **page 246**), but later iPods can also use an even more efficient file format unique to Apple. By 2005, more than 1.5 million songs, and even the album art that goes with them, were available for downloading through Apple's iTunes website. Despite the sleek white box and ultra-cool user interface, the iPod did not contain any new technology, just a hard disk drive and a little computer to control it and decode the music. With its distinctive image and ability to find any tune in seconds, it quickly displaced the suddenly very clunky Walkman. (✳ *see* **page 233**)

More moons for Jupiter

2002

Scott S. Sheppard, David Jewitt

In 2002, astronomers from the University of Hawaii revealed that the planet Jupiter has even more moons than we thought. Using a 3.6-m (140-in) telescope atop a Hawaiian volcano, they spotted 11 new satellites. This took the total number of known satellites up to 39 – far more than for any other planet in the solar system. It is perhaps a bit of an exaggeration to call these moons – they are not large, round bodies, but relatively small, irregularly shaped lumps of rock that were somehow captured by the giant planet's huge gravitational field. By 2013, 67 moons had been found orbiting Jupiter.

IPOD *Since 2001, the basic iPod has acquired enough capacity for 10,000 tunes, and a colour screen that can show photos and album art.*

Single-atom transistor

2002

Paul McEuen, Dan Ralph

The first transistor built around a single atom was created by scientists at Cornell University in 2002. Buried inside a specially designed molecule was a lone atom of cobalt. When the molecule was hooked up to an electronic circuit, the cobalt atom responded to a control voltage by changing the current through the device. This is only what an ordinary transistor would do, but the invention could be a step towards something new – molecular electronics. This technology promises circuits built by chemical synthesis in the future, to replace the current technique of etching shapes on to silicon.

Synthetic virus

2002

Jeronimo Cello, Aniko V. Paul, Eckard Wimmer

Any virus can easily mass-produce itself by using the genetic machinery in the cells of a suitable victim. In 2002 though, a team from the State University of New York was the first to synthesize a virus from scratch. Using the genome (the genetic make-up) of the polio virus downloaded from the Internet, they made a copy using ordinary chemicals.

Super-tough fibre

2003

Ray Baughman

The plastic fibres in bullet-proof vests are tough, but in 2003, scientists at the University of Texas and Trinity College, Dublin, spun a fibre 17 times tougher. It was made from carbon nanotubes – tubular molecules consisting entirely of carbon – dispersed in a soft plastic. Possible uses include better safety belts and explosion-proof blankets.

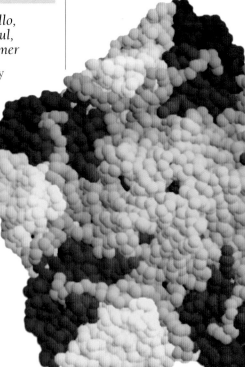

Outer coat made of four different proteins (false colour)

SYNTHETIC VIRUS *The polio virus has 20 five-sided faces around its genetic core.*

2002 The traditional currencies of many European countries cease to be accepted for payment as 12 Euro-zone nations switch their coins and banknotes to the Euro. Money in other forms has been Euro-based since 1999.

2003 The US, Britain, and other nations invade Iraq. Within three weeks, Saddam Hussein and his Ba'ath party are toppled, leaving the country free of its cruel dictator, but devastated and under the control of foreign troops.

Water on Mars

2004

NASA

In 2003, NASA landed two robot rovers, *Spirit* and *Opportunity*, on Mars. Their job was to explore the planet, looking in particular for signs of past life. *Opportunity* was the first to find geological evidence of water that had flowed long ago. In 2004, *Spirit* found even clearer signs of water. Although these rovers didn't actually find liquid water, the presence of sedimentary rocks and water-cut shapes show that water must once have been present. In 2013, *Curiosity* – a rover launched in 2011 – heated soil from the planet's surface and detected water vapour. The dust on Mars contains two per cent water, which is bound to chemicals in the soil.

WATER ON MARS *Opportunity (left) sent back images (above) showing layers of sediment and the effects of rippling water on rock.*

Oldest planet

2003

Donald Backer, Stephen Thorsett, Steinn Sigurdsson

Although the universe is about 13.7 billion years old, the planets in our Solar System were formed a mere 4.5 billion years ago. In 2003, the existence of a planet formed 12.7 billion years ago – a billion years after the universe – was confirmed by the Hubble space telescope. Planet PSR B1620-26C – or Methuselah (named after the oldest living person in the Bible) – belongs to a star system 5,600 light years from Earth. The planet showed up as a "wobble" in some star data many years before it was caught on camera.

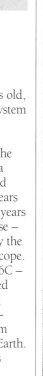

OLDEST PLANET *Floating 600 km (380 miles) above Earth, the Hubble telescope can detect remote objects like Methuselah normally hidden by our atmosphere.*

2004 An earthquake in the Indian Ocean creates a huge, fast-moving wave called a tsunami, causing terrible destruction in the coastal areas of surrounding countries. Nearly a quarter of a million people lose their lives.

2005 Sir Bob Geldof organizes Live8 – 11 concerts designed to put pressure on world leaders to help Africa by cancelling debt, increasing aid, and trading more fairly. More than 1000 musicians are seen by billions on 182 networks.

Low-cost mine clearance

2005

Paul Richards

The world is littered with landmines, which kill or maim more than 15,000 people every year. Getting rid of them was costly until 2005, when British engineer Paul Richards, based in South Africa, invented MineBurner. Instead of explosives, it uses bottled gas and oxygen to cut into landmines and destroy them, making disposal much cheaper.

Smartphone

2007

Steve Jobs, Jonathan Ive

In 2007, Apple launched the iPhone, which had an operating system, iOS, making it into a handheld computer on which the Internet could be accessed and phone calls could be made. The phones can also run apps whose functions include organization, news, social networking, and games. With an iconic design similar to the hugely popular iPod and a touchscreen, iPhones were in great demand. Soon, other mobile phone companies created smartphones with similar designs.

First lab-grown, synthetic organ transplant

2011

Alexander Seifalian, Harvard Bioscience, Dr Paolo Macchiarni

The world's first successful transplant of a synthetic organ grown in a laboratory was performed in July 2011. A plastic, Y-shaped model of the patient's trachea, or windpipe, was created, and then lined with the patient's stem cells. This meant his body would accept the synthetic organ. This operation paved the way for organ transplants that don't need a donor. Previous synthetic transplants were created from a patient's body tissue or a segment from a donor organ.

Higgs boson particle

2012

François Englert, Peter Higgs

On 4 July 2012, scientists at the CERN laboratory in Switzerland found a particle that could be the Higgs boson, a subatomic particle theorized to be responsible for the fact that objects have mass. In the 1970s, its existence was proposed by Peter Higgs and François Englert. Although the found particle is yet to be confirmed as the Higgs boson, Higgs and Englert were awarded

SMARTPHONE *The first iPhone was made mostly of aluminium and had a simple design, which quickly became iconic.*

HIGGS BOSON PARTICLE *The Large Hadron Collider is a huge machine in which particles were smashed together to find the Higgs boson.*

the Nobel Prize in Physics in 2013 for its likely discovery.

Life in the deep

2013

Mark Lever

Life, it seems, can exist almost anywhere there is water. A team of scientists studied rock samples from the oceanic crust, taken from under 2.6 km (1.6 miles) of ocean and 350–580 m (1150–1900 ft) below the sea bed. They discovered microbes living in the rock. With no light, oxygen, or nutrients, these microbes appear to live off energy from chemical reactions between rock and water. This is a potential major ecosystem that may exist throughout the oceanic crust, which covers 60 per cent of the Earth. Similar lifeforms may live on other planets.

Earth-like planets

2013

Erik A. Petigura, Andrew W. Howard, Geoffrey W. Marcy

In 2013, a team of astronomers studying data from NASA's Kepler space observatory discovered more than 3000 possible planets outside our solar system. Many of these were found to orbit at the right distance from their stars to support Earth-like temperatures that could make them habitable for life. Based on the data, it was estimated that our entire Milky Way galaxy may contain as many as 40 billion such planets.

EARTH-LIKE PLANETS *As a planet moves between its star and us, the star's brightness dips a little. Kepler finds planets by looking for these dips.*

2008 The bankruptcy of the huge Lehman Brothers bank is the start of a worldwide financial crisis.

2009 Barack Obama becomes the first African American to be elected President of the USA.

2010 Starting in Tunisia, demonstrations and protests, the "Arab Spring", challenge the governments of the Arab world.

2013 Nelson Mandela, the first black president of South Africa, dies. Billions of people watch his funeral.

INTO THE
FUTURE

THE BEST PART of this book remains unwritten – because it hasn't happened yet. Inventions and discoveries will continue to shape our world in ways we cannot predict. Once, people could say that some things never change. Now, with our increasing power over life and death, even that certainty is gone. We live in interesting times.

Index of Inventions & Discoveries

Index of Inventors & Discoverers

Picture credits & acknowledgements

The author would like to thank the staff at the Science Museum for their valuable help, especially: Neil Brown, Sam Evans, Ela Ginalska, Kevin Johnson, Ghislaine Lawrence, Bob McWilliam, and Peter Morris. Also: Louise Pritchard and everyone at Bookwork, who made this book happen; plus Caryn Jenner for proofreading.

The publisher would like to thank the following for their kind permission to reproduce their photographs: Position Key: c=centre; b=bottom; l=left; r=right; t=top
Courtesy of Apple: 249bl. Advertising Archives: 166bl, 180tc, 184br, 190tl, 193cl, 229cl.
AKG London: 38cl, 56–57t, 71, 74t, 79tr, 83br; Erich Lessing 15tr, 18tr; Gilles Mermet 43tr; Instrumentmuseum, Berlin 116; Paris Bibliotheque Nationale 64tl; Postmuseum, Berlin 129cr.
Alamy Images: ZUMA Press, Inc. 250bl. Ancient Art & Architecture Collection: 39cr, 39br, 11tr, 24bl, 26br, 29cr, 32–33t. Antiquarian Images: 38tl. The Art Archive: 58; Biblioteca Nazionale Marciana Venice/Dagli Orti 52bl. Ashmolean Museum: 35c. Bradbury Science Museum: Los Alamos 208cra, 208cr. Bridgeman Art Library, London / New York: 105tl; Bible Society, London 59tr; Bibliothèque Nationale, Paris 69tr; Christie's Images, London 66tl; Down House, Kent 143cr; Giraudon 62tr; Natural History Museum, London 79tc. British Library: 22bl, 23br, 55, 76bc. British Museum: 7r, 8l, 12tc, 16–17, 19, 22b, 22tl, 22tc, 22cl, 23tr, 24–25t, 26tl, 27, 30cl, 44t, 46br, 48tl, 49tr, 60bl. Corbis: 41bc, 59b, 70, 95br, 96c, 98tl, 105b, 112–3, 140bl, 174tr, 183cr, 247b, 63cr; Martial Trezzini/EPA 250cc; Minnesota Historical Society 118cl. The Culture Archive: 134tl, 149cr. Danish National Museum: 53. Dreamstime.com: Pressureua 241b. Mary Evans Picture Library: 2–3t, 12cl, 31tr, 63bl, 66bl, 66bc, 80–81, 104, 131tr, 132bl, 135, 184c; Engraving by Emile Baynard 2tl, 6, 18br; Illustrated London News 2tc, 40. Football Museum: 51l. Linton Gardiner: 182bl3. Getty Images: Simon Dawson/Bloomberg 243. Glasgow Museum: 202bc. Ronald Grant Archive: 20th Century Fox 236br. Robert Harding Picture Library: 92bl; Dr. Denis Kunkel/Phototake NYC 95tr; Ellen Rooney 41c. Hulton Archive: 3tl, 3tc, 118–9, 138, 172. Museum of London: 12tl. NASA: 249tl; JPL/Cornell 249l, 249br; Kepler Mission/Wendy Stenzel 250br. National Maritime Museum: 14–15b, 37tr, 86–87b, 102t, 106br. Natural History Museum: 14bl.

Peter Newark's Pictures: 76cla. Robert Opie Collection: 160tl, 195cl, 196, 198tl. Christine Osborne: 13r. Quadrant Picture Library: The Flight Collection 226–7. Royal Horticultural Society, Wisley: Lindley Library 21. Saint Bride Printing Library: 76clb. Saxon Village: Crafts 69ca. Science & Society Picture Library: 2tr, 4–5, 7c, 7l, 8–9b, 10–11c, 10b, 16cl, 17tr, 20r, 24bl, 30–31, 33br, 34tl, 34–35, 37c, 42cl, 44bl, 45, 47, 52tr, 54b, 60–61, 60r, 62cl, 65c, 67tc, 68c, 73r, 73tl, 74–75, 75br, 78, 80cl, 80t, 82c, 82b, 84–85, 84tl, 85c, 86tl, 86–87cb, 88, 89tl, 89br, 90, 91tc, 91r, 92, 92–93, 93tr, 93c, 96tl, 97b, 99cr, 100bl, 101, 102–103b, 103cr, 106tl, 107br, 108–9, 109tr, 110–1, 111tr, 112tl, 114–5t, 115tr, 115b, 117, 119, 120cl, 120bl, 120bc, 121tr, 121br, 122–3, 124, 125cl, 125t, 126br, 126–7, 128, 130cl, 131cr, 131bc, 132tl, 133cl, 133t, 134bl, 137c, 137t, 139tr, 139tc, 140c, 141, 144tl, 144–5, 145, 146b, 148–9, 149tc, 150tl, 150–1b, 152bl, 152tl, 152c, 153br, 154cl, 153cr, 154–5, 155tr, 156tr, 156cr, 156bl, 157, 159, 160–1, 161r, 162bl, 162br, 163tl, 163r, 164–5, 165cr, 166ca, 166–7, 168bl, 168–9, 169c, 169br, 170tl, 170bc, 170cl1, 170cl2, 171tr, 171br, 173tr, 173bl, 174bl, 175br, 176bl, 176br, 177, 178clb, 179tr, 180c, 181ll, 181r, 182tl, 185tr, 185bl, 186b, 187, 188–9, 189br, 190–1, 191tr, 192cla, 192cl, 193br, 194–5, 195tr, 197br, 198br, 199cl, 200cb, 200–1b, 201, 202cl, 203tc, 203br, 205tl, 205br, 206tl, 208tl, 208tr, 209b, 210tl, 210br, 211, 213bc, 213cr, 214l, 215br, 215tl, 218tl, 218–9, 219ca, 219cra, 220tl, 220–1b, 221tr, 222cl, 222bc, 224tc, 225l, 226tl, 227c, 228cr, 228bc, 230tc, 230–1, 231tr, 232bl, 232–3t, 233tr, 233br, 234tl, 240tl, 240bc, 241cl, 242tl; Graseby Medical 186c; NASA 94, 188bl, 174–5. Science Photo Library: endpapers, 3tr, 48cl, 66tl, 178bc, 179cra, 189cr, 202cb, 203tr, 204tl, 207br, 212f, 216tl, 216tc, 217tr, 221ca, 223, 229tr, 236t, 244cla, 244cl, 244cb, 244bc, 246, 247tr, 248bl; CNRI 242cb; James M. Hogle, Harvard Medical School 248br. Statens Historika Museum: Stockholm 50–51. Superstock Ltd.: 46tl, 77tr. Topham Picturepoint: 245cr. TRH Pictures: 199tc. Art Directors & TRIP: 39tr, 85tr, 236l, 33c. University Museum of Archaeology and Anthropology, Cambridge: 50br. University of Archaeology and Anthropology: 20c. Matthew Ward: 182bl1, 182bl2. Barrie Watts: 192bl1, 192bl2, 192bl3.
All other images © Dorling Kindersley. For further information see: www.dkimages.com
Illustrations by Peter Dennis.